D0866989

The Black Book of the American Left

The Black Book of the American Left

The Collected Conservative Writings of David Horowitz

Volume VII
The Left in Power: Clinton to Obama

Second Thoughts Books
Los Angeles

First American edition published in 2015 by Second Thoughts Books.

Manufactured in the United States and printed on acid-free paper. The paper used in this publication meets the minimum requirements of ANSI/NISO Z39.48 1992 (R 1997) *(Permanence of Paper).*

Book design and production by Catherine Campaigne; copy-edited by David Landau; research provided by Mike Bauer.

FIRST AMERICAN EDITION

LIBRARY OF CONGRESS CATALOGING-IN-PUBLICATION DATA

Horowitz, David, 1939–
The black book of the American left : the collected conservative writings of David Horowitz / by David Horowitz.
volumes cm.
Includes bibliographical references and index.
ISBN 978-1-941262-10-8 (hardback)
1. Social movements—United States—History. 2. Radicalism—United States. 3. Anti-Americanism—United States. 4. Horowitz, David, 1939– Political and social views. I. Title.
HX86.H788 2013
335.00973 2013000496

10 9 8 7 6 5 4 3 2 1

Contents

INTRODUCTION

The Left in Power

This seventh volume of the *Black Book of the American Left* reviews the administrations of three presidents and the transformation of the Democratic Party from a party of the American center into a party of the political left. The magnitude of this change can be measured in the distance Democrats have traveled since the presidency of John F. Kennedy, once a liberal icon. The Kennedy policies—militant anti-Communism, hawkish defense, a capital gains tax cut and balanced budget—are now firmly identified with the Republican right. At the same time, Barack Obama's Democrats are committed to the agendas of the left: income redistribution, socialized health schemes, and military retreat abroad.

Going into the 2016 elections, the views held by the Democratic leadership on national security were virtually indistinguishable from those of the Progressive Party, whose 1948 presidential campaign behind the candidacy of Henry Wallace defined itself by opposition to American "militarism" and rejection of the Cold War policies the Democratic Party was then pursuing against the Communist threat.

A salient but often resisted fact about this era is that progressives supported the Communist enemy in its conflicts with the United States. In other words, progressives worked as apologists, appeasers and enablers on behalf of a global movement openly dedicated to the destruction of their own country. Understanding this mentality is crucial to understanding the progressive political outlook and the movement that followed from it—specifically, the will to jettison America's allegedly outdated constitutional structures, and to cripple American power—all in the name of furthering economic equality and social justice.[1]

The 1948 progressives failed to defeat Harry Truman or achieve their foreign policy objectives, and became marginal to the political dramas of the next decade. Then, in the 1960s, a younger generation of progressives created a political movement that described itself as a "New Left." But while New Leftists developed an innovative rhetoric to distance themselves from their Communist forbears, they were in fact mobilized behind the same anti-individualist, anti-capitalist and anti-American agendas as the Communist movement from which they sprang.[2]

As the Sixties progressed, the New Left became more and more overtly radical until, in 1968, activists staged a riot at the Democratic Party convention to destroy the candidacy of Hubert Humphrey over his support for an anti-Communist war. Following the convention debacle and Humphrey's electoral defeat, New Left activists moved from the streets into the ranks of the party. With the support of the Democrats' 1972 presidential candidate, George McGovern, who had begun in his political career in the 1948 Henry Wallace campaign, the New Left radicals were able to take commanding positions in the party's congressional apparatus, and eventually in its national leadership.

As the activists acquired power, their aggressive tactics achieved a series of political victories: the betrayal of the Vietnamese and Cambodians by the "Watergate class" of congressional Democrats who cut off military and economic aid to the anti-Communist regimes; the appeasement of Communist insurgencies in Central America and obstruction of the Reagan administration's anti-Communist policies such as support for the *Contras;* the betrayal of Iraq and sabotage of the war on terror; the

---

[1]These continuities are analyzed at length in Volume 1 of this series, *My Life and Times,* and Volume 2, Chapter 1: "The Mind of the Left."
[2]Ibid.

thirty-year assault on the nation's borders; the undermining of public health measures during the AIDS epidemic; the traducing of the civil rights movement and its transformation into a lobby for race-based policies and racial preferences; the subversion of the modern research university and the suborning of its liberal arts divisions into training centers for the Democratic Party and the radical cause; and finally the rise of a campus support movement for Islamists and anti-Semites. These victories—documented in previous volumes of the present series—culminated in the election of Barack Obama in 2009 and the institutionalizing of the policies of the left in government over the next 8 years.[3]

President Obama was born, bred and trained in the progressive movement. His mentors were Communists and their progressive successors. On entering the Oval Office, he launched his administration with a global "apology tour," conceding America's "guilt" not only towards the Muslim world, but also towards surviving members of the Soviet bloc in Central America.[4] The signature foreign policies of his administration were retreats from America's battlefronts against Islamic terrorists in Afghanistan and Iraq; tepid and therefore ineffectual responses to terrorist forces in the Middle East; support for Palestinian terror regimes in the West Bank, Gaza and Egypt, this last under the Muslim

---

[3]An omission from this list, and from these volumes generally, is the left's environmental movement, a quasi-religious effort to vastly expand governmental controls over energy and the economy. Important as this movement has been to the advance of socialist progressivism, I have not addressed it except in one article "From Red to Green," published first in *National Review* and then in the book I co-authored with Jacob Laksin, *The New Leviathan,* 2012. This is because, in my judgment, the radical environmental movement has been well covered by other conservative writers.

[4]Nile Gardiner, Ph.D. and Morgan Lorraine Roach, "Barack Obama's Top 10 Apologies: How the President Has Humiliated a Superpower," *Heritage Foundation,* June 2, 2009, http://www.heritage.org/research/reports/2009/06/barack-obamas-top-10-apologies-how-the-president-has-humiliated-a-superpower; David Horowitz and Jacob Laksin, *The New Leviathan,* 2012, Chapter 2, "The Making of a President."

Brotherhood; and a major foreign policy effort to bring America's mortal enemy, the Islamic Republic of Iran, into the community of nations, fund its terrorist regime and provide its leaders with a legitimized path to nuclear power.

Bill Clinton had been the first Democratic president with political roots in the so-called "antiwar" movement, although he himself was not an ideological leftist in the way his wife and political partner was. Accordingly, the opening chapter of this volume focuses on the views of Hillary Clinton and the cohort of leftists she brought to the White House. Leftists figured prominently in the Clinton entourage, and their agendas became prominent themes of an administration that eventually presided over the most massive breach of military security in American history—a story told in the last three chapters of Part I of this volume and now all but forgotten. This breach and the policies associated with it could not have been implemented if the political atmosphere had been confined to a few individuals, even as influential as Mrs. Clinton.

Important chapters in the Democrats' defection from the bipartisanship which had characterized American foreign policy during the postwar years is told in other volumes of this series, in particular the essay "How the Left Undermined America's Security Before 9/11," which appears in Volume 3, *The Great Betrayal.* It describes the shift in Democratic Party attitudes on national security from the McGovern campaign through the Clinton years. Domestic effects of the progressive party line, which became a defining feature of Democratic politics over the next several decades, are analyzed in Volumes 5 and 6.

Just as the end of the Vietnam War created an opportunity for the progressive left to re-enter the Democratic Party after its break in 1948, so the Iraq War served as a political context for it to push the party towards more and more extreme agendas. The ground for this development, described in Part 2 of the present volume, was laid in the demonization of George Bush and the Republicans, for staying the course in Iraq despite the Democrats' defection from a war they had authorized. The part played by the left in this dramatic turn of Democratic policies was first described in my book *Unholy Alliance* (2004), which examined the still-poorly-understood events leading up to the invasion of Iraq and the growing sympathies of the political left for Islamist agendas.[5]

The present volume occupies a climactic place in the *Black Book* series, which can be viewed as a running analysis of the movement that produced the Obama presidency, and has had such a traumatic impact on the American future. The outlook shaping this movement is described in Part III, Chapter 3 of this volume, "Rules for Revolution," which examines the political bible of the Obama left, Saul Alinsky's *Rules for Radicals.* In its original pamphlet form, "Rules for Revolution" has been distributed and sold to more than three million people, and is thus the most popular work I have written.

Because the selections for the present volume were made with an eye to describing this momentous transformation, merely topical pieces have been omitted and, consequently, it is not as complete a collection of my writings from those years as it might have been. As in previous volumes, the selections have been edited and revised for readability, but the perspectives have been left unaltered.

---

[5]As previously mentioned, Volume 3 of this series, *The Great Betrayal,* provides a running account of the reversal and the Democrats' unprecedented sabotage of an American war in progress. A third book, *Party of Defeat* (2008), co-authored with Ben Johnson, also deals with these events, and includes the essay "How the Left Undermined America's Security Before 9/11." In 2014 I published *Take No Prisoners,* which deals with some of the same subject matter from the perspective of political tactics that conservatives might use to confront the Democratic agendas. One chapter from that book, "How Obama Betrayed America," is included in the present volume.

PART I

Clintonn

I

First Lady of the Left

Hillary Clinton is America's most prominent leftist. This is not an obvious idea even to leftists, especially those who think of themselves as radicals. Purists of the creed are likely to regard both Clintons as opportunists and sellouts of their cause. But the left is not and has never been a political monolith, and its radical factions have always attacked each other, often ferociously.

It is possible to be a socialist, radical in one's agendas, and yet moderate in the means one regards as practical to achieve them. To change the world, it is first necessary to acquire cultural and political power. These transitional goals may often be accomplished by indirection and deception more effectively than by frontal assault.[1] Political stratagems that appear moderate and compromising to radical factions of the left may present an even greater threat to those who oppose them. In 1917, Lenin's political slogan was not "Socialist Dictatorship! Firing Squads! Gulags!" It was "Peace! Land! Bread!"

Hillary Clinton as America's "first lady of the left" is not an obvious subject to many conservatives either. Since conservative

---

Originally published June 22, 2000, http://archive.frontpagemag.com/Printable.aspx?ArtId=24376.

[1]This is in fact the tactical advice that forms the core of Saul Alinsky's *Rules for Radicals.* Alinsky was an early icon for Hillary and in this book provided the strategic guide for the political left following the collapse of Communism. See Part III, I, Chapter 4 of this volume, "Rules for Revolution."

politics begins with the defense of America's constitutional order, this is a far more significant matter. Underestimating the foe on any battlefield can be a fatal fault, and politics is no exception. This problem is exemplified by *The Case Against Hillary Clinton,* an elegantly crafted portrait of Mrs. Clinton by former Reagan speechwriter Peggy Noonan.[2] Its focus is not Mrs. Clinton's *kitsch* Marxism or perverse feminism or cynical progressivism. Instead it is her narcissism, the psychological nexus in which Noonan finds the key to Hillary Clinton's public persona. It is almost as though Mrs. Clinton's politics were merely instrumental to her career, as changeable as her famous hairstyles. "Never has the admirable been so fully wedded to the appalling," Noonan writes of the subject and her faithless spouse. "Never in modern political history has such tenacity and determination been marshaled to achieve such puny purpose: the mere continuance of Them."

The wit is sharp but the point well wide of the mark. There are many unprincipled narcissists in politics. But there has never been a White House so thoroughly penetrated by the political left. Noonan's psychological characterization is surely correct. But if Hillary and Bill Clinton were unable to draw on the commitment and support of the political left—if they were Republicans, for example—there would be no prospect of a continuance of Them.

Ever since I abandoned the utopian illusions of the progressive cause, I have been struck by how little the world outside the left seems to actually understand it. How little those who have not inhabited the progressive mind are able to grasp the ruthless cynicism behind its idealistic mask, or the fervent malice that drives its hypocritical passion for "social justice." No matter how great the crimes progressives commit, no matter how terrible the future they labor to create, no matter how devastating the catastrophes they leave behind, the world outside the faith—conservatives included—seems ever ready to forgive them their "mistakes" and grant them the grace of "good intentions." It would be difficult for

---

[2]Peggy Noonan, *The Case Against Hillary Clinton,* 2000.

me to recall the number of times I have been introduced on conservative platforms as "a former civil rights worker and peace activist in the 1960s." I have been described this way despite having written a detailed autobiography that exposes these self-glorifying images of the left as so many political lies. Like many New Left leaders whom the young Mrs. Clinton once followed, and who are her comrades today, I regarded myself in the 1960s as a Marxist revolutionary. No matter what slogans we chanted or ideals we proclaimed, our agendas always extended beyond the immediate issues we championed to the destruction of the constitutional order of the society in which we lived.

New Left progressives, including Hillary Clinton and her husband's acting deputy attorney general Bill Lann Lee, were involved in supporting, protecting or making excuses for violent anti-American radicals abroad, like the Vietcong, and anti-American criminals at home like the Black Panthers.[3] We did this at the time—just as progressives still do now—in the name of "social justice" and a dialectical world-view that made this deception appear ethical and the fantasy seem possible. "If you can successfully camouflage your own pathology and hatred with a concern for the poor and the downtrodden," observes Jamie Glazov, an astute student of the left, "then there will always be a progressive milieu to support and defend you."[4] Huey Newton, George Jackson, Angela Davis, Bernardine Dohrn, Kathy Boudin, Sylvia Baraldini, Mumia Abu-Jamal, Rigoberta Menchú and innumerable other leaders of the left all discovered this principle in the course of their criminal careers.

There is a superficial sense, of course, in which leftists were also civil rights and (less plausibly) peace activists—and that is

[3]Cliff Kincaid, "Hillary Clinton's Biggest Cover-Ups," *Accuracy in Media*, August 11, 2003, https://www.aim.org/publications/aim_report/2003/15.html.

[4]David Horowitz, "Hillary Clinton and 'The Third Way': How America's First Lady of the Left Has Bamboozled Liberals and Conservatives Alike," *FrontPageMag.com*, June 22, 2000, http://archive.frontpagemag.com/readArticle.aspx?ARTID=24376.

certainly the way I would have described myself at the time, particularly if I were speaking to a non-left audience. It is certainly the way Mrs. Clinton and my former comrades in the left refer to themselves and their pasts in similar contexts today. But they are lying. The first truth about progressive missionaries is that the issues they fight for are not the issues. What drives all their agendas is the fantasy of a social transformation that will lead to a paradise of social justice. The first truth about progressive missionaries is that they are liars, although not in the ordinary way, which is to say by choice. They are liars by necessity. Because it is the political lie that gives their cause its life.

Why, if you believed as they do, would you tell the truth? If you took seriously your role as social redeemer and a member of humanity's vanguard, if you possessed the knowledge that you were certain would lead to a better world, why would you tell people a truth that might hinder this cause or even derail it? What makes you part of a vanguard is precisely your possession of a knowledge not shared by those outside it—who therefore cannot be trusted with the truth.

A perfect example of this mental process was recently on display in a video-taped lecture made during the Obama administration's rollout of "Obamacare"—the most ambitious socialist plan to date. Jonathan Gruber, an MIT professor and key architect of the plan, was taped explaining the strategy behind its authorizing bill: "This bill was written in a tortured way to make sure [the Congressional Budget Office] did not score the mandate as taxes. If CBO scored the mandate as taxes, the bill dies, okay? . . . If you made it explicit that healthy people pay in and sick people get money, it would not have passed, okay? Lack of transparency is a huge political advantage. And basically, you know, call it the stupidity of American voters or whatever. But basically that was really, really critical to getting the thing to pass." Gruber's justification for lying? "I'd rather have this law than not."[5] This was not just

[5]Gruber: "Lack of Transparency Is a Huge Political Advantage," October 17, 2013, https://www.youtube.com/watch?v=G790poLcgbI; http://ldi.upenn.edu/ahec2013/agenda.

the strategy of Gruber and the bureaucrats drafting the legislation. In order to sell the plan to the American people, President Obama himself lied on numerous occasions about its fundamental provisions—"If you like your doctor, you can keep your doctor. Period." Or, "You can keep your plan, period."[6] In sum, it is necessary to lie to the people in order to pass progressive laws, and the lie is justified by "the greater good."

If everyone shared progressives' understanding of the present and how to transform it, the "vanguard" would not be a vanguard. They would no longer inhabit the morally charmed world of revolutionary elites, whose members alone have seen the light and whose mission is to lead others toward it by whatever means necessary. If you were active in the so-called "peace" movement of the Sixties or in the radical wing of the civil rights causes, you would not want to tell the truth that no, you were not really a "peace activist," except in the sense that you were against *America*'s war. Why would you want to draw attention to the fact that you didn't oppose the Communists' war, and were gratified when America's enemies won? What you were really against was not war at all, but American "imperialism" and American capitalism. That's why you wanted to "Bring the Troops Home," as your slogan said. Because if America's troops came home, America would lose and the Communists would win. And the progressive future would be one step closer.

But you never had the honesty–then or now–to admit that. Or to confront the millions of corpses left in the wake of the Communist victory you worked so hard to achieve. You told the lie at the time to maintain your influence and increase your power to do good (as only the chosen vanguard can). And you keep telling the lie for the same reason. It is because America is a democracy that the left's anti-American "progressive" agendas can only be achieved by deceiving the people. This is the cross the left has to

---

[6]Montage: "If You Like Your Plan, You Can Keep Your Plan," June 15, 2009–January 27, 2010, https://www.youtube.com/watch?v=Tv-uFnjha1I.

bear: the better world is only achievable by lying to the very people they propose to redeem.

The heart of what it means to be a part of the progressive mission, and the source of its gratification, is this: You see yourself as a social redeemer; you feel anointed, heroic by having taken up the cause and "speaking truth to power." In other words, to be progressive is really the most satisfying narcissism of all.

That is why it is of little concern to progressives that their socialist schemes have run aground, burying millions of human beings along with them. That is why they don't care that their panaceas have caused more human suffering than all the injustices they have opposed. That is why they never learn from their so-called mistakes. It is why the continuance of Them is more important than any truth.

Despite the homage the contemporary left pays to post-modernist conceits, despite their belated and half-hearted display of critical sentiment towards Communist regimes, they are very much the ideological heirs of Stalinist progressives who supported the greatest mass murders in human history but who remember themselves as civil libertarian opponents of McCarthy and victims of a political witch-hunt. Only the dialectically gifted can even begin to follow the logic involved.

To appreciate the continuity of communism in the mentality of the left, consider how many recent Hollywood promotions of the Communists in their industry, and how many academic apologies for Stalinist crimes—in fact, the vast majority of recent academic texts on the subject—have been premised on the Machiavellian calculations and Hegelian sophistries I have just described. Naturally, today's leftists are smart enough to distance themselves from Soviet Communism. But the Soviet dictator Nikita Khrushchev was already a critic of Stalin forty years ago. Did his concessions make him less of a Communist? Or more?

Nonetheless, conservative misunderstanding of the left is only in part a product of the left's own deceits. It also reflects conservatives' inability to understand the religious nature of the progressive faith and the power of its redemptive idea. Conservatives often ask me about the continuing role and influence of the Communist Party, since they observe quite correctly the pervasive presence of so many familiar totalitarian ideas in our academic and political culture. However, though still around and sometimes influential in the left, the Communist Party has been a minor player for nearly fifty years. How, then, can there be a communist left (small "c") without a Communist Party? The answer is that it was not the Communist Party that made the left but the (small "c") communist idea. It is an idea as old as the Tower of Babel—that humanity can build a highway to Heaven. It is the idea of returning to an Earthly Paradise, a garden of social harmony and justice. It is the idea of a *tikkun olam* as it is framed by Jewish progressives—a healing of the cosmic order. It is the Enlightenment illusion of the perfectibility of man. And it is the siren-song of the serpent in Eden: "Eat of this Tree of the Knowledge of Good and Evil, and you shall be as God."

The intoxicating vision of a social redemption achieved by Them is what creates the left, and infuses the believers with self-righteousness. The same idea can be found in the Social Gospel that impressed the youthful Hillary Clinton at the United Methodist Church in Park Ridge, Illinois. She encountered it again among New Leftists at Yale and in the Venceremos Brigade in Communist Cuba, where she was a pro-Castro volunteer; she embraced it in the writings of the New Left author of the "politics of meaning" after she had become America's First Lady.[7] It is the idea that drives her comrades in the Children's Defense Fund, the National Organization for Women, the Al Sharpton House of Justice and the other progressive causes which look to her as a political leader. For these self-appointed social redeemers, the avowed goal—"social justice"—is not about rectifying particular injustices,

[7]Lee Siegel, "All Politics Is Cosmic," *The Atlantic,* June 1996, http://www.theatlantic.com/magazine/archive/1996/06/all-politics-is-cosmic/376610/.

which would be practical and modest, and therefore conservative. Their crusade is about rectifying injustice in the very order of things. "Social Justice" for them—as for the communists before them—is about a world reborn, a world in which prejudice and violence are absent, in which everyone is equal and equally advantaged and without fundamentally conflicting desires. It is a world that can only come into being through a restructuring of human nature and of society itself.

Even though they are too prudent and self-protective to identify this future as a revival of the communist fantasy, that is what it is. It is a world that has never existed and never will. As the gulags and graveyards of the last century attest, to attempt the impossible is to invite the catastrophic. But the fall of Communism has taught the progressives who were its supporters very little. Above all, it has failed to teach them the connection between their utopian ideals and the destructive consequences that flow from them. In characteristic fashion, the left has once again been showing its "abstract contempt for ordinary experience," as writer Lee Siegel put it. The fall of Communism has had a cautionary impact only on the overt agendas of the political left. They have learned to conceal their true ambitions, lest they jeopardize their quest for the power to achieve them.[8]

No matter how opportunistically the left's agendas have been modified, however, no matter how circumspectly its goals have been set or generous its concessions to political reality, the faithful have not given up the quest for social redemption—for a world in which human consciousness is changed, human relations refashioned and social institutions transformed, so that "social justice" can prevail.

The transformation progressives seek is ultimately total; consequently the power they require must be total as well. Such a

---

[8]On abstract contempt, see Siegel, *ibid.* With regard to concealing true ambitions, this is the gravamen of Saul Alinsky's *Rules for Radicals,* the handbook for Hillary's generation of progressives. See "Rules for Revolution" Part III, chapter 1 below.

redemption cannot be achieved as a political compromise, but only by the submission of those who resist it. Their social transformation requires the permanent entrenchment of the saints in power. Therefore, everything is justified that serves to achieve the continuance of Them.

In Peggy Noonan's portrait of Clinton, one can trace the outlines of the progressive persona I have just described. Noonan observes that the liberalism of the Clinton era is very different from the liberalism of the past. Clinton-era liberalism is manipulative and deceptive and not so interested in what real people think because "they might think the wrong thing." That is why Hillary Clinton's failed plan to socialize American health care was the work of a progressive cabal that shrouded itself in secrecy to the point of illegality. Noonan labels Clinton-era politics "command and control liberalism," using a phrase with a totalitarian ring. But, like so many conservatives I have come to know, Noonan is finally too decent and too generous to fully appreciate the pathology of the left. She begins her inquiry by invoking Richard Nixon's observation that only two kinds of people run for high office in America, "those who want to do big things and those who want to be big people." She identifies both Clintons as "very much, perhaps completely, the latter sort."

Regarding the husband, Peggy Noonan is probably right. I do not think of Bill Clinton as a leftist inspired by ideas of a socially just world, or as having even a passing interest in the healing of cosmic orders. He is more readily understood as a narcissist fully absorbed in the ambitions of self, who chameleon-like assumes the coloration of his environments and the constituencies on which his fortunes depend.

Hillary Clinton is not so slippery. In her actions one can clearly observe an ideological spine that creates political difficulties her husband is able to avoid. This is not to deny the force of her personal ambitions or the power of her self-regard. But these attitudes are to be expected in any number of elites— especially one like the left, which is based on moral election.

For this reason, it would be difficult to separate the narcissistic from the ideological in the psychology of political missionaries. Do they advance the faith for the sake of the faith, or because advancing the faith will earn them the adoration of saints? Do the Lenins of history sacrifice normal life in order to achieve "big things" or because they hunger for the canonization their achievements will bring? It is probably impossible to finally answer the question. Despite their lifelong collaboration, Bill and Hillary Clinton are different political beings. Her marital rages are provoked by a mate whose adolescent lusts put their collective mission at risk and are probably a good measure of just where the difference lies.

"In their way of thinking," Noonan observes of the Clintons, "America is an important place, but not a thing of primary importance. America is the platform for the Clintons' ambitions, not the focus of them." The implication is that if they were principled emissaries of a political cause, the ambition to do big things for America would override all others. Instead, they have focused on themselves and consequently made the American political landscape itself "a lower and lesser thing." They have "behaved as though they are justified in using any tactic in pursuit of their goals," including illegality, deception, libel, threats and "ruining the lives of perceived enemies...." They believe, she says, "they are justified in using any means to achieve their ends for a simple and uncomplicated reason. It is that they are superior individuals whose gifts and backgrounds entitle them to leadership." They do it for themselves; for the continuance of Them.

But the fact is that all progressives do it. The missionaries of the progressive causes, the Gloria Steinems, Patricia Irelands, Kate Michelmans, Betty Friedans and Hillary Clinton herself, were all willing to toss their feminist movement overboard to give Bill Clinton a pass on multiple sexual harassments, and on a career of sexual predation that reflects his enduring contempt for the female gender. Indeed, the Clinton-Lewinsky defense accord, which the feminists signed onto, can be looked on as feminism's version of the Nazi-Soviet Pact. Their calculation was both simle and crude. If Clinton were removed, Hillary would go too. But she was their link to patronage and power, and they couldn't imagine losing that. Their partisans were finally in control of the White House, and the conservative enemies of their beautiful future were not. That trumped whatever principles they had.

Almost a decade earlier, in the name of the very principles they so casually betrayed for Clinton, the same feminists organized the most disgraceful lynching of a public figure in American history. Despite fiercely proclaimed commitments to the racial victims of American persecution, they launched a vicious campaign to destroy the reputation of Clarence Thomas, an African-American nominee for the Supreme Court who had risen, unblemished, from dirt-shack poverty in the segregated South to the nation's highest tribunals. They did it knowingly, cynically, with the intent to destroy him in his person and ruin his public career. Has there ever been a more reprehensible witch-hunt in American public life than the one organized by these feminist leaders who then emerged as vocal defenders of the White House predator? Was there ever a more sordid betrayal of common decency and feminist principle than this defamatory outrage for which no apology has been or ever will be given?

What was the sin Clarence Thomas committed to earn such punishment? The allegation that he had talked inappropriately (and privately) ten years earlier to a female lawyer, and made her uncomfortable, appears laughable in the post-Lewinsky climate of presidential gropings and borderline rapes that the same feminists accommodated to protect their political accomplice. Thomas's real crime, as everybody understood, was his commitment to constitutional principles that progressives despised. They hated these principles because the Constitution was written by conservatives for the express purpose of preventing the realization of egalitarian schemes.[9]

[9]Federalist 10.

Noonan is right that the focus of Hillary Clinton's ambition is not her country. But it is not just herself, either. It is also a place that does not exist. It is the fantasy of a world that progressives will create when they have accumulated enough power to change this one.

That is why Hillary and Sidney Blumenthal, her fawning New Left Machiavelli, call their philosophy the politics of "the Third Way."[10] That is what distinguishes it from the "triangulation" strategy Dick Morris used to resurrect Bill Clinton's presidency, which was a strategy of compromise. Morris guided Clinton in appropriating specific Republican policies towards a balanced budget and welfare reform as a means of securing his re-election. Triangulation fails to project the sense of promise that intoxicates the imaginations of self-styled "progressives," which is why Hillary and Sidney call their politics "the Third Way."

The Third Way is a familiar term from the lexicon of the left. It has a long and dishonorable pedigree in the catastrophes created by messianic socialists in the 20th century. It is the most ornate panel in the tapestry of deception I described earlier in this essay. In the 1930s, Nazis used the Third Way to characterize their own brand of national socialism as equidistant between the "internationalist" socialism of the Soviet Union and the capitalism of the West. Trotskyists used the Third Way as a term to distinguish their own Marxism from Stalinism and capitalism. In the 1960s, New Leftists used "the Third Way" to define their politics as an independent socialism located somewhere between the Soviet gulag and America's democracy. But as the history of Nazism, Trotskyism and the New Left have shown, there is no "Third Way." There is the capitalist, democratic way based on private property and individual rights; and there is the socialist way of group identities, group rights, a relentless expansion of the political state, restricted liberty and diminished opportunity.

---

[10]Andrew Leigh, "The Rise and Fall of the Third Way," *Australian Quarterly,* Vol. 75, No. 2, March—April, 2003, pp. 10–15, 40.

The Third Way is not a path to the future. It is just the suspension between these two destinations. It is a bad-faith attempt on the part of people who are incapable of giving up their socialist dreams to escape the taint of their discredited past.

Is there a practical difference in the *modus operandi* of Clinton narcissism and Clinton messianism? I think there is. It is the difference between "triangulation" as a compromise to achieve practical ends, and the Third Way, which is a cynical deception to ensure the continuance of Us, until we acquire enough power to transform everyone else. It is the difference between the politics of achieving what is viable, and the politics of changing the world.

A capsule illustration of these different political ambitions can be found in the book *Primary Colors,* which describes, in a thinly veiled fiction, Bill Clinton's road to the presidency.[11] *Primary Colors* is an admiring portrait not only of the candidate, but of the dedicated missionaries—the true-believing staffers and the long-suffering wife—who serve Clinton's political agendas, but at the price of enabling the demons of his self. These staffers—political functionaries like Harold Ickes and George Stephanopoulos—serve as the flak-catchers and "bimbo cruption" controllers who clean up his personal messes and shape his image for a gullible public. They enable him to succeed politically. But they are also the idealists who design his message.

It is *Primary Colors'* insight into the minds of these missionaries that is particularly revealing. The missionaries see Clinton clearly as a flawed and often repellent human being. They see him as a lecher, a liar and a man who would destroy an innocent person in order to advance his own career. Yet through all the sordidness and lying, the personal ruthlessness and disorder, the idealistic missionaries faithfully follow and serve the leader. They do it not because they are themselves corrupted through material rewards. The prospect of fame is not even what drives them. Think only of

---

[11]Anonymous, *Primary Colors,* Random House, 1996. The author was subsequently revealed to be the reporter Joe Klein, a Clinton supporter.

Harold Ickes, personally betrayed and brutally cast aside by Clinton, who nonetheless refused to turn on him, even after the betrayal. Instead, Ickes kept his own counsel and protected Clinton, biding his time and waiting for Hillary. Then he joined her staff to manage her Senate campaign.

The idealistic missionaries in this true tale bite their tongues and betray their principles, rather than betray him. They do so because in Bill Clinton they see a necessary vehicle of their noble ambition and intoxicating dreams. He, too, cares about social justice, about poor people and blacks—or so he makes them believe. In *Primary Colors,* a not-so-fictitious staffer says about the not-so-fictitious candidate: "I have seen better speakers and heard better speeches, but I don't think I'd ever heard . . . a speaker who measured his audience so well and connected so precisely."[12] Clinton's staffers, an audience whom he is manipulating day and night, will serve him and lie for him and destroy for him, because he is the vessel of their hopes. Because he "cares," Bill Clinton is the vital connection to the power they require to achieve the redemption. Because the keys to the state are within Clinton's grasp, in their eyes he is the only prospect for advancing the progressive cause. Therefore, they will sacrifice anything and everything—principle, friends, country—to make him succeed.

But Bill Clinton is not like those who worship him, corrupting himself and others for a higher cause. Unlike them, he betrays principles because he has none. He will even betray his country, but without the slightest need to betray it for something else—for an idea, a party, or a cause. He is a narcissist who sacrifices principle for power because his vision is so filled with himself that he cannot tell the difference.

But the idealists who serve him—the Stephanopouloses, the Ickeses, the feminists, the progressives and Hillary Clinton—can indeed tell the difference. In *Primary Colors,* the Hillary character

---

[12]Ibid., p. 9.

says about her husband that "he could also be a great man ... if he weren't such a faithless, thoughtless, disorganized, undisciplined shit."[13] The cynicism of Hillary and others flows from the very perception they have of right and wrong. They do it for higher ends. They do it for the progressive faith. They do it because they see themselves as political saints on a mission to save the world from the evils that assail it. It is this terrifyingly exalted ambition that fuels their spiritual arrogance and justifies their sordid collusion in often reprehensible and occasionally criminal means.

And that is the reason they hate conservatives. They hate them because they are killers of the dream. Because they are defenders of a Constitution that thwarts their cause; because a reactionary commitment to individual rights, to a single ethical standard, to a limited state, obstructs their progressive design. Conservatives who think progressives are misinformed idealists will forever be blind-sided by progressive malice—by the cynicism of those who claim to be guided by principles only to traduce them, by the viciousness of those who champion sensitivity, by the intolerance of those who call themselves liberal, and by the ruthless disregard for the well-being of the downtrodden by those who preen themselves as their saviors. Conservatives are caught by surprise because they see progressives as merely misguided, when in fact they are constitutionally misdirected. They are the messianists of a religious faith—a false faith and a self-serving religion. Since the noble future that justifies their existence can never be realized, what really motivates progressives is a modern idolatry: their limitless passion for the continuance of Them.

---

[13]Ibid., p. 17.

2

Gays March On The Pentagon

(with Peter Collier)

Bill Clinton came to power in a time of international crisis. Bosnia was under genocidal attack. Somalia was occupied by U.S. forces under siege from al-Qaeda. The regime in Iraq was already breaching the truce that had ended the Gulf War. But Clinton could not focus on these nations during his first and most important days in office. The only nation he cared about was Queer Nation. And the first enemy he chose to confront was the U.S. military.

By forcing the issue of gays in the military as the first item on his presidential agenda, Clinton showed a disquieting lack of political savvy, the one quality he was supposed to possess above all others. But this was not just an anomaly of ineptitude. Clinton raised the issue of gays for the same reason that he stocked the administration with his wife's politically correct appointees. While he was selling himself as a commonsense centrist during the recent election, he was also selling his soul to the leftwing pressure groups that have deformed his party over the last twenty-five years. As the furor over the gay issue erupted, gay activists made it clear they knew that the political battle was not about morality but payoff. Gays and lesbians had supported Clinton at a higher rate even than blacks and now their time had come.

Originally published February 1993, *Heterodoxy* magazine, http://www.discoverthenetworks.org/Articles/1993%20February%20Vol%201,%20No.pdf.

Clinton's astonishingly banal statement that he intended to be the first president to lead on a "civil rights" issue shows not only how much a prisoner this alleged pragmatist can be of the myths of the Sixties, but how perversely even those myths have been deformed over the last quarter-century. That decade which the president has courted with embarrassing unctuousness might have been launched with the notion of "making America better," but it ended with a commitment to "bring America down" (Abbie Hoffman). This is the legacy of the Sixties identity that is at work today promoting gays in the military. From ACT UP to Queer Nation, from the pro-Castro head of the Armed Services Committee, Berkeley Congressman Ronald V. Dellums, to its ranking member, anti-military crusader Patricia Schroeder, the crowd that is pressing the confrontation with military tradition is a crowd that has been defiantly opposed to the military mission itself over the past quarter-century. Does Ron Dellums or Pat Schroeder lie awake at night worrying what the impact of this or any policy will be on the effectiveness of America's military shield? Of course not. Both regularly proposed cutting America's military by half during the height of the Cold War with the Soviet Union; they both promoted the idea that America's role in the Cold War was generated by paranoia and nativism rather than the threat posed by an imperial aggressor. When the Red Army was invading Afghanistan, Ron Dellums was denouncing the Carter White House as a place of "evil" and as the principal menace to world peace. The only enemy Pat Schroeder ever saw on America's horizon were Navy fliers accused of sexual harassment.[1]

It is reflexively claimed by supporters of gays in the military, from the president on down, that the issue is simply a matter of fairness and equity. It is no different, they insist, from Harry Truman's decision in 1948 to end racial segregation in the military. That analogy is, of course, deeply insulting to black soldiers in the

---

[1]See Volume 5 in this series, *Culture Wars,* 2015, Part IV, Feminist Assaults, Chapter 1, "The Unforgiving."

same way that the trendy parasitism of other self-identified victim groups who compare their travails to slavery is insulting to the black experience. If fairness in dealing with homosexuals in public were an issue comparable to that of black Americans during segregation, then gay congressmen Barney Frank—whose lover ran a prostitution business out of Frank's home—and Gerry Studds, who confessed to statutory rape with a congressional male page, would have been subjected to the same inquisition as Bob Packwood faces for lesser heterosexual offenses. But neither was. Clinton himself kept trying to drive the point home by repeating, in a kind of mantra meant to soothe the passions he had aroused, it is not what you are that matters but what you do. This is indeed an appropriate philosophy for all the civic institutions of America except apparently the military. Unlike many other institutions, the military does not exist to serve as an engine of social change. It exists to serve as an effective fighting machine to protect this country from its enemies.

If the issue was simply one of civil rights, why stop at gays? Why deny other minority groups that have been traditionally excluded from the military? The disabled, for example. Surely it doesn't take more than two hands to operate a computer or fire a missile. Is an American in a wheelchair less of an American for that? Should he/she be denied the right to serve one's country? Why is the president content with half-measures? If the military exists not to protect America but to liberate American society from racism, sexism, homophobia, ableism and other politically incorrect blemishes, why equivocate? Why not have a plan to integrate the entire rainbow into the military mission?

Theoretically, the military could find a place for almost any able-bodied or differently abled citizen—if it did not have to consider the financial cost, or the effect of such a policy on the military mission. But the military mission is precisely the factor that is absent in these concerns. The military, after all, is an institution that exists to make war, not love. It is for this reason that the principal rationale for the present exclusionary policy on gays, which is backed by the entire U.S. chain of command, is the threat to *military effectiveness* of integrating overt homosexuals into the armed forces. This threat is not reflective of a phobia, homo or otherwise. It comes from a recognition of the nature of the sexual bond—one of the most powerful and uncontrollable factors in human affairs.

The military command believes that the introduction of the sexual factor into its fighting units would have an incalculable and potentially disastrous impact on military effectiveness. Unit cohesion, the ability of individual soldiers to weld themselves into a unified force prepared to die for each other and kill an enemy, would obviously be called into question if sexual forces were allowed to operate between the individuals within the unit—forces which allowed servicemen to see themselves as lovers and competitors rather than soldiers whose only job was achieving their objectives.

Sexual attraction is a threat not only to combat cohesion *effectiveness* but to ordinary military discipline and order. This is why segregation still prevails in the military between women and men among enlisted personnel in the areas of housing and hygiene, as across a whole spectrum of military assignments and pursuits. Even with this segregation, the inclusion of women in the military has had a demonstrably negative impact on military effectiveness. To cite just one fact, the rate at which women were undeployable (that is, failed to fulfill their military assignments) in the Persian Gulf War was four times that of males. The principal reason was pregnancy. Thanks to the previous pressures of feminists like Ms. Schroeder, there were no dishonorable discharges for these pregnancies as military code mandates.[2]

It would be possible, of course, to end the existing segregation: to put women and men in the same quarters, for example, and then try to regulate the interactions between them in a manner that is conducive to military order. But no one in his/her right

---

[2]This became a significant problem during the Iraq War; see http://www.washingtontimes.com/news/2004/jun/15/20040615-115647-8125r/?page=all .

mind would propose this as a feasible possibility. Instead, everyone ranging from the president to feminist organizations is as happy with gender segregation (hypocritical though this is at the abstract level at which these critical issues are publicly discussed) as they would be dismayed at the suggestion of comparably segregating all-homosexual military units. Yet they blithely propose for men mutually attracted to each other solutions that would not work between men and women. We are supposed to believe that open homosexuals—for whom, after all, sexual behavior is the key to identity—could be easily integrated into units in which heterosexuality is not only the dominant orientation but also an elemental part of the fighting élan. In the background of such an assumption can be heard the totalitarian clicking of word-processors, turning out manuals for an effort in sensitivity training that will make the Normandy Beach landings look easy by comparison.

Homosexual men have distinguished themselves as honorable, even heroic soldiers in the service of this country. Yet they have done so only after agreeing to submerge their homosexual identity in their identity as servicemen. Only a generation such as the present one, infected by the malicious clichés of the Sixties, would consider this some sort of psychological mutilation. Only a generation like the present should claim that the central issue in bringing gays into the military is civil rights and not behavior. We are witnessing a power play here. There is a reason that the president and his gay advisers have chosen to make their stand on this ground, As Dennis Altman, gay historian of the gay liberation movement in *The Homosexualization of America,* writes: "The greatest single victory of the gay movement over the past decade has been to shift the debate from behavior to identity, thus forcing opponents into a position where they can be seen as attacking the civil rights of homosexual citizens rather than attacking specific and (as they see it) antisocial behavior."[3]

---

[3]Dennis Altman, *The Homosexualization of America,* St. Martin's Press, 1982.

In the present debate the Pentagon brass have been portrayed as Neanderthals trapped in bigotries of the past. In fact, the generals are probably the only ones thinking realistically in this case. They know that the rules against open homosexuality have not only protected morale but also, by closing a dangerously volatile issue, protected those homosexuals who have chosen to serve in this volunteer army. They know that the military has been one of the few institutions in America relatively untouched by AIDS, and that such a status is absolutely critical to the military mission. (Under the new dispensation it would be hard to imagine that men would give their wounded comrades mouth-to-mouth resuscitation, let alone try to haul their bleeding bodies to safety). They know too that simply lifting the ban on homosexuals is only the first step in a process that would soon make the military into a political battleground involving agitation for quotas of homosexual officers, demands of benefits for domestic partners, and remaking of military hospitals to be able to handle the panoply of diseases that result from practices like "rimming" and "fisting" which have made gay medicine into a petrie dish where exotic cultures grow.

To ascribe knowledge to the Pentagon brass is not to grant them clairvoyance. After all, the generals of the gay movement have already made clear that this is exactly the sort of Blitzkrieg they intend to wage. Inclusion of gays in the military is the beginning. The members of the gay power structure have already said that they will oppose any exclusion of gays from combat units or ships or any situation where their identity-behavior may be thought to impact military effectiveness in a negative way. "That's unacceptable," Tanya Domi, director of the civil rights project of the National Gay and Lesbian Task Force, told *The New York Times*. "We stand absolutely opposed to any segregation of gay men and lesbians in the military."[4] So the prospect now is

[4]Eric Schmitt, "The Gay Troop Issue; Pentagon Aides to Study Option of Segregation for Gay Soldiers," *The New York Times*, January 31, 1993, http://www.nytimes.com/1993/01/31/us/gay-troop-issue-pentagon-aides-study-option-segregation-for-gay-soldiers.html.

that, wherever gays are present, military objectives and activities will come under the jurisdiction of the Equal Employment Opportunities Commission and the courts, and the scrutiny of the whole battery of legal experts and lawyers marshaled by the National Lawyers Guild Military Law Task Force, the ACLU Gay and Lesbian Rights Project, and other left-wing organizations which have historically demonstrated their unrelenting hostility to the U. S. military and its purpose in the first place.

Gay activists have also made it clear that they intend to implement the entire agenda of affirmative action mischief in the military. Here is a letter to the superintendent of West Point from a Clinton volunteer and ACT UP member. "Lifting the ban is not enough.... We intend to sue in Federal court as soon as the ban is lifted to insure compensatory representation in the service academies. In particular we intend to get a ruling mandating a set number of places for homosexuals in the Air Force Academy, the Naval Academy and West Point."[5]

There is more. In the current reformulation of what constitutes civil rights, AIDS carriers and sufferers are postulated as a protected minority whose rights must be observed. Thus, Ernesto Hinojos, director of education for the Gay Men's Health Crisis, has already announced: "Being positive for the human immunodeficiency virus, which causes AIDS, does not mean someone is unfit to serve."[6]

Obviously the intent here is not making the military fair and equitable but remaking the military altogether. Queer activist Frank Browning, author of a new book titled *The Culture of Desire,* concedes that this is the case: "I agree with Colin Powell admitting gays into the military will have a negative impact on

---

[5]Dan Coats, "Clinton's Big Mistake," *The New York Times,* January 30, 1993, http://www.nytimes.com/1993/01/30/opinion/clinton-s-big-mistake.html.

[6]Ernesto Hinojos, Letter to the Editor, *The New York Times,* January 31, 1993, http://www.nytimes.com/1993/01/31/opinion/l-gays-in-military-would-hurt-combat-efficiency-plain-talk-on-aids-510093.html.

military effectiveness. The difference between us is that I think that this is a good thing."[7]

Little wonder that, reflecting on the furor over gays in the military and extreme positions by gay activists like those cited above, the respected *Washington Post* columnist William Raspberry has observed that it is neither a dislike of homosexuals, nor a desire to exclude them from institutions like the military, that is driving the opposition to the Clinton policy. It is more a reaction against the radical and even apocalyptic character of what its proponents believe is a liberation agenda. "I'm guessing that if lifting the ban meant only that homosexual service personnel would no longer have to lie, no one would care very much," Raspberry writes, "But the fear is that something else would change, in unhealthy directions. There seems to be some larger fear that lurks just beyond our ability to define it—a sense that we may be about to release some deadly cultural genie."[8]

Exactly right. Over the last two decades, Americans have become familiar with this "cultural genie." This one is a far cry from the pleasant blue fellow in *Aladdin*. It may be hard to define its shape, but we know it by its works. In the early seventies it established public sexual gymnasia as "liberated zones" of the gay revolution. When a series of epidemics (some, like hepatitis B, quite deadly) swept through these zones, public health authorities who allowed themselves to be convinced that there was a civil rights issue at stake turned a blind eye to the physiological mayhem in deference to the demands of the same activists who are now proposing to deconstruct our current military traditions. The sexual behaviors which were the breeding grounds of the epidemic were declared off-bounds to public health officials by the same

---

[7]*The Heterodoxy Handbook*, David Horowitz and Peter Collier, eds., Regnery, 1994, p. 21.

[8]William Raspberry, "The Difference Between Homosexuals in the Military and Lifting the Military Ban," *Philly.com*, January 29, 1993, http://articles.philly.com/1993-01-29/news/25958468_1_military-ban-homosexuals-anti-gay-bigotry.

civil rights vigilantes who have now descended on the military. When AIDS began to cut a deadly swathe through the gay community, these activists rewrote the book on public health, blocking testing, reporting, contact-tracing and other tested epidemiological procedures in the name of privacy and other civil rights. Instead of proven methods for fighting an epidemic, we have AIDS education that fails to stress the dangers of anal intercourse (the source—if the government's HIV hypothesis is correct—of transmission in more than 95 percent of the sexually spread cases) and we have condoms.[9]

The recent tragic death of Arthur Ashe, who contracted AIDS through tainted transfusions, is a reminder of yet another triumph of gay disinformation. During the early days of the epidemic, when screening tests were ineffective, blood bank officials attempted to discourage potential gay blood donors—and groups like the San Francisco Coordinating Committee of Gay and Lesbian Services issued policy papers asserting that donor screening was "reminiscent of miscegenation blood laws that divided black blood from white."[10]

What have been the human and public costs of political correctness in the battle against AIDS? Has anybody attempted an accounting? The unleashed cultural genie has accomplished other works. High on the list was transforming the public arena regarding sexuality, making the bizarre and repellent plan the muzak of our lives. America would acknowledge extreme forms of homosexuality in the public arena. It would be forced to sit in on seminars in fisting at universities. It would be forced to act the unwilling voyeur and admire, for example, the "water sport" of one man urinating into another's mouth as art. It would be forced to accept these behaviors as normative and teach their authenticity

---

[9]A more recent study has this number at between 80 and 98 percent; see http://health.usnews.com/healthnews/news/articles/2012/07/20/biology-leaves-gay-men-highly-vulnerable-to-hiv-study .

[10]See Volume 5 of this series, *Culture Wars*, 2015, Part III, Sexual Politics.

in elementary and secondary schools, where children who were not yet sure how to brush their teeth would learn how the polymorphous perverse use a dental dam.

It would be short-sighted to understand the critical mass now mobilized behind admitting gays in the military simply as a product of the Clinton presidency, although this administration is well aware of the debt it owes gay groups who fueled its campaign with $3.4 million in contributions.[11] The current debate is rather the final step in a twenty-year-old agenda. It was in 1972 that more than 200 gay organizations put together their 12-point "Gay Rights Platform."[12] One point was: "Federal encouragement and support for pro-homosexual sex education courses in public schools; prepared and taught by gay men and women, presenting homosexuality as a valid, healthy preference and life-style." Another was: "Repeal all laws governing age of consent." But right up there near the top, in number two position, was: "Permit homosexuals to serve in the Armed Forces." The genie brings with him a package deal.

The homosexual power structure sees the issue of gays in the military as the tip of an iceberg whose lower depths it is quite willing to describe. "This isn't about just the military," said David Mixner, Clinton's adviser on gay issues, after the president was forced into a temporary compromise. "This is about homophobia in America. It's the beginning of a two-year, a three-year fight in 11 states [where various initiatives affecting gay rights are on the ballot] and in school-board rooms around the country."[13] The agenda is not about civil liberties; it is about transformation.

---

[11]Smith and Haider-Markel, *Gay and Lesbian Americans and Political Participation: A Reference Handbook*, ABC-CLIO, 2002, p. 151: "Estimates suggest that LGBT activists contributed at least $3.4 million to Clinton's victory."

[12]Dr. Scott Lively, *Redeeming The Rainbow*, Veritas Aeterna Press, 2009, p. 204.

[13]*The Heterodoxy Handbook*, op. cit., p. 23.

3

Conservatism Needs a Heart

What's happened to the triumph of conservatism? In the wake of Clinton's re-election, it is a question that has become the topic of the season on the political right. Recently, *The Weekly Standard* ran a cover symposium titled "Is There a Worldwide Conservative Crackup?" Conservative ideas appear to be ascendant, the editors point out, but the party that represents them is getting battered. In an essay in *The Wall Street Journal* titled, "What Ails Conservatism?" two of the right's articulate theorists, William Kristol and David Brooks, put it another way: "The era of big government may be over, but a new era of conservative governance hasn't yet begun. Why the delay?"[1]

The short answer is confusion in the ranks. Kristol and Brooks identify three tendencies representing the current conservative outlook: the anti-government, "leave-us-alone" faction; the family values movement, which wants to "re-moralize" society; and the federalists, who want to give power back to the states. What is missing in these agendas, according to the authors, is America itself. Individually, the tendencies may be healthy responses to the threats from the left. But what is missing is "a conservatism committed to national greatness." Let Clinton talk about building a

Originally published October 6, 1997, http://archive.frontpagemag.com/Printable.aspx?ArtId=24387; http://www.salon.com/1997/10/06/nc_06heart/.

[1]William Kristol and David Brooks, "What Ails Conservatism," *The Wall Street Journal*, September 15, 1997, http://www.wsj.com/articles/SB874276753849168000.

bridge to a multicultural, diverse, politically correct 21st century. "Conservatives should act to shape the next century as an American century."

But what additional electoral constituency do Kristol and Brooks imagine GOP leaders would attract if they came out as patriotic nationalists beating the drum of "American greatness?" Republicans are already presumed to be patriotic, and they sound the theme of American greatness often. But, since words are cheap, so does Bill Clinton. Moreover, Clinton is no stranger to the other conservative tendencies identified by Kristol and Brooks. After all, his key State of the Union line was: "The era of big government is over."[2] Family values constituted a major part of the most recent Democratic convention. And in his presidential acceptance speech, Clinton actually claimed credit for six of the ten points in the Republicans' "Contract With America."

The sad truth that the conservative handwringers seem to overlook is that Bill Clinton, their great antagonist, is presiding over a conservative agenda, however watered down it may seem. To most voters, Clinton appears to be balancing the federal budget, reforming the welfare system, toughening government attitudes toward crime and shrinking the liberal state. And Clinton has done one more thing which any right-wing party must do to win the political center and, with it, a majority of the American electorate. He has presented himself as a conservative with a heart.

What really ails conservatives is not that they lack the lift of an expansive national dream, but that they appear to have a mean spirit. Republicans present themselves as accountants whose principal concerns are budgets and marginal tax rates, rather than the human beings whose hearts as well as minds they need to win. For all the economic good times of the present, the country is distressed about declining schools, drugs, and an abusive popular culture. What do Republicans talk about? They talk about whether

[2]William J. Clinton, "Address Before a Joint Session of the Congress on the State of the Union," January 23, 1996.

there should be a flat tax, a value-added tax or a tax credit. Forget national greatness, whatever that inflated concept might mean. Republicans would be better off asking themselves why the American people want Bill Clinton to implement their agenda. It is because they trust Bill Clinton to do it with compassion. They like the fact that Clinton tries to identify himself with America's diverse constituencies, black and white, native- and foreign-born, the middle class, the disadvantaged and the poor.

Of course, there is great injustice in this perception. It is the liberal welfare state created by Clinton's party that has destroyed the inner-city family and created a culture of poverty that has blighted the lives of millions of children. It is the Democratic apologists on crime who have made our nation's once-safe streets a minefield of terrors for women and the young, especially in our poorer neighborhoods. It is the feel-good, relativist, anti-authority fashions of the progressive left that have brought America's schools low. And it is the teacher union mafia that has deprived poor children of the access to vouchers and the better education that private schools can offer.

Here is what would make a promising Republican platform: liberate the American people, particularly minorities and the poor, from the chains of progressive policies. But to be credible in advancing this agenda, conservatives have to readjust their priorities and refashion their political language to show people they actually care.

4

Political Roles Reversed

As in the natural world, seismic shifts in the political landscape occur below the surface. Only after accumulating a critical mass do they become visible. Until then, one can track their movement in the growing incoherence of the political language and in the terms we use to describe our political choices, like "liberal" and "conservative." As even the most casual observer must realize by now, these terms no longer identify a consistent set of political positions. Instead, they increasingly refer to policies that are often the opposite of what the terms themselves imply. Take the late, unlamented tobacco bill, the most passionate liberal cause of Clinton's second term. Why should this qualify as a liberal bill, except in the trivial sense that a coalition of self-identified "liberals" spawned the campaign in effect to outlaw the weed?

What is liberal about a bill that would use the power of the state to crush an industry that is otherwise legal, and whose customers voluntarily pay billions a year to purchase its product while knowing its medical consequencces? What is liberal about a strategy that would achieve such social agendas by regulating what people can see and hear, and by imposing a regressive tax whose burdens would fall principally on working people and the poor? But then, what is liberal about liberals *at all* anymore, except their attitudes toward hard drugs and sex?

Originally published July 27, 1998, http://archive.frontpagemag.com/readArticle.aspx?ARTID=22638.

This obsolescence of the political language serves to reveal how profoundly the parties themselves have changed; how much they have traded places. The opponent of the tobacco legislation, the "conservative" party, is in practice the party of liberal values—deregulatory, individualistic—and of social reform. It is Republicans who want to shrink the power of the federal bureaucracies and devolve it through the states to the people. It is the so-called liberal party that is dominated by a faction of political reactionaries and puritan busybodies fighting tooth and nail to expand the federal government and reinstitute the kind of moral prohibitionism that was proven bankrupt more than a half-century ago.

The reactionary character of the "progressive" agenda extends well beyond the tobacco follies. In the area of so-called civil rights legislation, it is liberals who have turned back the clock by instituting governmental race preferences. It is liberals who have promoted cultural separatism to the point that our most "progressive" and elite academic institutions have become the centers of segregated life right down to separate (but equal?) graduation ceremonies. It is liberals who are fighting a rearguard action to defend these political anachronisms even after they have been declared unconstitutional by the courts and rejected by electoral majorities at the polls.

It is not only civil rights issues that bring out the reactionary attitudes of the left. Liberals and progressives have had to be dragged over the bridge to the 21st century clinging to a welfare leviathan that in 30 years has only deepened and broadened the ranks of the poor, destroying families and community support systems for minorities trapped in the inner city. It is liberals who seem only able to repeat the past—the endless demands for money to fund systems that are morally and practically bankrupt; the resistance to reforms that would break up the educational bureaucracies which exploit minorities and the poor, whose children are the only ones still trapped in the public schools. It is liberals who fight to preserve bankrupt bilingual education programs that prevent children of immigrants from learning English, their best hope of unlocking the door to economic opportunity and the American dream.

By contrast, it is increasingly apparent that the conservative and Republican opponents of liberalism comprise the new party of social reform. It is conservatives whose self-conceived mission is to return power usurped by government to the American people; to chip away at a cultural and political status quo that has not worked, and has been rejected by the American public.

Liberalism now, and for some time, has been having great difficulty facing the social future. It is not for nothing that liberals were either promoters of, or at best ambivalent towards, the monstrous socialist experiment that collapsed in ruins just a decade past. Even liberals who rejected the means of socialism were willing to go along with the idea that social planning and redistribution of wealth were noble, progressive ideals. Now that the Marxist moment has passed, brutally exposed as a destructive social delusion, liberals are demonstrating that they are unable to replace it with a better idea.

The primary institutional bases of the left are the trade unions and the universities. The unions are a declining 19th-century behemoth, preoccupied these days with the threat of immigrant labor; with defending outmoded native industries against the competition of industrious foreigners; with retarding change in the private sector; and with expanding featherbeds in governmental agencies. The liberal arts divisions of American universities, whose closest antecedent is the medieval monastery, constitute the last natural refuge for the socialist left, a place where the catastrophe of Marxism may not register for another 100 years or more.

Beneath the surface, however, the tectonic plates of American politics have shifted. This event first registered on the political Richter scale in 1994 with the Republican victory in the midterm congressional elections. At the time, the odd, oxymoronic term employed to describe what had happened was "the conservative revolution." It was a term for which Newt Gingrich and his Republican radicals—such are the ironies of history—were made to pay a heavy political price by the liberal left—a fact that only underscored the obsolescence of the political terminology.

Thanks to the effective and hypocritical attacks on Gingrich by liberal reactionaries in the Democratic Party, and by the defenders of the *ancien régime* in the nation's press, there was a temporary slowing of the progressive tide that the Contract With America had unloosed. President Clinton was reelected in 1996. That was the superficial restoration. For it was only because of his surrender to Gingrich's balanced budget and welfare reforms—and possibly illegal campaign contributions from reactionary dictatorships overseas—that Clinton was able to win a second term. The simultaneous re-election of the Republican congressional majorities—the first time this had happened in 60 years—consolidated the underlying trend and established it as an epoch-making fact of American political life.

In the four years since the Gingrich revolution, 357 Democratic elected officials have switched parties, including the only Native American ever elected to the United States Senate. Just last month, Herman Badillo, the most prominent Puerto Rican political leader in New York City—a metropolis that was once a stronghold of Democratic liberalism and is now the power base of a Republican reform mayor—became a Republican too. For 30 years, Badillo had been a party-line liberal Democrat, as congressman, borough president and deputy mayor. But now he has had second thoughts. In a statement explaining his conversion, Badillo wrote:

> Many Democrats believe that some ethnic groups, such as Hispanics, should not be held to the same standards as others. This is a repellent and destructive concept, a self-fulfilling prophecy of failure. Fortunately, the ethnic groups hurt by these patronizing policies are beginning to understand that low standards mean low results—a realization that will move people in these groups to the GOP. Democrats don't see that this is happening, because they take their historic constituencies for granted. They believe that Hispanics will vote Democratic in the future because they voted Democratic in the past. In the Hispanic community,

> however, there is a real desire for change—the kind of change that Democratic policies cannot achieve. Democratic policies consistently harm minorities by permitting students to graduate from college without college-level skills, allowing crime to go unpunished and making welfare an absolute right regardless of one's willingness to work.[1]

It would be hard to find a more succinct summary of what has been happening under the surface of American politics for the last two decades, all in preparation for the political earthquake ahead.

Modern conservatism is a movement of "leave-us-alone" libertarians, middle-class entrepreneurs and ordinary American workers rebelling against the bureaucratic elitism of the welfare state. The liberal party, the party of trade-union apparatchiks and government bureaucrats, of academic monks and *kitsch* Marxists, is the party of political statism and racial spoils systems. It is the party of political bureaucrats and reactionaries. In contrast, the conservative party is the party of little people—small business entrepreneurs, blue-collar workers, upwardly mobile immigrants and cyberspace libertarians. It is a party described by Newt Gingrich as one that wants "to break down the old system and return the power it has usurped to the people for whom it was intended." In the context of American-style democracy, you can't get much more "revolutionary" than that.

---

[1]http://archive.frontpagemag.com/readArticle.aspx?ARTID=22638.

5

The African-American Amen Chorus

A revealing aspect of the current White House crisis is the racial gap in public opinion polls. When the world discovered in January that the president was having sex with a young intern, a *New York Times* poll found that 81 percent of blacks (compared to 58 percent of whites) still approved of the way the president was conducting his job. When asked whether the President shared the moral values of most Americans, fully 77 percent of blacks (twice as many as whites) said yes. Nine months later, after the discovery of the stained dress and the release of the Starr Report, 63 percent of blacks still thought the president—now a proven liar and philanderer—shared the nation's morality. This was nearly three times the number of whites—22 percent—who thought he did. This striking disparity, reflecting a unique community support for the president—even feminists are more ambivalent—has prompted several attempts to explain it.

According to a widely quoted comment by comedian Chris Rock, Clinton's African-American support is inspired by the fact that he is "the first black president." Explains Rock: "It's very simple. Black people are used to being persecuted. Hence, they relate to Clinton."[1]

Originally published, October 12, 1998, http://archive.frontpagemag.com/Printable.aspx?ArtId=24304; http://www.salon.com/1998/10/12/12horo/.
[1]http://snltranscripts.jt.org/96/96emono.phtml.

The comedian is not alone in these ruminations. In an article surveying African-American reactions, *New York Times* reporter Kevin Sack quotes NAACP head Julian Bond saying, "You just can't help but think that some of this [investigation of Clinton] is race-based," while Harvard Professor Alvin Poussaint reports that rumors have been circulating in the African-American community to the effect that Clinton "must have had black ancestry."[2] A full-blown expression of these attitudes is on display in the current *New Yorker,* where Nobel laureate Toni Morrison writes of the crisis: "African-American men seemed to understand it right away. Years ago, in the middle of the Whitewater investigation, one heard the first murmurs: white skin notwithstanding, this is our first black president. Blacker than any actual black person who could ever be elected in our children's lifetime. After all, Clinton displays almost every trope of blackness: single-parent household, born poor, working-class, saxophone-playing, McDonald's-and-junk-food-loving boy from Arkansas."[3]

Perhaps one has to be, as I am, a lapsed man of the left to react to the loopy anti-white attitudes laced into these cadences from our most celebrated and rewarded national literary figure. Blacker than any actual black person who could ever be elected in our children's lifetimes? Apparently, Colin Powell, the most popular presidential hopeful in polls taken only two years ago, isn't all that black, having been born into a two-parent household and—though poor in origins and familiar with discrimination—not known for his unhealthy food addictions or stereotypical musical tastes.

On the other hand, perhaps the liberal identification of blackness with victimization and social dysfunction isn't so wide of the

---

[2]Kevin Sack, "Testing Of A President: The Supporters; Blacks Stand by a President Who 'Has Been There for Us'," *The New York Times,* September 19, 1998, http://www.nytimes.com/1998/09/19/us/testing-president-supporters-blacks-stand-president-who-has-been-there-for-us.html.

[3]Toni Morrison, "The Talk of the Town," *The New Yorker,* October 5, 1998, p. 31, http://www.newyorker.com/magazine/1998/10/05/comment-6543.

mark in explaining the sympathy of political leftists like Morrison and Bond, or the support of the Congressional Black Caucus for the immoralist from Little Rock. Perhaps it reflects a resonance in the black community to the White House's cynical strategy of defining presidential deviancy down: "They all do it." Roosevelt, Kennedy, Eisenhower, Bush—they all lie and cheat, so why shouldn't our guy? This certainly seems to be the corrosive logic behind which some blacks have rallied behind criminal politicians, like corrupt and crack-addicted Washington Mayor Marion Barry. It could easily account for the undertones of racial paranoia—"they're out to get our guys"—that surfaced when African-American members of the Clinton administration, Ron Brown, Mike Espy and Hazel O'Leary, all came under investigation for irregularities in office.

Which is precisely the way Toni Morrison frames Clinton's problem: "When virtually all the African-American Clinton appointees began, one by one, to disappear, when the president's body, his privacy, his un-policed sexuality became the focus of the persecution, when he was metaphorically seized and body-searched, who could gainsay these black men who knew whereof they spoke?" According to Morrison, the message from white America is clear. "No matter how smart you are, how hard you work, how much coin you earn for us, we will put you in your place or put you out of the place."[4] Or, as the late Malcolm X, in his racist phase, once put it: "What do you call an educated Negro with a B.A. or an M.A., with a B.S., or a Ph.D.? The answer? You call him a nigger, because that is what the white man calls him, a nigger."[5]

Putting aside the racial paranoia of such attitudes coming from a black Nobel prizewinner in the era of Oprah Winfrey, one might still ask why Clinton should be "our guy" from an African-Amer-

---

[4]Ibid.

[5]Lionel Kimble, "What Do They Call A Black Person With A Ph.D.? . . . Or Why I Sit On The Sidelines," Chicago State University, March 27, 2013, http://csufacultyvoice.blogspot.com/2013/03/what-do-they-call-black-person-with-ph.html.

ican perspective. Isn't this the President Clinton who established his New Democrat credentials by delivering a verbal slap to Sista Souljah on the eve of his election, and banishing Jesse Jackson from the circle of his power? Isn't this the Clinton who betrayed his old friend and political soul mate, Lani Guinier, after nominating her to be his civil-rights chief, leaving her to the mercies of her political enemies while pretending ignorance of who she was and what she believed? Isn't this the Clinton whose vaunted "dialogue on race", the centerpiece of his strategy for redressing minority grievances, ended up drowned in his own sex scandal while the final report of his race commission called merely for more dialogue? Reviewing the report, liberal columnist Frank Rich summed up the administration's record on race as follows: "high ideals, beautiful show, one-night stand."

Indeed, isn't this the Clinton who brought Jackson back into the fold, and wrapped himself in the protective cloak of the black community and its historic symbols, only when he himself was in terminal trouble because of his sexual escapades, and only after he had lost whatever power he once may have had to seriously advance their agendas? Surely there have been few more repellent demonstrations of Clinton's user ethic than his traipsing off to Africa to apologize for slavery, Jackson and Maxine Waters in tow, in the heat of the Lewinsky scandal only after he had been trapped in his lies and become an international laughingstock. Then there was his performance on Martha's Vineyard—debasing the anniversary of Martin Luther King, Jr.'s March on Washington to make yet another unconvincing confession of regret that he had "sinned." These are the kinds of gestures that give tokenism a bad name.

Still, the most prominent voices of black leadership have joined willingly in these charades. There was John Lewis at the Martin Luther King, Jr. anniversary, solemnly and tearfully forgiving Clinton and urging the rest of the country to forgive him as well. It was terrible, apparently, for the rest of us to be so judgmental. This was the same John Lewis who not so long ago was denouncing Newt Gingrich and the congressional Republicans as

"Nazis" for attempting to reform a bankrupt and destructive welfare system.

This is what the melodramas of conspiracy and witch-hunt are really about: not racial persecution but political loyalties. The previously cited *Times* report also noted that "many of those interviewed said they not only subscribed to Hillary Rodham Clinton's statement that a 'vast right-wing conspiracy' had targeted her husband, but also that they believed the conspirators were motivated by a desire to reverse the gains made by blacks during the Clinton administration."[6] One paranoia is linked to another. Liberals and leftists from Waters to Morrison to Hillary Clinton have convinced the African-American community that Republicans are racists and want to reverse the gains of the civil-rights era. This is the really Big Lie that keeps blacks in Clinton's corner and safely secure on the liberal plantation.

If liberals really want instances of racial persecution, they need go no further than their own character assassination of Clarence Thomas in an episode of sexual McCarthyism (to use Alan Dershowitz's inflammatory phrase) whose charges, unlike those against Clinton, are unproven and unfounded. Where are the liberal apologies for this racial atrocity? Or consider a more unpalatable thought: the political persecution of Gingrich, which cannot be far from the Speaker's own reflections as he contemplates hearings that will determine the president's fate. Democrat leaders of the House, hoping to reverse the results of the Republican victory in the 1994 election, leveled 370 phony ethics charges against Gingrich before they got one ludicrous claim to stick—and I'm willing to bet there is not one in a hundred Gingrich-loathing liberals who can describe the specifics of the charge. Yet Gingrich was censured, fined, and politically destroyed outside his conservative base by what was little more than a liberal smear campaign, and there is not a single liberal now defending Clinton and bemoaning

[6]Kevin Sack, "Testing Of a President: The Supporters; Blacks Stand by a President Who 'Has Been There for Us'," op. cit.

the unfairness of his prosecution who has offered any second thoughts about this outrage.

That is because the outrage, like that against Thomas, serves their political agendas. In the present presidential crisis, Gingrich is the point-man for the "right-wing conspiracy" that is seeking to bring down a leader in order to "reverse the civil-rights gains of African-Americans." Cease to believe in this political mythology and what happens to the president, or to the leftist demagogues in the Congressional Black Caucus who are still wedded to every jot and tittle of the failed welfare state?

What if Republicans no longer function as racial bogeymen? What if African-Americans were to see that Republican policies like educational choice, and Republican values like personal responsibility, work to the benefit of the African-American community? What if they were no longer to vote 90 percent Democratic? What if they were to free themselves from the chains of a one-party system that feeds them tokens and shamelessly exploits their moral capital for its own venal agendas? These are the real stakes that keep the political melodrama alive, and prevent a taken-for-granted political community from fully entering the American polity and exercising its political power.

6

Clinton's Academic Shills

When the dust has finally settled on this lost year of American politics, there may be consolation in the fact that much of the damage is reparable, and that most of the scars inflicted on the nation will be readily healed. As a new election cycle rolls around, fresh faces will become the focus of public attention. President Clinton, along with his seductions and prevarications, will be gone. There will be renewed respect for the privacy rights of public figures. Even Congress will come together and, in a bipartisan moment, undo the independent counsel law that liberals contrived as a weapon against conservatives and conservatives turned into a weapon against liberals, and then against themselves.

But there is at least one institution that has thrust itself to the fore in this presidential crisis, which will not be so easy to repair. That institution is the American university, which in the midst of the presidential battle volunteered a battalion of academics to serve the sordid Clinton cause.[1] As the House Judiciary Committee was gearing up for impeachment in October, a full-page political ad appeared in *The New York Times* sponsored by an ad hoc committee called "Historians in Defense of the Constitution." The historians declared that in their professional judgment there

---

Originally published February 1, 1999, http://www.salon.com/1999/02/01/nc_01horo_2/.

[1]For more on this subject see *The Left In The University*, Volume 7 of this series.

was no constitutional basis for impeaching the president, and that to do so would undermine our political order.[2] The historians' statement was eagerly seized on by the president's congressional defenders and deployed as a weapon against his congressional accusers. In the none-too-meticulous hands of the pols, the signers became 400 "constitutional experts" who had exposed the Republicans' attempt at a "*coup d'état*."[3]

One of the three organizers of the statement, Sean Wilentz, even appeared before the House Judiciary Committee to warn the Republicans that "history will hunt you down" for betraying the American Founders. On the day his Senate trial began, Clinton referred reporters to the "constitutional experts" who had gone on record that he should not have been impeached.

The statement itself is something of a fraud. Its signers are not constitutional experts at all. One of them, Julian Bond, is not even a trained historian, though two universities—Maryland and Virginia—have appointed him a "professor of history." Now head of the NAACP, Bond is a leftist with a failed political career whose university posts were in effect political appointments.

Another signer, Henry Louis Gates, is not a historian but an essayist and a professor of literature. A third, Orlando Patterson, is a first-rate sociologist. Perhaps the three are affirmative action signers designed to increase the African-American presence on the list. All three, of course, are men of the left.

Wilentz is a socialist whose expertise is social, not political, history. A second organizer, C. Vann Woodward, is a distinguished historian of 19th- and 20th-century America but not a historian of the Constitution. The third, Arthur Schlesinger, Jr., is a partisan Democrat who has written adoring books on Andrew Jackson,

---

[2]Sean Wilentz, Arthur Schlesinger, C. Vann Woodward, "Dear Henry," *Salon.com,* January 21, 1999, http://www.salon.com/1999/01/21/newsc_28/.

[3]"Historians' Statement on Impeachment," *Washington Post,* October 28, 1998, http://www.washingtonpost.com/wp-srv/politics/special/clinton/stories/petition102898.htm.

Franklin Roosevelt and the Kennedy brothers, but not on the Constitution.

The same could be said for almost all the "historians in defense of the Constitution"—with a handful of exceptions like Pauline Maier, who has indeed studied and written about the founding, and Garry Wills. Others on the list have even fewer credentials than the organizers to pontificate on these matters. Todd Gitlin is a professor of sociology and cultural studies whose only contribution to historical knowledge is a tendentious book justifying the radical '60s from the perspective of a former president of SDS. Jonathan Weiner is a writer for *The Nation* whose major publication is a book on John Lennon's FBI file. Michael Kazin is another *Nation* writer whose work as a historian is on American populism. John Judis is a *New Republic* editor who wrote a biography of William Buckley and a book on 20th-century conservatives. Jeffrey Herf's expertise is modern German history; Robert Dallek and Bruce Kuklick are 20th-century diplomatic historians. Maurice Isserman is another *Nation* regular and a historian of the 20th-century American left.

Another signer, Ellen Du Bois, is typical of a large cohort in what have become the thoroughly politicized humanities. She is a professor of women's history at UCLA and a radical feminist. She is joined as a signer by other zealous feminists whose academic work has been the elaboration of feminist themes. These include Gerda Lerner, Linda Gordon, Ruth Rosen, Sara Evans, Christine Stansell (Wilentz's wife) and Alice Kessler-Harris. Two months after the *Times* ad appeared, while the House was pursuing its impeachment vote, a notice was posted on the Internet announcing that Du Bois would be a speaker (along with two other well-known leftists) at a "Reed College Symposium on the Joy of Struggle."[4] The symposium was a presentation of the Reed

[4]"On The Joy Of Struggle" Symposium To focus On Social Justice, Reed College, October 15, 1998, http://www.reed.edu/news_center/press_releases/1998–1999/.

College Multiculturalism Center and was co-sponsored by the Feminist Union, the Queer Alliance, Earth First, Amnesty at Reed, the Latino/a Student Association and the Reed student activities office.

Not all the signers of the "Historians in Defense of the Constitution" statement are radical ideologues, but the political inspiration of the gesture is unmistakable and reflects the ongoing intellectual corruption of the academy. By assembling 400 historians "in defense of the Constitution," the organizers imply that these well-known liberal and left-wing academics are defending the document's original intent. Since when, however, have liberals and leftists become defenders of the doctrine of original intent? Are any of the signers on record as opposing the loose constructionism of the Warren court? Were any of the scholars exercised when the Brennan majority inserted a nonexistent "right of privacy" into the Constitution to justify its decision in Roe vs. Wade? Were any of them defenders of Judge Robert Bork—the leading theorist of "original intent"—when a coalition of political vigilantes set out to destroy his nomination to the Supreme Court by trolling for his video-store purchases to see if he had rented X-rated films (talk about "sexual McCarthyism")?

Not only is the answer to all these questions negative, but dozens of the same historians, including organizers Schlesinger and Wilentz, are "veterans of the politicized misuse of history" (as Romesh Ponnuru put it in a recent *National Review* article), having previously signed a "historians' brief" to the Supreme Court in support of abortion. Concern for the original intent of the Constitution apparently enters these academic hearts only when it can be deployed against Republicans and conservatives. This probably explains why the office address listed at the bottom of the historians' statement is the Washington address of People for the American Way, a national lobby for the political left.

Partisan pronouncements by groups invoking the authority of a profession are treacherous exercises. They misrepresent what scholarship can do, such as deciding questions that are inherently controversial. More important, they cast a chill on academic discourse by suggesting there is a historians' party line. When Jesse Lemisch, a notable left-wing historian, tried to organize a counter-statement favoring impeachment (over Clinton's wag-the-dog policy in the Persian Gulf), he received vicious e-mails from his colleagues and Wilentz stopped speaking to him.

The politicization reflected in these episodes is a fairly recent development in academic life. Its origin can be traced to a famous battle at the annual meeting of the American Historical Association in 1969. At that meeting, a "radical caucus" led by Staughton Lynd and Arthur Waskow attempted to have the organization pass an official resolution calling for American withdrawal from the Vietnam War and an end to the "repression" of the Black Panther Party. Opposition to the resolution was led by Marxist historian Eugene Genovese and liberal historian H. Stuart Hughes. Four years earlier, Genovese had been a national *cause célèbre* when he publicly declared his support for the communist Viet Cong. He nonetheless opposed the radical call for such a resolution as a "totalitarian" threat to the profession and to the intellectual standards on which it was based.[5] H. Stuart Hughes, who had been an anti-Vietnam War candidate for Congress, joined in asserting that any antiwar resolution would "politicize" the AHA, and urging the members to reject it.

Hughes and Genovese narrowly won the battle, but eventually lost the war. The AHA joined other professional academic associations in becoming institutions of the political left. The politicization went so far that, a few years ago, philosopher Richard Rorty smugly applauded the fact that "the power base of the left in America is now in the universities, since the trade unions have largely been killed off."[6] In a *Nation* editorial ("Scholars on the

---

[5]See http://www.newrepublic.com/book/review/what-politics-does-history .

[6]*The Heterodoxy Handbook,* David Horowitz and Peter Collier, eds., Regnery 1994, p. vii.

Left," Feb. 1, 1999) Jon Wiener, one of the signers of the historians' statement, boasts that "three members of the *Nation* family" have just been elected to head three powerful professional associations—the American Historical Association, the Organization of American Historians and the Modern Language Association—with a combined membership of 54,000 academics.

Eric Foner, Columbia professor and president-elect of the American Historical Association, is the scion of a family of well-known American Communists—a supporter of the Rosenbergs, a sponsor of Communist Party stalwarts Angela Davis and Herbert Aptheker, a lifelong member of the radical left and, recently, an organizer of the secretaries' union at Columbia and would-be architect of an alliance between intellectuals and the working class. David Montgomery, the new president of the Organization of American Historians, is described in *The Nation* as "a factory worker, union organizer and Communist militant in St. Paul in the Fifties."[7] Montgomery's ties to labor remain strong, and he was active in the Yale clerical workers' strike and other campus and union struggles.

Edward Said is a former member of the Palestine Liberation Organization's governing council and was the most prominent apologist in America for PLO terrorism until he fell out with Yassir Arafat over the Oslo peace accords, which he regarded as a "sellout" to the Israeli imperialists. An icon in the leftist academy, Said's overrated work is little more than warmed-over Marxism. As historian Keith Windschuttle observes: "Even Lenin has a more convincing explanation of imperialism than Said"—and adds, with examples: "Said's inept handling of historical material is evident throughout the book."[8]

---

[7]See http://www.thenation.com/article/david-montgomery-grand-master-workman/ .

[8]Keith Windschuttle, "Edward Said's Orientalism Revisited," January 1999, http://www.newcriterion.com/articles.cfm/Edward-Said-s—ldquo-Orientalism-rdquo—revisited-2937.

The deeper problem in this episode is the serious absence of intellectual diversity on university faculties. Such diversity would provide a check on the *hubris* of academic activists like Wilentz and his co-signers. The fact is that leftists in the university, through decades of political hiring and promotion, and through systematic intellectual intimidation, have virtually driven conservative thought from the halls of academe. Now a Communist ideologue like Angela Davis can be officially invited to speak at a quality institution like Brandeis and be paid $10,000 for her effort, while a conservative like Jeanne Kirkpatrick, invited to the same institution, will be asked by administrators not to come because they are unable to guarantee her safety.[9] Columbia University will host an official reception honoring Herbert Aptheker, a Communist Party apparatchik and apologist for the Soviet rape of Hungary, but will close down a conference featuring University of California trustee Ward Connerly because he holds politically incorrect views against racial preferences.[10]

An inquiry made to one of the handful of known conservatives allowed to teach a humanities subject at Princeton confirms the following suspicion: in Wilentz's history department, not a single conservative is to be found among 56 faculty members. If he believes in the original intent of the Constitution to create a pluralistic society, that is something for Professor Wilentz to be concerned about.

---

[9] See http://www.dartblog.com/data/2014/05/011496.php .

[10] David Horowitz, "Fascism by Any Other Name," *Salon.com*, December 7, 1998, http://www.salon.com/1998/12/07/nc_07horo/.

7

Moral Issues in Politics

In the aftermath of the Senate impeachment trial of President Clinton, the nation has been struggling to move on, to put the scandal and the partisan standoff over the impeachment process behind it and to get on with the political business at hand. Both left and right have stakes in moving forward, particularly as a new election cycle approaches. With a few exceptions, the consensus on both sides reflects this desire. Nonetheless, closure is not a foregone conclusion.

One distraction has been the testimony of Juanita Broaddrick, previously known as Jane Doe #5, whom the president allegedly raped in an Arkansas hotel room twenty years ago. Another is Monica Lewinsky's TV appearance and the publication of her gossipy book. Both have poured fuel on old fires. Some suicidal Republicans, Bill Kristol most prominent among them, have called for new congressional investigations into the Broaddrick charges. In a *Weekly Standard* cover editorial that asks "Can't we just move on?" Kristol throws down this regrettable gauntlet: "The only honorable answer to the question is no."[1] Democrats, on the other hand, have responded to the new charges with equally familiar agnostic attitudes toward the allegations themselves, coupled with pleas to bury the whole mess, so that once again they appear in a group as partisan defenders of the reprobate.

Originally published March 15, 1999, http://archive.frontpagemag.com/Printable.aspx?ArtId=22452; http://www.salon.com/1999/03/15/nc_15horo/.

[1]http://www.weeklystandard.com/Content/Protected/Articles/000/000/009/650pntsu.asp.

The real problem underlying this stasis is that none of the major players really wants to examine the events of this deeply troubling year in a way in which they would have to admit where they went wrong. Mercifully, there is one group that has actually begun to do just that and, as unlikely it may seem, it is the Christian Right. In a reaction triggered by the impeachment failure, several leaders of the Christian political community have begun to discuss whether religious conservatives should now withdraw from the political process altogether. In a stunning confession of misjudgment, Paul Weyrich—the man who gave the Moral Majority its name—has announced that his movement's 25 year-long political effort has been based on an assumption that he now realizes was an error. This is the assumption that the majority of the American people share his moral outlook. Weyrich puts it this way: "If there really were a moral majority out there, Bill Clinton would have been driven out of office months ago."[2]

This is certainly correct, and refreshing. (Would that more politicians had the courage to admit publicly they were wrong.) Weyrich's view of his political failure, and of America's unreceptive attitude towards his moral viewpoint, is quite stark. "We got our people elected. But that did not result in the adoption of our agenda. The reason, I think, is that politics itself has failed. And politics has failed because of the collapse of the culture. The culture we are living in becomes an ever-wider sewer. In truth, I think we are caught up in a cultural collapse of historic proportions, a collapse so great that it simply overwhelms politics."[3]

Weyrich is certainly wrong about America. In the popular culture, it is the year of romance (*Shakespeare in Love*) and duty, honor, country (*Saving Private Ryan*). As for the civic culture, every social indicator Bill Bennett and other conservatives have

---

[2]Paul M. Weyrich, "Letter to Conservatives," *National Center for Public Policy Research*, February 16, 1999, https://www.nationalcenter.org/Weyrich299.html.

[3]Ibid.

used to describe its downward arc through the era of liberal irresponsibility is currently headed in the right direction. Crime rates, teenage pregnancies and out-of-wedlock births are on the decline. Combine that with full employment, and it would be more appropriate to say that things haven't been better for a long time. Only someone attached to an irrecoverable past, and therefore hostile to change as such, could react so negatively towards a culture that is doing all right by any reasonable measure.

But Weyrich is certainly correct about religious conservatism like his. In fact he is right about religious politics across the board. One of the most enduring negative consequences of the Sixties was the injection of chiliastic ambitions into the normal political culture. The utopian idea of a "liberation" that would encompass both the personal and the social has roots not only in Karl Marx and the Paris Commune, but in Martin Luther and the Puritan settlement. "The personal is political," a Sixties slogan that originated with the feminist left, could just as well describe the moral aspirations of the Christian Right. Moreover, it could easily stand as a summary statement of the attitudes that created the impeachment debacle.

"The great debates in American politics," according to Christian right candidate Gary Bauer, "end up being essentially moral debates." In his current stump speech, Bauer likes to compare the anti-abortion crusade to Abraham Lincoln and the anti-slavery struggle. It is, he cries, "the soul of the Republican Party."[4] In fact the abortion issue is not the soul of the Republican Party so much as its most divisive issue. In comparing abortion to slavery, moreover, Bauer conveniently overlooks the fact that the slavery issue was too morally divisive to be resolved by the political process. It took a bloody civil war to do that. If civil war is what Gary Bauer wants, he should be prepared to say so and to recognize his brotherhood with other radicals of the past, including the Sixties activists who used that same analogy to identify , and legitimize, their war

[4]http://www.ontheissues.org/Gary_Bauer.htm#Civil_Rights.

with America. This is not the voice of responsible politics and has no place in a pluralistic polity, let alone a party that regards itself as "conservative."

Everyone who subscribes to the idea of American pluralism thereby accepts the idea that there are limits to what politics can accomplish, and to what is proper advocacy in a democratic society. Democracies work through coalitions, achieved through compromises that are both moral and political. Compromise is the condition of their civil stability and peace. To articulate what is, in effect, the political equivalent of a call for civil war in a democracy like ours is nihilistic and destructive. The fundamental premise of pluralism is that morally incompatible communities agree to live with each other and respect their differences, and work together through political compromise.

That is why the new sober turn in religious conservatism is to be welcomed. The religious right has contributed greatly to the renewed public sense of responsibility and accountability in America over the last few decades, a fact the secular culture seems incapable of acknowledging. But now several of its leaders are beginning to recognize that their movement may be approaching the limits of what it can hope, politically, to achieve. Paul Weyrich concedes that the majority of Americans do not share his values and, unlike Bauer, accepts that the political agendas of a democracy are necessarily circumscribed by the shared values of its constituencies. Those who are unhappy with those values must turn to avenues other than politics for the answers they seek. Moral goals can only be achieved by persuading a majority to adopt them, not by seeking political power to enforce them.

A new book by two former leaders of the Moral Majority makes the point clearly: "Those who are looking in whole or in part to the Government to correct the problems of America are looking in the wrong place." As one of the authors explained to a reporter for *The New York Times*, "moral transformation will come one person at a time, one family at a time, one street at a time, one community at a time. It will not come from the

Government."[5] This is exactly right, and political moralists on both sides of the aisle—including the sin-taxers in the White House who want to save citizens from their bad habits—would do well to heed it. The failure to do this is what led to the political fiasco of the impeachment process. Now that the evidence is in, few people would deny that President Clinton is morally corrupt and that his corruption has had serious consequences for his office and for the general welfare of the American people. What could have been done to deal with this problem and how was it botched? These are critical questions because it is the manner in which the corruption of the presidency was dealt with on all sides that lies at the heart of the present political impasse.

In the first place it is important to recognize the origins of the problem in the president's response to the exposure of his behavior. Once this happened, Clinton should have acknowledged that he had compromised his office and his own ability to fulfill his responsibilities. Then he should have resigned. He should have resigned not because he was morally impure or exceptionally dishonest (although he was both), but because of the damage that would inevitably ensue to the nation and his party if he decided to stay. That was, after all, why Nixon stepped down when he did, instead of taking the fight to the bitter end, as some advised him. Unfortunately, neither his responsibility to party nor country seems to have mattered to Clinton, who has not infrequently exhibited certain classic sociopathic traits.

Absent a presidential conscience, the leaders of the Democratic Party should have stepped into the vacuum and attempted to persuade Clinton to leave. Once again, there is a parallel with Nixon. It was Barry Goldwater and Howard Baker who finally informed Nixon it was time to leave. Had Democrats followed their

---

[5]Gustav Niebuhr and Richard L. Berke, "Unity Is Elusive As Religious Right Ponders 2000 Vote," *The New York Times*, March 7, 1999, http://www.nytimes.com/1999/03/07/us/unity-is-elusive-as-religious-right-ponders-2000-vote.html.

example and joined the chorus of 150 mainly liberal American newspapers who did call on Clinton to resign, his departure would have been almost inevitable.

That didn't happen, however. Instead Democrats went into a defensive mode in which they lost all connection to any discernible principle other than partisan political interest. It is only one of the many bizarre aspects of these events that, while they marched in lockstep, Democrats were able to pin the "partisan" label on their Republican opponents. Given the resistance of the president and his party to an appropriate remedy, his political opponents responded with a series of miscues that greatly compounded the already existing crisis. Special Prosecutor Ken Starr, to pick the most important offender, should never have entered the murky waters of the Paula Jones case in an attempt to make his own against the president. The sexual harassment law that allows prosecutors to probe the intimate personal histories of defendants is a brainchild of moralists on the left. In particular, it is the work of the same feminists these events have discredited by slamming them up against a human complexity that remains forever out of reach of their ideological catch-phrases. The bottomless probing into the emotional quicksand of human relationships is the very stuff of "sexual McCarthyism." It is a pursuit that conservatives above all should find both abhorrent and dangerous.

It is true that, as Republicans claimed, the president lied under oath. But it is also true, as the Democrats maintained, that the lies were about sex and that the law, as the saying goes, is sometimes an ass. Particularly a law devised by radical feminists to ensnare demonized males. What Clinton's lies revealed about his lack of character is one thing. Whether the crime he was shown to have committed actually merited his removal is quite another. This question is now moot, because the House Republicans failed to convince the American public that the president needed to go.

The impeachment process is political, not a legal or moral exercise. For all their political courage and their concern for constitutional principle, the House Republicans and the Republican Party failed in the only political task that really mattered: to persuade the American public that the president should be removed. Therefore, the appropriate course for them was to concede the terrain and admit defeat, as Paul Weyrich has done. They could have done so after the November elections sent a strong message as to where the American people stood. They did not believe their president; they were pretty well convinced he had committed a crime; but they did not want him removed. Instead Republicans pushed the process where it could not go and inevitably came up short-handed. This effort won them respect from a rank-and-file convinced that the president should be impeached, and gratified to see their party stand up for principle. But it also wasted precious political capital and precious months of political time.

Now that the impeachment process is over, there are some conservatives who do not want to move on and who are calling for renewed investigations into the Broaddrick allegations. But if the last year has taught us anything, these calls should be ignored. Disturbing though the claims of Mrs. Broaddrick may be, they are irrelevant to the political process and should be disregarded by those who have a responsibility to govern. The reason is simple. No one will ever know what happened between Mrs. Broaddrick and Bill Clinton in that hotel room, and no one can assess how it affects the president's conduct of his political office now.

Whatever happened to Juanita Broaddrick happened twenty years ago was not reported then, while she herself has lied about it, under oath. Even the courts—which are the appropriate venue for establishing the truth or falsehood of such charges—recognize the extreme difficulty of establishing facts so long after the event by imposing a statute of limitations, which the Broaddrick incident has already exceeded. The political process, beset by partisan agendas, is certainly incapable of doing do so.

Without the possibility of ascertaining the truth, a congressional investigation would be just another partisan smear campaign similar to the Democrats' successful campaign to remove Senator Bob Packwood. The fact that feminists have begun to rally to Mrs. Broaddrick's cause—now that the president who champions their political agendas can no longer be removed—should be a caution to Republicans who entertain these ideas.

This entire destructive course in America's political life began, of course, with the most disgraceful episode in the history of American liberalism—the public lynching of Justice Clarence Thomas over the unproven and unprovable allegations of a probably spurned and certainly spiteful woman seven years in the past. One of the chief lessons of the Clinton scandal is that the Anita Hill era is over. Another should be: good riddance.

8

Misdemeanors or High Crimes?

On one hundred occasions in the last three years, including innumerable campaign appearances and three State of the Union addresses, the President of the United States has looked the American people in the eye and assured them that, because of his policies, "There are no more nuclear missiles pointed at any children in the United States."[1] If you are Bill Clinton, the truth of this statement probably depends on what "are" means. But the rest of us—for our own sake and for the sake of our children—must recognize the president's statement to be a morally repulsive and dangerous lie.

The shred of truth out of which Clinton has woven his politically useful lie is a meaningless, post-Cold War agreement between Russia and the United States not to target one another's cities. But even if Russia were not a country in a state of near dissolution, its people now enraged because of NATO's "aggression" against their Slavic brethren and historic allies in Serbia, the stark military reality is that US intelligence services normally have no way of telling what targets Russia's leaders have actually chosen for their nuclear warheads. In fact, it would take exactly fifteen

---

Originally published June 1, 1999, http://archive.frontpagemag.com/Printable.aspx?ArtId=24280; http://www.salon.com/1999/05/28/espionage/.

[1]Bill Clinton uttered this phrase, in one form or another, a total of 86 times while he was in office. Allahpundit, "Obama: Hey, Let's Eliminate Nuclear Weapons," *Hot Air.com,* July 16, 2008, http://hotair.com/archives/2008/07/16/obama-hey-lets-eliminate-nuclear-weapons/.

seconds for Russian commanders to re-target any of the hundreds of strategic missiles tipped with multiple nuclear warheads that are ready to go.

By every military index available, the Russians are energetically planning for the possibility of nuclear war with the United States. And they are not alone. Thanks to technology transfers courtesy of the Clinton administration, China and North Korea are also armed with long-range missiles capable of reaching the American mainland, and they are not parties to the non-targeting agreement. According to a recent CIA report, thirteen of China's eighteen current nuclear warheads are believed to be aimed at American cities. Thanks, finally, to six years of tenacious, dedicated opposition by the Clinton administration to the Strategic Defense Initiative, America has no defense against incoming missiles and no prospect of deploying one for many years.

By every reasonable measure, the post-Cold War world is a dangerous one; perhaps even more dangerous, because our potential adversaries are more numerous and less predictable, than during the Cold War itself. That is the conclusion any responsible commander-in-chief would draw, and what he would tell the nation whose security depends on him. It is the assessment that any responsible administration would have acted on in the last seven years. But the actual response of the Clinton administration during those years, as documented by the veteran military reporter Bill Gertz in his disturbing new book, *Betrayal,* are very different indeed:[2]

- While the Clinton administration has cut America's military by 40 percent and dramatically drawn down America's nuclear forces, the general in charge of Russia's rocket forces has publicly boasted that his are still at 90 percent of their combat effectiveness during the Cold War. The same general admits

---

[2]Bill Gertz, *Betrayal: How the Clinton Administration Undermined American Security,* Regnery, 1999.

that his nuclear command and control systems are already stretched 71 percent beyond their life expectancy (and thus susceptible to unauthorized acts by rogue commanders).

- While threats from nuclear proliferation and nuclear terrorism continue to grow, Clinton has used his veto power to resist every effort by Republicans in Congress to authorize an anti-missile defense program. This opposition was mounted in the name of will o' the wisp "arms control" agreements with the Russians—who have never in the past respected them—and under the assumption that there was no imminent threat of a missile attack to the United States. In pursuit of these chimeras, as Gertz has documented, Clinton was willing to go behind the back of his own Pentagon and collude with the Russians in blocking the development of a U.S. anti-missile system. This attitude only changed with the discovery of the recent nuclear spy leaks and imminent publication of the Cox report, putting a practical remedy for America's defenseless condition well into the future.
- While the Clinton administration has stopped all development of its own nuclear weapons and is in the process of drawing down America's existing forces, and while Clinton's Department of Energy chief, in charge of nuclear weapons development, has publicly assailed America's "bomb-building culture" and declassified information on 204 nuclear tests for the benefit of potentially hostile powers, Russia and China are engaged in a full-scale nuclear arms race to develop and expand their own nuclear arsenals. The expressed purpose of these large-scale nuclear buildups is to gain military superiority over the United States.
- While the United States has largely closed down its own underground military shelters, Russian rulers are devoting massive resources (in a country on the verge of famine) to building an underground nuclear bunker the size of Washington, D.C., which is capable of holding 30,000 people. The evident purpose of this bunker is to allow the Russian elite to survive a nuclear attack so

that Russia can prevail in an all-out nuclear war. Meanwhile, Clinton is sending a billion dollars to Russia earmarked for its "nuclear disarmament program," even though the government's own General Accounting Office has already determined that millions of these dollars are going to Russian scientists working to build new nuclear weapons for the Russian military.

Now the Cox report has revealed that, even while the Clinton Administration was steadfastly "engaging" China as a friendly power, the Chinese were systematically plotting to penetrate the Democratic Party, subvert America's electoral process, and—with the help of the president himself—infiltrate the administration and steal America's advanced weapons arsenal.[3] The bottom-line result is chillingly captured in *The Wall Street Journal*'s summary of the bipartisan report: "The espionage inquiry found Beijing has stolen U.S. design data for nearly all elements needed for a major nuclear attack on the U.S., such as advanced warheads, missiles, and guidance systems. Targets of the spying ranged from an Army anti-tank weapon to nearly all modern fighter jets. Most wasn't done by professionals, but by visitors or front companies. Lax security by the Clinton Administration is blamed in part, and satellite makers Hughes and Loral are criticized."[4]

Loral and Hughes are the companies that provided the Chinese with the technology to deliver their nuclear payloads. They were able to accomplish this with indispensable assistance provided by the Clinton White House that allowed them to circumvent technology controls instituted for national-security purposes by previous administrations. Loral and Hughes are large Clinton campaign contributors. In fact, the head of Loral is the largest electoral contributor in American history.[5]

---

[3]http://www.house.gov/coxreport/chapfs/over.html.

[4]Hsuan Chung-wen, "Cox Report Findings Expose Fallacy Of Wishful Thinking," *Taiwan Today*, June 11, 1999, http://taiwantoday.tw/ct.asp?xItem=17242&CtNode=103.

[5]http://partners.nytimes.com/library/politics/052498clinton-donate.html.

Pennsylvania representative Curt Weldon, who is chair of the National Security subcommittee on military research and development, and is fluent in Russian, took the care to tabulate the presidential lies mentioned at the top of this article; he has characterized the six years of Clinton's administration as "the worst period in our history in terms of undermining our national security."[6] In May, Weldon traveled to Russia in company with ten other congressmen. On that trip, in his presence, a Russian general threatened the assembled congressmen, warning that if the United States put ground troops in Kosovo, Russia could detonate a nuclear device in the lower atmosphere off the eastern United States. The resulting magnetic pulses would fry every computer chip in the country, shutting down phones, airplanes, electrical grids, and so on until the country was thrown into absolute chaos. This threat was not made during the Cold War by a ruler of the former Soviet Union. It was made by a Russian general within the last month.[7]

These revelations are disturbing enough; but in the initial reaction to the Cox report, the elements of complacency and denial that surfaced may be even more troubling. Before the report was even issued, the Clinton cover-up squad had begun its famous spin cycle. The public has been told by the Clinton team, for example, that the damage resulting from all this spying is not great because China has only eighteen missiles and we have 6,000.

Well, that is this year. The theft has given China a twenty-year jump in its nuclear weapons development—an eternity in terms of modern technologies. What happens five or ten years from now, when the Beijing dictatorship has hundreds of missiles aimed at American cities and decides that it wants Taiwan? What consolation

---

[6]Congressional Record, Volume 145, Number 24, February 10, 1999, p. H581, http://www.gpo.gov/fdsys/pkg/CREC-1999-02-10/html/CREC-1999-02-10-pt1-PgH578.htm.

[7]David Horowitz, *Hating Whitey: And Other Progressive Causes,* Spence Publishing, 1999, p. 263.

would it be to people in Los Angeles, who have already been threatened with a nuclear attack over the Taiwan issue, should Beijing decide to launch even one missile in their direction, given the fact that their president has denied them a missile defense?

In the event of such an attack, would Washington be willing to trade seventeen American cities (and that's just this year) in a retaliatory nuclear exchange to defend Taiwan? On the other hand, if historical experience is any guide, the Communists just might. In Vietnam, the Communists were willing to sacrifice two million of their own citizens—a figure comparable to 72 million US deaths—to achieve their victory, while 58,000 proved to be too great a sacrifice for Americans in pursuit of the opposite result. The Chinese Communists have already killed an estimated 50 million of their own population in their pursuit of a revolutionary future. Is the risk of China's willingness to pay another awful price, to achieve what its leaders consider a worthy objective, one that can be just brushed off?

In addition to making the false and irresponsible claim that the thefts reported by the Cox committee are not so serious, Clinton and his spinners have argued that they themselves are not really guilty because "everyone does it." Shame on Democrats who have gone along with this argument, as they did with similar mendacities during the impeachment process. This is not about a squalid presidential affair but over reckless and perhaps criminal behavior affecting the very lives of the American people. Yes, nuclear spying took place in previous administrations, and in every administration no doubt since the invention of the atom bomb. The difference was that previous administrations cared about such leaks, plugged them, and prosecuted the offenders—and did not accept millions of dollars in illegal campaign contributions from the military and intelligence services of foreign powers that threatened them. Previous administrations did not lift security controls that supplied the thieves with additional vital military technologies. Or systematically disarm their own military forces while this was happening. Or vigorously oppose the development of necessary defenses for their own people. But the Clinton administration has.[8]

One of the key technological breaks China received, without having to spy to get it, was the deliverance of supercomputers once banned from export for security reasons. Supercomputers underpin the technology of nuclear and missile warfare, and not only for firing and controlling the missiles. A supercomputer can simulate a nuclear test and is thus crucial to the development of nuclear warheads. But, according to a *Washington Post* editorial: "In the first three quarters of 1998 nine times as many [supercomputers] were exported [to China] as during the previous seven years."[9] This transfer was authorized three years after the spy thefts were detected. What rationale—besides stupidity, greed, or some other equally indefensible motive—could justify this? What responsible president or administration official, at any relevant level in any government, would allow the massive transfer of national-security assets like these to a dictatorship they knew had stolen their country's most highly guarded military secrets? And if they did do it, why did they?

Was this ominous result connected to the Chinese Communist cash-flow to the Clinton-Gore campaign? If not, what was the payoff the Chinese expected? What was the payoff they received? And who in the administration is responsible for the cover-ups, the laxity and the leaks that made the Chinese conspiracy work as effectively as it did? Is there, for example, any connection between this security disaster and fact that Sandy Berger, the president's national security advisor, was a lobbyist for Chinese companies before being appointed to his post?[10] Or that he and other top Clinton officials

---

[8]Richard D. Fisher, "Time to Heed the Cox Commission's Wake-Up Call," *Heritage Foundation,* Executive Memorandum #602, June 3, 1999, http://www.heritage.org/research/reports/1999/06/time-to-heed-the-cox-commission.

[9]"The Cox Report: Chapter 3 High Performance Computers," *Washington Post,* May 25, 1999, http://www.washingtonpost.com/wp-srv/politics/daily/may99/coxreport/chapter3.htm.

[10]http://www.americanthinker.com/articles/2010/05/the_senator_from_sandy_berger.html.

responsible for this mess have in the past been left-leaning skeptics about Communist threats, and radical critics of American power?[11]

In the immediate handling of this national-security disaster a profound disservice has been done to the American people by both political parties. Shell-shocked by Democratic attacks during the impeachment process, Republicans on the Cox committee, in the name of bipartisanship, became complicit in an essential part of the cover-up. This was the decision to de-couple the spy scandal and the technology transfers from the Clinton money trail to Beijing. This removed a large potential area of conspiracy from the perspective of the report.

In all, 105 witnesses to the illegal funding of the Clinton-Gore campaign by people connected to the Chinese military and Chinese intelligence either took the Fifth Amendment or fled the country to avoid cooperating with investigators. They did this with the tacit acquiescence if not active help of the Clinton administration. Americans have a right to know what they are hiding and why the Clinton administration has, at very minimum, not cared that they are.

Bipartisanship is a problem at this stage of the inquiry because the Democratic Party and administration are up to their ears in the entire scandal; and Democrats have in the past shown they will put party before country when their president is under attack. Perhaps, once the implications of the Cox report sink in, there will be Democrats who will break their lockstep defense of Clinton to consider the vital security interests of the nation as well. All Americans must surely hope that this will happen. Thus far, however, the entire debate has taken place in a surreal atmosphere of politics as usual: the partisan defense of the White House, the denial of the magnitude of the nuclear danger, the political de-coupling of the Chinese plot to infiltrate and influence the Clinton-

[11]Horowitz, *Hating Whitey,* op. cit., p. 265.

Gore administration, and the failure even to acknowledge that what is at stake, is certainly a massive betrayal of the American people's trust by its national security leadership.

In the days that follow, the American people may want to revisit questions they recently disposed of, and subject them to the light of the unfolding national-security drama. Is bad character an impeachable offense? Does reckless behavior and lying under oath indicate a leader is unfit to be commander-in-chief? Whatever their answers, and whatever the results of the investigations now in progress, one thing is certain: the already revealed facts will redraw the legacy of this presidency as the most reckless and dangerous in our time.

9

A Question of Loyalties

Even as the government prepared to release the Cox report, revealing how the Communist dictatorship in Beijing had stolen the design information for every advanced nuclear weapon in the U.S. arsenal, the Democratic National Committee was announcing the appointment of its new "political issues director"—Carlottia Scott, a former mistress of the Marxist dictator of Grenada and an ardent supporter of America's Communist adversaries during the Cold War.

What could the DNC have been thinking, to make such an appointment at such a political juncture? And what might this tell us about the roots of the nation's security crisis—the dramatic erosion of America's defenses and military credibility in the midst of an ill-conceived and ineptly fought war, and the theft of its nuclear arsenal by an adversary the Administration thinks of as a "strategic partner,"[1] while its Communist leaders regard America as their "international archenemy?"[2]

Carlottia Scott was for many years the chief aide to Congressman Ron Dellums, a Berkeley radical who, with the approval of

---

Originally published June 6, 1999, http://archive.frontpagemag.com/Printable.aspx?ArtId=24282; http://www.salon.com/1999/06/07/scott/.

[1]Charles Krauthammer, "The Real China Scandal," *The Washington Post*, p. A35, May 28, 1999, http://www.clintonlibrary.gov/assets/storage/Research-Digital-Library/speechwriters/orzulak/Box002/42-t-7585791-20080702f-002-008-2014.pdf (p.62).

[2]Jeff Jacoby, "Ten Years after Tiananmen, China Is Still Tyrannical," *The Boston Globe*, p. A23, June 3, 1999, http://www.clintonlibrary.gov/assets/storage/Research-Digital-Library/speechwriters/orzulak/Box002/42-t-7585791-20080702f-002-008-2014.pdf (p. 57).

the congressional Democratic leadership, was appointed first to the Armed Services Committee and then to the chair of its subcommittee on Military Installations, which oversees U.S. bases worldwide. The Democratic leadership apparently saw no problem in the fact that, every year during the Cold War with the Soviet empire, Congressman Dellums introduced a "peace budget" requiring a 75 percent reduction in government spending on America's defenses. Nor did they have any problem with Dellums' performance during the Soviet invasion of Afghanistan, which occurred on Democrat Jimmy Carter's presidential watch. As Soviet troops poured across the Afghanistan border and President Carter called for the resumption of the military draft, Dellums told a "Stop the Draft" rally in Berkeley that "Washington DC is a very evil place," and that the only arc of a crisis that he could see was "the one that runs between the basement of the west wing of the White House and the war room of the Pentagon."[3]

Among the government documents retrieved from the fallen Marxist regime in Grenada were the love letters of Dellums' chief aide—and now the Democratic Party's political issues director—Carlottia Scott, who wrote them to its anti-American dictator Maurice Bishop. In them Scott advised Bishop that "Ron has become truly committed to Grenada.... He's really hooked on you and Grenada and doesn't want anything to happen to building the

[3]Speech to Berkeley students at an anti-war demonstration in 1980; cited in a speech by David Horowitz, "The 'Peace' Movement," to the Conference of the Law and National Security Committee of the ABA, Washington, D.C., January 31, 1991, http://discoverthenetworks.org/Articles/The%20Peace%20Movement.htm; The "arc" was a reference to Jimmy Carter's National Security Adviser Zbigniew Brzezkinski's remark in December 1978, that "An arc of crisis stretches along the shores of the Indian Ocean, with fragile social and political structures in a region of vital importance to us threatened with fragmentation. The resulting political chaos could well be filled by elements hostile to our values and sympathetic to our adversaries." ("The Crescent of Crisis," *Time*, January 8, 1979.).

Revolution and making it strong.... The only other person that I know of that he expresses such admiration for is Fidel."[4]

Bishop and Fidel were not the only Communists in the Americas favored by Dellums. About the time these letters were retrieved, Dellums was opening his congressional office to a Cuban intelligence agent who proceeded to organize support committees in the United States for the Communist guerrilla movement in El Salvador.[5] Yet, on his retirement, the Clinton administration's Secretary of Defense, William S. Cohen, bestowed on Ron Dellums the highest civilian honor the Pentagon can award "for service to his country."

After Dellums's retirement, Carlottia Scott became the chief of staff to Dellums' successor, Berkeley leftist Barbara Lee. I met Barbara Lee in the 1970s when she was a confidential aide to Huey Newton, the "Minister of Defense" of the Black Panther Party, whose calling card was the Red Book of Chinese dictator Mao Zedong, and who was responsible for several unsolved murders in the Bay Area. Also among the documents liberated from Grenada were the minutes from a politburo meeting attended by Barbara Lee and the Marxist junta. The minutes state that "Barbara Lee is here presently and has brought with her a report on the international airport done by Ron Dellums. They have requested that we look at the document and suggest any changes we deem necessary. They will be willing to make the changes."[6]

The airport in question was being built by the Cuban military and, according to U.S. intelligence sources, was designed to accommodate Soviet warplanes. The Reagan administration regarded the airport project as part of a larger Soviet plan to establish a military base in the hemisphere, and administration officials

---

[4]http://www.centerforsecuritypolicy.org/2009/04/08/my-darling-comrade-leader-barbara-lee-friends-coddling-dictators-2/.

[5]Peter Collier and David Horowitz, *Destructive Generation,* Summit, 1989, pp. 188–189.

[6]*The Grenada Papers,* Paul Seabury and Walter A. McDougall, eds., Institute for Contemporary Studies, 1984, Ch. V, *Propaganda and Public Relations Work in the United States.*

invoked its construction as a national-security justification for the invasion that followed. In an effort to forestall such an invasion, and as head of the Military Installations subcommittee of the House, Dellums made a "fact-finding" trip to Grenada and issued his own report on the airport, alleging that it was being built "for the purpose of economic development and is not for military use." Dellums's report also made the political claim that the Reagan administration's concerns about national security in regard to the airport were "absurd, patronizing and totally unwarranted."[7]

In other words, the captured minutes of the politburo meeting show that Ron Dellums and his aide Barbara Lee colluded with the dictator of a Communist state to cover up the fact that the Soviet Union was building a military airport that posed a threat to the security of the United States.

Despite this history, and with the approval of her Democratic colleagues in the House, Barbara Lee is now a member of the House International Relations Committee, which deals with issues affecting the security of the United States. With equal disregard for national security, the Democratic Party has now made Carlottia Scott—former chief aide to both Dellums and Lee, and thus an abettor of these treacherous schemes—the new political-issues director of the Democratic National Committee. When I asked a leading Democratic political strategist, who is not a leftist, how it was possible that the leaders of the Democratic Party could appoint someone like Carlottia Scott to such a post at such a time, he replied: "You have to understand that in the 1960s these people were chanting "Ho, Ho, Ho Chi Minh, the NLF Is Gonna Win!"

The left-wing culture of the Democratic Party and the Clinton administration is at the heart of the current national-security crisis. People who never conceded that the Soviet Union was an evil empire, who never grasped the dimensions of the Soviet military threat, who regarded America's democracy as imperialist and as morally convergent with the Soviet state, who insisted (and still

---

[7]Ibid.

insist) that the ferreting out of Soviet loyalists and domestic spies during the early Cold War years was an ideological "witch-hunt," who opposed the Reagan military buildup and the development of an anti-ballistic missile system in the 1980s, and who consistently called for unilateral steps to reduce America's nuclear deterrent, could hardly be expected to take the post-Cold War threat from the Chinese Communist dictatorship seriously. And they have not.

In fact, the current national-security crisis may be said to have begun when President Clinton appointed an anti-military, environmental leftist, Hazel O'Leary, to be Secretary of Energy in charge of the nation's nuclear-weapons labs. O'Leary promptly surrounded herself with other political leftists (including a self-described "Marxist-Feminist") and anti-nuclear activists, appointing them as assistant secretaries with responsibility for the nuclear labs. In one of her first acts, O'Leary declassified eleven million pages of reports on 204 U.S. nuclear tests, a move she described as an action to safeguard the environment and as a protest against a "bomb-building culture."[8]

Having made America's nuclear-weapons secrets available to adversary powers, O'Leary then took steps to relax security precautions at the labs under her control. She appointed Rose Gottemoeller, a former Clinton National Security Council staffer with extreme anti-nuclear views, to be director in charge of national-security issues. Gottemoeller had been previously nominated to fill the post, long vacant in the Clinton administration, of Assistant Secretary of Defense for International Security Policy. But her appointment was successfully blocked by congressional Republicans because of her radical disarmament views. The Clinton response to her rejection was to appoint her to be in charge of security for the nation's nuclear-weapons labs.

---

[8]ohmlaw98, "Downside Legacy at Two Degrees of President Clinton," *alamo.girl.com*, Rev. July 14, 2000, http://alamo-girl.com/0241.htm; According to a *Washington Post* account from December 8, [1993], O'Leary's goal was to expose secrets from "an unresponsive bureaucracy wedded to a bomb-building culture." [as she stated at a press conference].

The architect of America's China policy over the course of the current disaster has been Clinton's national security adviser, Sandy Berger. Berger began his political life as an anti-Vietnam war protestor and member of the radical "Peace Now" movement, which regards Israel as the aggressor in the Middle East. Berger first met Clinton as an activist in the McGovern for President camp, the most left-wing Democratic presidential campaign in American history. Berger's law practice, prior to his appointment, was lobbying for the business arm of China's Communist dictatorship.[9]

Is it surprising that a political leftist and business lobbyist for China's rulers should take steps to lift the security controls which previously protected U.S. military technology? Or that, under his tenure, invitations to the White House should be extended to agents of Chinese intelligence and China's military, or that appointments like that of John Huang to posts with a top security clearance should be considered reasonable?[10] Is it surprising, given the politics of the Clinton managers, that the administration should place its faith in arms-control agreements that depend on trustworthy partners, while strenuously opposing measures to develop anti-ballistic missile defenses that do not? Even now, *after* the revelations of China's thefts, Berger and the Clinton administration are still opposing the implementation of anti-ballistic missile defense programs, while pressing to keep China's Most Favored Nation trading status.

Nor is it surprising that a party wedded to left-wing illusions should work so assiduously to obstruct the investigations of the

---

[9]Horowitz, *Hating Whitey,* op. cit., pp. 271–272.

[10]John Huang, a Chinese-born American, was a friend of Bill Clinton's from their Little Rock days. He was the vice president and Far East area manager for the Worthen Bank. In 1994, through the intervention of Hillary Clinton, he was made a top official in the Commerce Department, where he was the only official in that department to have been given a top security clearance. He had access to all the information an agent would need to strip America of the supercomputer technologies vital to the development of advanced weapons systems. He had been identified as a spy by the CIA but, like Wen Ho Lee, had been protected by the Clinton Justice Department.

Clinton-Gore campaign's debts to the Chinese dictators, or should be so irresponsibly complacent in the face of the revelations of the Cox report.[11] There is perhaps nothing more alarming for the prospects of the two-party system in the wake of the Cox disclosures than the wall of denial that has been hastily and irresponsibly erected around these issues by Democratic leaders like Tom Daschle. To say, as the Senate Minority Leader has, that there is nothing really new in these revelations—as though previous administrations had dismantled vital security procedures, taken illegal monies from foreign intelligence services, blocked investigations when the illegalities were revealed, presided over the evaporation of the nation's nuclear weapons advantage, abetted the transfer of missile technologies that can strike American cities, and opposed the development of weapons systems that could defend against such attacks—is patently absurd.[12]

At the heart of the current crisis is, in fact, a White House that has loaded its administration with officials deeply disenchanted with, if not actively hostile to. America's character and purposes. Behind that White House and still supporting its cover-up is a party that lacks proper pride in America's national achievement and loyalty to America's national interests. This is a party whose leader has spent enormous political capital apologizing to the world for America's role in it. This is an administration whose leader has now embroiled his country in a war in Europe that is about no national interest and is guided by a multilateral alliance he cannot control. This is a party that, even in the face of the most massive breach of security in America's history, is still taking the position that "everybody does it."

---

[11]http://www.nytimes.com/1999/05/27/opinion/essay-follow-up-the-cox-report.html.

[12]Horowitz, *Hating Whitey,* op. cit., p. 272.

10

The Manchurian Presidency

With the publication of the Cox report, we have learned that seven years of the Clinton administration coincided with the most massive breach of military security in American history; that as a result of the calculated degrading of security controls at America's nuclear laboratories, the Chinese Communists have been able to steal the designs of our arsenal of nuclear weapons, including our most advanced warheads; that as a result of the 1993 Clinton decision to terminate the COCOM security controls denying sensitive technologies to nuclear proliferators and potential adversary powers, the Chinese Communists have been given the secrets of our intercontinental ballistic missile systems, along with previously restricted computer hardware.[1] This allows them for the first time to target cities in the United States. In a little over five years, the Chinese Communist dictatorship has been able to close a technology gap of twenty years and to destroy a security buffer that had kept America safe from foreign attacks on its territorial mainland for more than a hundred.

Throughout its entire history until 1957, the United States was protected from such attacks by two oceans that provided a natural

---

Originally published June 22, 1999, http://archive.frontpagemag.com/Printable.aspx?ArtId=24284;
http://www.salon.com/1999/06/21/manchurian/.

[1]Edward Timperlake and William C. Triplett II, *Year of the Rat: How Bill Clinton Compromised U.S. Security for Chinese Cash*, Regnery, 1998, pp. 143, 146.

barrier insulating it from potential aggressors. In 1957 the Soviet Union acquired an intercontinental missile technology that erased this advantage. Since then, the only real protection the United States has enjoyed has been its technological edge in developing more sophisticated warheads and more accurate missiles than its potential opponents. The edge offered the possibility that America might prevail in a nuclear war, and discouraged pre-emptive strikes. The catastrophe that has occurred on the Clinton watch is summed up in the fact that this edge has now vanished, probably never to be regained.

America's new vulnerability to nuclear attack is a reality not merely in respect to China, but vis-à-vis every rogue state that China has chosen to arm. Along with Russia, China is the chief proliferator of nuclear, missile and satellite technologies to other governments. The governments it has chosen to benefit in this way are notorious stockpilers of biological and chemical weapons. Among them are the most dangerous and dedicated enemies of the United States: Iraq, Iran, and Syria.[2] Yet, even after the release of the Cox report, the attitude of the Clinton administration is still one of hear-no-evil, see-no-evil. The official line of the Democratic leadership is, "it's no big deal"—presumably because, at the moment, China only has a few nuclear weapons actually deployed. Far from acknowledging the catastrophe that has occurred, or recognizing the dangers it creates, the Clinton White House has hurried to resume export sales of the same previously restricted technologies, to reassert the "strategic partnership" it promoted with the very dictatorship that has declared America its "number one adversary," and has stripped us of our military shield.[3]

Indeed, the government's awareness of many of the losses dates back several years, during which the Clinton reaction was exactly the same: continue on the destructive course. According to Congressman Curt Weldon, who is a member of the Cox Committee, at least fifteen government officials have experienced the wrath of the

---

[2]Ibid., p. 142.
[3]Charles Krauthammer, "The Real China Scandal," op. cit.

Clintonites because they tried to protect America's secrets from being transferred to China. One case was described in a recent *Wall Street Journal* article by a former security official, Michael Ledeen. According to documents obtained by Ledeen, a mid-level government arms-control bureaucrat was asked in 1997 to provide a memo supporting the administration's certification that China was not a nuclear proliferator and could be provided with advanced technologies. This request was made on the eve of a visit from China's Communist dictator, Jiang Zemin. The bureaucrat refused and wrote that the agreement the Clinton administration was about to sign "presents real and substantial risk to the common defense and security of both the United States and allied countries."[4] The official added that China was actively seeking American secrets and that "China routinely, both overtly and covertly, subverts national and multilateral trade controls on militarily critical items."

This patriot was immediately told by his superiors to revise his memo or lose his job. Sadly, he complied with the order and rewrote the document to state that the proposed Clinton trade agreement "is not inimical to the common defense or the security of the United States."

In keeping with its relentless defense of an indefensible policy, the Clinton administration has failed to prosecute the very spies who have been identified as being responsible for the most critical thefts of American military secrets, and has slapped the wrists of others. Wen Ho Lee, the man responsible for the most damaging espionage, is known to have downloaded millions of lines of computer code revealing the designs of our most advanced nuclear warheads.[5] But Wen Ho Lee today is a free man. Peter Lee, who

---

[4]Scott L. Wheeler, "Clinton Gave China 'False Certification' on Nukes," *World Net Daily*, August 25, 2003, http://www.wnd.com/2003/08/20451/.

[5]David Johnston, "Suspect in Loss of Nuclear Secrets Unlikely to Face Spying Charges," *The New York Times*, June 15, 1999, http://www.nytimes.com/1999/06/15/world/suspect-in-loss-of-nuclear-secrets-unlikely-to-face-spying-charges.html.

gave Communist China our warhead testing techniques and the radar technology to locate our submarines—until then the most secure element of our nuclear deterrent—is also free, having served only a year in a halfway house for his treason.[6]

Wen Ho Lee was actually protected while performing his dirty work. When government agents requested a wiretap on Wen Ho Lee's phone, the request was denied by Clinton Justice. The Clinton DOJ had never previously denied a wiretap request. In explaining why it had not prosecuted Lee, the department claims its evidence only shows that Lee downloaded the classified information onto a non-secure computer, from which others unknown may have picked it up. But, as defense expert Angelo Codevilla pointed out, "by this logic no one could be prosecuted for espionage for putting stolen documents into a dead drop, such as a hollow tree, for later pickup by foreign agents."[7] Of course, the administration lacks even this transparent excuse in the case of Peter Lee, who did in fact give the information directly to the Communists.

Why is the Clinton administration feverishly covering up for the Communist Chinese and protecting its leaders and their spies from the wrath that should surely follow their theft of America's most guarded secrets? Unlike China, for example, the state of Israel is a democracy and a proven ally of the United States. Yet when an Israeli agent named Jonathan Pollard was discovered stealing secrets whose dimensions did not even approach the seriousness of these thefts (no technologies, for example, were involved), he was given a life sentence amidst the most solemn anathemas from the officials of the government he betrayed.[8]

The evidence is compatible with only one conclusion: the reason Bill Clinton is protecting China's spies and their Communist

---

[6]Timperlake and Triplett, op. cit., p. 131; Also see *The Wall Street Journal,* March 7, 1997.

[7]Angelo M. Codevilla, "China's New Hostages," *The Washington Times,* June 7, 1999, http://www.jonathanpollard.org/1999/060799.htm.

[8]Ibid.

masters is that, in protecting them, he is protecting himself. Clinton's China strategy is fully intelligible only in the frame of Clinton's strategy on other matters: the president has triangulated with China's Communist government in pursuit of his own political interest at the expense of the United States. This is not about loyalties that Bill Clinton might have to Communist ideology or Communist dictators. On this, Clinton's record is clear: he has no loyalties except to himself.[9] It is the solipsistic nihilism that we have come to know as the very essence of Bill Clinton that has made this treachery possible, even inevitable.

Clinton's triangulation with Communist China has been charted by two national-security professionals with the help of the Thompson committee investigations into illegal campaign contributions. In *Year of the Rat,* Bill Triplett and Ed Timperlake show that the roots of the Clinton betrayal lie in relationships that go back to Arkansas, and the fact that Bill Clinton owes his political life to the Chinese Communists through their agents, business associates and friends. *Year of the Rat* begins with the authors' observation that the number one funder of the Clinton-Gore 1992 presidential campaign was an Arkansas resident and Chinese banker named James Riady, who has been a friend of Bill Clinton's for twenty years. Riady is the scion of a multi-billion-dollar financial empire, which is a working economic and political partnership with China's military and intelligence establishment. The Riadys gave $450,000 to Clinton's presidential campaign and another $600,000 to the Democratic National Committee and Democratic state parties.[10]

But the importance of the Riadys to Clinton's ascent is far greater than even these contributions suggest, and not merely because the Chinese network, in which the Riadys are only one important factor, extends through thousands of companies and individuals whose contributions no one has as yet attempted to

---

[9]Ibid.; also see Timperlake and Triplett, op. cit., p. 1.
[10]Timperlake and Triplett, op. cit., pp. 10, 27, 34.

track. Without the Riadys, Clinton would not have won the Democratic nomination in the first place, and would not have been in a position to benefit from their later largesse. In the presidential primaries of 1992, in fact, the Riadys were the crucial factor that stood between Clinton and defeat. After losing the New Hampshire primary, the candidate faced a critical test in New York. He had also run out of money. At this critical juncture, James Riady stepped in to arrange a $3.5 million loan to the Clinton campaign.[11] New York proved to be the last real competition that Clinton faced on his path to the nomination.

When the Arkansas governor stepped onto the national scene, he and Riady were not new acquaintances. They had met in 1978, when Clinton was attorney general and had not yet become governor of the state. They were introduced by Clinton's chief political backer, Jackson Stephens, the head of Stephens, Inc., one of the largest private investment firms outside of Wall Street. "Thus began, a friendship," write Timperlake and Triplett, "that has lasted twenty years, and has spread a web of intrigue, financial corruption, and foreign influence into American government."[12]

James Riady had begun his American banking career earlier in the Seventies as an intern at Stephens, Inc. Later the two became partners in the Worthen Bank of Little Rock,[13] the very same bank that subsequently experienced a mysterious fire, which destroyed records being sought by Kenneth Starr and other Whitewater investigators in their inquiries into Hillary Clinton's Rose Law Firm activities.[14] It was also through the Worthen bank that Riady arranged the $3.5 million credit to Clinton's failing primary campaign. The Riady relationship extended beyond the Clintons themselves to their friends and to Hillary's associates at Rose, including its head Joe Giroir, and a White House aide named Mark

[11]Ibid., p. 10.
[12]Ibid., pp. 9, 35.
[13]Ibid., pp. 9–10, 25.
[14]Ibid., pp. 34, 38.

Middleton, who later invoked the Fifth Amendment when he was called before the Thompson committee.[15] It was the Riadys who provided a $100,000 job for the indicted Webb Hubbell, at the moment when he had indicated to the Starr prosecutors that he might be ready to talk.[16] After the payment from Riady and others, Hubbell changed his mind and chose jail instead.

Understanding the security disaster that has befallen the United States requires an understanding of the fact that the leakage of America's secrets proceeded along two parallel tracks. One was espionage; the other was a political-economic track through the legal commercial activities of the United States government and in particular through its political oversight of these commercial activities. Past administrations had created and enforced formal controls of sensitive technologies that the Clinton team now systematically dismantled. Political contributors to the Clinton-Gore campaigns played key roles in promoting the dismantling process.

A central figure in the economic track of Chinese activities was the vice president and Far East area manager for the Worthen Bank, a Chinese-born American named John Huang, who was a friend of Bill's from Little Rock days. Triplett and Timperlake make a strong case that it was through the personal intervention of Hillary Clinton that in 1994 John Huang was made a top official in the Commerce Department, where he had access to all the information an agent would need to strip America of the supercomputer technologies vital to the development of advanced weapons systems. Huang also inexplicably retained his top security clearance in the Commerce Department when he left the government.[17]

The decision to leave the government for a position at the Democratic National Committee was made for Huang at a meeting in

---

[15]Ibid., pp. 10–11.
[16]Ibid., pp. 20, 36, 40.
[17]Ibid., pp. 31, 43–50.

the Oval office attended by the president, Huang, James Riady, Riady partner and former Rose law firm head Joe Giroir, and presidential aide Bruce Lindsey.[18] This meeting took place three days after the president had decided on a strategy to rescue his failing political fortunes, which had reached a nadir following the Democrats' historic defeat in the congressional elections of 1994 and Newt Gingrich's ascension to the speakership of the House. It was the first Republican majority in the House in 48 years.

Designed by the president's new political advisor, Dick Morris, the strategy involved a massive television advertising campaign directed against Gingrich and the Republican House. The campaign has been directly credited with turning the political tide and ensuring the re-election in 1996 of the Clinton team. The chief fundraiser for this campaign was John Huang.[19]

It should be evident from these facts (and they could easily be amplified) that the alliance Bill Clinton has made with the Riadys and their China network is the key to his political survival and success. It has had consequences for American politics and security so far-reaching that no brief summary can begin to describe them. In 1996, to pick an illustrative example, the Long Beach City Council granted a lease on the demobilized Long Beach Naval Station to a Chinese company named COSCO, which is little more than the naval arm of the Chinese Communist Army and is a major arms supplier to dictators and terrorists.[20] Its cargoes have included rocket fuel for Pakistan, helping to destabilize the Indian peninsula, and nuclear components for Iran, a volatile factor in the Middle East. In 1996 a COSCO ship was seized in Oakland, California, by U.S. Customs agents, who discovered a cargo of 2,000 assault weapons intended for sale to Los Angeles street gangs.

Why would the Long Beach City Council approve a lease to such a company, particularly if the relevant oversight officials in

---

[18]Ibid., pp. 64–70.
[19]Ibid., pp. 26–27, 64, 68, 78.
[20]Ibid., pp. 188–203.

Washington had alerted them to the nature of the COSCO enterprise? But the relevant oversight officials in Washington did not alert Long Beach to the danger posed by COSCO. On the contrary, they encouraged the deal.

In the 1996 election campaign, Johnny Chung—another middleman for the China network and for COSCO in particular—gave $366,000 to the Democratic Party.[21] It was subsequently returned after the campaign finance scandal surfaced and it was clear that it had come illegally from foreign sources. Among the sources was a Chinese intelligence officer, Lieutenant Colonel Liu Chaoying, the daughter of China's highest-ranking military officer.[22] On the eve of the 1996 elections, a White House official named Dorothy Robyn made a conference call to the Long Beach City Council and applied direct pressure to push the deal with COSCO through. Robyn told the council that the "national interest would best be served if the [COSCO] plan proceeds." The chief competitor for the lease, whose application was denied by the White House pressure, was the U.S. Marine Corps.[23]

Nine months before the COSCO lease was sealed, a crisis had developed in the Taiwan Strait. Elections were being held in Taiwan, and the mainland Communist regime, which claims sovereignty over Taiwan, was launching intermediate range ballistic missiles with blank warheads in the direction of the island, an act of blatant intimidation. The Clinton administration had interposed two aircraft carriers from the Seventh Fleet, ostensibly to remind the Communists that Taiwan was an American ally. At that moment, an old Little Rock friend of Bill Clinton's appeared in Washington with a $460,000 donation to the Presidential Legal Defense Trust that Clinton had set up to defray his legal expenses in the Paula Jones sexual-harassment case. The friend also brought his own broken-English personal message: "Any negative outcomes of

---

[21]Ibid., pp. 83, 187–188, 199–202, 206.
[22]Ibid., pp. 83–84, 137, 187, 206–207.
[23]Ibid., p. 196.

the U.S. decision in the China Issue will affect your Administration position especially in the campaign year."

The messenger was Charlie Trie, owner of the Fu Lin Restaurant in Little Rock. Trie was also a member of the Four Seas Triad, a billion-dollar Asian crime syndicate allied to Chinese military and intelligence agencies.[24] Clinton's written reply to Trie's blackmail was addressed "Dear Charlie" and assured him and his Communist bosses in Beijing that the interposition of the aircraft carriers was "not intended as a threat to the Peoples Republic of China," but as "a signal to both Taiwan and the PRC that the United States was concerned about maintaining stability in the ... region."[25]

The network of businessmen, agents, and gangsters that links Bill Clinton to China's Communist dictatorship is interwoven with every element of the greatest security disaster in American history. It is as though the Rosenbergs were in the White House, except that the Rosenbergs were little people and naïve, and consequently the damage they were capable of accomplishing was incomparably less. It could even be said in behalf of the Rosenbergs that they did not do it for themselves, but out of loyalty to an ideal, however pathetic and misguided.

Bill Clinton has no such loyalties—not to his family, his party, or his country. As is evident from the disclosures that have already come to light, the damage he has done is without precedent and will dwarf even the legacy of national embarrassment that he earned for himself in the Lewinsky affair. The wounds he has inflicted on this nation, and every individual within it, with consequences unknown for future generations, cannot be said to have been inflicted for ideological reasons or even out of some perverse dedication to a principle of evil. The destructiveness of Bill Clinton has emerged out of a need that is far more banal—to advance the cause of a self-absorbed and criminal self.

---

[24]Ibid., pp. 110–112.
[25]Ibid., p. 115.

PART II

Bush

I

"W" on His Game

"I was born in Midland Texas, which is closer to Los Angeles than it is to Houston. You could say I'm a westerner. People in Midland were individualists, risk-takers. We had a saying: 'The Sky's the limit!' Strike oil and you can realize your dream. I want an America that is prosperous, where every single individual has access to the American dream."

George W. Bush was speaking to twenty supporters at lunch in the governor's mansion in Austin. His delivery was more passionate than when I had seen him a year before. He was in his rhythm and confident, obviously buoyed by the energies of the presidential campaign. His war chest was larger than those of his opponents, and the response to his candidacy—so new that his exploratory committee had opened its offices on the day we arrived—could hardly have been better. Even *The New Republic,* which had fired its editor for being too critical of Clinton, had an issue on the stands whose cover story was titled "What 'W' Stands For," and had answered by pretty much suggesting it was not "Wishy Washy" but "Wise."

I like George Bush. He's quick-witted and personable, good-humored and direct. Confident as his game now is, I found when I interviewed him in Austin that he still answers a question with "I don't know. I have more to learn about that area. But I'm going to conduct myself in office in a way that is responsible, that restores

---

Originally published May 6, 1999, http://www.salon.com/1999/05/06/bush_2/; http://archive.frontpagemag.com/Printable.aspx?ArtId=24273.

its dignity and that includes all Americans." Bush has core convictions that are strong and he is obviously a man of religious faith. But he is also convincingly tolerant, genuinely open and warm-hearted towards people with whom he disagrees.

He has made, for example, the strongest statements of any Republican candidate about including homosexuals in the American family, and treating them with Christian charity and civic respect. "I was taught," he said in response to Senator Lott's remarks comparing homosexuality with kleptomania and other sins, "that we should look after the beam in our own eye before searching for the mote in someone else's." He has the charisma of a national leader, but a personal style that is down home and down-to-earth. He is both relaxed and disciplined, which shows how seriously he is taking the task ahead of him. Most surprising to me, he's a Republican comfortable in his own skin.

I first met Bush over a year ago. Since then I've often been asked *The New Republic* question by conservatives wary of the Republican establishment, which has a tendency to confuse noblesse oblige with core ethical and political principles. In such situations, I find myself recalling my first meeting with Bush, which was a lunch with his staff at the governor's mansion. He had invited me because of the book *Destructive Generation* I had written with Peter Collier and also my autobiography *Radical Son.* These had influenced some of his thinking on the damage done to the moral and ethical fabric of American society by the more malign currents of the Sixties. His political theme was "responsibility"—a value that needed to be restored to the common culture after the wreckage of that decade and its aftermath.

Most of the meeting was as relaxed as his style, but at one point he became emotionally agitated and we clashed over a political episode in Texas that was still unfolding. This was the Graglia affair, which was another reason for my appearance in the state. The *Hopwood* decision ending racial preferences at the University of Texas Law School had recently been handed down. I had just spoken at the university in defense of Professor Lino Graglia, whose strong opposition to racial preferences had provoked demonstrations, including one led by Jesse Jackson.[1] The Hispanic caucus of the state legislature was calling for Graglia's head. This put Bush in a difficult position, since conservatives were defending Graglia and he had set out to win 50 percent of the Hispanic vote in the next gubernatorial election, whose campaigns were already underway.

Graglia had especially angered the Hispanic and African-American communities with remarks they regarded as insensitive. He had been lured by a reporter into explaining why certain minorities' grades were behind those of other groups, a disparity that made racial preferences in admissions to college seem a necessary form of affirmative action. Graglia had said that such groups were handicapped by cultures that apparently didn't have a problem with academic failure. When I discussed this with Graglia, a Sicilian by birth, he told me this had been a problem in his own cultural background, which gave little support to his academic ambitions.

In our head-to-head, Bush was as critical of Graglia as I was strong in his defense. The principle of a single standard was vital. Members of Bush's own staff had been offended by Graglia's remarks, which, as I tried to explain, had been distorted in the press. The press had reported him as saying that some ethnic groups were cultures of failure and their children couldn't learn. We argued back and forth but the governor gave no ground, and we dropped the subject.

Afterwards, I asked myself why he had gotten so upset. I concluded that the emotion reflected his discomfort at being jammed between the principle and the politics. This set him apart from many establishment Republicans, who wouldn't understand a principle if they tripped over it. But I also respected the fact that Bush was determined not to abandon the Hispanic and African-

[1]http://www.nytimes.com/1997/09/16/us/texas-law-professor-prompts-a-furor-over-race-comments.html.

American communities. He was going to make Hispanics and African- Americans feel integral parts of his political community and his political coalition. For if Americans were going to embrace the principle of a single standard for all, then all communities of the American spectrum would have to be persuaded to embrace that principle too.

Later, I was able to confirm in a private conversation with him that I had been right in my interpretation of our encounter. The entire episode reminded me of an observation about leadership that had been made by the Jewish philosopher Martin Buber, who said: A great leader has to be far enough ahead of his people so that he can lead them, but not so far ahead that he loses them.

2

Al Gore's Missile-Defense Dodge

The most important national security debate since the end of the Cold War has suddenly become a leading issue in the presidential campaign. It is the debate over whether we are going to build a missile defense that will provide Americans with a shield against attack by weapons of mass destruction. The result of this debate will affect the security of every man, woman and child among us for generations to come.

Like most issues that come up in the heat of an electoral campaign, the missile debate has been characterized by obfuscation. Even informed voters may feel that a correct decision involves political considerations which are impossibly complex, and technical issues that only a specialist could understand. But it is not as difficult as it seems. What is really at issue, as in all questions that are political, is the nature of human society—in this case, the correct balance between legitimate suspicion, bridge-building and prudent self-defense. Here, the Clinton-Gore administration has shown a naïveté that is characteristic of liberalism but, in this context, is also dangerous.

For two terms, the Clinton-Gore administration has anchored America's security in a system of arms control agreements that were concluded in the past with the now defunct Soviet Union. The most important of these agreements is the Anti-Ballistic

---

Originally published June 26, 2000, http://archive.frontpagemag.com/Printable.aspx?ArtId=24377; http://www.salon.com/2000/06/26/missile_defense/.

Missile Treaty of 1972, which Clinton has referred to as "a cornerstone of strategic stability."[1] In order not to break this treaty and anger the Russians, the Clinton administration has for eight years resisted the development and deployment of an anti-ballistic missile system that would protect Americans. In the last month, however, with an election looming in which the Republican candidate has declared this posture unacceptable, the Clinton-Gore team has roused its lawyers to find a loophole in the treaty so that it can propose its own baby step in the direction of an anti-ballistic defense, while claiming that this will not remove the "cornerstone" it has used as an excuse for doing virtually nothing until now.

The purpose of the 1972 ABM Treaty was to stabilize the balance of terror by ensuring that, if one of the two powers launched a nuclear first strike against its rival, the other would have the ability to strike back unhindered by an anti-missile defense. This is the doctrine known as MAD (for Mutual Assured Destruction). The arms-control advocates in the Clinton-Gore camp claim that this arrangement worked in the past to preserve nuclear peace during the Cold War, and therefore should work in the future as well. Opponents of this doctrine—let's call them the deterrence camp—believe that the history of 20th-century conflicts, including the Cold War, shows that MAD is a dangerous illusion in a world composed of sovereign states whose interests are profoundly at odds. and whose reliability in keeping agreements is problematic to say the least.

This history is absolutely crucial to framing a judgment in the contest between a Republican candidate who wants to forge ahead with a comprehensive missile defense, and a Democratic candidate who wants to proceed very cautiously (if at all) because his chief concern is calming the fears of foreign leaders, rather than protecting American security.

---

[1]Kim R. Holmes, Ph.D. and Baker Spring, "Clinton's ABM Treaty Muddle," *Heritage Foundation,* July 7, 1995, http://www.heritage.org/research/reports/1995/07/clintons-abm-treaty-muddle.

History shows us that the arms-control approach to national security frequently fails. In the aftermath of World War I, the world's democracies attempted through a series of international accords to control the ability of nations to develop aggressive military capabilities, particularly sea power—the aggressive weapon *du jour.* These arms control agreements culminated in the Kellogg-Briand Pact, which outlawed war as "an instrument of national policy."[2] It was signed in 1928 by virtually every nation—11 years before Hitler's invasion of Poland and the start of World War II.

In the years preceding the outbreak of war, the democracies of the West adhered to the arms-control agreements they had signed, while the totalitarian powers—the aggressors, Germany and Japan—did not. In fact, it is probable that the aggression itself was inspired by the perception of German and Japanese leaders that their opponents had tied their own hands behind their backs.

The same pattern was evident during the Cold War, when the Soviet Union systematically violated its arms control agreements, in particular the same Anti-Ballistic Missile Treaty of 1972 that Clinton and Gore regard as the "cornerstone of strategic stability." In fact, Russia has a deployed anti-ballistic missile system around Moscow, in violation of the treaty.[3] But Washington chooses to overlook the violation, because it is only a partial system and making an issue of it would cause an international crisis. As a result, the chief effect of the 1972 ABM treaty has not been to control the development of defensive missile systems by our adversaries but to hamstring the United States—and prevent us from doing the same.

---

[2]"The Kellogg-Briand Pact, 1928," *U.S. Department of State Office of the Historian,* https://history.state.gov/milestones/1921-1936/kellogg.

[3]"Treaty on the Limitation of Anti-Ballistic Missile Systems," Signed: May 26, 1972, Entered into Force: October 3, 1972, *nti.org,* http://www.nti.org/treaties-and-regimes/treaty-limitation-anti-ballistic-missile-systems-abm-treaty/.

The ABM Treaty had an even more deleterious impact, since it also provided an incentive to the Soviet rulers to attempt to develop a first-strike capability against which the United States would have no defense. Thus the ABM Treaty's unintended consequence was not only not to control the arms race but to escalate it, and to put the United States at a dangerous disadvantage.[4]

Fortunately, in 1980 voters elected Ronald Reagan, whose administration was ready to meet this challenge head- on. Reagan ignored the arms-controllers and disarmers who had mobilized the nuclear freeze movement with Soviet support, and deployed cruise missiles to Europe to neutralize the Soviet advantage. He then announced the Strategic Defense Initiative—the so-called "Star Wars" program—whose goal was to build a space-based, anti-missile defense system, which was maliciously derided by arms-control Democrats and the liberal press as a kind of Hollywood gimmick.

Thanks to the stalling of the Clinton-Gore administration, SDI has never been fully perfected or deployed, although successful missile kills have been achieved. But even the embryonic SDI managed to play a significant role in ending the Cold War. Reagan's determination to proceed with such a system forced the Soviet leadership to confront the fact that its bankrupt economic system could not underwrite the next stage of the arms race. This caused the Kremlin to initiate a series of reforms (perestroika and glasnost) that caused the entire Soviet system to unravel, culminating in the fall of the Berlin Wall.[5]

In contrast to the arms-control enthusiasts on the Clinton-Gore team, deterrence advocates including George W. Bush believe

---

[4]Baker Spring, "The Comprehensive Test Ban Treaty: In Arms Control's Worst Tradition," *Heritage Foundation,* October 7, 1999, http://www.heritage.org/research/reports/1999/10/the-comprehensive-test-ban-treaty.

[5]Peter Schweizer, *Victory: The Reagan Administration's Secret Strategy That Hastened the Collapse of the Soviet Union,* Atlantic Monthly Press, 1994.

that in a world of sovereign states, most of them ruled by dictators, American security must not rest on unenforceable agreements but on America's ability to maintain a superiority of arms that will discourage potential aggressors. In the current stage of weapons development, that means deploying an effective and comprehensive missile defense system.

During the Cold War there were only two nuclear superpowers with missiles capable of crossing the oceans. Today, 36 nations possess ballistic missiles, five with intercontinental reach; 17 nations are believed to have chemical and or biological-warfare programs; eight are known to possess nuclear weapons and four are believed to be close to developing them. As a result of years of Clinton-Gore inaction, Americans have no defense against even a single incoming missile tipped with a nuclear, biological or chemical warhead. Since a nation as desperate and poor as North Korea has already demonstrated an ability to reach the United States with a ballistic missile, and since the ability to shoot down one such missile has already been achieved, deterrence advocates view this dereliction and delay by the Clinton-Gore security team as unconscionable—comparable to its laxity in the area of national security that has resulted in the theft of America's nuclear secrets to Communist China and its allies.

In response to the Bush initiative, the arms controllers have claimed that building such a system would upset our allies and undermine the 1972 ABM Treaty—never mind that it was signed with the Soviet Union, which no longer exists, or that the Soviet Union, when it did exist, systematically violated its terms. And never mind that China has never signed the ABM Treaty. The Clinton-Gore administration does not want to implement a defense that might upset the governments of either Russia or China, or our allies. A truly effective missile defense system will of course be opposed by all other states (including our allies), since its purpose is to neutralize their aggressive abilities.

Is there any other way to guarantee our security? In the deterrence view, achieving a comprehensive missile defense is not only worth the diplomatic price; the opposition one can expect from other nations is the very reason for the defense itself. States do not share common interests, and can only be trusted to pursue their own; therefore, any other kind of defense entails risks that are unacceptable. There is one qualification to this proposition, and that is that democracies, which are open societies and therefore far less likely to cheat on agreements, provide a partial exception. Bush has already accommodated this exception by proposing to include our democratic allies in the missile shield.

The security issue was joined in the presidential campaign as a result of Bush's May proposal to build a sea-based and space-based anti-missile defense system that would provide an effective shield against missile attack for the United States and its allies, and that would itself be invulnerable to attack. The Bush plan would in effect implement the Strategic Defense Initiative launched by Reagan. In his May speech Bush accused the Clinton-Gore administration of denying the need for a national missile defense system and delaying its development. For seven years the administration had refused to act on this issue, until finally the Republican Congress authorized the development of an anti-missile defense system last year and Clinton signed the bill. He did so, however, with the caveat that he would defer a decision on whether to actually develop such a system until this August, less than six months before the end of his term.

In the last few weeks, the Clinton-Gore administration has finally become a convert to some form of missile defense—cynics might say a form sufficient to cover Gore's political vulnerability, but not the American people's military vulnerability. Gore has proposed a limited, land-based missile defense system, which would be built in Alaska, and would be sufficient to deter rogue states like North Korea and Iran. But North Korea and Iran are really client states of China. Like most of Gore's proposals, this one seems focus-group-designed for the election season.

Until recently, the American voter was blissfully unaware of the derelictions of the Clinton-Gore team on the missile defense issue. It was the successful launch of a North Korean Taepo Dong ICBM, capable of reaching Alaska and probably California, that has brought the issue to the fore. The United States, today, has no defense against North Korea's Taepo Dong missile. If the American people were to become aware of the fact that eight years of administration inaction had made them vulnerable to a nuclear attack by North Korea, that awareness could very well impact the tracking polls.

This is just the tip of an iceberg of bad national security news that the Clinton-Gore administration, abetted by a friendly press, has managed to keep under the surface of the political waters. What if the American electorate began to ask other questions? For example: What happened to America's technological advantage in nuclear weaponry? Why are underdeveloped rogue states like North Korea, Iraq, Iran and even Libya potentially in possession of technologies that can overwhelm America's defenses? Might this have some relation to the policies of the Clinton-Gore "strategic partners" in Moscow and Beijing, who have systematically spread those technologies to their allies in Iran, Iraq, Libya and North Korea? Might this security disaster be the result of the systematic removal of security controls by the Clinton-Gore White House, which allowed American missile, satellite and computer technologies to be transferred to the Communist regime in China, which in turn gave (or sold) them to its allies in Iran, Iraq, Libya and North Korea? And might all this have something to do with the infamous Buddhist Temple affair and the long-term funding of the Clinton-Gore electoral machine by illegal monies flowing directly or indirectly from the Chinese regime?[6] Would we not know more about these issues except for the refusal of over 100 witnesses to testify before congressional investigating committees—the same witnesses

[6]Edward Timperlake and William C. Triplett II, *Year of the Rat: How Bill Clinton Compromised U.S. Security for Chinese Cash,* Regnery, 1998, pp. 71–76.

who were abetted and encouraged in their resistance by the Clinton-Gore team?

When, in the 1930s, Japan disregarded the pieties of the Kellogg-Briand Pact to build an aggressive force and attack Pearl Harbor, America was ultimately protected by its geography—the vast expanse of the Pacific Ocean, which no aircraft at the time could traverse without refueling. As a result, America was provided with a chance to regroup and make up the arms deficit caused by its adherence to the agreements it had so myopically relied on. During the Cold War and the early stages of missile technology, America enjoyed a significant edge over its adversaries that partially made up for the loss of this geographical advantage because of the development of air power.

But the Clinton-Gore administration's voluntary release of all the secrets of America's nuclear tests, combined with the systematic theft of the secrets that were left as a result of its lax security controls, effectively wiped out America's technological edge. Since China is the world's No. 1 proliferator of nuclear secrets, this catastrophe also seriously diminished America's advantage over such scrupulous observers of international accords as Saddam Hussein, Kim Jong Il and Muammar Qaddafi. Now, the Clinton-Gore team is actually proposing that America share its anti-ballistic missile technologies with some of these nations.[7] Appeasement of Russian and Chinese sensibilities is apparently more important than achieving the most effective defense America can build. The appeasers' argument is that if we don't accommodate the Russians and Chinese, there will be a new arms race and a new Cold War.

But there already is an arms race with Russia and China, and the lesser "rogue states" as well. If there is not, why did China, for example, feel the need to steal our nuclear secrets? Why did the Chinese regime invest so much money in the Clinton-Gore

---

[7]https://www.centerforsecuritypolicy.org/2000/06/01/how-to-share-u-s-missile-defense-protection-deploy-sea-based-anti-missile-systems-2/.

campaigns? Why did it press so hard to have the administration remove the security controls that govern commerce and thus gained our Chinese adversary access to previously banned missile and satellite technologies and super-computers? The answer to these questions is both obvious and ominous, and a good reason for supporting the presidential candidacy of George W. Bush.

3

The Bad Fight

(with Peter Collier)

When Al Gore finally conceded the election, he was showered with hosannas by the media for his "statesmanlike," even "elegant" withdrawal speech. This would have been true if it had come 38 days earlier. But coming when it did, after he had opened Pandora's Box and let out Jesse Jackson, Bob Beckel, Connie Roberts, the Broward County canvassing board, the Florida Supreme Court and all the other monstrosities of the post-election nightmare, Gore's statement was a cynical attempt to sprinkle perfume over the smell of vomit.

One truth should not be lost in the false calm following this storm, a time when the realities we have witnessed are submerged in the smarmy praise lavished on the vice president for finally accepting the inevitable. There was nothing noble about Gore's concession because there was nothing noble in his post-election fight to seize the presidency. No principle about the popular will was affirmed in Florida. No vision of America was served. No higher truth about democracy was honored.

Despite the talk about "the will of the people" and "counting every vote," what took place in Florida was Al Gore's personal pathology played out in an ambiguous post-electoral context. Pundits talked ominously about the possibilities of the Republicans and Democrats exercising "nuclear options" in their respective

Originally published in the November/December 2000 issue of *Heterodoxy,* http://www.discoverthenetworks.org/Articles/2000%20nov-dec.pdf.

struggles to win, and then thanked our lucky stars that such a thing didn't occur. But in fact Gore pursued a scorched-earth policy from the beginning. He ran for the Presidency like a rat in heat, employing any stratagem, no matter how despicable, in the quest for victory. Any *post mortem* of Decision 2000 must look back beyond what happened after November 7 and remember the terrorizing telephone messages beamed into the homes of seniors, and the nauseating James Byrd ad run by Gore's lackeys in the NAACP.

And his post-election campaign was equally desperate. On the night of November 7, he unleashed the dogs of war. Some of them still run wild in the streets. John Lewis, in an absurd analogy that debases the entire history of the civil rights movement, compares Florida to Selma. Jesse Jackson, shakedown artist *par excellence* who showed in Florida that there is no light between him and Al Sharpton and Louis Farrakhan, raved incoherently about Bush's "Nazi tactics."[1]

In America today, only black demagogues could get away with this sort of thing. And only Gore and the other overseers of the liberal plantation would act as their facilitators. What the post-election showed beyond doubt was that, however much he tried to distance himself from Bill Clinton and that dollop of semen on the blue Gap dress, Al Gore is Clinton's authentic political heir. In his eight years as president, Clinton divided the nation, sullied the White House and diminished the authority of the Oval Office. And in his reckless attempt to stage a post-election coup, Gore continued Clinton's assault on American institutions.

We must not lose the history of what actually happened in Florida. By dispatching within hours of the closing of the polls a small army of political operatives to Florida to subvert the results, Gore threw the nation into electoral chaos and unleashed an

---

[1]Hal Lindsey, "Living In A Parallel Universe," *World Net Daily*, December 13, 2000, http://www.wnd.com/2000/12/5680/.

unprecedented effort to de-legitimize the process by which Americans elect their president.

His post-election campaign was far better organized than the one that had lost him the election on November 7. First, there was the calculated effort to inflame the nation over the now-infamous "butterfly" ballot, only later to be deemed lawful by Florida courts. Blacks and Jews perhaps had voted for Pat Buchanan! Gore operatives' cries of outrage found willing megaphones in individuals such as filmmaker Michael Moore who, in one of the acts of true moral imbecility of the post-election furor, moaned about victims of the Holocaust being forced, apparently because of a sinister plot by Palm Beach Democratic election officials, to vote for a Holocaust denier.

After he had waved the bloody shirt of "disenfranchisement" and gotten the nation's attention, Gore allowed the butterfly ballot to sink into the oblivion from which it should never have been raised. Gore—who was, we were repeatedly assured, in control of every detail, making dozens of calls a day and spamming his minions with email—then moved on to the real prize: the "undercount" in the three most heavily Democratic counties in the state. This led to the weeks-long *intifada* of legal sophistries, after-the-fact rule changes and dimpled ballot absurdities. Regiments of the vice president's operatives invaded heavily-controlled Democratic enclaves and forced election bureaucrats to start counting anything in sight that resembled a vote, making a mockery of the American system. In doing so, they turned the fate of an entire nation over to the chicaneries of a Chicago-style political ward like the one presided over for half a lifetime by Gore campaign chief William Daley's father Richard. It was only because of the sudden and surprising resistance of Republican rank-and-filers that the son was not able to perform an homage to the old man by stealing another election 40 years later.

It was only two years ago, in Miami's Dade County—the largest fish pond for the elusive votes in this disgraceful endeavor—that authorities removed an elected Democratic mayor because the county's Democratic machine had elected him with the votes of the dead. But rigging a mayoral election is nowhere near as cynical as trying to change the outcome of votes for the leader of the free world. And this is what Al Gore tried to do. The assault on the truth that had begun with the Derridaean vapors of the postmodern university and spread into the Clinton White House—"depends on what the meaning of is is"— had now been injected into the electoral system itself: depends on what you mean by "a vote."

As a result of Gore's disgraceful campaign in Florida, the most basic institutions of our government have been called into question, and the legitimacy and authority of the next presidency will be profoundly subverted. The election process has been constructed in such a way as to reveal only naked power relationships. How will public reverence, let alone respect, for elections be restored? What Al Gore has accomplished in a few short weeks is the impeachment not only of the integrity of local precincts, but of the entire machinery of American elections. Not just for now, but into the foreseeable future.

To fully appreciate the sewer of cynicism into which Gore has plunged a stupefied nation, one has only to look to the systematic effort by his legal mob to deprive overseas military personnel of their votes. These were not rogue raids into the enemy camp, any more than the bogus effort to toss out votes in Seminole County, but a calculated effort by the campaign itself. Gore lawyers fanned out across the Florida counties and descended on the precincts where the military votes were being received. Armed with a legal memo circulated by Team Gore, they set about browbeating ordinary citizens attempting to count the incoming votes into believing—falsely—that the law disallowed military ballots without postmarks.

By the time the dust partially settled, the Gore team had managed to get 1,527 of 3,733 overseas absentee ballots thrown into the trash. That was pushing 50 percent. However, in the handful of Democrat-controlled counties, which Gore had targeted for his plans to overturn the national election, the percentage of disallowed absentees was astronomical. In Democrat-run Broward County, Gore's crew was able to get 304 overseas ballots rejected out of a total of 396 cast.

Gore apparently thought he could do this in the dark. Once the military ballots became the subject of public outrage, he tried to avoid a potential public-relations nightmare by sending out Joe Lieberman to further debase himself by wringing his hands over the equivalent of "no controlling legal authority." Interviewing Lieberman on NBC's *Meet the Press* Sunday, Tim Russert asked: "Will you today, as a representative of the Gore campaign, ask every county to re-look at those ballots that came from armed services people and waive any so-called irregularities or technicalities which would disqualify them?" Lieberman replied: "I don't know that I have that authority. I don't believe I do legally, or in any other way."[2]

Meanwhile, Democrats like Sen. Bob Kerrey, a military hero trotted out by Gore to defend the indefensible, explained that, of course, Democrats do not approve of the disenfranchising of military personnel. When it was pointed out by MSNBC's Chris Matthews that they had done just that, Kerrey replied: "I haven't accused Republicans of being anti-Semitic or anti-African-American," thus backhandedly accusing Republicans of being anti-Semitic and anti-black because of the butterfly ballot.

This was not a rogue statement by Kerrey. Racial McCarthyism, it could be said, was the most potent theme of Al Gore's Florida electoral success story. During the campaign, millions of dollars worth of Democratic ads painted George W. Bush as a supporter of racial lynch mobs—personally responsible for a series of legal lynchings of convicted black prisoners in Texas. It was Willie Horton in reverse, and the success of this reprehensible campaign

---

[2]Christopher Caldwell, "Thoroughly Corrupt in the Citrus State," *NYPress.com*, December 5, 2000, http://www.nypress.com/thoroughly-corrupt-in-the-citrus-state/.

could be measured by the 65 percent increase in the black vote in Florida over the previous presidential election, with an otherwise inexplicable 93 percent of that vote going to Gore.

It was a fitting climax to a campaign that had begun half a year earlier with Gore's embrace of Al Sharpton, and his insinuation that left-leaning former Sen. Bill Bradley was a closet racist. It was almost anticlimactic when Gore, in an act of political and racial nihilism, deployed the nation's racial arsonist in chief, Jesse Jackson, to proclaim: "Once again, sons and daughters of slavery and Holocaust survivors are bound together with a shared agenda, bound by their hopes and their fears about national public policy."[3] The subtext was far from subtle: Bush Republicans are crypto-slavemasters and Nazis. The election must be won by any means necessary.

This is Al Gore's legacy—not the sonorous words of concession summoning up Thomas Jefferson and Abraham Lincoln. This is the rancor we will now have to live with.

In the aftermath of this speech, which one can only hope will be the last Gore will ever give on the presidential stage, many commentators noted optimistically that in America we achieve even our most difficult electoral transitions without the involvement of armies. This is true. But if the tale is told honestly, 2000 will be remembered as the election in which the Gore forces deployed the moral equivalent of tanks in the streets, and almost won.

---

[3]Mark Fineman, "Blacks, Jews 'Must Stand Together' on Tally, Jackson Says," *Los Angeles Times,* November 13, 2000, http://articles.latimes.com/2000/nov/13/news/mn-51159.

4

First Blood

A graphic image in the *Los Angeles Times* by its editorial cartoonist, Conrad, encapsulates in succinct fashion the ugly spectacle unfolding on the left side of the political spectrum, where a frenzied paranoia has taken hold of opponents of the new administration. The title of Conrad's cartoon is "Some of Bush's Cabinet Choices"[1] and pictured its frame are five older white males (one actually doddering) whom the artist has dressed in suits and dunce caps. A sixth male completes the line-up in Ku Klux Klan hood and robe. Even the terminally challenged can't miss this point: Republicans are racist idiots.

Does it ever occur to liberals, who dream up and publish this poisonous stuff, that they have become mirror images of that which they profess to fear: hate-mongers, witch-hunters and, yes, racists? Can one even imagine the *Times* printing a cartoon that showed six *female, black* and *Hispanic* Bush cabinet nominees wearing dunce caps? In the politically correct culture, there is license to assault only whites and males this way. Conrad, it should not go unnoticed, is a Pulitzer Prize winner. Does character assassination, even as crass as this, have an impact? You bet. A liberal friend of mine—a Hollywood person who wouldn't be able to tell you the name of the governor of California, let alone the

---

Originally published January 8, 2001, http://www.salon.com/2001/01/08/lynch_mob/; http://archive.frontpagemag.com/Printable.aspx?ArtId=24409.
[1]*Los Angeles Times,* January 3, 2001.

Attorney General nominee—called me the other day to say: "I hear Bush has nominated a Ku-Kluxer to his cabinet."

The facts, in case anyone is interested, are these: Bill Clinton sent 28 African-American nominees to the Senate Judiciary Committee for confirmation as federal judges. One nomination was withdrawn. John Ashcroft—the Bush cabinet member portrayed with the Ku Klux Klan hood—voted to confirm 26 of those remaining. As Missouri governor, he signed into law a state holiday honoring Martin Luther King, Jr.; made the home of Scott Joplin Missouri's only historic site honoring an African-American; created an award honoring black educator George Washington Carver; named a black woman to a state judgeship; and led the fight to save Lincoln University, which was founded by black soldiers.

As for being qualified for the post, John Ashcroft was Attorney General and then Governor of the state of Missouri. He was a United States Senator, and a member of the Senate Judiciary Committee, for six years. He is by all accounts an honest man and ethical public servant. He never gave orders that incinerated 80 innocent people, mainly women and children, as Clinton's attorney general, Janet Reno, did in Waco Texas. He has never been accused of obstructing justice, or failing to investigate situations in which, say, a vice president of the United States appeared to have lied under oath in the judgment of at least three different Justice Department officials. He never had sex with a college-age government employee, or any government employee, or committed perjury before a grand jury as President Clinton did. He was never accused of taking bribes or misusing government funds, as at least three of the last administration's cabinet members have been accused of doing. In a lifetime of public service, he has never displayed racial, gender or ethnic prejudice towards any group.

Opposing a nominee because you disagree with his or her political positions is one thing. To slander that person as a bad human being—implying he is a racist, homophobe or misogynist, even though there is no basis for saying so other than your disagreement with his politics—is quite another. This is the kind of gutter attack that was on display during the presidential campaign in the NAACP's reprehensible TV ads, insinuating that George Bush defended lynchers and in effect killed James Byrd a second time. The NAACP is quickly becoming the National Association for Defaming Other People.

The left, of course, is aware of the bad company it's keeping as it witch-hunts opponents on the basis of stray quotes, garbled positions and remote associations. So it often pretends it is doing something else. Thus, NAACP president Kweisi Mfume claimed to be against Ashcroft only because he had "consistently opposed civil rights."[2] As a senator, Mfume said, "he received a grade of 'F' on each of the last NAACP report cards because of his anti-progressive voting record, having voted to approve only three of 15 legislative issues supported by the NAACP and other civil rights groups."[3] But "progressive" and "civil rights," in the usage of Mfume and the NAACP, turn out to be code words for "left" and "far left," and have little to do with civil rights as Martin Luther King, Jr. and the civil rights movement of his day understood them. Among the 12 "civil rights" issues that Ashcroft and the NAACP disagree on are Clinton's impeachment (two votes on this), an expanded role for the federal government in education, a raise of the minimum wage and gun- show background checks. Disagree with us on these matters, and we'll tag you as a racist.

The gay left's attack on Secretary of the Interior nominee Gail Norton is an extreme instance of this method. Norton is a libertarian, and therefore hardly anti-gay. But she supported "Amendment 2" in Colorado, which the gay left didn't like. In opposing her nomination, its spokespersons are accusing her of supporting legislation that would take away the civil rights of gays. This is false.

---

[2]"Democrat Vows 'Fair Hearing' for Nominee Ashcroft," *Reuters,* December 24, 2000, http://www.greatdreams.com/pol2000.htm.

[3]"NAACP to Oppose Ashcroft Nomination for Attorney General," *U.S. Newswire,* December 22, 2000, http://www.greatdreams.com/pol2000.htm.

The issue in Colorado was not over civil rights but over special rights exclusive to gays. What is wrong with special rights? Well, until the special-rights crowd came along, every sexually transmitted disease was treated with standard public health methods like testing and contact tracing. But the gay left demanded special rights for gays not to be tested, and not to have their sexual partners warned after they were diagnosed with AIDS. They demanded the right to keep the public sexual gymnasia, which functioned as incubators of infection, open as centers of "gay liberation." The consequences? An epidemic that has so far killed two hundred thousand young Americans, mostly gay, and is still going strong.[4]

The left-wing smear attacks on all Bush's conservative nominees—John Ashcroft, Gail Norton and Linda Chavez—have been as bad as anything Senator McCarthy ever attempted, and with even less foundation; the vast majority of McCarthy's targets actually were pro-Soviet, whereas the targets of the "civil rights" crowd are not the least bit anti-black. A column in the *Los Angeles Times* by Clinton shill Robert Scheer had this to say about the Attorney General nominee: "Ashcroft's hysterical attacks on Clinton [Scheer is referring to the fact that Ashcroft supported impeachment] and his fervent embrace of the right-wing social agenda led him to explore a bid for the presidency as the ultra-right alternative to Bush."[5] Scheer himself is an ultra-leftist, a former acolyte of Lin Piao, the author of *Long Live the Victory of the People's War*.[6] His motives are transparent, like those of the other character assassins in the pack. He doesn't like the election result and is determined to bloody the administration and weaken it from the start.

---

[4]See Volume 5 in this series, *Culture Wars*.

[5]Robert Scheer, "A Far-Right Nominee Who's All Wrong," *The Nation*, January 8, 2001, http://www.thenation.com/article/far-right-nominee-whos-all-wrong.

[6]See Volume 2 in this series, *Progressives*, "Scheer Lunacy at the *Los Angeles Times*.."

As former Clinton Labor Secretary Robert Reich explains in *The New York Times*, this is all part of a "civil war" that the left has been waging for decades.[7] Reich traces the problem back to 1987, "when Ronald Reagan's nomination of Judge Robert H. Bork to the U.S. Supreme Court was rejected by the Democratic-controlled Senate after an extensive media campaign by his opponents."[8] It was more than a media campaign. It was a witch-hunt that involved rifling through the nominee's garbage for personally incriminating material, subpoenaing his bills from a video store to see if he could be accused of watching pornographic tapes, and bald-faced lies told by Teddy Kennedy and Gregory Peck—the latter in TV ads that depicted Bork as a heartless reactionary who wanted to take away the rights of every vulnerable group in the population. Conceded Reich: "George W. Bush may sincerely want to 'reach out' to congressional Democrats, but the Democrats don't want to reach back."

The coalition that has geared up to tar and feather Bush's conservative nominees is exactly the same lynch-mob that ten years ago conducted the most disgraceful campaign of character assassination in American history against Supreme Court nominee Clarence Thomas. The coalition includes the whole familiar civil-rights gang, including Nan Aron of the Alliance for Justice, Ralph Neas of People For the American Way, Kate Michelman of NARAL, Patricia Ireland of NOW, Jesse Jackson, Al Sharpton and Kweisi Mfume. The decade that has gone by since the attack on Thomas ought to have proved to everyone by now that these racial and sexual McCarthyites are unprincipled hypocrites and liars. It is now obvious, for example, that every charge they made against Thomas to smear his reputation was made in bad faith. At the time Thomas was nominated to a seat on the Supreme Court, he

---

[7]*The New York Times*, December 29, 2000.

[8]Linda Greenhouse, "Bork's Nomination Is Rejected, 58–42; Reagan 'Saddened'," *The New York Times*, October 24, 1987, http://www.nytimes.com/1987/10/24/politics/24REAG.html?pagewanted=all.

had been an upstanding civil servant for twenty years. He had risen to great heights from great adversity, growing up in a dirt shack in Georgia when the South was still segregated. In all that time, he had not had a single blemish on his public record. But that didn't faze the Democrats who went straight for his jugular.

The pretext they employed was that, in a private conversation ten years earlier, he had used off-color language to a Yale civil rights lawyer. Just think of it! The left was beside itself. They said he had committed an outrage against a helpless female who was unable to speak up for herself. They said Thomas had abused his position as her employer and also his power. They said he had committed a crime against all women. They called for his head in the name of all women. In the end, they were unable to defeat his nomination. But they succeeded in staining his reputation and neutralizing him as a public force—which is their agenda against Bush and his nominees today.

But the same lynch-mob reacted very differently a few years after the Thomas episode, when Bill Clinton was caught having actual sex with a White House employee. His victim was not a Yale lawyer with an expertise in civil rights, but a confused college-age intern. It was also revealed that Clinton had groped a widow, demanded a sexual favor from a state employee and forced himself on a campaign worker. Unlike Clarence Thomas, who refused to attack the character of his accuser, Clinton and his agents systematically set out to destroy the reputations of each of his female targets as they came forward to speak about their abuse. He even went so far as to lie in a court of law to carry out this assault.

However, when confronted with Clinton's sexual abuses, the same posse of feminists, civil rights activists and liberals, who had slandered Thomas, said: "It's OK. He's just a man. Boys will be boys." They did more than give Clinton a pass. They leapt to his defense. Congressional Democrats, who had preened themselves on being the social conscience of the nation, went to the wall to keep a guilty male in power. They said: "It's *only* sex."

Through a long process of self-degradation, a once-venerable civil rights coalition has transformed itself into a national shakedown operation—one that specializes in witch-hunts for the Democratic Party. The process is simple. Like Senator McCarthy, you dig up an interview that someone may have given to an obscure magazine a long time ago. Then you find a quote from a different article in the magazine that seems, on the surface, offensive. You use this to accuse your target of being a closet racist. Repeat the lie and the word "racist" enough times, and you will find millions of half-awake citizens who will soak up the message. And they will spread the word: "Bush has appointed a Ku-Kluxer to his cabinet."

5

How Leftists Play the Race Card

One hundred days into the Bush administration, few would deny that Washington is a changed town. In contrast to Bill Clinton—a political quick-change artist—the new president has already made good on his two principal promises to voters during the recent election—a large tax refund to citizens overcharged for the expense of government, and a change of tone in the nation's capital. Bush has also delivered on the political front, appointing the most diverse cabinet in the nation's history and establishing "compassionate" issues like education and support for faith-based charities as government priorities. In fact, in his first 100 days, both the president and his cabinet have done more to reach out to minorities and citizens left behind than any Republican administration since that of Abraham Lincoln. Those of us who voted for George Bush can take confidence and pride in this aspect of his governance, too.

That is the Washington aspect of the story. But out in the country, the signs are not so encouraging and the future looks less bright. George Bush may have changed the tone in Washington for the better. But in the rest of the nation, Democrats have continued to change it for the worse.

Just after the Florida election drama drew to a close, an African-American staffer for one of the Republican House leaders was having a Christmas dinner with his family when his twelve-

---

Originally published May 7, 2001, http://archive.frontpagemag.com/Printable.aspx?ArtId=24426 http://www.salon.com/2001/05/07/tone/.

year-old niece asked this question: "Now that Bush has been elected President, am I going to be treated as three-fifths of a human being?"[1]

The same anecdote, with slight variations, has been reported from all ends of the country. A teacher at a rural black elementary school in South Carolina e-mailed me that her students were asking the same question as the staffer's niece; and also whether—since Bush was now president—they would be made slaves again. In the April 30 issue of *The Weekly Standard,* Eric Cohen reports taking a group of black fourth- and fifth-graders from a Washington housing project to an outing in the nation's capital. The trip occurred just after the inauguration. A few days earlier, a man had been arrested for firing shots at the White House. Cohen asked the children what they thought of their new president.

"'When I heard about the shooting I was pretty happy,' said one of the boys with a laugh. 'I thought Bush might have got shot.'" Other comments were just as bitter; "President Bush is going to put us all back in slavery." "He's going to round up all the black people and kill them."[2]

Where could these black youngsters be getting ideas like that? The Democratic Party, perhaps? The Democratic Party's presidential candidate? The leadership of the civil rights movement? The inescapable answer is: all three.

It was the Democratic Party and the NAACP that sponsored millions of dollars of ads on television and black talk radio accusing George Bush of killing a lynch victim a second time, supporting hate crimes,[3] incarcerating "75 percent of minority youth in Texas," and maliciously executing blacks and Hispanics on death row. And it was Al Gore who, in an election campaign attack on Bush's alleged

---

[1]See "Al Gore, George Bush, and the Three-Fifths Clause," http://www.wallbuilders.com/libissuesarticles.asp?id=132.

[2]Eric Cohen, "Race and the Republicans," *The Weekly Standard,* Vol. 6, No. 31, April 30, 2001, http://www.weeklystandard.com/Content/Protected/Articles/000/000/011/422smysm.asp.

[3]"Ignored Byrd Hate Crime Bill Despite Plea by Byrd's Family," *Issues 2000,* http://www.onthcissues.org/George_W__Bush_Crime.htm.

judicial preferences, repeated the libel claiming that the framers of the Constitution regarded a black person as "three-fifths of a human being." This is one of the most widely believed myths in black America today. In fact, it was the anti-slavery framers who insisted on the three-fifths figure in order to diminish the electoral power of the slave South. And it was Democratic and NAACP spokesmen in Florida who described the voting-booth mess as a "return to slavery."

In sum, every element of the anti-Republican paranoia rampant in African communities throughout this nation was deliberately planted there by the Democratic Party and the civil rights leadership. Nor did the racial slanders end with George Bush's election. The nomination of John Ashcroft for attorney general was turned into a Star Chamber proceeding reminiscent of 17th-century Salem, when a man without blemish on his public record was interrogated as though he were a modern-day witch: *Mr. Ashcroft, are you now or have you ever been pro-slavery?* Have we all lost our senses? Slavery has been dead 136 years, and there has never been a movement to revive it. Thousands of *free* African-Americans actually fought *for* the Confederacy. Yet John Ashcroft was nearly denied the attorney generalship of the United States because, in an interview with an obscure historical journal, he praised the loyalty of Confederate leaders to *their* cause!

The fact is that, in the nation's public political arena, we *have* lost our senses. Or, rather, have been beaten senseless by the racial McCarthyism of the left. Republicans—and others—had better learn how to combat this latter-day witch-hunting hysteria—or surrender the fight in advance to any political opponent who is willing to employ a race-baiting attack.

John Ashcroft is now paying penitential visits to black churches to demonstrate that he really is not a witch. He has announced that ending "racial profiling"—a principal demand of the race-baiting left—will be a top Justice Department priority. Will this political appeasement of his persecutors work? The visits to black churches are good in themselves—it's time that Republicans reached out in a big way to African-American communities.

But they will not buy John Ashcroft peace. Not unless he surrenders to the left and gives up his conservative ideas.

The same rule applies to the Bush administration, which has also signed on to the campaign against "racial profiling." George Bush is a good and decent man. There is more racial animus in a single speech of Kweisi Mfume or Jesse Jackson or Al Sharpton than in all the words that George Bush has uttered in his entire life. Yet these men and the Democratic Party have willfully caused black children all over America to think of George Bush as a "racist" who would put them back in chains. This will not go away with symbolic gestures like visiting churches or genuflections to left-wing causes like ending "racial profiling." It will only go away when the demagogues are exposed—when those under attack are willing to call racial McCarthyism by its proper name and fight back on the issues themselves.

The symbolic aspect of the administration's gesture on racial profiling is sound. It is saying, "We hear your concern." The problem is that there is no way to end "racial profiling" as the NAACP and Democrats define it, except by giving up the fight against crime. Black males are stopped and arrested in far greater numbers than they make up in the population, because black males commit violent crimes in far greater numbers than they make up in the population. Black males, who represent 6 percent of the population, commit more than 40 percent of the violent crimes. In New York City, based on victim reports, a black male is 13 *times* more likely to have committed a violent crime than a white male. How are the police going to avoid stopping a greater percentage of black males than white, if they are to protect citizens from the criminals who prey on them? Readers who do not understand this proposition should read Heather MacDonald's "The Myth of Racial Profiling," in the current issue of the Manhattan Institute's *City Journal* from which the following data are taken.[4]

[4]Heather Mac Donald, "The Myth of Racial Profiling," *City Journal,* Spring 2001, http://www.city-journal.org/html/11_2_the_myth.html.

The anti-racial profiling crusade began with a New Jersey Turnpike stop of suspected African-American drug dealers. Under a deafening media barrage powered by the Jesse Jackson-Al Gore-Al Sharpton-NAACP noise machine and amplified by Bill Bradley, Al Gore and the Democratic Party machine, the Republican administration in New Jersey caved to the anti-profiling cause. A report was produced that appeared to confirm that there was indeed racial profiling by New Jersey cops. The report's conclusion was based on the fact that 53 percent of the people stopped and searched by officers looking for drug dealers were black, while blacks make up only 13.5 percent of the population in the state. When an embarrassing photo of Republican governor Christie Todd Whitman frisking a black suspect was published in the press, she and her attorney general, Peter Verniero, capitulated to the demagogues and certified the statistics assuring the public that this racial profiling was unacceptable and would be stopped. In February 1999, to emphasize the point, Whitman fired the head of the state police.

The problem, however, is that 60 percent of the drug dealers in New Jersey are black. In other words, the percentage of stops was prudent law enforcement. Race had nothing to do with it.

In an atmosphere in which racial demagoguery has made politics surreal, facts like these do not appear to present a problem. Testifying on racial profiling before the Senate Judiciary Committee in 2000, New Jersey Senator Robert Torricelli assured the committee: "Statistically, it cannot bear evidence [sic] to those who suggest, as our former superintendent of state police suggested, that certain ethnic or racial groups disproportionately commit crimes. They do not."[5]

Well, Senator, actually they do. As MacDonald points out, blacks make up over 60 percent of arrests in New Jersey for drugs and weapons violations. "Against such a benchmark," she writes,

---

[5]Ibid.

"the state police search rates look proportionate." MacDonald also points out that 64 percent of the homicide victims in drug turf wars are black and 60 percent of victims and perpetrators in drug-induced fatal brawls are black—which computes with the fact that 60 percent of the drug offenders in state prison are also black. "Unless you believe that white traffickers are less violent than black traffickers, the arrest, conviction, and imprisonment rate for blacks on drug charges appears consistent with the level of drug activity in the black population."

The result of ignoring these realities and outlawing racial profiling in the state of New Jersey? MacDonald reports that, since the Whitman surrender, "Drug arrests dropped 55% on the Garden State Parkway in New Jersey in 2000, and 25% on the turnpike and parkway combined." The inescapable conclusion: unless you believe that drug dealers have responded to these facts by decreasing their own activity, the civil rights leadership, the Democratic Party and their Republican appeasers have increased the flow of narcotics to New Jersey's inner-city African American communities, with all the destructive consequences that implies.

If Attorney General Ashcroft and the Bush administration follow the pattern of appeasement and proceed down the politically correct path to the world the Democrats are demanding, two things are certain. The mainly minority victims of minority criminal predators will multiply, and the Democratic Party, waving the bloody shirts of racial persecution and Republican insensitivity, will march to victory at the polls. Think of Christie Todd Whitman as the poster-girl of racial profiling. Would her capitulation to the left have prompted the constituencies seduced by its myth to vote for her in the next election? There are only two ways to combat this political pathology. The first is to fight it on the only ground feasible, which is that of reality. The facts must be aired; the demagoguery must be exposed. The second is to beat back the racial McCarthyites by calling them to account.

Let's begin with the reality. Racial profiling is only an injustice if it is profiling solely on the basis of race. There have been recent cases of rogue police officers and even rogue departments, which target minorities such as blacks *because* they are black. This is offensive and inexcusable, and the Ashcroft Justice Department should take every measure available to see that it is stopped. But where profiling means that race is but one element in a clearly defined criminal dossier, it must be defended on the merits, because—among other things—it is the best way to protect minorities themselves.

That is the way to present the case for sound police methods against the attacks of the racial McCarthyites. While blacks do commit over 40 percent of the violent crimes, the overwhelming majority of their victims are black as well. It is to protect vulnerable communities, which are overwhelmingly black, that non-racist profiling is also necessary. Unless politicians like Ashcroft have the courage to explain this, and stand up to their ideological opponents, the left will roll over them, people will suffer—and these people will be mainly poor and black.

The profiling dilemma is characteristic of the challenge the Bush administration—and Republicans generally—face on the racial front. If Republicans are to succeed, they must not succumb to the illusion—as they did during the election—that they can fly under the radar, avoiding the issue and ignoring the Democrats' racial attacks. In the next election, this will not be an option because the political dynamics have changed as result of the last election.

The results show that, for Democrats, the race issue is not a tactic they can do without. In the last election, Democrats needed 92 percent of the black vote—and the inflammatory race-baiting that secured it—just to stay even. Now George Bush has appointed the most diverse cabinet in American history, moved into the black community with a faith-based initiative, and shown that he is ready to contend with Democrats everywhere for the minority vote. This means that now more than ever the race card represents political survival, which for political animals like Democrats is life itself.

6

Who Is Guilty?

The guilty ones are often the first to point the finger. Now the same Democrats who for eight years slashed the military, crippled the CIA, blamed America for the enemies it made, opposed the projection of American power into terrorist regions like Afghanistan and Iraq, dismissed acts of war as individual misdeeds, rejected legitimate airport security measures as "racial profiling," defended a commander-in-chief who put his libido above the security of his citizens, and still oppose essential defense measures like detaining suspects in Guantanamo and imposing immigration controls—these same obstructers and appeasers are now in full war cry against the president and are hoping to pin him with responsibility for the September 11 attack.

Not every Democrat is as anti-American as Rep. Cynthia McKinney (D-GA), who sits with Democratic connivance on the International Relations Committee and spent the week before 9/11 joining hands in South Africa with Iranians and other Islamo-fascists to condemn the United States; then came home to accuse Bush of plotting 9/11 so that his friends in the Carlyle Group could make war profits on defense contracts. But more mainstream Democrats—the Leahys, the Boxers, other equally left and determined antagonists of American power—are far more significant players in the debacle of 9/11. And no one is more singularly

---

Originally published May 20, 2002, http://archive.frontpagemag.com/Printable.aspx?ArtId=24460; http://www.salon.com/2002/05/17/blamegame/.

responsible for America's vulnerability on that fateful day than the Democratic president, Bill Clinton, and his White House staff.

Appropriately, then, the crowning irony of the present Democratic attack is that it is the Clinton administration, not George Bush, who knew of the plot to use airliners as bombs to blow up American buildings; that they knew it in 1995; that they did nothing about it; and that they kept this information from the Bush security team.

But first, the background:

> The first World Trade Center bombing was on February 26, 1993, one month into the Clinton administration. The terrorists—Egyptians and Palestinians—blew a hole six stories deep beneath the North Tower, intending to topple it onto the South Tower and kill 250,000 people. It was—in the words of the definitive account—the most ambitious terrorist attack ever attempted, anywhere, ever."[1] Clinton did nothing. He did not even visit the site. Worse, he allowed the attack to be categorized as a criminal act by individuals, even though its mastermind—as the administration soon discovered—was an Iraqi intelligence agent named Ramzi Yousef.
>
> The second attack took place 10 months later in Mogadishu, Somalia. It was an attack on American military forces who were in country to bring food to the starving Somalis. In the battle, which has been memorialized in the film *Black Hawk Down*, 18 American soldiers were killed and the body of one was dragged through the streets in a gesture designed to humiliate the world's greatest superpower. Clinton's response? He turned tail and ran.
>
> In 1995, Ramzi Yousef was captured in the Philippines with plans to use commercial airliners to blow up CIA headquarters, among other targets. This al-Qaeda plot was termed "Operation Bojinka," which means "the big bang."[2] After the discovery of "Operation Bojinka," Al Gore was appointed to head a task force to tighten airport security. Its key recommendations, which

---

[1]Laurie Mylroie, *Study of Revenge*, AEI Press, 2000, p. 1.
[2]http://www.prisonplanet.com/bust_and_boom.html.

> would have prevented 9/11, were rejected by the White House on grounds that they might be construed as "racial profiling."[3]
>
> In 1996, the Khobar Towers, a barracks housing U.S. soldiers in Saudi Arabia, was blown up by Iranian and Palestinian terrorists acting on behalf of al-Qaeda. Nineteen U.S. servicemen were killed, but the Saudis refused to cooperate in tracking down the killers. The Clinton administration did nothing.
>
> In 1998, the year of Lewinsky, al-Qaeda blew up the U.S. embassies in Kenya and Tanzania—under any circumstances an act of war. Two hundred forty-five people were killed and 6,000 injured, mainly Africans. Clinton's response? The infamous strike on a medicine factory in the Sudan and a spray of missiles onto an emptied terrorist camp in Khost, Afghanistan.
>
> In October 2000, al-Qaeda attacked the U.S.S Cole, an American warship, killing 17 servicemen. Another act of war. The Clinton response? Nothing.
>
> Every year that these terrorist attacks were taking place, Democratic congressional leaders supported bills to cut U.S. intelligence funding and/or hamstring CIA operations, and/or prevent the tightening of immigration controls—all of which would have strengthened American defenses against an al-Qaeda attack.
>
> Meanwhile, the principal ally of Saddam Hussein was the architect of suicide bombing, the creator of the first terrorist training camps, and the apostle of terror as a redemptive social cause—namely, Yasser Arafat. That same terrorist was regarded as a "partner in peace" and was the most frequent guest at the Clinton White House of all foreign heads of state.

Despite the fact that Republicans had fought Democrats for eight years over the military and intelligence budgets, over immigration and security issues, despite the alliances that leftwing Democrats had made with America's enemies at the UN, despite the obstructionism of Senate Judiciary chairman Patrick Leahy in opposing domestic security measures and efforts by the Justice

---

[3]Seymour Hersh, "Mixed Messages," *The New Yorker,* May 27, 2002, pp. 40–48 http://www.freerepublic.com/focus/news/690278/posts.

Department to bring al-Qaeda to heel, Republicans refused to point a partisan finger on issues of war and peace. Now their self-restraint has come back to haunt them as the Democrats seek to shift the blame they have done so much to earn to the shoulders of their political opponents.

The Democratic attack on George Bush is based on an intelligence analysis he received a month before 9/11, which indicated that al-Qaeda terrorists were planning to hijack planes. The described threats in this analysis came under the category "general," meaning they did not specify time, place or method, and were uncorroborated. The reports the president received in the months prior to 9/11 described targets that were mainly overseas—in the Arabian Peninsula, Israel, Italy, Paris, Rome and Turkey. On the slim reed of the existence of a possible hijacking threat in the United States—included with all these others—the Democrats have built their treacherous case.

Yet hijackings occur and have occurred for forty years. On most occasions they are stopped. Nine of the 9/11 hijackers were hauled out of airport security lines as they were boarding the fatal flights that September. But because airport security had not been tightened—and could not be tightened without a battle royal with Democrats over "racial profiling"—the al-Qaeda hijackers were allowed to continue and carry out their sinister design. Shutting down the U.S. airline industry, or sounding a national alarm that would produce the same effect, on the basis of a reported possible hijacking, is something no administration has ever done in 40 years of hijacking incidents. Yet this is the logic behind the Democrats' present investigation.

If the Bush White House had known what the Clinton administration knew—that al-Qaeda had plans to use commercial airliners as *bombs* and fly them into buildings—specifically the CIA—this would be a serious charge. But the Bush people did not know it, because the Clinton team had never told them.

Although the Clinton security team knew that Operation Bojinka included blowing up the CIA building in Langley, Virginia, it kept this information from the rest of the government. When Dale Watson, chief of the FBI's International Terrorism Operations Section, testified before the Senate Judiciary Committee in February 1998, he withheld this vital information. He identified Operation Bojinka only as a plot to blow up U.S. air carriers, and assured the senators that the FBI had the situation under control.

It is possible that Clinton never received the information about Operation Bojinka. His lack of interest in national security matters throughout the course of his administration has been noted by many, including his chief political advisor Dick Morris and his journalist-biographer Joe Klein. February 1998—the date of the FBI testimony—is also the month after Monica Lewinsky became a national celebrity.

The fact that Bush didn't know about plans to hijack planes and run them into tall buildings was confirmed by Condoleezza Rice at her recent press conference:

> ***Dr. Rice:*** Hijacking before 9/11 and hijacking after 9/11 do mean two very, very different things. And so focusing on it before 9/11—perhaps it's clear that after 9/11 you would have looked at this differently, but certainly not before 9/11.[4]
> ***Q:*** And no discussion in this briefing, or any others, about the possibility of al-Qaeda hijacking, and the fact that there have been active investigations into the possibility of a CIA building plot, or an Eiffel Tower plot. Never came up?
> ***Dr. Rice:*** It did not come up.

On September 10, 2001 a document landed on the President's desk that he had commissioned months before. It was a plan to dismantle and destroy al-Qaeda and had taken months to prepare. It was necessary because the Clinton administration had drawn up no such plan in the eight years before. The charge now being laid by the Democrats against the nation's commander-in-chief, as he

[4]"What Did Bush Know of Warnings Before 9/11?," *CNN Transcripts*, Aired May 18, 2002, http://www.cnn.com/TRANSCRIPTS/0205/18/tt.00.html.

attempts to protect its citizens against the next certain terrorist attack, is worse than unconscionable. It is one more Democratic stake driven into the heart of the nation's security. Limiting the damage, and defending his authority in order to protect Americans from further harm, is now the daunting task before the president and his team.[5]

[5]http://www.9-11commission.gov/report/911Report_Exec.htm ; see especially section "1998 to September 11, 2001."

7

The Doctrine of Pre-Emption

Even as American forces complete their liberation of Iraq and the world celebrates their victory, domestic opponents of the Bush administration have stepped up their attacks on the national security policy that led to the result. In particular, they have challenged the doctrine of military "pre-emption," which is the policy of readiness to initiate action in order to quell an imminent threat; in short, to take the battle to the enemy camp.

Opponents argue that pre-emption is a radical departure from previous American foreign policies; that it is an immoral doctrine; and that it sets a dangerous example for other nations. These objections are held to be so grave as to justify fracturing the traditional bipartisan consensus on national defense and dividing the home front—even in the face of enemies who are supporters of terror, armed with weapons of mass destruction, and motivated by religious fanaticisms that appear impervious to rational dissuasion or traditional military deterrence.

At the very outset, there is a problem in taking these arguments as seriously as their proponents intend them. The same voices raised no similar complaint during the eight foreign policy years of the Clinton administration. Yet every use of military force by the Clinton administration can be reasonably said to have been an act of pre-emption according to the standards invoked in the

---

Originally published April 15, 2003, http://archive.frontpagemag.com/Printable.aspx?ArtId=18696.

present liberal attack. These military actions include the missile strikes on the Sudan, Afghanistan and Iraq, and the air attacks of the Kosovo War whose goal was a regime change in Belgrade.

The 1998 missile strike on the Sudan was an unannounced, unprovoked attack that destroyed that Third World nation's only medicine factory. Yet it provoked no opposition outcry on the left. The Clinton air strike violated every principle of the current liberal critique of Bush foreign policy. The target of the attack was an alleged chemical weapons factory—which, the administration subsequently had to concede, contained no chemical weapons facility. There were no inspections, UN or otherwise, preceding the attack to determine whether the factory was actually producing chemical weapons, as the Clinton White House claimed. There was not even a presidential phone call, to the head of a state with whom the United States had diplomatic relations, to request such an inspection.

The strike on the Sudan was ordered without a UN resolution, without congressional authorization and without approval from the Joint Chiefs of Staff, who actually opposed it. Yet no critic of the current Bush foreign policy on Iraq expressed concern over the aggression. This is in dramatic contrast to the present critique of a war policy that is based on 12 years of disregarded UN resolutions and thwarted UN inspections, and two congressional resolutions (under two presidents) supporting a regime change by force.

The 1998 decisions by the Clinton Administration to fire 450 cruise missiles into Iraq and 72 into Afghanistan were justified by no attack on the United States on the part of Afghanistan or Iraq, and were not authorized by either Congress or the United Nations. The Clinton air war against Iraq was initiated in response to the expulsion of UN inspectors by Saddam Hussein. But no act of Congress or a UN Security Council resolution legitimized this military assault.

Clinton's attack on Afghanistan was justified by administration officials as a response to the blowing up of two U.S. embassies in Kenya and Tanzania by unknown terrorists. But the Clinton

Administration provided no more evidence of a connection between Afghanistan and those attacks than was provided by the Bush administration of the connection between the World Trade Center bombing and Iraq. In both cases, the judgment to launch a military response was made by those charged with responsibility for America's national security. But in only one case did the absence of a proven connection become the basis for a critique of the action.

The Clinton-led attack on Yugoslavia was a pre-emptive war that was not even justified as "national defense." Slobodan Milosevic and the government of Yugoslavia did not threaten, let alone attack the United States. There were no Serbian terrorist organizations linked to attacks on the United States or American citizens; nor was Yugoslavia accused of harboring such organizations. Slobodan Milosevic and the government of Yugoslavia were never regarded by anyone as constituting a national security threat to the United States or the NATO alliance.

Yet, without provocation, the Clinton administration organized a coalition attack on Yugoslavia from the air and proceeded to bomb targets in that country until a regime change was achieved. The targets included the capital city of Belgrade, with as large a civilian population as Baghdad. Yet there was no UN resolution authorizing this attack, nor did liberal critics of the present Bush policy complain about the lack of one. Nor was there a congressional declaration of war or authorization, as there was in Iraq, for the use of force. The attack on Yugoslavia was a pre-emptive war to save the lives of Albanian Muslims. There was no other rationale for conducting it, nor did anyone in the United States or Europe ask for one.

Nor is there anything new in the doctrine of pre-emption itself. The First World War, in fact, was a pre-emptive war from the American point of view. America did not enter the war because it was attacked; it wasn't. Nor had Germany declared war on the United States. For three years Americans had watched the war from the sidelines. It was a European conflict in which America had had no national stake. Then, in 1917, the United States decided to go to war to prevent a German victory, claiming that its goal was "to make the world safe for democracy."

The second war with Germany was different, but only slightly. The very same people who now claim to oppose pre-emption have long faulted the United States for remaining neutral during the Spanish Civil War. If fascism had been defeated in Spain, they argue, there might not have been a Second World War at all. It's an interesting point. But it is also an argument for a pre-emptive policy.

Lives could have been saved—in fact, tens of millions of lives—if the United States and the Western powers had taken the initiative and used force to stop Hitler early—in the Rhineland, in Austria and in Czechoslovakia, before he was able to amass the military strength that made the Second World War inevitable. The war against Hitler was itself pre-emptive. It is true that Hitler declared war on the United States after the attack on Pearl Harbor. But Hitler did not attack the United States. The United States went to war with Hitler to pre-empt the possibility of a German attack on the United States.

Thus, pre-emptive war has made sense in the past. Why should not the same prudent defense policy make sense now? In fact, it has. The pre-emptive war against Iraq actually began a dozen years ago, at the end of the Gulf War, when the United States and Britain instituted "no-fly zones" to protect the Kurds from potential poison gas attacks. This was an invasion of Iraqi air space. But no one besides Iraq and its allies objected, and the Kurds thrived under the protection.

The threat of pre-emptive war is a form of protection. It tells Iran and Syria—the sponsors of Hezbollah, Hamas and al-Qaeda terrorists who have killed American citizens—that the consequences of their covert aggressions can be deadly to them. Syria and Iran have already done no less than the Taliban regime in Afghanistan when we attacked it. Should the United States tie its hands and force its citizens to wait for another World Center-scale attack before allowing them a response?

Critics of the war in Iraq claimed that the Administration should have allowed Saddam Hussein more time to continue his evasion of the UN resolutions and focus on the nuclear threat from North Korea instead. What credibility would American demands to North Korea have had, however, if we had continued to appease Saddam and ignore his defiance of UN resolutions? Far from being a distraction, the pre-emptive war against Saddam Hussein has enhanced the ability of the United States to deter North Korea from its sinister plans.

In sum, the arguments against the doctrine of pre-emption are historically baseless and logically incoherent. On the other hand, they present obstacles to a national consensus that can prove dangerous. Division at home on matters of national security is the surest way to undermine the credibility of an American deterrent and create the possibility of an enemy assault. Critics should think twice before encouraging such outcomes.

8

The Liberal Hate Campaign

In the entire span of this nation's political history, there has never been a hate campaign as massive, as nasty, and as personally vicious as the one directed against President George Bush. Part of this hate is a product of the generic politics of destruction practiced by Democratic Party leaders in every election cycle as a matter of course.

In the 2000 campaign, the Democrats placed ads in black communities across the country accusing Bush of killing a black lynch victim "a second time," and even recruited the daughter of the lynch victim to do the voiceover. This year, the Democrat who would be president is touring the country telling black audiences that George Bush won the election in Florida by stealing a million black votes—an ugly, racially divisive and mendacious charge which, if Republicans were behind it, would elicit howls of foul play from the national media instead of their present silence.[1] Not a single actual victim of such theft has been identified by civil rights organizations or by the Kerry campaign, because none exists. The Civil Rights Commission and the press investigated these charges at the time and found them baseless.

This article originally appeared in the *Philadelphia Inquirer* as one of a series of 21 guest op-eds on the election, October 13, 2004, http://archive.frontpagemag.com/Printable.aspx?ArtId=11010.

[1]Larry Elder, "A Million Black Voters Disenfranchised," *Townhall.com*, August 12, 2004, http://townhall.com/columnists/larryelder/2004/08/12/a_million_black_voters_disenfranchised/page/full.

But it is the specifically personal attacks on Bush that reveal the ferocity of liberal hate in this political season. For two years, George Bush has been derided as a "moron," a "dummy," and a Dick Cheney "puppet" by liberal elites. He has been accused of being a military "deserter," despite the failure of the media to prove this charge in four election campaigns, despite his logging 574 air hours in a plane dangerous enough to be referred to as "the widow-maker," and despite his honorable discharge from the service. As president, he has been denounced as a traitor who has "betrayed" Americans, a liar, a corrupt manipulator who misled America and sent its young and innocent to battle in full knowledge that their mission was fraudulent and their deaths needless.

It has been charged that the sole reason he sent American youth to die was to line the pockets of his corporate Texas cronies. He has been accused in advance of being responsible for any dirty nuclear bomb that terrorists might detonate in the United States. Not a single Democrat has stood up to deplore the recklessness of these smears, or to speculate on how such attacks might affect the fortunes of the troops under the president's command. Instead of fulfilling their role as neutral arbiters of the facts, the media have regularly given these destructive and despicable accusations a free pass.

The personal attacks on Bush began even before the war in Iraq started—a war which was authorized and justified by Bill Clinton and Al Gore and ratified by the majority of congressional Democrats who voted for the Iraqi Liberation Act of 1998; then ratified again in the congressional Authorization of Force Act of October 2002. John Kerry signed on to both resolutions before he turned his back on them because Howard Dean was passing him in the presidential primary polls. These attacks on a President carrying out a bipartisan policy began with an unconscionable personal strike by Senate Minority Leader Tom Daschle on the very eve of the war. Even as American troops moved into harm's way to enforce United Nations Resolution 1441—an ultimatum that called on Saddam to disarm or else—Daschle claimed that Bush's "failed diplomacy," not Saddam's intransigence, was responsible for the war.[2]

I have been invited to respond to today's *Inquirer* editorial, which takes aim not at the Democrat hate-mongers but at their target, describing him as a vindictive politician with an "enemies list." How's that for a fair-minded press! *Inquirer* editors have every right to be partisan; but what kind of judgment would make a man more sinned against than sinning, and responsible for the security of us all, the butt of an editorial like this?

The *Inquirer* editorial rehashes a discredited canard about Joseph Wilson and his wife who, it claims, were punished by Bush for revealing that he had lied about Saddam's attempt to get nuclear materials from Niger. Yet a bipartisan Senate Intelligence Committee investigated Wilson's charges and rejected them, concluding that the president's statement was "well-founded." Wilson's story was evidently a political dirty trick to undermine the rationale for the war, but the media are so consumed by their own anti-Bush passions that they can't even play fair a year and a half later, after the accusation they endorsed turned out to be false.

If George Bush loses this election to a man who has been on all sides of the issue of war and peace, and has shifted his positions according to which way the political winds blow, Americans will surely suffer consequences in the coming months of the war on terror. But then they will have only themselves to blame, along with media that did not meet their most fundamental obligation to stay above the political fray and tell the American people the truth.

---

[2]Carl Cameron, "Lawmakers Rally Around President Bush," *FoxNews.com*, March 18, 2003, http://www.foxnews.com/story/2003/03/18/lawmakers-rally-around-president-bush.html.

9

Counsels of Cowardice

A political ad was placed in *The New York Times* by the radical organization MoveOn.org, a group that has provided a platform for attacks on the Bush administration by Howard Dean, Al Gore and members of the Kerry-Edwards campaign. The ad was an open letter, purportedly from college students, and began: "President Bush Will You Call On Us To Die?"[1]

This was not really criticism of the president's policy choices or of America's war to liberate Iraq, but rather a frontal attack on both. In addition to its blunt and unwarranted assertion that service to one's country was equivalent to a death sentence, it falsely insinuated that the president was planning a military draft, which would make the service as involuntary as—well—a death sentence. Finally, it demanded that the president provide "a plan to end the war," and did so without expressing the slightest concern about the war's outcome.

In other words, in the midst of America's armed conflict with a terrifying enemy, the MoveOn.org ad was an incitement to self-interest, cowardice and defeat. The ad ended with a parsing of John Kerry's famous question about Vietnam, a war he first abandoned

---

Originally published October 25, 2004, http://archive.frontpagemag.com/Printable.aspx?ArtId=10854.

[1]MoveOn/History, *SourceWatch.org,* http://www.sourcewatch.org/index.php?title=MoveOn/History; Originally quoted in *Voice4Change.org,* June 2003, http://www.voice4change.org/stories/showstory.asp?file=030623~www.asp.

and then turned against: "Most importantly, when will we know that the last of our friends has died?"[2]

What has happened to the moral fiber of this country, that a group as close to the center of American political life as MoveOn.org would counsel cowardice, selfishness and defeat in the midst of a war with an enemy as ruthless and determined as the terrorists in Iraq? The war in Iraq was authorized in congressional resolution by both political parties. It is a war to enforce a unanimous Security Council ultimatum, and sixteen ignored Security Council resolutions before that. It is a war to depose one of the worst tyrants of the modern world, whose removal is a policy requested by two successive American presidents, again representing both political parties. It is a war in which every enemy of the United States is ranged on the other side. What has happened to the moral fiber of this country, that an organization like MoveOn.org—along with many leaders of the Democratic Party—should actively seek to sabotage this war by turning America's youth against it, and by demanding a retreat from the field of battle without condition?

The retreat from Vietnam and Cambodia that Mr. Kerry did so much to encourage thirty years ago had an unhappy ending that critics of this war seem eager to forget. That retreat resulted in the deaths of two-and-half million Indochinese peasants whom the Communists slaughtered when they came to power.[3] This is the infamous bloodbath whose prospect John Kerry dismissed as a possibility when he debated swift boat veteran John O'Neill on the

---

[2]youthpolitik, MoveOn Student Action: Open Letter to President Bush on Iraq War, *youthpolitik.blogspot.com*, September 19, 2004, http://youthpolitik.blogspot.com/2004/09/please-sign-this-petition-if-you-agree.html; http://dialogic.blogspot.no/2004/09/moveon-student-action-open-letter-to.html.

[3]http://www.heritage.org/research/reports/1980/04/indochina-five-years-of-communist-rule ; see also Becker, *When the War Was Over: Cambodia and the Khmer Rouge Revolution*, Public Affairs, 1998.

Dick Cavett show.[4] John Kerry was proved wrong then. What if the proponents of retreat from Iraq are proven wrong this time?

If the United States were to lose the battle for Iraq—and a retreat without condition would ensure that—there would be a similar bloodbath. Every Iraqi who has fought for freedom, every ally of America in Iraq will be put to the sword by Abu al-Zarqawi and his terrorist cohorts—many quite literally. The terrorist government of Iran, whose jihadists are now engaged in fighting our troops alongside the agents of Saddam Hussein, will emerge from our retreat as the dominant force in a radicalized Middle East. Revenge against the crusaders will be high on its agenda.

It is time for us to take seriously the counsels of doom in our midst. The threat we face is not only external. American troops can defeat any army on the field of battle. What America cannot do is win the war on terror if the forces of selfishness, cowardice and defeatism divide us at home.

[4]"Complete Kerry/O'Neill Debate" (transcript), *Dick Cavett Show*, June 30, 1971, http://www.wintersoldier.com/index.php?topic=KerryONeill; Complete video of the *Dick Cavett Show*, *C-Span*, June 30, 1971, https://www.youtube.com/watch?v=9j4AP2GW7Ac.

10

Party of Defeat

Most conversations about the coming elections focus on the question of which candidate is more suited to lead the nation as it confronts the challenges and threats ahead. A better question would be to ask whether there is one party—the Democratic Party—which has demonstrated in word and deed that it is unfit to lead the nation in war at all. Criticism of government policy is essential to a democracy. But in the last five years the Democratic Party has crossed the line from criticism of war policy to fundamental sabotage of the war itself—a position no major American party has ever taken in the face of a foreign enemy until now.

In July 2003, just four months into the war in Iraq, the Democratic National Committee ran a national TV ad whose message was: "Read His Lips: President Bush Deceives the American People."[1] This began a five-year, unrelenting campaign to persuade Americans and their allies that "Bush lied, people died"—that the war was "unnecessary" and "Iraq was no threat." In other words: for five years, the leaders of the Democratic Party have been telling Americans, America's allies and America's enemies that their own country was an aggressor nation that had violated

---

Originally published June 4, 2008, http://archive.frontpagemag.com/Printable.aspx?ArtId=31214.

[1]Byron York, "Democrats' Iraqi Attack Ad," *National Review,* July 11, 2003, http://www.nationalreview.com/article/207479/democrats-iraqi-attack-ad-byron-york.

international law, and was in effect an outlaw—the "bad guy"—in the war with the Saddam Hussein regime.

The first principle of psychological warfare is to destroy the moral character of the opposing commander-in-chief and discredit his nation's cause. Yet this is a perfect summary of the campaign that has been waged for the length of this war by the entire Democratic Party leadership; Joe Lieberman being an honorable exception who was driven out of his party for his pains.

The one saving grace for Democrats would be if their charges were true—if they were deceived into supporting the war, and if they had turned against it only because they realized their mistake. But this charge is demonstrably false. The claim that Bush lied in order to dupe Democrats into supporting the war is itself the biggest lie of the war.

Every Democratic Senator who voted for the war had on his or her desk before the vote a 100-page report, called "The National Intelligence Estimate,"[2] which summarized all America's intelligence on Iraq that was used to justify the war. We live in a democracy; consequently, the opposition party has access to all our secrets. Democrats sit on the Senate Intelligence Committee, which oversees all of America's intelligence agencies. If any Democrat on that committee, including Senator John Kerry, had requested any intelligence information on Iraq, he or she would have had that information on his or her desk within 24 hours. The self-justifying claim that Bush lied to hoodwink the Democrats is a fraudulent charge with no basis in reality.

The Democrats changed their views on the war for one reason and one reason alone. In June 2003, a far-left Democrat named Howard Dean was poised to win the Democratic Party presidential

---

[2]"Iraq's Continuing Programs for Weapons of Mass Destruction" (excerpted from the October 2002 National Intelligence Estimate), Federation of American Scientists, http://fas.org/irp/cia/product/iraq-wmd.html; the complete National Intelligence Estimate from October 2002 can be viewed here: http://fas.org/irp/cia/product/iraq-wmd-nie.pdf.

nomination by running on the claim that America was the bad guy in the war in Iraq, and he would get us out.

The charge that Iraq was no threat is another false claim of the Democratic attack on America's war to defend itself. Typical of Democratic Party leaders, former vice president Al Gore now says that "Iraq posed no threat" because it was a "fragile and unstable" nation. But if this were true, the same argument would apply to Afghanistan on September 10, 2001. Afghanistan is half the size of Iraq and a much poorer, more unstable nation; it has no oil; its government did not invade two countries and use chemical weapons on its own citizens, as Saddam did. Yet by providing a safe harbor to terrorists, Afghanistan made possible the murder of 3,000 Americans in half an hour and allowed Osama bin Laden to do what the Germans and the Japanese had failed to accomplish in six years of the Second World War: kill Americans on American soil.

That's why, in February 2002, a year before the war in Iraq, Al Gore was saying that "Iraq is a virulent threat in a class by itself" and that President Bush should "push the limit" to do what was necessary to deal with Saddam Hussein.[3]

But the most self-serving and deceptive of the lies told by the Democratic leadership is this: you can support the troops and not support the war. No, you can't. You can't tell a 19-year-old, who is risking his young life in Fallujah and who is surrounded by terrorists who want to kill him, that he shouldn't be there in the first place; that he's with the "bad guys"—the aggressors, the occupiers, who have no moral right to be in Iraq. You can't do that and *not* undermine his morale, encourage his enemies, deprive him of allies, put him in danger.

That is exactly what the Democrats have done in five years of America's war to deny the terrorists victory in Iraq. Such a party is unfit to lead this nation in war. To place it in a position to do so would be to invite a tragedy of epic proportions.

---

[3]"Iraq No Threat?," *The Trentonian,* July 22, 2008, http://www.trentonian.com/article/TT/20080722/OPINION/307229975.

PART III

Obama

1

Candidate of the Left

A candidate may well change his ... position on, say, universal health care or Bosnia. But he ... cannot change the fact—if it happens to be a fact—that he ... is a pathological liar. ...

—Christopher Hitchens

Christopher Hitchens is normally able to make sharp distinctions between reality and fiction, but this talent seems to have abandoned him in his current electoral ruminations, which have led him to support the presidential candidacy of Barack Obama. Perhaps his instincts have been blunted by the new company he is keeping among the bigoted hysterics of the left, to whom distinctions appear as mere distractions from the path of Truth. Here is Christopher on Governor Sarah Palin: "The Republican Party has placed within reach of the Oval Office a woman who is a religious fanatic, and a proud boastful ignoramus." On November 4, advises Hitchens, those who care for the Constitution and reason will "repudiate this wickedness and stupidity." Wickedness and stupidity are more aptly reflected in baseless, mean-spirited remarks like this.

Christopher has become famous for his recent book *God Is Not Great.* Anti-God is not great either, Christopher. While you refuse to cut Governor Palin some slack in an election season, look at the

---

Originally published October 31, 2008, http://archive.frontpagemag.com/Printable.aspx?ArtId=32913; for the biographical facts of Obama's actual life see Stanley Kurtz, *Radical-in-Chief,* Threshold, 2010.

gaping latitude you provide her opponent. Obama's election (should it come to pass) will not put him a heartbeat away from the presidency but in the cockpit as commander-in-chief. This makes your burden of responsibility much greater, particularly since as a man of the left you understand exactly who Obama is.

Some years ago, you wrote a memorable book about Bill Clinton called *No One Left to Lie To.* When you wrote it, you shared many of Clinton's political agendas but parted ways with him over his moral corruption. Your defection turned on the issue of presidential character. You were repelled by Clinton's easy ways with the truth. Obama's lies make Clinton's pale by comparison. Consider that Obama's closest counselor and spiritual guide over a twenty year period is a racist, Jew-hating, terrorist-loving acolyte of Minister Farrakhan. When asked how this could be, Obama responded he had no idea who Jeremiah Wright really was. What Clinton lie comes close to that one in brazen coolness? Or this one: *My name is Barack Hussein Obama; I grew up the son of a Muslim father and went to a Muslim school in an Islamic state, but I wasn't raised as a Muslim—I've always been a Christian.* I do not believe being raised as a Muslim should matter. But I believe the lie should.

For his entire adult life, Obama's closest political allies have been pro-Soviet leftists—like state Senator Alice Palmer, who chose Obama as the politically appropriate figure to inherit her state senate seat; or anti-American radicals like Bill Ayers, who organized a terrorist army in the 1970s with the intention of launching a race war in America and bringing down the "empire." Others may be under the illusion that the Weather Underground was organized to protest the Vietnam War. But you know better. Ayers and his comrades were still bombing during the year of America's bicentennial, 1976, and into the Jimmy Carter administration. They were still in the trenches four years after our withdrawal from Vietnam because their agenda was a war to destroy the imperial beast, America.

"I was eight years old when Ayers set his bombs," is Obama's excuse for the friendship. (More likely he was several years older.) But Ayers's reputation as a radical bomber was legend in the Hyde Park "liberal" community, where Obama met him and embraced him as a political comrade and ally. It was in Ayers's living room that Obama launched his campaign for Alice Palmer's left-wing seat. It was Ayers's father who got Obama his job at the law firm of Sidley Austin, and it was Ayers himself who hired Obama to spend the $50 million Ayers had raised to finance an army of anti-American radicals drawn from ACORN and other nihilistic groups to recruit Chicago school children to their political causes.

When confronted by his association with Ayers, Obama had another, by now characteristic memory lapse. Ayers was just a "guy in the neighborhood" whose children went to school with his. Not likely, since Ayers's children are significantly older than his. And, in any case, as a fellow leftist he would know exactly who the famous Billy Ayers was. What other crucial facts about his life, and what other essential clues to his character, has Obama lied about? Or perhaps more appropriately: *What has he not lied about?* For example: what about Syrian criminal Tony Reszco, who gave him his house and received what political favors in return? If you ask Obama, he never read all those front-page news stories about Rezsko's indictments.

And, of course, nobody ever bothered to ask Obama why a pro-Soviet-camp-follower like Alice Palmer would want to give her senate seat to him rather than some other worthy to carry on her pro-Communist agendas. But we can pretty well guess Obama's answer if anyone had. When you peel away the subterfuges and get down to the facts, what you are left with is a life-long radical posing as a political liberal to win the trust of a larger constituency.

Obama is also a ruthless machine politician who chose the Daley mafia over inner-city school kids and crushed an incipient reform movement he himself had been part of. When the chips are down, his loyalty is to the machine; but when he runs for office it is as a political idealist. In his heart, he is a radical distressed that the Constitution presents obstacles to socialist theft; but when he runs for office he is a constitutionalist posing as a political centrist. The balancing act is superb. His chief economic adviser this presidential run is Austan Goolsbee, an economic centrist, while Paul Volcker, a much-admired conservative, has joined his campaign. Both men would do a Republican administration proud. But once he is securely in power, where will they be?

The economy is probably not where your own heart is. Consider, then, the global war against Islamic fanatics, which is far from over. Those fanatics are not people who want to "teach the argument" in public schools, like Sarah Palin. Their remedy for disagreement is not discussion but decapitation. Where is Obama on the war between barbarism and civilization? He was for keeping Saddam Hussein in power, when the entire Clinton national security team was against it. He was for capitulation on the battlefield once the war started, which would have left the Iraqis to the tender mercies of Abu Musab al-Zarqawi and his terrorist crew. In regard to foreign policy, where he knows he is vulnerable, his deceptions are predictably world-class. In practice he has spent his political life in league with anti-American, "antiwar" radicals who make no secrets among their friends as to the nature of their agendas. As a sitting U.S. senator, he was an appeaser of America's enemies. But as a candidate *poseur* he is able to pull off the credible impression that he is a tough-minded realist.

And maybe he is. Or maybe he's not any of these things, because all that anyone knows for certain about Barack Obama is that he is not what he seems. Who is the real Barack Obama? His intentions, like those of many, are a mystery. But what we do know about his deeds is bad.

We know that he is a man without loyalty. Wright, Ayers, Grandma—throw them under the bus. When his benefactor Alice Palmer changed her mind about passing him her senate seat, he refused to give it back. When she and two other black candidates attempted to challenge him in the primaries, he went to court to prevent them from running at all. He preferred to disenfranchise their supporters than win an election. When TV anchors posed uncomfortable questions to him and his running-mate, he had his campaign threaten their stations with reprisals. Michael Barone has written eloquently about the emerging "Obama thugocracy." What counter-evidence could you possibly produce against this concern? You have embraced a Machiavellian liar and Olympic charmer, remarkably disciplined as a political actor. Should he become president, will you or anyone else be able to call him to account?

Here's another thing to think about. Consider what those who have known Obama best and longest think of all that bobbing and weaving on issues that are fundamental to America's future. Despite his tacks to the center— despite his brave words about standing up to Iran and his claims to be ready to defend Israel's democracy—every anti-Israel, anti-American, pro-Iranian communist in America is supporting Barack Obama; every pro-Palestinian leftist, every former Weatherman terrorist—many of whom are active in his campaign, some even on his campaign website; all Sixties leftists and their disciples, whose hope all their lives has been that America would lose its wars, because in their perverse view America is the Great Satan; every black racist follower of Louis Farrakhan, who said recently that when Obama speaks you are "hearing the voice of the messiah"; every "antiwar" activist who wanted us to leave Saddam in power and then lose the war in Iraq; everyone who believes that America is the bad guy and that our enemies are justly aggrieved; every member of ACORN, the most potent survivor of the Sixties left, which thinks nothing of conducting massive electoral fraud because it has massive contempt for the American way—every one of these radical forces, without exception and without defection, is pulling for Barack Obama, along with al-Jazeera and Vladimir Putin and the religious fanatics of Hamas and the PLO. Have you asked yourself what it is that you think you know, that they don't?

Of course all these leftists with their hostile agendas might be mistaken about Barack Obama. His distinctive talent, after all, is to appear all things to all men and women. In the end Obama may be so faithless, disloyal and unprincipled as to turn his back on everything he has ever stood for and everyone who has ever supported him for the last twenty years. He may throw them all under the bus along with Reverend Wright, radical Ayers, and racist Grandma. But how certain of that can you be? Can you even be sure that Wright and Ayers will not be invited back into the fold once the prize is achieved? What do you know that the anti-American, anti-Israel left in this country and abroad, which also supports Obama, does not?

I am stunned that you would give all these facts a pass in casting your vote for the mysterious stranger, and use Sarah Palin's mild, mainstream religious faith as an excuse to condemn her and endorse him. Unlike Obama's political commitments, Palin's faith has been a consistently private aspect of her life.(Is there an act of her governorship you can point to that was dictated by the "religious fanaticism" you ascribe to her on the basis of a single appearance she made in a church she has long since left? There is none. I am not so much surprised as dispirited by your thoughtless attacks on the religious faith of this woman, who has the support of Democrats and Republicans in her state, and who is seeking high office in a nation whose core principle, as you know better than most, is religious tolerance.

Perhaps it is precisely a misapplication of America's tolerance that is the problem here. Perhaps it is this misuse of a good thing that itself has given rise to the passionate hatreds which are directed unfairly at Palin and McCain. These hatreds are justified by their protagonists as a defense of the first presidential candidate who is black. Perhaps, in the rush to elect a black president, there is too much tolerance for lies, too much willingness to give a pass to Obama in matters where he should not get a pass—to ignore so many obviously troubling facts.

I am dispirited that you, who wrote so movingly about your own post-9/11 love for this country, would attack in such an unrestrained and incoherent manner a woman whose candor in expressing similar love has earned her the contempt of the left. Leftists, of course, refuse to consider themselves nationalists or patriotic defenders of a tolerant country. They think of themselves as "citizens of the world" whose allegiances are to international courts and organizations, and to a United Nations dominated by dictators and racists, by women-hating, gay-hating, Jew-hating, Christian-hating and, yes, atheist-hating regimes. All of this doesn't matter to them when they are faced with truly dangerous individuals like Sarah Palin.

Think again, Christopher. Vote for Obama if you want to, but don't debase yourself by thinking—and hating— in lockstep with the left. Since your adoption of this country, you have written thoughtful appreciations of several of its Founders. You know, more than most, that religious freedom—and respect—is the foundation of all the freedoms we enjoy in this country, including the freedom of people to hate it. One thing you can count on from John McCain and Sarah Palin is that they will defend their country and its Constitution against enemies, global and domestic, who hate it and seek its demise. What can you count on from Barack Obama?

2

From Red to Green

Even as its own inhumanity and inefficiency consume revolutionary socialism in the East, a specter can be seen rising from its ashes in the West. The colors are no longer red but green, the accents are those of Malthus rather than Marx, but the missionary project is remarkably intact. The planet is still threatened, the present still condemned, redemption through radical politics still presses: Better green than dead. In environmentalism radicals have found a new paradigm for the paradigm lost.

Thus, the official program of France's Green Party echoes Rosa Luxemburg's apocalyptic cry: "The future will be green or will not be at all." And the program of Germany's Greens exhibits the distinctive accents of the totalitarian voice: "The politics of radical ecology embraces every dimension of human experience ... the old age is giving way to the new." Or, in the blunter expression of the founder of American "social ecology," Murray Bookchin: "We can't heal the environment without remaking society."

The old radical Adam is back: the apocalyptic ambition, the destructive resentment, the totalitarian project. "From all the knowledge we now have about environmental issues," writes Jonathon Porritt, a spokesman for Britain's Ecology Party and the director of Friends of the Earth, "the inevitable conclusion is that our way of life cannot be sustained ... we cannot go on living as

---

Originally published as "Making the Green One Red," *National Review*, March 19,1990; despite the article's earlier provenance, the radical environmentalism it describes only later became a centerpiece of government policy during the Obama administration; hence its placement here.

we do now." The revolutionary agenda requires a revolutionary strategy. When Porritt hears politicians saying they care for the environment and therefore want to achieve "sustainable growth," it leaves him "spitting with rage."[1] We cannot continue, he says, "with [our] same material living standard and at the same time be warriors on behalf of the planet."

Thus radical ecology leads to the familiar threat. The virtuous state must control and restrict social wealth and redistribute it according to the radical creed. In the radical view, property—the foundation of free societies—is mere theft, whose spoils are to be divided up. As Porritt argues: "We in the West have the standard of living we do only because we are so good at stripping the Earth of its resources and oppressing the rest of the world's people in order to maintain that wealth." To achieve ecological balance means "progressively narrowing the gap to reduce the differences between the Earth's wealthiest and poorest inhabitants" until there are "more or less equal shares for all people." Karl Marx described this prescription aptly 150 years ago.

Jonathon Porritt is a leader of the "moderate" wing of the radical environmental movement. David Brower, the founder of Porritt's organization, departed some years ago to create the more radical Earth Island Institute in Berkeley. In 1989 Brower took his place alongside *comandante* Daniel Ortega as co-sponsor of the fourth biennial meeting of the International Congress on the Hope and Fate of the Earth in Managua. One thousand delegates from more than 70 nations met at the Olof Palme Center to denounce the United States and the other "imperialist" predators of the free world, and to launch a new movement of "solidarity environmentalism" by establishing alliances with radicals in Third World countries. According to a report in Brower's magazine:

[1]Apparently a typical reaction of this writer; see, for example, Porritt's statement quoted in *The Green City: Sustainable Homes, Sustainable Suburbs* by Nicholas Low and others, Routledge 2005, p. 72.

> The consensus at the Congress was that 'solidarity environmentalism' is the only kind that makes sense.... Would George Bush and Margaret Thatcher be able to call themselves environmentalists if the effort to protect the ozone layer and stop global warming was linked to the Third World movement's demands for a new, more equitable international economic system, an end to the Third World debt, and curbs on the free action of multinational corporations?[2]

In Managua the political symbolism of the Green united front was all in place: Swedish social democracy, British eco-socialism, Third World Marxism-Leninism, and American auto-nihilism. This development reflects the fact that the Green Movement has grown to its present dimensions out of the crisis of the left; in particular, the necessity of establishing a face-saving distance from the catastrophe of Marxist liberation in the socialist bloc.

To avoid the taint of the socialist past, the Green parties of Europe and even primitive communists like Porritt constantly emphasize that their movement is "neither left nor right," and distinguish the "politics of ecology" from the "politics of industrialism" (i.e., of economic growth) that characterize both capitalist and socialist societies. But from a historical perspective, it would be more accurate to say that the Green movement is a phenomenon of both the political left and the political right, uniting in itself the two traditions of radical totalitarian revolt against liberal order in the 20th century—Communism and fascism—and aspiring to be the third wave of the gnostic assault against freedom in our lifetime.

The fascist roots of the Green movement are well known. National Socialists were naturists long before the post-Khrushchev left discovered ecology; and the Nazis have been justly described as "the first radical environmentalists in charge of

---

[2]See references to Brower at http://archive.frontpagemag.com/readArticle.aspx?ARTID=11365.

a state."[3] Indeed the enthronement of biological imperatives, of the virtues of blood and soil and the primitive communities of the *Volk*, the pagan rejection of the Judeo-Christian God and the radical anti-humanism featured in the philosophy of the Greens are even more obviously derivative of fascist than Marxist political traditions. But despite tensions that exist between the deep ecologists of the environmental right and the eco-socialists of the left, they are indissolubly joined in the common embrace of a single illusion: the gnostic idea that humanity has been alienated from its natural self and that its redemption can be achieved by political means; an idea that implies a declaration of war by a chosen few against the historical existence of all.

Thomas Lovejoy has expressed the radical anti-humanism of the Greens in a statement reminiscent of Susan Sontag's infamous indictment of the white race as the "cancer of history" during the Sixties: "The planet is about to break out into a fever and we are the disease."

Appearing at first as a new ideological wrinkle, this turns out to be the same old anti-humanism of the radical tradition, the very malevolence that has brought it to its present grief. In the environment, the left has found a victim to champion that cannot reject it, a victim that will provide endless justification for its destructive agendas. This is the truly new element in the Green revolution: a constituency—nature—that cannot speak for itself. The conflict between vanguard and victim that has plagued generations of the left has been thus eliminated. What remains is the hubris of self-appointed saviors for whom the human condition is not a reality we must come to terms with, but rather material to be subdued and transformed.

---

[3]Marxists acknowledge this view even in contesting it. http://www.hartford-hwp.com/archives/25b/012.html

3

Obama's Communist Czar

Those who were surprised by the White House appointment of Van Jones—a self-described "communist," and proponent of the idea that the Katrina catastrophe was caused by "white supremacy"—haven't been paying attention to developments on the left since the fall of Communism, or to president Obama's extensive roots in its political culture. Van Jones is the carefully groomed protégé of a network of radical organizations—including Moveon.org—and of Democratic sponsors like billionaire George Soros and John Podesta, former Clinton chief of staff and co-chair of the Obama transition team.

At the time of his appointment as the President's "green jobs" czar—and despite a very recent 10-year history of "revolutionary" activity—Jones was a member of two key organizations at the very heart of what might be called the executive branch of the Democratic Party. The first is the Center for American Progress, which was funded by Soros and the Clintons, and is headed by Podesta. The second is the Apollo Alliance, on whose board Jones sits with Podesta, Carol Browner and Al Gore. This is a coalition of radicals, left-wing union leaders and corporate recruits, which had a major role in designing Obama's green-economy plans, including the "cash for clunkers" program. The New York director of the Apollo Alliance, who will be writing its applications for tens of millions of dollars in "stimulus" funds, is Jeff Jones—no relation of Van's,

---

Originally published September 11, 2009, http://archive.frontpagemag.com/Printable.aspx?ArtId=36267.

but a co-leader of the terrorist Weather Underground along with Obama's close friend and political ally William Ayers.

According to his own account, Van Jones became a "communist" during a prison term he served after being arrested during the 1992 Los Angeles race riots. For the next ten years Jones was an activist in the Maoist organization STORM—"Stand Together to Organize a Revolutionary Movement." When STORM disintegrated, Jones joined the Apollo Alliance and the Center for American Progress Democrats. As he explained in a 2005 interview, he still considered himself a "revolutionary, but just a more effective one." "Before," he told the interviewer, "we would fight anybody, any time. No concession was good enough; ... Now, I put the issues and constituencies first. I'll work with anybody, I'll fight anybody if it will push our issues forward.... I'm willing to forgo the cheap satisfaction of the radical pose for the deep satisfaction of radical ends."[1]

Pursuing the deep satisfaction of radical ends is the clear subtext of Jones's 2007 book, *The Green Collar Economy,* which comes with a Forward by Robert F. Kennedy, Jr. and enthusiastic blurbs from Nancy Pelosi and Al Gore. According to Jones, the Katrina tragedies were caused by global warming, white supremacy, free-market economics and the "war for oil" in Iraq. This "perfect storm" of social evils deprived poor blacks of the protection of adequate levees and private vehicles, which would have allowed them to escape. The fact that a fleet of public buses was available, but that the black mayor and the black power structure in New Orleans failed to deploy them, goes unmentioned in Jones' indictment of white racism. Instead, "The Katrina story illustrates clearly the two crises we face in the United States: radical socioeconomic inequality and rampant environmental destruction." To deal with these crises, the author asserts,

[1]Eliza Strickland "The New Face of Environmentalism," *East Bay Express,* November 2, 2005, http://www.eastbayexpress.com/gyrobase/the_new_face_of_environmentalism/Content?oid=290098&showFullText=true.

"we will need both political and economic transformation—immediately."

How did John Podesta and Al Gore and Barack Obama come to be political allies of a far-left radical like Van Jones—a 9/11 conspiracy "truther" and a supporter of the Hamas view that the entire state of Israel is "occupied territory?" To answer this question requires an understanding of developments within the political left that have taken place over the last two decades—in particular the forging of a "popular front" between anti-American radicals and mainstream liberals in the Democratic Party. The collapse of Communism in the early Nineties did not lead to an agonizing reappraisal of its radical agendas among many who had supported it in the West. Instead, its survivors set about creating a new socialist international which would unite "social justice" movements, radical environmental groups, left-wing trade unions and traditional communist parties—all dedicated to the revival of utopian dreams.

The new political force made its first impression at the end of the decade, when it staged global demonstrations against the World Trade Organization and the World Bank. The demonstrations erupted into large-scale violence in Seattle in 2001 when 50,000 Marxists, anarchists and environmental radicals, joined by the giant left-wing unions AFSCME and SEIU, descended on the city, smashed windows and automobiles, and set fire to buildings to protest "globalization"—i.e., the world capitalist system.

In the direct aftermath of the 9/11 attacks, the anti-globalization forces morphed into what became known as the "antiwar" movement. An already scheduled anti-globalization protest on September 29 was re-named and redirected against America's plans to attack al-Qaeda and the Taliban. The new "peace" movement grew to massive proportions in the lead-up to the war in Iraq; but it never held a single protest against Saddam's violation of 17 UN arms control resolutions, or his expulsion of the UN arms inspectors. It did, however, mobilize 35 million people in worldwide protests against America's "imperialist war for oil." The orchestrators of the demonstrations were the same leaders and the same organizations, the same unions and the same "social justice" groups that had been responsible for the Seattle riots against the World Trade Organization and the international capitalist system.

A second watershed came in the run-up to the 2004 elections, when billionaire George Soros decided to integrate the radicals—including their political organization, ACORN—into the structure of Democratic Party politics. Together with a group of like-minded billionaires, Soros created a "Shadow Party" whose purpose was to shape the outcome of the 2004 presidential race. "America under Bush," Soros told *The Washington Post,* "is a danger to the world, . . . " To achieve his goal, Soros created a galaxy of "527" political organizations headed by left-wing union leaders like SEIU chief Andrew Stern and Clinton operatives like Harold Ickes. As its policy brain he created the Center for American Progress.[2] (The "527" groups are named for the section of the IRS code allowing them to register with the Federal Election Commission.)

Soros failed to achieve his goal in 2004 but went on working to create new elements of the network, such as the Apollo Alliance. Four years later the Shadow Party was able to elect a candidate who had spent his entire political career in the heart of this movement. Obama's electoral success was made possible by the wide latitude he was given by the press and the public, partly because he was the first African-American with a chance to be president and partly because his campaign was deliberately crafted to convey the impression that he was a tax-cutting centrist who intended to bring Americans together to find common solutions to their problems. When confronted with his long-term associations and working partnerships with anti-American racists like Jeremiah Wright and anti-American radicals like William Ayers,

---

[2]See below, Chapter 6, *From Shadow Party to Shadow Government.* Also see David Horowitz and Richard Poe, "The Shadow Party: How George Soros, Hillary Clinton, and Sixties Radicals Seized Control of the Democratic Party," Nelson Current, 2006.

Obama denied the obvious and successfully sidestepped its implications.

Just eight months into his presidency, however, a new Barack Obama has begun to emerge. With unseemly haste Obama has nearly bankrupted the federal government, amassing more debt in his first eight months than all his predecessors combined. He has appeased America's enemies abroad and attacked America's intelligence services at home. He has rushed forward with programs that require sweeping changes in the American economy and is now steamrolling a massive new health-care program that will give the government unprecedented control of its citizens.

Among the hallmarks of this new radical regime was the appointment of Van Jones; but there was now concealing how that appointment stood out for its sharp departure from political normalcy. In his White House role, the radical Jones would have represented the president in shaping a multibillion-dollar stimulus package which could easily function as a patronage program of particular interest to his political allies in the "Apollo Alliance," ACORN and the left-wing unions.

In the classic manual for activists on how to achieve their radical goals, Obama's political mentor Saul Alinsky wrote: "From the moment an organizer enters a community, he lives, dreams, eats, breathes, sleeps only one thing, and that is to build the mass power base of what he calls the army."[3] As the president's green jobs commissar, Van Jones had entered the trillion-dollar community of the federal government and would soon have been building his radical army. The rest of us should be wondering who his sponsors were within the White House. Then we should ask ourselves what they are planning next.

---

[3]Saul Alinsky, http://www.discoverthenetworks.org/individualProfile.asp?indid=2314.

4

Rules for Revolution

Barack Obama is an enigma. He won the 2008 presidential election claiming to be a moderate, saying he wanted to bring Americans together and govern from the center. But since he took office, his actions have been far from moderate. He has apologized to foreign dictators abroad for sins he alleges his own country committed. He has appointed a self-described communist and an admirer of Mao Zedong to top White House posts. He has used the economic crisis to take over buisnesses and has attempted to nationalize the health care system. In his first nine months in office, these actions have already made his presidency one of the most polarizing in history.

Many Americans have gone from hopefulness, through unease, to a state of alarm as the president shows a radical side that was only partially visible during his campaign. To understand Obama's presidency, Americans need to know more about the man and the nature of his political ideas. In particular, they need to become familiar with a Chicago organizer named Saul Alinsky and the strategy of deception he devised to promote social change.

Of no other occupant of the White House can it be said that he owed his understanding of the political process to a man and a philosophy so outside the American mainstream, or so explicitly ded-

---

Originally published November 25, 2009, http://www.frontpagemag.com/2009/david-horowitz/barack-obama%E2%80%99s-rules-for-revolution-the-alinsky-model-by-david-horowitz/; This is an edited version that was included as a chapter in *Radicals: Portraits of a Destructive Passion*, Regnery, 2012.

icated to opposing it. Alinsky wrote a famous political manual outlining his method for advancing radical agendas. It was originally titled "Rules for Revolution," which is an accurate description of its content; but later Alinsky changed the title to *Rules for Radicals,* a politically more palatable title. Its ideas, however, remained the same and provide eye-opening clarity on the words Obama uttered on the eve of his election in 2008, when he told his followers: "We are five days away from fundamentally transforming the United States of America."[1]

Saul Alinsky was born in Chicago in 1909 and died in California in 1972. His preferred self-description was "rebel"; his entire life was devoted to organizing a revolution in America to destroy a system he regarded as oppressive and unjust. By profession he was a "community organizer," the same term employed by his most famous disciple, Barack Obama, to describe himself. Alinsky came of age in the 1930s and was drawn to the world of Chicago gangsters, whom he had encountered professionally as a sociologist. He sought out and became a social intimate of the Al Capone mob and of Capone enforcer Frank Nitti, who assumed leadership of the mob when Capone was sent to prison for tax evasion in 1931. Later Alinsky said, "[Nitti] took me under his wing. I called him the Professor and I became his student."[2]

While Alinsky was not oblivious to the fact that criminals were dangerous, like a good leftist he held "society"—capitalist society in particular—responsible for creating them. In his view, criminality was not a character problem but a result of the social environment—in particular the system of private property and individual rights which radicals like him were determined to change.

Alinsky's career as an organizer spanned the period in which the Communist Party was the major political force on the

---

[1]"Obama: We Are 5 Days from Fundamentally Transforming America," http://www.youtube.com/watch?v=_cqN4NIEtOY.
[2]Sanford Horwitt, *Let Them Call Me Rebel,* Knopf, 1989, p. 20.

American left. Although he was never formally a Communist and did not share the party's tactical views on how to organize a revolution, his attitude towards the Communists was fraternal and he saw them as political allies. In the 1969 afterword to his book *Reveille for Radicals* he explained his attitude in these words: "Communism itself is irrelevant. The issue is whether they are on our side..."[3]

Alinsky's unwillingness to condemn communists extended to the Soviet empire—a regime that murdered more leftists than all their political opponents put together. This failure to condemn communism—his biographer describes him as an "anti-anti-communist"—contrasts dramatically with the extreme terms in which he was willing to condemn his own country as a system worth "burning."[4]

Communists played a formative role in the creation of the CIO—the "progressive" coalition of industrial unions—led by John L. Lewis and then Walter Reuther. In the late 1940s, Reuther purged the Communists from the CIO. Reuther was a socialist but, unlike Alinsky, an anti-communist and an American patriot. In *Rules for Radicals,* Alinsky, a deracinated Jew, refers to the ferreting out of Communists, who were in practice Soviet agents, as a "holocaust"—even though in the McCarthy era only a handful of Communists ever went to jail. By his own account, Alinsky was too independent to join the Communist Party but instead became a forerunner of the left that emerged in the wake of the Communist fall. Like leftists who came of age after the Soviet collapse, Alinsky understood that there was something flawed in the communist outlook. But, also like them, he never really examined what those flaws might be. In particular he never questioned the Marxist view of society and human nature, or its goal of a utopian future, and never examined its connection to the epic crimes that

[3]Saul Alinsky, *Reveille for Radicals,* Vintage edition 1969, p. 227 (Original was published by University of Chicago Press, 1945).
[4]Saul Alinsky, *Rules for Radicals,* Random House, 1971, p. xiii.

Marxists had committed. He never asked himself whether the vision of a society determined to engineer social equality was itself the source of the totalitarian state.

Instead, Alinsky identified the problem posed by Communism as inflexibility and "dogmatism" and proposed as a solution that radicals should be "political relativists"—that they should take an agnostic view of means and ends. For Alinsky, the revolutionary's purpose is to undermine the existing system and then see what happens. The Alinsky radical has a single principle—to take power from the "Haves" and give it to the "Have-nots." What this amounts to in practice is political nihilism—a destructive assault on the established order in the name of those whom the revolutionary elite, in the fashion common to dictators, designate as "the people.". This is the classic revolutionary formula in which the actual goal is power for the political vanguard, whose members get to feel good about themselves because they are acting in the name of the voiceless and the powerless.

Alinsky created several organizations and inspired others, including his training institute for organizers, which he called the Industrial Areas Foundation. But his real influence was as the Lenin of the post-Communist left. Alinsky was the practical theorist for progressives who had previously supported the Communist cause; *Rules for Radicals* was a guide that would allow them to regroup after the fall of the Berlin Wall and mount a new assault on the capitalist system. It was Alinsky who wove the inchoate relativism of the post-Communist left into a coherent outlook and helped to form the coalition of Communists, anarchists, liberals, Democrats, black racialists, and social-justice activists who launched the anti-globalization movement just before 9/11, created the anti-Iraq War movement, and finally positioned one of their own to enter the White House. As Barack Obama summarized these developments at the height of his campaign: "We are the ones we've been waiting for."[5]

---

[5]"Obama 'We Are the Ones We Have Been Waiting for'," https://www.youtube.com/watch?v=3EWLeKGI0ro.

Infiltrating the institutions of American society and government—something the "countercultural" radicals of the 1960s were reluctant to do—was Alinsky's *modus operandi.* While Tom Hayden and Abbie Hoffman and Jerry Rubin were confronting Lyndon Johnson's Pentagon as antagonists and creating riots at the Democratic convention, Alinsky's organizers were insinuating themselves into Johnson's War on Poverty program and directing federal funds into their own organizations and causes. The Sixties left had no connection to the labor movement. But Alinsky did. The most important radical labor organizer of the time—César Chavez, leader of the United Farmworkers Union—was trained by Alinsky and worked for him for ten years.

Alinsky also shaped the future of the civil rights movement after the death of Martin Luther King. When racial unrest erupted in Rochester, New York, Alinsky was called in by activists to pressure Eastman-Kodak to hire more blacks, a form of racial extortion that became a standard of the civil rights movement under the leadership of Jesse Jackson and Al Sharpton. Alinsky also pioneered the alliance of radicals with the Democratic Party, which ended two decades of confrontation climaxing in the convention riot of 1968. Through Chavez, Alinsky had met Robert Kennedy, who supported his muscling of Kodak executives. But the Kennedys were only one of the avenues through which Alinsky organizers now made their way into the inner circles of the Democratic Party. In 1969, the year that publishers reissued Alinsky's first book, *Reveille for Radicals,* a Wellesley undergraduate named Hillary Rodham submitted her 92-page senior thesis on Alinsky's theories; she had interviewed him personally for the project.[6] In her conclusion Hillary compared Alinsky to Eugene Debs, Walt Whitman and Martin Luther King, Jr.

Hillary's thesis was titled: "There Is Only the Fight: An Analysis of the Alinsky Model." In this title she had singled out the

---

[6]Bill Dedman, "Reading Hillary Rodham's Hidden Thesis," *NBC News,* May 9, 2007, http://www.nbcnews.com/id/17388372/#.VV-Ln2DbJJQ.

single most important Alinsky contribution to the radical cause—his embrace of political nihilism. An SDS radical once wrote, "The issue is never the issue. The issue is always the revolution." In other words, the cause—whether inner-city blacks or women—is never the real cause, but only an occasion to advance the real cause. The real agenda is the accumulation of *power* to make the revolution. Gaining power is the all-consuming focus of Alinsky and his radicals.

Guided by Alinsky principles, post-Communist radicals are not idealists but Machiavellians. Their focus is on means rather than ends, and therefore they are not bound by organizational orthodoxies in the way their admired Marxist forebears were. Within the framework of their revolutionary agenda, they are flexible and opportunistic and will say anything (and pretend to be anything) to get what they want, which is resources and power.

The following anecdote about Alinsky's teachings, as recounted by *The New Republic*'s Ryan Lizza, nicely illustrates the focus of Alinsky radicalism: "When Alinsky would ask new students why they wanted to organize, they would invariably respond with selfless bromides about wanting to help others. Alinsky would then scream back at them that there was a one-word answer: 'You want to organize for *power!*'[7] In *Rules for Radicals,* Alinsky wrote: "From the moment an organizer enters a community, he lives, dreams, eats, breathes, sleeps only one thing, and that is to build the mass power base of what he calls the army."[8] The issue is never the issue. The issue is always the revolution—*power.*

Unlike communists who identified their goal as a Soviet state—and thereby generated opposition to their schemes—

[7]Ryan Lizza, "The Agitator," *The New Republic,* March 9, 2007, http://www.pickensdemocrats.org/info/TheAgitator_070319.htm. The source of the anecdote is Horwitt, op., cit.
[8]*Rules for Radicals,* op. cit., p. 113.

Alinsky and his followers organize their power bases without naming the end game, without declaring a specific future they want to achieve—socialism, communism, a dictatorship of the proletariat, or anarchy. Without committing themselves to concrete principles or a specific future, they organize exclusively to build a power base, which they can leverage to manipulate, destroy, or transform the existing social order. By refusing to commit to principles or to identify a goal, they have been able to organize a coalition of all the elements of the left who were previously divided by disagreements over means and ends.

The demagogic banner of the revolution is "democracy"—a democracy which upends all social hierarchies, including those based on merit. Alinsky built his initial power base among the underclass and the urban poor. The call to make the last ones first is a powerful religious imperative. But in politics it functions as a lever to upset every social structure and foundation. For Alinsky radicals, policies are not important in themselves; they are instrumental. They are means to expanding the political base and accumulating power.

To Alinsky radicals, "democracy" means getting those who are in, out. Their goal is to mobilize the poor and "oppressed" as a battering ram to bring down the system. Hillary concludes her thesis with these words: "Alinsky is regarded by many as the proponent of a dangerous socio/political philosophy. As such, he has been feared—just as Eugene Debs or Walt Whitman or Martin Luther King has been feared, because each embraced the most radical of political faiths—democracy." But democracy as understood by the American founders is *not* "the most radical of all political faiths"—or, if it is, they regarded it as dangerous enough to put checks and balances in its way to restrain it.

When Hillary graduated from Wellesley in 1969, she was offered a job with Alinsky's new training institute in Chicago. She opted instead to enroll at Yale Law School, where she met her husband and future president, Bill Clinton. But in March 2007 *The Washington Post* reported that she had kept her connections to the

Alinsky movement even in the White House, from which she gave Alinsky's army support.[9]

Unlike Hillary Clinton, Barack Obama never personally met Saul Alinsky. But as a young man he became an adept practitioner of Alinsky's methods. In 1986, at the age of 23 and only three years out of Columbia University, Obama was hired by the Alinsky team to organize residents on Chicago's South Side "while learning and applying Alinsky's philosophy of street-level democracy."[10] The group Obama joined was part of a network that included the Gamaliel Foundation, a religious group that operated on Alinsky principles. Obama became director of the Developing Communities Project, an affiliate of the Gamaliel Foundation, where he worked for the next three years on initiatives that ranged from job training to school reform to hazardous waste cleanup. A reporter who researched the projects sums them up in these words: "the proposed solution to every problem on the South Side was a distribution of government funds..."[11]

Three of Obama's mentors in Chicago were trained at the Alinsky Industrial Areas Foundation, and for several years Obama himself taught workshops on the Alinsky method.[12] One of the three, Gregory Galluzo, shared with Ryan Lizza the actual manual for training new organizers, which he said was little different from the version he used to train Obama in the 1980s. Lizza wrote: "It is filled with workshops and chapter headings on understanding power: 'power analysis,' 'elements of a power organization,' 'the

[9]"As first lady, Clinton occasionally lent her name to projects endorsed by the Industrial Areas Foundation (IAF), the Alinsky group that had offered her a job in 1968. She raised money and attended two events organized by the Washington Interfaith Network, an IAF affiliate." Peter Slevin, "For Clinton and Obama, a Common Ideological Touchstone," *The Washington Post,* March 25, 2007, http://www.washingtonpost.com/wp-dyn/content/article/2007/03/24/AR2007032401152_pf.html.

[10]Ibid.

[11]David Freddoso, *The Case Against Barack Obama,* Regnery, 2008, cited in Barack Hussein Obama, http://www.discoverthenetworks.org/individualProfile.asp?indid=1511.

[12]Lizza, op. cit.

path to power.' Galluzo told me that many new trainees have an aversion to Alinsky's gritty approach because they come to organizing as idealists rather than realists. The Alinsky manual instructs them to get over these hang-ups. 'We are not virtuous by not wanting power,' it says. 'We are really cowards for not wanting power,' because 'power is good' and 'powerlessness is evil.'"[13]

According to Lizza, who interviewed both Galluzo and Obama, "the other fundamental lesson Obama was taught was Alinsky's maxim that self-interest is the only principle around which to organize people. (Galluzo's manual goes so far as to advise trainees in block letters: 'Get rid of do-gooders in your church and your organization.') Obama was a fan of Alinsky's realistic streak. 'The key to creating successful organizations was making sure people's self-interest was met,' he told me, 'and not just basing it on pie-in-the-sky idealism. So there were some basic principles that remained powerful then, and in fact I still believe in.'" On Barack Obama's presidential campaign website, one could see a photo of Obama in a classroom "teaching students Alinskyan methods. He stands in front of a blackboard on which he has written, 'Power Analysis' and 'Relationships Built on Self Interest,..'"[14]

Until he became a full-time elected legislator in 1996, Obama focused his political activities on the largest radical organization in the United States, ACORN, which was built on the Alinsky model of community organizing. A summary of his ACORN activities was compiled by *The Wall Street Journal*:

> In 1991, he took time off from his law firm to run a voter-registration drive for Project Vote, an ACORN partner that was soon fully absorbed under the ACORN umbrella. The drive registered 135,000 voters and was considered a major factor in the upset victory of Democrat Carol Moseley Braun over incumbent Democratic Senator Alan Dixon in the 1992 Democratic Senate primary. Mr. Obama's success made him a hot commodity on the

---

[13]Ibid.
[14]Ibid.

> community organizing circuit. He became a top trainer at ACORN's Chicago conferences. In 1995, he became ACORN's attorney, participating in a landmark case to force the state of Illinois to implement the federal Motor Voter Law. That law's loose voter registration requirements would later be exploited by ACORN employees in an effort to flood voter rolls with fake names. In 1996, Mr. Obama filled out a questionnaire listing key supporters for his campaign for the Illinois Senate. He put ACORN first (it was not an alphabetical list).[15]

After Obama became a U.S. Senator, his wife, Michelle, told a reporter, "Barack is not a politician first and foremost. He's a community activist exploring the viability of politics to make change." Her husband commented: "I take that observation as a compliment."[16]

Saul Alinsky is the Sun-Tzu for today's radicals, his book a manual for their political war. As early as its dedicatory page, Alinsky provides revealing insight into the radical mind by praising Lucifer as the first rebel: "Lest we forget, an over-the-shoulder acknowledgment to the very first radical: from all our legends, mythology, and history (and who is to know where mythology leaves off and history begins—or which is which), the first radical known to man who rebelled against the establishment and did it so effectively that he at least won his own kingdom—Lucifer."

Thus Alinsky begins his text by telling readers exactly what a radical is. He is not a reformer of the system but its would-be destroyer. In his own mind the radical is building his own kingdom, which to him is a kingdom of heaven on earth. Since a kingdom of heaven built by human beings is a fantasy—an impossible dream—the radical's only real-world efforts are those aimed at subverting the society he lives in. He is a nihilist.

---

[15]John Fund, "Acorn Who?," *Wall Street Journal,* September 21, 2009, http://www.wsj.com/articles/SB10001424052970204488304574427041636360388#.

[16]Lizza, op. cit.

This is something that conservatives generally have a hard time understanding. As a former radical, I am constantly asked how radicals could hate America and why they would want to destroy a society that compared to others is tolerant, inclusive and open, and treats all people with a dignity and respect that is the envy of the world. The answer to this question is that radicals are not comparing America to other real-world societies. They are comparing America to the heaven on earth—the kingdom of social justice and freedom—which they think they are building. And compared to *this* heaven, even America is hell.

In my experience, conservatives are generally too decent and too civilized to match up adequately with their radical adversaries—too prone to give them the benefit of the doubt, to believe there is goodness and good sense in them that will outweigh their determination to take down the existing social order. Radicals talk of justice and democracy and equality. They can't really want to destroy a democratic and liberal society, more equal than others, which has brought wealth and prosperity to so many people.

Oh yes, they can. There is no goodness that trumps the dream of a heaven on earth. And because America is a real-world society, managed by real and problematic human beings, it will never be equal, or liberal, or democratic enough to satisfy radical fantasies—to compensate their longing for a perfect world, and their unhappiness in this one.

In *The 18th Brumaire,* Marx himself summed up the radical's passion by invoking a comment of Goethe's Mephistopheles: "Everything that exists deserves to perish." The essence of what it means to be a *radical* is thus summed up in Alinsky's praise for Satan: to be willing to destroy the values, structures and institutions that sustain the society in which we live.

The many names of Satan are also a model for the way radicals camouflage their agendas by calling themselves, at different times, communists, socialists, new leftists, liberals, social justice activists and *progressives.* My parents, who were card-carrying Communists, never referred to themselves as Communists but always as "progressives," as did their friends and political comrades. The "Progressive Party" was created by the Communist Party to challenge Harry Truman in the 1948 election because he opposed the spread of Stalin's empire. The Progressive Party was led by Roosevelt's vice president, Henry Wallace, and was the vehicle chosen by the Communists to lead their followers out of the Democratic Party, which they had joined during the "popular front" of the 1930s. Progressives rejoined the Democrats during the McGovern campaign of 1972. With the formation of a hundred-plus member Progressive Caucus in the U.S. Congress, and the ascension of Barack Obama to the presidency, they have now become its most important political force.

Alinsky's tribute to Satan as the first radical is further instructive because it reminds us that the radical illusion is an ancient one and has not changed though the millennia. Recall how Satan tempted Adam and Eve to destroy their paradise: If you will rebel against God's command, "You shall be as gods." This is the radical hubris: *We can create a new world. Through our political power we can make a new race of men and women who will live in harmony and peace and according to the principles of social justice. We can be as gods.* And let us not forget that the kingdom the first radical "won," as Alinsky so thoughtlessly puts it, was *hell.* Typical of radicals not to notice the ruin they leave behind.

This, in a nutshell, is why conservatives are conservative and why radicals are dangerous: because conservatives pay attention to the consequences of actions, including their own, while radicals don't.

One kind of hell or another is what radicalism has in fact achieved since the beginning of the modern age, when it conducted the first modern genocide during the French Revolution. The Jacobins who led the revolution changed the name of the cathedral of Notre Dame to the "Temple of Reason" and then, in the name of Reason, proceeded to slaughter every Catholic man, woman and child in the Vendée region to purge religious "superstition" from the planet. The Jacobin attempt to liquidate Catholics and their faith was the precursor of Lenin's destruction of 100,000 churches in the Soviet Union to purge Russia of reactionary ideas. The "Temple of Reason" was replicated by the Bolsheviks' creation of a "People's Church" whose mission was to usher in the "worker's paradise." This mission led to the murder not of 40,000 as in the Vendée, but 40 *million* before its merciful collapse—with progressives cheering its progress all the way and then mourning its demise.

The radical fantasy of an earthly redemption takes many forms, with similar results:

- The chimera of "sexual liberation" caused leftists to condemn and ban the proven public-health methods for combating AIDS—testing and contact tracing—as "homophobic," leading directly to the preventable deaths of more than 300,000 gay men in the prime of life.[17]
- The crusade to rid mankind of the scourge of DDT, which was launched in the 1960s by the American environmentalist Rachel Carson, led to a global ban on the use of DDT and the return of malaria. This has resulted in the deaths of 100 million children, mainly black Africans under the age of five.[18]
- The left's campaign to build a welfare utopia under the umbrella of the "Great Society" destroyed the inner- city black family, spawned millions of fatherless black children, and created intractable poverty and a violent underclass which is still with us today.[19]

Conservatives think of war as a metaphor when applied to politics. For radicals, it is no metaphor; the war is real. That is why, when partisans of the left go into battle, they set out to destroy

---

[17]David Horowitz, "A Radical Holocaust," *DiscoverTheNetworks*, May 31, 2006, http://www.discoverthenetworks.org/Articles/z-RADICAL%20HOLOCAUST.htm.

[18]Rachel Carson, http://www.discoverthenetworks.org/individualProfile.asp?indid=1866.

[19]Breakdown Of The Black Family And Its Consequences, http://www.discoverthenetworks.org/viewSubCategory.asp?id=1261.

their opponents by stigmatizing them as "racists," "sexists," "homophobes" and "Islamophobes." It is also why they so often pretend to be what they are not—"liberals," for example—and rarely say what they mean. Deception for them is a military tactic in a war whose goal is to eliminate the enemy.

Alinsky's *Rules for Radicals* is first of all a comradely critique of the Sixties' New Left. What bothers Alinsky about Sixties' radicals is their honesty—which may have been their only redeeming feature. While communist leftists pretended to be Jeffersonian democrats and "progressives" and formed "popular fronts" with liberals, the New Left radicals disdained these deceptions, regarding them as displays of dishonesty and weakness. To distinguish themselves from such popular-front politics, Sixties radicals said: "We are *revolutionaries* and proud of it."

New Left radicals despised and attacked liberals and created riots at Democratic Party conventions. Their typical slogans were "Up against the wall motherf-ker" and "Off the pig", telegraphing exactly how they felt about those who opposed them. By contrast, the most basic principle of Alinsky's advice to radicals is to *lie* to their opponents and disarm them by pretending to be moderates and liberals. Deception is the Alinsky radical's most important weapon, and it has been a prominent one since the end of the sixties. Racial arsonists such as Al Sharpton and Jeremiah Wright pose as civil rights activists; anti-American radicals such as Bill Ayers pose as progressives; socialists pose as liberals. The mark of their success is reflected in the fact that conservatives collude in the deception and call them liberals, too.

Alinsky writes of the "revolutionary force" of the 1960s that its activists were "one moment reminiscent of the idealistic early Christians yet they also urge violence and cry 'Burn the system down!' They have no illusions about the system, but plenty of illusions about the way to change our world. It is to this point that I have written this book."[20]

[20]*Rules for Radicals,* op. cit., p. xiii.

I once had a Trotskyist mentor named Isaac Deutscher who was critical of the New Left in the same way Alinsky is. He said that American radicals such as Stokely Carmichael were "radical" in form and "moderate" in content; that they spoke loudly but carried a small stick. Instead, he said, they should be moderate in form and radical in content. In the same vein, Alinsky chides New Leftists for being "rhetorical radicals" rather than "realistic" radicals. New Leftists scared people but didn't have the power to back up their threats. The most important thing for radicals, according to Alinsky, is to deal with the world as it is. "As an organizer I start from the world as it is, *as it is,* not as I would like it to be. That we accept the world as it is does not in any sense weaken our desire to change it into what we believe it should be—it is necessary to begin where the world is if we are going to change it to what we think it should be. That means working in the system."[21]

This is the Alinsky quote which Michelle Obama selected to sum up her husband's vision at the convention that nominated him for president in August 2008. Referring to a visit he had made to Chicago neighborhoods, she said: "And Barack stood up that day, and he spoke words that have stayed with me ever since. He talked about 'the world as it is' and 'the world as it should be.' And he said that, all too often, we accept the distance between the two and we settle for the world as it is, even when it doesn't reflect our values and aspirations." She concluded: "All of us are driven by a simple belief that the world as it is just won't do—that we have an obligation to fight for the world as it should be."[22]

When he became president, Barack Obama named Van Jones, a self-described "communist" and Alinsky disciple, to be his special assistant for "green jobs," a key position in the administration's

[21]*Rules for Radicals,* op. cit., p. xix.

[22]"Michelle Obama's Remarks at the Democratic Convention" [Transcript], *The New York Times,* August 26, 2008, http://www.nytimes.com/2008/08/26/us/politics/26text-obama.html?ei=5124&en=48bdd187be31e21e&ex=1377489600&partner=permalink&exprod=permalink&pagewanted=print&_r=0.

plans for America's future. In a 2005 interview, Jones had explained to the *East Bay Express* that he still considered himself a "revolutionary, but just a more effective one." "Before," he told the *Express*, "we would fight anybody, any time. No concession was good enough ... Now, I put the issues and constituencies first. I'll work with anybody, I'll fight anybody if it will push our issues forward ... I'm willing to forego the cheap satisfaction of the radical pose for the deep satisfaction of radical ends."[23]

The issue is never the issue; the issue is always the revolution. It was the Alinsky prescription perfectly expressed. "These rules," explains Alinsky, "make the difference between being a realistic radical and being a rhetorical one who uses the tired old words and slogans, calls the police 'pig' or 'white fascist racist' or 'motherf-ker and has so stereotyped himself that others react by saying, 'Oh, he's one of those, and then promptly turn off.'"[24] Instead, advance your radical goals by camouflaging them; change your style to appear to be working within the system.

Alinsky's long-term goal is no different from that of the radicals who called for "Revolution Now" in the 1960s. He just has a more clever way of achieving it. There's nothing new about radicals camouflaging their agendas as moderate in order to disarm their opposition. That was exactly what the 1930s "popular front" was designed to accomplish. It was devised by Communists pretending to be democrats, in order to form alliances with liberals who would help them acquire the power to shut the democracy down. It was also Lenin's idea, from whom Alinsky appropriated it in the first place.

Lenin is one of Alinsky's heroes. Alinsky invokes Lenin in the course of chiding the rhetorical radicals over a famous Sixties slogan, which originated with the Chinese Communist dictator Mao Zedong. The slogan was "political power grows out of the barrel of a gun." During the 1960s, it was a favorite cry of the Black

---

[23]"The New Face of Environmentalism," op. cit.

[24]*Rules for Radicals*, op, cit., p. xviii.

Panthers and other radical groups. Regarding this, Alinsky comments: "'Power comes out of the barrel of a gun' is an absurd rallying cry when the other side has all the guns. Lenin was a pragmatist; when he returned to what was then Petrograd from exile, he said that the Bolsheviks stood for getting power through the ballot but would reconsider after they got the guns."[25]

In other words, vote for us now, but when we become the government it will be a different story. One man, one vote, one time. This is the political credo of all modern totalitarians, including Hitler, who was elected chancellor and then made himself Führer and shut down the voting booths. Despite Alinsky's description, however, Lenin was a pragmatist only within the revolutionary framework. As a revolutionary, he was a dogmatist in theory and a Machiavellian monster in practice. He was engaged in a total war, a notion he used to justify every means he thought necessary to achieve his goals—including summary executions, concentration camps which provided the model for Hitler's, and the physical "liquidation" of entire social classes.

"[The] failure of many of our younger activists to understand the art of communication has been disastrous," writes Alinsky. What he really means is that their *honesty* is disastrous—their failure to understand the art of *mis*-communication. This is the precise art that he teaches radicals who are trying impose socialism on a country whose people understand that socialism destroys freedom. Don't sell it as socialism; sell it as "progressivism," "economic democracy" and "social justice."

The strategy of working within the system until you can accumulate enough power to destroy it was what Sixties radicals called "boring from within." It was a strategy that the New Left despised, even as Alinsky and his followers practiced it. Alinsky and his followers infiltrated the War on Poverty, made alliances with the Kennedys and the Democratic Party, and secured funds from the federal government. Like termites, they set about to eat away at

---

[25]Ibid., p. 37.

the foundations of the building in expectation that one day they could cause it to collapse. Alinsky's advice can be summed up in the following way. Even though you are at war with the system, don't confront it as an opposing army; join it and undermine it from within. To achieve this infiltration you must work inside the system for the time being. Alinsky spells out exactly what this means: "Any revolutionary change must be preceded by a passive, affirmative, non-challenging attitude toward change among the mass of our people."

In other words, it is first necessary to sell the people on change itself, the "audacity of hope," and "yes we can." You do this by proposing moderate changes that open the door to your radical agendas: "Remember: once you organize people around something as commonly agreed upon as pollution, then an organized people is on the move. From there it's a short and natural step to political pollution, to Pentagon pollution." It is not an accident that the Green Czar appointed by President Obama to jump-start the anti-pollution revolution was an Alinsky disciple.

The first chapter of Alinsky's manual is called "The Purpose" and is designed to lay out the radical goal. Its epigraph is taken from the *Book of Job*: "The life of man upon earth is a warfare...." This is not an invitation to democratic politics as understood by the American Founders. The American system is about tolerance and compromise, and bringing disparate factions into a working partnership. The Founders devised a system of checks and balances to temper the passions of the people and prevent factions from going to war. This is the reality of American democracy; revolutionary warfare against it must be conducted through deception. The rules for the organizers of revolutions, as laid down by Alinsky, are rules for deception.

Alinsky's book could easily be called *Machiavellian Rules for Radicals,* after the man who devised principles of statehood and advice for rulers in his book *The Prince.* In Alinsky's view, the difference between the unethical behavior counseled by Machiavelli and the unethical behavior he would like to see practiced by radicals lies solely in the fact that their political enemies are different. "*The Prince* was written by Machiavelli for the Haves on how to hold power," Alinsky writes. "*Rules for Radicals* is written for the Have-Nots on how to take it away."[26] For Alinsky, politics is a zero-sum exercise. No matter what Alinsky radicals say publicly or how moderate they appear, they are at war. This provides them with a great tactical advantage, since other actors in the political arena are not at war. The other actors actually embrace the system that commits all parties to compromise and to the peaceful resolution of conflicts. It commits them to a pragmatism of ends as well as means. Not every wish can be satisfied.

By contrast, Alinsky radicals have an unwavering end, which is to attack the so-called Haves until they are finally defeated. In other words, to undermine the system that allows them to earn and possess more than others. Such a system, according to the radicals, is one of "social injustice," and what they want is "social justice." The unwavering end of radicals is a communism of results. For tactical reasons radicals will make many compromises along the way; but their unfailing purpose—the vision that guides them—is to conduct war against a system that in their view that makes social injustice possible. When you are in a war—when you think of yourself as in a war—there is no middle ground. Radicals perceive opponents of their causes as enemies on a battlefield, and they set out to destroy them by demonizing and discrediting them. Personally. The politics of personal destruction is an inevitable weapon of choice for radicals. If your goal is a just world, then the moral code you live by requires you to wage war without quarter.

Because conservatives embrace the system, they believe in its rules of fairness and inclusion. But these rules can also be used by its cynical enemies to destroy it. As Alinsky's hero Lenin put it, "The capitalists will sell us the rope to hang them." Or, as Alinsky's own "fourth rule of power tactics" puts it: "Make the enemy live up to their own rules." There is no real parallelism in the war

[26]Ibid., p. 3.

which radicals have declared. One side is fighting with a no-holds-barred, take-no-prisoners battle plan against the system, while the other is trying to enforce its rules of fairness and pluralism. This is the Achilles' heel of democracies, and all radical spears are aimed in its direction.

At first it might seem paradoxical that an American president who has been the beneficiary of an electoral process second to none in its openness and inclusion should have been a veteran advocate and functionary of an organization like ACORN, which has been convicted of the most extensive election fraud in American history. But this is perfectly intelligible once the Alinsky method is understood. ACORN activists have contempt for the election process because they don't believe in the electoral system as it is constituted in a capitalist democracy. To them, elections are already a fraud—an instrument of the rich or, as Alinsky prefers to call them, the Haves. If the electoral system doesn't serve "the people" but is only an instrument of the Haves, then election fraud is justified as the path to a future that will serve the Have-Nots. Until conservatives begin to understand exactly how dishonest radicals are—and why—it will be hard to defend the system under attack. For radicals the noble end—creating a new world—justifies any means. And if one actually believed, as they do, that it is possible to create heaven on earth, what institution would one not be justified in destroying to realize that future?

What makes radical politics a war is the existence of an enemy who must be eliminated. For Alinsky radicals, that enemy is the "Haves," who "oppress" and rule the "Have-Nots." The Haves sit on the top of "hierarchies" of class, race and gender. From the radicals' viewpoint, although America is called a democracy, it is really a "Have society." Alinsky explains: "The setting for the drama of change has never varied. Mankind has been and is divided into the Haves, the Have-Nots, and Have-a-Little, Want Mores." (p.18) This maxim is just another Alinsky theft, in this case from Karl Marx whose *Communist Manifesto* famously begins: "The history of all hitherto existing society is the history of class struggles. Freeman and slave, patrician and plebian, lord and serf, guild-master and journeyman, in a word, oppressor and oppressed, stood in constant opposition to one another, carried on an uninterrupted, now hidden, now open fight, a fight that each time ended, either in a revolutionary reconstitution of society at large, or in the common ruin of the contending classes."

This was rubbish when Marx wrote it—deadly rubbish considering the tens of millions of individuals slaughtered by those who believed it—and it is still rubbish. But it remains the bedrock of radical belief, the foundation of all its destructive agendas. The idea that the world is divided into the Haves and the Have-Nots, the exploiters and the exploited, the oppressors and the oppressed, leads directly to the idea that liberation lies in the elimination of the former and thus the dissolution of the conflict. This, according to radicals, will lead to the liberation of mankind. In fact, it led directly to the deaths of 100 million people who were murdered by radicals in power on the way to their dream.

"In this book," Alinsky explains, "we are concerned with how to create mass organizations to seize power and give it to the people."[27] Power is to be "seized"—the word is revealing. The present system will not allow justice to be realized, so sooner or later immoral, illegal, even violent means are required to achieve it. In the myth created by Marx, which all radicals continue to believe, the market system is a zero-sum game where one man's gain is another's loss. Because the Haves will defend what they have and thus deprive the Have-Nots of what they want, they must be destroyed before justice can be achieved. That is why radicals are organized for war—a deceptive guerrilla war to begin, and a total war to end.

Take another look at the opening of the *Communist Manifesto.* The history of all previous societies, Marx claims, is the history of "class struggle," of war between the Haves and the Have-Nots. Marx names them through time: freeman and slave, patrician and

---

[27]Ibid.

plebeian, lord and serf, guild-master and journeyman, oppressor and oppressed. In Marx's schema the capitalists in our era are the new oppressors, and wage-workers the new oppressed. Post-communist radicals have added women, racial minorities and even sexual minorities to the list. But to compare women and minorities in a democracy to slaves and serfs, or capitalists to slave owners and feudal lords, as Marx and his disciples do, is delusional.

There are tens of millions of capitalists in America and they rise and fall with every economic wave. Where are the Enrons of yesteryear and where are their bosses? If proletarians can become capitalists and capitalists can be ruined, there is no class struggle in the sense that Marx and his disciples claim, no system of oppression, no Haves and Have-Nots and no need for revolution. The same is truer and even more obvious where racial minorities and women are concerned. In the last decade America has had a black president, two black secretaries of state, three women secretaries of state, a chief law enforcement officer who is black, and so on and so forth. No slave or serf ever held such positions, or could. The radical creed is a religious myth—the most destructive in the history of mankind.

In a democracy like ours, the notion that there are Haves and Have-Nots is akin to the particular religious myth advanced by Manicheans who viewed the world as ruled by the devil and who saw history as a struggle between the ruling forces of evil and the liberating forces of light. In the radicals' religion, the "Haves" are also a category identical to that of "witches" in the Puritan faith—agents of the devil—and they serve the same purpose. The purpose is to identify one's political enemies as instruments of evil to justify the war against them. It is true that there are *some* Haves—that is, individuals who have inherited wealth and merely *have* it. In other words, there are individuals who are not active investors creating more wealth for themselves and others. There are also *some* Have-Nots—people who were born to nothing and because of character or social dysfunction have no way of changing their circumstances. But it is false to describe our social and economic divisions in these terms, or to imply that there are immovable barriers to individuals that prevent them from bettering themselves and increasing their wealth. If there is social mobility, if a person can move from one rung of the economic or social ladder to the next, there is no hierarchy and there is no justification for the radical war.

In the real world of American democracy, social and economic divisions are between the Cans and the Can-Nots, the Dos and the Do-Nots, the Wills and the Will-Nots. The vast majority of wealthy Americans, as a matter of empirical fact, are first-generation wealthy and have created what they possess. In the process of creating wealth for themselves, they have created wealth for hundreds and sometimes thousands or even hundreds of thousands of others. But to describe the wealthy as wealth earners and wealth creators—that is, to describe them accurately—is to explode the whole religious fantasy that gives meaning to radical lives, inspires the radicals' war, and has been the source of the most repressive regimes and the greatest social disasters in the history of mankind.

Because the radical agenda is based on a religious myth, a reader of any radical text, including Alinsky's, will constantly come across statements that are so absurd that only a co-religionist could read them without laughing. Thus, according to Alinsky: "All societies discourage and penalize ideas and writings that threaten the status quo." The statement, of course, is again lifted directly from Marx, this time from his *German Ideology,* which claims that "the ruling ideas are the ideas of the ruling class." From this false claim, Alinsky proceeds to the following howler: "It is understandable therefore, that the literature of a Have society is a veritable desert whenever we look for writings on social change." According to Alinsky, this is particularly true of American society, which "has given us few words of advice, few suggestions on how to fertilize social change."[28]

---

[28]Ibid., p. 7.

On what planet did this man live? Where do his disciples now agitate, that they could miss the narratives of subversion, "resistance" and "change" which have been familiar themes of our culture and dominant themes of our school curricula, our media and our political discourse since the 1960s? But Alinsky presses on: "From the Haves, on the other hand, there has come an unceasing flood of literature justifying the status quo." Really? Curricula in virtually every liberal arts college are dedicated precisely to social change.[29] The explicit goal of our most prestigious schools of education is promoting "social change," and even more specifically "social justice." The mission statements of entire universities express a devotion to social change, which is also the routine subject of commencement addresses, often given by anti-capitalist radicals such as Angela Davis and unrepentant terrorists such as Bernardine Dohrn. The newest mass medium—the Internet—features heavily trafficked websites such as Daily Kos and MoveOn.org dedicated to promoting the Alinsky program of taking wealth and power from the so-called Haves in the name of "Have-Nots."

Finally there is the inconvenient fact—for this particular myth—that America's first black president, a community organizer, leader of an Alinsky organization and lifelong associate of political radicals, was able to run a successful campaign on a platform of changing the *status quo,* not defending it.

Sanford Horwitt prefaces his biography of Alinsky, *Let Them Call Me Rebel,* with an anecdote he felt illuminated Alinsky's method. In this anecdote, Alinsky shares his wisdom with students wishing to protest the appearance on their campus of the first George Bush, then America's representative to the UN during the Vietnam War:

> College student activists in the 1960s and 1970s sought out Alinsky for advice about tactics and strategy. On one such occasion in

---

[29] Indoctrination Studies, http://www.discoverthenetworks.org/viewSubCategory.asp?id=522#Curricular_Studies.

> the spring of 1972 at Tulane University's annual week-long series of events featuring leading public figures, students asked Alinsky to help plan a protest of a scheduled speech by George Bush, then U.S. representative to the United Nations, a speech likely to be a defense of the Nixon Administration's Vietnam War policies. [author's note: the Nixon administration was then negotiating with the North Vietnamese Communists to arrive at a peace agreement.] The students told Alinsky that they were thinking about picketing or disrupting Bush's address. That's the wrong approach, he rejoined—not very creative and besides, causing a disruption might get them thrown out of school. He told them, instead, to go hear the speech dressed up as members of the Ku Klux Klan, and whenever Bush said something in defense of the Vietnam War, they should cheer and wave placards, reading 'The K.K.K. supports Bush.' And that is what the students did with very successful, attention-getting results.[30]

This vignette tells us everything we really need to know about Alinsky's ethics and his attitude towards means and ends. Lenin once said that the purpose of a political argument is not to refute your opponent "but to wipe him from the face of the earth." The mission of Alinsky radicals is a mission of destruction. It didn't matter to Alinsky that the Vietnam War was not a race war, that millions of South Vietnamese opposed the Communists. It didn't matter to Alinsky who George Bush actually was or what he believed because in a war the objective is to kill the enemy and destroy the system he represents. Therefore seize on any weapon, in this case a symbol for one of the greatest evils in American history, and use it to obliterate the enemy of the hour. If America's cause in Vietnam is the Ku Klux Klan, then its cause is evil and America is evil. If George Bush is the Ku Klux Klan, no more needs to be said. These are the methods of political discourse that Stalinists perfected and that radicals—parading as liberals— continue to use to this day.

---

[30]*Let Them Call Me Rebel,* op. cit., pp. xv–xvi.

The most important chapter of Alinsky's manual is called "Means and Ends," and is designed to address Alinsky's biggest problem: How to explain to radicals, who think of themselves as creating a world of perfect justice and harmony, that the means they must use to get there are Machiavellian—deceitful, conniving, and ruthless? The radical organizer, Alinsky explains, "does not have a fixed truth—truth to him is relative and changing; *everything* to him is relative and changing. He is a political relativist."[31] And that will do it. Being a radical in the service of the higher good is a license to do anything that is required to achieve that good.

Liberals share radicals' utopian agendas of a just and peaceful world but are hampered because they have scruples. They support radical ends but because they are principled they don't like the means radicals use to get to their ends. As a result, Alinsky's contempt for them is boundless. In his first book, *Reveille for Radicals,* he wrote: "While liberals are most adept at breaking their own necks with their tongues, radicals are most adept at breaking the necks of conservatives."[32] In contrast to liberals, who in Alinsky's eyes are constantly tripping over their principles, the rule for radicals is that the ends justify the means. This was true for the Jacobins, for the Communists, for the fascists and now for the post-Communist left.

This is not because radicals begin by being unethical people. On the contrary, their passion for a future that is ethically perfect is what drives their political agendas, and also what causes many to mistake them for idealists. But the very nature of this future—a world without poverty, without war, without racism, without "sexism"—is so desirable, so noble, so perfect in contrast to everything that exists as to justify any and every means to achieve it. If the radicals' utopia were actually possible, it would be criminal *not* to deceive, lie, and murder to advance the radical cause which is, in effect, a redemption of mankind. If it were possible to provide every man, woman and child on the planet with food, shelter and

---

[31] *Rules for Radicals,* op. cit., pp. 10–11.
[32] *Reveille for Radicals,* op. cit., p. 21.

clothing as a right, if it were possible to end bigotry and human conflict, what sacrifice of principle or self would not be worth it?

The German philosopher Nietzsche had a phrase for this: "Idealism kills." And of course the great atrocities of the modern era, whether Nazi or Communist or Islamist, have been committed by people who believed in a future that would save mankind. When you are overthrowing the existing order, you must break the rules to do it. The nobler the end, the easier it is to justify breaking the rules to get there. Thus, to be really committed to being a radical is to be committed to being an outlaw. During the sixties, SDS leader Tom Hayden once described the utility of the drug culture to me, although he claimed he was not a part of it. Once you get a middle-class person to break the law, he said, thinking of students, they are on their way to becoming revolutionaries.

In the sixties, radicals were generally proud of the idea that they were linked to criminals. Gangsters such as John Dillinger and films such as *The Wild Bunch* and *Bonnie and Clyde,* which celebrated American outlaws, were popular among them. Abbie Hoffman's *Steal This Book* was a manifesto of the creed. Obama friend and Weatherman leader Bernardine Dohrn's tribute to the murderer Charles Manson was its extreme expression.

This romance continues to be expressed in radicals' affinity for criminals and their causes at home and abroad, as it was in Alinsky's early attraction to Capone's enforcer Frank Nitti. The Stalinist historian Eric Hobsbawm gave the radicals' romance an academic veneer in a book about Sicilian criminals, whom he described as "primitive rebels"—in other words, revolutionaries *avant la lettre.* Among the chapters of *Primitive Rebels* is one titled "Social Bandits." In Hobsbawm's description, these criminals were avatars of "social justice," their activity "little more than endemic peasant protest against oppression and poverty."[33] Hobsbawm claimed that the activity of the "mob" was "always

[33]Eric Hobsbawm, *Primitive Rebels,* Manchester University Press, 1959, p. 5.

directed against the rich"—in other words, okay.[34] The French radical Pierre-Joseph Proudhon gave license to radicals to steal and destroy in socialism's most famous epigraph: "Property is Theft." In reality, of course, it is socialism that is theft.

Another reason radicals believe that their goals justify criminal means—and can be relied on to lie, steal votes and justify murder when committed by their political friends—is that they're convinced they are engaged in a permanent war whose goal is the salvation of mankind. In *this* context restraint of means can easily seem finicky. Alinsky's entire argument is an effort to answer liberals who refuse to join the radical cause with the objection "I agree with your ends but not your means." To this Alinsky replies that the very question of whether "the end justifies the means?" is "meaningless." The real question, according to Alinsky, is: "Does this particular end justify this particular means?"[35] But this is disingenuous, since radicals are in a permanent war and "the third rule of the ethics of means and ends is that in war the end justifies almost any means."[36]

Writes Alinsky: "The man of action views the issue of means and ends in pragmatic and strategic terms. He has no other problem." In other words, Alinsky's radical is not going to worry about the legality or morality of his actions, only their practical effects. If they advance the cause, they are justified. "He asks of ends only whether they are achievable and worth the cost; of means, only whether they will work." If one proceeds by criminal and immoral means, it might be asked, won't that corrupt one's cause and determine its outcome? After all, Marxists killed 100 million of their own citizens, in peacetime, justifying every step of the way by the end they were attempting to achieve—a just world.

Here is how Alinsky answers the question about immoral means: *Everybody does it.* "To say that corrupt means corrupt the ends is to believe in the immaculate conception of ends and principles. The

[34]Ibid., p. 7.
[35]*Rules for Radicals,* op. cit., p. 24.
[36]Ibid., p. 29.

real arena is corrupt and bloody. Life is a corrupting process ... he who fears corruption fears life." Since life is corrupt, everyone is corrupt and corruption is just business as usual—Chicago style. "In action," Alinsky writes, "one does not always enjoy the luxury of a decision that is consistent both with one's individual conscience and the good of mankind. The choice must always be for the latter."[37]

But who is to determine what is good for mankind? The Russian writer Fyodor Dostoevsky famously wrote that "if God does not exist then everything is permitted." What he meant was that if human beings do not have a conception of the good that is outside themselves, then they will act as gods with nothing to restrain them. Alinsky is already there: "Action is for mass salvation and not for the individual's personal salvation. He who sacrifices the mass good for his personal salvation has a peculiar conception of 'personal salvation;' he doesn't care enough for people to be 'corrupted' for them."[38] In other words, the evil that radicals may do is already justified by the fact that they do it for the salvation of mankind.

Note the scare-quotes Alinsky puts around the verb "corrupted," a signal that he does not believe in moral corruption because he does not believe in morality. Or, more precisely, his morality begins and ends with the radical cause. The sadistic dictator Fidel Castro, one of Alinsky's radical heroes, summarized this principle in a famous formulation: "Within the revolution everything is possible; outside the revolution nothing is possible." The revolution—the radical cause—is the way, the truth and the life.

The singer John Lennon understood that the practical end was in fact the crucial missing element in these calculations. "You say you want a revolution," he wrote, "well, you know, we'd all like to see your plan." The fact is that, going back to Rousseau and

---

[37]Ibid., p. 25.
[38]Ibid.

Marx, revolutionaries have never had a plan. The ones who did, and who tried to build utopian communities, failed. But the really serious revolutionaries, the ones prepared to burn down the system and put their opponents up against the wall, have never had a plan. What they had—and still have—is a vague idea of the kingdom of heaven they propose to create—in Marx's case "the kingdom of freedom," in Alinsky's "the open society," in the case of the current left, "social justice."

These ideas are sentimental and seductive enough to persuade their followers that it is all right to commit fraud, mayhem and murder—usually in epic doses—to enter the promised land. But otherwise, revolutionaries never spend two seconds thinking about how to make an actual society work. How to keep people from committing crimes against each other; how to get them to put their shoulders to the wheel; how to provide incentives that will motivate individuals to produce wealth. But if there is no viable plan, then it is the means used to get there that make the revolution what it is. Each step of the way creates the revolutionary world. What radicals like Saul Alinsky create is not salvation but chaos.

5

Rules for Revolution Applied

(with Liz Blaine)

The burden of the national debt has become so great that even Barack Obama's Secretary of State Hillary Clinton describes it this way. "I think that our rising debt level poses a national security threat and it poses a national security threat in two ways: It undermines our capacity to act in our own interests and it does constrain us where constraint may be undesirable. And it also sends a message of weakness, internationally."[1]

According to the Congressional Budget Office, in the first nineteen months of Obama's presidency, the national debt increased by $2.5260 *trillion.*[2] The debt is a higher percentage of the gross national product now than at any time since World War II. Yet Secretary of State Clinton did not ask why the president she serves has spent the savings of present and future generations so prodigally. Perhaps because the answer would have been too discomforting.

Originally published on October 22, 2010 as "Breaking the System: The Obama Team's Strategy for Changing America," http://www.frontpagemag.com/2010/frontpagemag-com/breaking-the-system-the-obama-teams-strategy-for-changing-america/.

[1]"A Conversation with U.S. Secretary of State Hillary Rodham Clinton," Council on Foreign Relations, September 8, 2olo, http://www.cfr.org/world/conversation-us-secretary-state-hillary-rodham-clinton/p34808.

[2]Terrence Jeffrey, "Obama Added More to National Debt in First 19 Months Than All Presidents from Washington Through Reagan Combined, Says Gov't Data," *cnsnews.com,* September 8, 2010, http://www.cnsnews.com/news/article/obama-added-more-national-debt-first-19-months-all-presidents-washington-through-reagan.

It is true that on taking office the Obama administration was faced with a dangerous financial crisis, and that the massive government intervention to prevent a meltdown known as "TARP" was proposed by the previous Republican regime. But the subsequent explosion of sovereign debt under Obama's rule was neither inevitable nor the result of forces beyond his administration's control. The decision to spend more than a trillion dollars following the initial intervention, and to load on massive government programs incurring many trillions in future debt, was both avoidable and deliberate. This government expansion can only be understood as a calculated strategy to promote long-held leftist ambitions. White House chief of staff Rahm Emanuel gave a flippant endorsement to these designs when he said of the country's deepening financial woes in 2009, "You never want a serious crisis to go to waste."

This progressive version of crisis management has allowed the White House to use America's economic troubles as an excuse to shackle the government with financial burdens, while encumbering the private sector with new government controls. "Bailouts" and "stimulus packages" become an excuse to stage takeovers in private industry; high insurance premiums become an excuse to move America closer to a socialized medical system. National bankruptcy becomes a way to bind future generations to government dependency and to cripple "imperial" America in the world at large.

Using economic and social crises to engineer radical changes that would otherwise be politically unacceptable is not something that Barack Obama and his advisers thought up when they arrived in Washington. It is the implementation of a strategy that the radical left devised forty years ago and has been consciously developing ever since. The goal of this strategy as articulated by its leftist authors is to dismantle America's private enterprise system and implement a socialist redistribution of wealth.

The strategy was first proposed in 1966 by two Marxist professors at Columbia University named Richard Cloward and Frances

Fox Piven.[3] Their initial idea was to recruit enough people to the welfare rolls in New York City to bankrupt the welfare system, thus eliminating the safety net and precipitating a social and financial crisis, which could be exploited to propose radical change. Their larger goal was to take this strategy national with the idea of weakening the capitalist system they were bent on destroying. Cloward and Piven published their plan in *The Nation* magazine, a left-wing publication with a long history of supporting Communist causes. Their manifesto quickly galvanized activists who understood immediately that they had a sharp new weapon in their arsenal.[4] They called their new idea the "crisis strategy" and, alternatively, the "flood-the-rolls, bankrupt-the-cities" plan. Over the next four decades their proposal became the go-to strategy in the radical playbook.

The Cloward-Piven plan called for "cadres of aggressive organizers" to create street actions by the poor that would create "a climate of militancy." Fearful of the prospect of racial violence just then beginning to set America's inner cities on fire, politicians would desperately embrace the idea of a federally guaranteed "living income" for nonworking people—or so the plan surmised. Following up on their proposal, Cloward and Piven recruited a radical organizer named George Wiley to lead their newly formed "National Welfare Rights Movement" to implement the strategy.[5]

By 1969, the National Welfare Rights Movement claimed a dues-paying membership of 22,500 families, with 523 chapters

[3]Richard Poe, "The Cloward-Piven Strategy," *DiscoverTheNetworks*, 2005, http://www.discoverthenetworks.org/Articles/theclowardpivenstrategypoc.html.

[4]Frances Fox Piven and Richard Cloward, "The Weight of the Poor: A Strategy to End Poverty," *The Nation*, May 2, 1966 (reprinted March 8, 2010), http://www.thenation.com/article/weight-poor-strategy-end-poverty; and David Horowitz and Richard Poe, *The Shadow Party*, Thomas Nelson, 2007, p. 106.

[5]George Alvin Wiley, http://www.discoverthenetworks.org/individualProfile.asp?indid=1769.

across the nation.[6] The strategy was vindicated when, by 1974, the number of single-parent households on welfare soared from 4.3 million to 10.8 million in relatively good economic times.[7] Their greatest success was in New York. Newly-elected liberal Mayor John Lindsay capitulated to every Wiley demand. New York's welfare rolls were soon growing at the unsustainable rate of 50 percent annually. "By the early 1970s, one person was on the welfare rolls in New York City for every two working in the city's private economy," Sol Stern reported in the *City Journal.*[8] In 1975, as a direct result of its reckless welfare spending, New York City—the financial capital of the world—was forced to declare bankruptcy.[9] The entire state of New York nearly went down with it. The Cloward-Piven strategy was now a proven success, and a signal to radical community organizers everywhere that this was a path to the fundamental changes in American society they had so long desired.

The National Welfare Rights Organization was generously funded by federal War on Poverty money. But after Richard Nixon was elected in 1968, these funds began to dry up and the organization itself began to falter. Wiley resigned in 1971 and the organization disintegrated, to be replaced by a new community-organizing force founded by one of Wiley's disciples, Wade Rathke.[10] It was called the Association of Community Organizations for Reform

---

[6]Mark Toney, "Revisiting the National Welfare Rights Organization," *Colorlines,* Volume 3, Number 3, November 29, 2000, http://www.colorlines.com/articles/revisiting-national-welfare-rights-organization; William Borders, "Welfare Militant On the Way Up: George Alvin Wiley," *The New York Times,* May 27, 1969, http://query.nytimes.com/gst/abstract.html?res=9406E0D9123AEE34BC4F51DFB3668382679EDE.

[7]Sol Stern, "ACORN's Nutty Regime for Cities" *City Journal,* Spring 2003, http://www.city-journal.org/html/13_2_acorns_nutty_regime.html.

[8]Ibid.

[9]Floyd Norris, "Orange County Crisis Jolts Bond Market, *The New York Times,* December 8, 1994," http://www.nytimes.com/1994/12/08/business/orange-county-s-bankruptcy-the-overview-orange-county-crisis-jolts-bond-market.html.

[10]Wade Rathke, http://www.discoverthenetworks.org/individualProfile.asp?indid=1773.

Now, or ACORN, and was the vehicle for the rise of Barack Obama, who became its general counsel in the 1980s.[11] ACORN spread to over 100 U.S. cities and acquired 400,000 dues-paying members. An avowedly anti-capitalist organization, it focused on fighting for a so-called "living wage," which was a minimum wage set at a higher level than the national standard.

Partisans of the Cloward-Piven idea soon found a new area to apply the strategy and founded a second movement in tandem with ACORN to take up "the unfinished work" of the Voting Rights Act of 1965. The new voting rights movement, which was launched in 1982, was spear-headed by Project Vote, an ACORN front group, and Human SERVE, created by Cloward and Piven.[12] All three of these organizations—ACORN, Project Vote and Human SERVE—set to work lobbying for the so-called Motor-Voter law, which would allow people to register to vote when they received their driver's licenses, and against laws which would require proof of citizenship at the polls.

Just as they had swamped America's welfare offices in the 1960s, the Cloward-Piven organizers now sought to overwhelm the nation's understaffed and poorly policed voting system. When President Clinton signed the National Voter Registration Act on May 20, 1993, Cloward and Piven stood behind him, in places of honor, at the ceremony. ACORN and its front group Project Vote set to work flooding the polls with phony ballots and bogus registrations. Election officials who dared to complain were intimidated with lawsuits and cries of "racism."[13] The law quickly led to what John Fund of *The Wall Street Journal* called "an explosion of phantom voters," swamping the voter rolls with dead or non-

[11]Association Of Community Organizations For Reform Now (ACORN), http://www.discoverthenetworks.org/groupProfile.asp?grpid=6968; Matthew Vadum, *Subversion, Inc.*, WND Books, 2011.

[12]Richard Poe, "Project Vote," *DiscoverTheNetworks*, 2005, http://www.discoverthenetworks.org/Articles/pvextprofile.html.

[13]"Vote Fraud, Intimidation and Suppression in the 2004 Presidential Election," American Center for Voting Rights (ACVR), August 2, 2005.

existent people with names such as Mickey Mouse and calling the integrity of the electoral system into question.[14]

But the greatest impact of the Cloward-Piven bankrupt-the-system-strategy was made through the 1977 Community Reinvestment Act, which, using the rubric of increasing "racial equality," required banks to extend credit to high-risk borrowers in low-income, mostly minority areas. Madeline Talbott, a Chicago ACORN leader, openly boasted of using her organization's clout to force the city's banks into loans to house buyers who lacked the ability to pay them. She also hired a young Barack Obama to train her staff.[15] Obama solidified his ties with ACORN as he moved up the political ladder in the city, funneling money to the group through the Woods Fund and the Chicago Annenberg Challenge as a member of those boards. He also defended ACORN members when they became targets of federal election fraud investigations.[16]

The Community Reinvestment Act became a wedge to loosen credit requirements for mortgages at all levels. Any bank wishing to expand or to merge with another was required to first demonstrate that it had complied with the new loosened standards. Final approval for bank expansions or mergers could be held up or derailed entirely by complaints—however frivolous or unfounded—when groups like ACORN accused a bank of being "racist" and having failed to follow the loose lending standards required by the Community Reinvestment Act.[17] As their campaign progressed, the ACORN organizers found that banks would tell them they could only reduce their credit standards by a little since Fannie Mae and Freddie Mac, the federal mortgage giants, refused to buy up the risky loans for sale on the secondary

---

[14]John Fund, *Stealing Elections: How Voter Fraud Threatens Democracy,* Encounter, 2004.

[15]Stanley Kurtz, "O's dangerous Pals," *New York Post,* September 29, 2008, http://nypost.com/2008/09/29/os-dangerous-pals/.

[16]Ibid.

[17]Richard Poe, "ACORN: History, Activities, and Agendas," *DiscoverTheNetworks,* 2005, http://www.discoverthenetworks.org/Articles/acornhistory.html.

market.[18] Unless Fannie and Freddie were willing to relax their credit standards as well, local banks would never make home loans to customers with bad credit histories or with too little money for a down payment.

So ACORN's Democratic friends in Congress moved to force Fannie Mae and Freddie Mac to follow suit and also dispense with normal credit standards.[19] Despite their 1994 takeover of Congress, Republicans continued to fund ACORN. Their efforts to cut back the Community Reinvestment Act were consistently stymied when ACORN representatives came to Congress to lobby against revising that law as racist. They also lobbied to expand the reach of quota-based lending to Fannie, Freddie and the rest of the financial system.[20]

In June 1995 the Clinton administration announced a comprehensive strategy to push homeownership in America to new heights. Fannie and Freddie were assigned massive subprime lending quotas, which would rise to about half of their total business by the end of the decade.[21] The ACORN lobby was represented by a young attorney named Barack Obama.[22]

Democratic politicians took payoffs from Fannie and Freddie in the form of large campaign contributions in return for turning a blind eye to the mortgage giants' risky behavior, and for expanding "affordable housing mandates."[23] Daniel Mudd, CEO of Fannie

---

[18]Fannie Mae Foundation, http://www.discoverthenetworks.org/funderprofile.asp?fndid=5197&category=78; and Freddie Mac Foundation, http://www.discoverthenetworks.org/funderProfile.asp?fndid=5196.

[19]Stanley Kurtz, "ACORN at Root of Financial Mess," *Fox News,* October 10, 2008, http://www.foxnews.com/story/2008/10/10/kurtz-acorn-at-root-financial-mess.html.

[20]Stanley Kurtz, "Spreading the Virus," *New York Post,* October 13, 2008, http://nypost.com/2008/10/13/spreading-the-virus/.

[21]Ibid.

[22]Buycks-Roberson v. Citibank Fed. Sav. Bank, *University of Michigan Law School,* http://www.clearinghouse.net/detail.php?id=10112.

[23]Hans Bader, "Clinton Pressure to Promote Affordable Housing Led to Mortgage Meltdown," *Competitive Enterprise Institute,* September 16, 2008, https://cei.org/blog/clinton-pressure-promote-affordable-housing-led-mortgage-meltdown.

Mae from 2005 to 2008, publicly referred to Barack Obama and the Democrat Congressional Black Caucus as the "family" and "conscience" of Fannie Mae when describing their partnership.[24] Not surprisingly, the top recipients of Fannie and Freddie's campaign contributions were Democrats.[25] In just two years as a U.S. Senator, Barack Obama received $126,349 in campaign contributions from Fannie and Freddie. During his Presidential campaign Obama's advisors included former Fannie Mae CEO's Frank Raines and Jim Johnson.[26]

As a young community organizer in 1992, Barak Obama served as a lead organizer for Project Vote, ACORN's voter mobilization subsidiary, which employed the Cloward-Piven Strategy to overwhelm, paralyze and discredit the voting system through fraud, protests, propaganda and litigation.[27] Obama successfully represented ACORN in a 1994 redlining suit against Citibank, helping ACORN to expand Community Reinvestment Act (CRA) authority.[28] In 1995, he represented ACORN in a suit forcing the state of Illinois to implement the federal "motor voter" bill. As a U.S. senator, in 2006, Obama voted "present" when a bill was put on the floor that would have stopped Fannie and Freddie from accepting more toxic loans.[29]

---

[24]James Simpson, "Barack Obama and the Strategy of Manufactured Crisis," *American Thinker,* September 28, 2008, http://www.americanthinker.com/articles/2008/09/barack_obama_and_the_strategy.html.

[25]Lindsay Renick Mayer, "Update: Fannie Mae and Freddie Mac Invest in Lawmakers," *Open Secrets,* September 11, 2008, https://www.opensecrets.org/news/2008/09/update-fannie-mae-and-freddie/.

[26]Lynn Wooley, "Obama's Friends at Fannie Mae," *Human Events,* October 1, 2008, http://humanevents.com/2008/10/01/obamas-friends-at-fannie-mae/.

[27]Adam Doster, "Growing the Pie," *Illinois Times,* August 6, 2008, http://illinoistimes.com/article-5162-growing-the-pie.html.

[28]Barack Hussein Obama, http://www.discoverthenetworks.org/individualProfile.asp?indid=1511.

[29]Ed Morrissey, "Obama Voted 'Present' on Fannie/Freddie Reform," *Hotair.com,* October 15, 2008, http://hotair.com/archives/2008/10/15/obama-voted-present-on-fanniefreddie-reform.

As a presidential candidate, Obama paid Citizens Services, Inc., an offshoot of ACORN, over $800,000 for "Get-Out-the-Vote" projects during the Democrat primaries. He denied any association with the group and minimized its activities to the FEC as limited to "polling, advance work, and staging major events." He would go on to deny the FEC access to his list of political donors who had contributed the maximum legal amount to his campaign, and hand over the list to ACORN with the aim of collecting additional political donations through ACORN for use in his presidential campaign.[30]

In June 2008 Democratic Senator Chuck Schumer leaked a memo questioning the solvency of the IndyMac bank, triggering a deposit run on IndyMac that led to its failure.[31] This was followed by the collapse of large financial institutions and a gathering storm in the markets until September 15 when, in a matter of hours, a colossal drawdown of money market accounts in the U.S. caused the disappearance of $550 billion from the U.S. banking system.[32] To avert a general financial meltdown, the Bush administration sponsored a $700 billion Troubled Asset Relief Program (TARP) bill to bail out endangered companies.[33]

---

[30]Anita MonCrief, "Obama, ACORN and Stealth Socialism: Dire Domestic Threat," *NetRightDaily*, May 26, 2010, http://netrightdaily.com/2010/05/obama-acorn-and-stealth-socialism-dire-domestic-threat/.

[31]Ari Levy and David Mildenberg, "IndyMac Seized by U.S. Regulators; Schumer Blamed for Failure," *Bloomberg*, July 12, 2008, http://www.bloomberg.com/apps/news?pid=newsarchive&sid=aAYLeK3YAie4; and Lawrence B. Lindsey, "The Fannie and Freddie Follies," *DiscoverTheNetworks*, http://www.discoverthenetworks.org/Articles/The%20Fannie%20and%20Freddie%20Follies.html.

[32]John Sweat, "Who Was Behind the Attack on Our Economy—Just Before the Election?," *Family Security Matters*, February 17, 2009, http://www.familysecuritymatters.org/publications/id.2539/pub_detail.asp.

[33]Katalina Bianco, "A Retrospective of the Troubled Asset Relief Program," *Business.cch.com*, https://business.cch.com/bankingFinance/focus/News/TARPwhitepaper.pdf.

As president, Obama used these TARP bailout funds to finance government takeovers of GMAC, Fannie Mae, Freddie Mac, and AIG, to acquire a large share of Citigroup and to hand controlling interest of Chrysler to the United Auto Workers Union. By July 2010, U.S. taxpayer support for the financial system had grown to around $3. 7 trillion, a 23 percent increase over 2009.[34] The expenditure was due largely to the government's pledge to supply capital to Fannie Mae and Freddie Mac, and to guarantee more mortgages to support the housing market. The Treasury Department provided $145 billion of capital to Fannie Mae and Freddie Mac, and hundreds of billions more in potential liability, until the cost of fixing the mortgage companies has grown to an estimated $1 trillion.[35] It was called the "mother of all bailouts" and transpired without congressional action, oversight, or public scrutiny.

As though oblivious to the effects of these policies, President Obama announced reforms to the Community Reinvestment Act, which provided for an expansion of the same irresponsible lending practices that had led to the collapse of the mortgage industry. The Obama reform gave enforcement of compliance rights to community activists, i.e., to ACORN and its allies.[36] During the ensuing wave of house foreclosures, Francis Fox Piven advocated civil

---

[34]John M. Brandow, Beverly Chase, Luigi L. De Ghenghi, John L. Douglas, William J. Fenrich, Edmond T. FitzGerald, James F. Florack, Randall G. Guynn, Michael Kaplan, Yukako Kawata, Leor Landa, Kyoko Takahashi Lin, Jean M. McLoughlin, Annette L. Nazareth, Jennifer G. Newstead, Barbara Nims, Reena Agrawal Sahni, Margaret E. Tahyar, Linda Chatman Thomsen, Danforth Townley, and Raul F. Yanes, "A Guide to the Laws, Regulations and Contracts of the Financial Crisis," *DavisPolk*, September 23, 2009, http://www.davispolk.com/sites/default/files/files/Publication/d1ab7627-e45d-4d35-b6f1-ef356ba686f2/Preview/PublicationAttachment/2a31cab4-3682-420e-926f-054c72e3149d/fcm.pdf.

[35]Jonathan Berr, "Treasury to Discuss the Futures of Fannie Mae and Freddie Mac," *Daily Finance,* July 27, 2010, http://www. dailyfinance.com/2010/07/27/treasury-fannie-mae-freddie-mac-conference-future/.

[36]Howard Husock, "The Trillion-Dollar Bank Shakedown That Bodes Ill for Cities," *City Journal,* Winter 2000, http://www.city-journal.org/html/10_1_the_trillion_dollar.html.

disobedience by desperate homeowners as a way to leverage the crisis to their benefit. "If millions of people, a couple of million, refuse to go along with foreclosure proceedings, and refuse to pay off those mortgages that are underwater, that will be enormous pressure on the banks. And if they do it in the form of a social movement, if they do it with pride and audacity, if they do it with a sense of self-righteousness, the political leaders of this nation will not be able to ram them up."[37] ACORN immediately established a nationwide Home Defenders campaign in which it organized homeowners to refuse to move out of foreclosed homes, or in some cases move back in.[38]

When the federal government seized control of bankrupt Fannie and Freddie in September 2008 under a legal process called "conservatorship," the government was permitted to amend the TARP agreements through the end of 2009 without the consent of Congress. Not willing to let the opportunity go to waste, President Obama signed an executive order on Christmas Eve authorizing unlimited access to TARP funds for the next three years to cover Fannie and Freddie's financial losses. There is no limit on taxpayer exposure from continued risk-taking by the publicly funded lenders, furthering the chance of damage caused by the mortgage giants and threatening more destabilization to the housing, mortgage and banking industries. Citing Fannie and Freddie's conservatorship status, the Obama administration defiantly refuses to inform Congress or the people as to how the endless funds given to the mortgage giants are spent.

The timing of President Obama's executive order on Labor Day weekend was not incidental. It was part of an effort to hide the unlimited slush fund from taxpayer visibility by announcing it

---

[37] F. Vincent Vernuccio and Matthew Vadum, "Financial Attack: SEIU Plans Days of Rage against Wall Street," *Capital Research Center,* July 4, 2011, http://capitalresearch.org/2011/07/13401/.

[38] Michelle Malkin, "Obama's Housing Entitlement Campaign & ACORN's Civil Disobedience Mob," michellemalkin.com, February 18, 2009, http://michellemalkin.com/2009/02/18/acorn-and-obama-together-again/.

over the national holiday. In conjunction with the president's executive order, Fannie Mae and Freddie Mac announced they would pay up to $42 million in executive compensation to their officers for 2009.[39] The payments were made in cash, not the type of stock-deferred payment recommended for other bailed-out institutions. In spite of the administration's demand for the regulation of executive compensation in private industry and institutions receiving TARP funds, Obama's pay czar, Kenneth R. Feinberg, defended Fannie and Freddie's extravagant cash bonuses for work poorly done.[40]

Under the Cloward-Piven strategy, the first step in fundamentally changing America is to dramatically weaken the system by undermining its economic supports. Using numerous bailouts, stimulus packages, and perpetual massive government spending, Obama has more than tripled the national deficit since 2008, from $455 billion to a projected $1.6 trillion in 2010, a figure that does not include unfunded liabilities for Medicare, Social Security, Fannie Mae and Freddie Mac, or the government's unfunded budget for 2010.[41] The president's own forecasts project the national debt will reach $20 trillion by the end of the current decade, yet the total U.S. economy is just over $14 trillion.[42] The government is currently borrowing $0.41 of every dollar it spends.[43]

When a government is faced with a debt it cannot pay, it has four choices: borrow, tax, print or default. Obama's excessive

---

[39]Steven Davidoff Solomon, "Fannie's Christmas Eve Surprise," *The New York Times*, January 4, 2010, http://dealbook.nytimes.com/2010/01/04/fannies-christmas-surprise/.

[40]Nick Timiraos, "Obama's Pay Czar Defends Fannie, Freddie Compensation Deals," *The Wall Street Journal*, December 31, 2009, http://blogs.wsj.com/developments/2009/12/31/obamas-pay-czar-defends-fannie-freddie-compensation-deals/.

[41]"W.H., Congress Project Record Deficits," *CBS News/AP*, August 25, 2009, http://www.cbsnews.com/news/wh-congress-project-record-deficits/.

[42]Ibid.

[43]Andrew Taylor, "White House Predicts Record $1.47 Trillion Deficit," *Salon/AP*, July 23, 2010, http://www.salon.com/2010/07/23/us_record_deficit/.

spending has limited the U.S. government's ability to borrow; the administration's response to America's mounting debt is to print ever-greater quantities of money, inflating the money supply.[44] As the money supply increases, the currency devalues, leading to inflation, the decline in the purchasing power of money or increase in the level of consumer prices. When the bill comes due to repay Obama's trillions in borrowed debt, the government will have to either raise taxes to devastating levels or promote inflation by printing money. The radicals around Obama know what their priority is. Former Obama green czar Van Jones recently called for Washington to stop worrying about deficits and take more money from businesses. "This is a rich country ... There's plenty of money out there; don't fall into the trap of this whole deficit argument. The only question is how to spend it."[45]

Despite the breathless pace of his legislative agendas, the president recently complained: "Change has not come fast enough."[46] To overcome the popular opposition to his agendas, Obama is aggressively pressing to "maximize the vote" by granting amnesty to upwards of 30 million illegal immigrants. Hundreds of thousands of illegal immigrants have been fraudulently registered as voters under the Motor Voter bill, but granting blanket amnesty ensures a flood of millions more as they cross the borders to sign up for the government entitlements that come with American citizenship. In 2010, Representative Barney Frank and Senator Chuck Schumer unveiled legislation mandating 'universal voter registration' under which any person whose name is on any federal roll at

---

[44]James Grant, "Is the Medicine Worse Than the Illness?," *The Wall Street Journal,* December 20, 2008, http://www.wsj.com/articles/SB122973431525523215.

[45]Chris Moody, "Van Jones: Stop Worrying about the Deficit. The Government Can Just Take More Money from Rich Companies," *The Daily Caller,* July 24, 2010, http://dailycaller.com/2010/07/24/van-jones-stop-worrying-about-the-deficit-the-government-can-just-take-more-money-from-rich-companies/.

[46]"State of the Union Speech," Barack Obama, *The Huffington Post,* January 27, 2010, http://www.huffingtonpost.com/2010/01/27/state-of-the-union-2010-full-text-transcript_n_439459.html.

all—be it a list of welfare recipients, food stamp recipients, unemployment compensation recipients, licensed drivers, convicted felons, property owners, etc.—would automatically be registered to vote in elections.[47] Deputy Assistant Attorney General Julie Fernandez, a political appointee, instructed DOJ attorneys that the administration has no interest in enforcing the provision of the law requiring dead, duplicate and ineligible registrations to be removed from the voter rolls.[48]

ACORN and its affiliates are an integral part of the Democratic push for expanded electoral rolls. ACORN was under investigation in at least 13 states for voter registration fraud during the 2008 presidential election but the Obama administration amended the $140 million Mortgage Reform and Anti-Predatory Lending Act to allow ACORN to receive federal funds even while under investigation.[49] After Republicans in Congress pressed for a ban on ACORN's federal funding due to financial misrepresentation and videotaped evidence of members advising possible partners to hide illegal activity, the Obama administration quietly restored the group's funding while Americans were distracted by the congressional healthcare vote.[50] Obama and the Democrats included $100

---

[47]Cloward-Piven Strategy, http://www.discoverthenetworks.org/groupprofile.asp?grpid=7522.

[48]J. Christian Adams, "Lawlessness at the DOJ: Voting Section Told Not To Enforce Purging the Dead or Ineligible from Voting Rolls," *PJ Media*, July 8, 2010, http://pjmedia.com/blog/lawlessness-at-the-doj-voting-section-told-not-to-enforce-purging-the-dead-or-ineligible-from-voting-rolls/.

[49]Kevin Mooney, "ACORN Drops Tarnished Name and Moves to Silence Critics," *Washington Examiner*, June 20, 2009, http://www.washingtonexaminer.com/acorn-drops-tarnished-name-and-moves-to-silence-critics/article/135492; Kevin Mooney, "ACORN Got $53 Million in Federal Funds Since 94, Now Eligible for Up to $8 Billion More," *Washington Examiner*, May 4, 2009, http://www.washingtonexaminer.com/acorn-got-53-million-in-federal-funds-since-94-now-eligible-for-up-to-8-billion-more/article/37998.

[50]Matthew Vadum, "While America Is Distracted by Healthcare, Obama Admin Restores Acorn Funding," *Live Leak*, March 19, 2010, http://www.liveleak.com/view?i=d65_1269025000.

million for ACORN in the original $700 billion TARP bailout package, and an additional $5.2 billion in taxpayer funds in the stimulus package for leftist community organizing groups including ACORN.[51]

Barack Obama is a lifetime student and practitioner of the Cloward-Piven strategy. The toxic bailouts, stimulus packages, and entitlement programs enacted by his administration are generating an increasingly unsustainable debt. His expansion of entitlement programs means increased entitlement benefits and an exponential growth in the number of beneficiaries, so that an already burdened government is loaded with additional obligations and unfunded mandates. Permanently high levels of unemployment are further straining the system by increasing dependency on big government and the Obama administration's decision to extend benefits to two years. President Obama and the leftists in his administration are fully aware of the effects of their actions, yet they are determined to stay the course they have set for themselves. The Cloward-Piven strategy is his means to achieve the maximum amount of change in the minimum amount of time, even if it means a single term in office. The question is: what does it mean for the rest of us if the course he has set is not reversed?

---

[51]David A. Patten, "Obama's Bill Hands ACORN $5.2 Billion Bailout," *Newsmax*, January 27, 2009, http://www.newsmax.com/Headline/obama-bailout-bill/2009/12/12/id/341743/.

6

Obama and the War Against the Jews

(with Jacob Laksin)

No other country in the world faces an array of existential threats such as the nation of Israel confronts daily. The world's only Jewish state is also its most precarious. Geographically tiny, Israel is surrounded by theocracies that reject its very existence as a "nakba"—a catastrophe—and call for its destruction. To carry out these malignant ambitions, anti-Israel Islamists have mobilized three rocket- wielding armies, sworn to wipe Israel from the face of the earth.

First and most aggressive among them is the Gaza-based Hamas, a fanatical religious party committed in its official charter to obliterating Israel and killing its Jews. Hamas is the creation of the Muslim Brotherhood, the inspirer of al-Qaeda and the global Islamic jihad, whose official motto declares: "Death in the service of Allah is our highest aspiration." In Gaza, Hamas has created a terrorist state and a national death cult whose path is martyrdom and whose goal is openly proclaimed: "O, our children: The Jews—brothers of the apes, assassins of the prophets, bloodsuckers, warmongers—are murdering you, depriving you of life

Originally published June 25, 2010, http://www.frontpagemag.com/2010/david-horowitz-and-jacob-laksin/obama-and-the-war-against-the-jews/.

after having plundered your homeland and your homes. Only Islam can break the Jews and destroy their dream."[1]

Given that hatred for Jews is the animating passion of the Hamas militants, their response to Israel's unilateral withdrawal from Gaza in 2005 was not surprising. Far from greeting this as a gesture of peace, Hamas regarded the Israeli withdrawal as a surrender to its terrorist attacks and an opportunity to escalate them. In the days and months following the withdrawal, Hamas launched 6,500 unprovoked rocket strikes on towns and schoolyards in Israel until the Israelis decided to strike back.

Israel's eastern border is home to the al-Aqsa Martyrs' Brigade, the Palestine Liberation Organization and other terrorist groups, armed and protected by the Palestinian Authority, the so-called "moderate" wing of the Palestinian *jihad.* Like Hamas, the Palestinian Authority officially rejects Israel's existence and the right of its Jews to self-determination. Like Hamas, the Palestinian Authority provides a curriculum for Gaza's schoolchildren that teaches them to hate Jews and aspire to kill them, seeking martyrdom and sainthood in the process. In line with these genocidal goals, all Palestinian schoolchildren are taught from maps of the region from which Israel has been erased.[2]

On Israel's northern border, in Lebanon, is Hezbollah, the "Party of God," which is busily stockpiling tens of thousands of Iranian rockets in anticipation of the war of annihilation it has promised to wage against the Jewish state. Created by Iran's Republican Guard and supplied by Syria's (officially) fascist dictatorship, Hezbollah is the largest terrorist army in the world. Like Hamas, it makes explicit its hatred for the Jews and its agenda in regard to them—to "finish the job that Hitler started". Its fanatical

---

[1]Alan Johnson, "Hamas and Antisemitism," *The Guardian,* May 15, 2008, http://www.theguardian.com/commentisfree/2008/may/15/hamasandantisemitism.

[2]"High School Map with Palestinian Flag Erasing Israel," *Palestinian Media Watch,* January 24, 2006, http://www.palwatch.org/pages/allmaps.aspx?sort=s&fld_id=&doc_id=5013.

leader, Hassan Nasrallah, leads thousands of believers in chants of "Death to Israel, Death to America." He has said, "If Jews all gather in Israel, it will save us the trouble of going after them worldwide."[3] Under the complicit eye of UN "peacekeepers," Hezbollah continues to amass rockets whose sole purpose is the obliteration of Israel. In May 2006, Nasrallah boasted: "Today all of Israel is in our range.... Ports, military bases, factories—everything is in our range."[4]

But it is Hezbollah's sponsor—the totalitarian, soon to be nuclear-armed state of Iran—that presents the most disturbing threat to Israel's existence. Its blood-soaked dictators have been targeting Israel for destruction since 1979, when Iran became an Islamic republic and its theocratic ruler, the Ayatollah Khomeini, identified Israel and America as "the Little Satan" and "the Great Satan." Its former president Akbar Hashemi Rafsanjani has publicly announced his support for nuclear war against the Jewish state, reasoning that since Iran is more than 70 *times* the size of Israel it could survive a nuclear attack while Israel could not.[5]

Iran's current leader, Mahmoud Ahmadinejad, has called for America and Israel to be "wiped from the map"—and there is no apparent dissent from the other 56 Islamic states that make up the Organization of the Islamic Conference. Amateur semanticists insist that Ahmadinejad's words were mistranslated; that he really meant both countries should be "erased from the pages of history." But this is a distinction without a difference. For what can that threat possibly mean if Israel or America should continue to exist? Meanwhile, Iran continues to build long-range nuclear missiles that could be used for just such a purpose, and no serious effort to

---

[3]Elena Lappin, "The Enemy Within," *The New York Times,* May 23, 2004, http://www.nytimes.com/2004/05/23/books/the-enemy-within.html?sec=&pagewanted=all.

[4]Amos Harel, Avi Issacharoff, *34 Days: Israel, Hezbollah, and the War in Lebanon,* Palgrave Macmillan, 2008, p. 48.

[5]Mitchell Bard, *Will Israel Survive?* Palgrave Macmillan, 2007, p.77.

check that ambition has been made by the international community or by the United States.

Where, indeed, does the international community stand in the face of this brazen preparation to bring about a second Holocaust of the Jews? Since the creation of the state of Israel in 1948, the Arab states have conducted three unprovoked, aggressive, conventional wars against it, along with a continuous terrorist war that began in 1949. Yet between 1948 and 2004 there were 322 resolutions in the UN General Assembly condemning the victim, Israel, and not one that condemned an Arab state.[6]

The United Nations is today dominated by the Organization of the Islamic Conference, a group that was established in 1969 at a summit convened, according to its website, "as a result of criminal arson of the al-Aqsa Mosque in occupied Jerusalem"—in other words, as a result of the criminal Jews. The Organization of the Islamic Conference regularly passes one-sided resolutions that condemn Israel, particularly for its efforts to combat Palestinian terrorism and disrupt Palestinian weapons-smuggling into Gaza. The UN's most notorious assault on Israel was the so-called "Goldstone Report," which was commissioned by the UN Human Rights Council in September 2009 and which condemned Israel's belated response to the unprovoked Hamas rocket attacks.

Relying on the testimony of Hamas terrorists, the Goldstone report charged that Israel had deliberately targeted Palestinian civilians and had committed war crimes in Gaza. Outside the precincts of the Islamic propaganda machine, however, Israel's record is that of a nation more protective of enemy civilians than any other. In testimony ignored by the Goldstone Report, Col. Richard Kemp, the former commander of British forces in Afghanistan, noted that "During Operation Cast Lead [the Israeli response to the Hamas attacks], the Israel Defense Forces did more to safeguard the rights of civilians in a combat zone than any other

---

[6]Dennis Prager, "Explaining the Arab-Israeli Conflict through Numbers," *dennisprager.com*, July 27, 2004, http://www.dennisprager.com/explaining-the-arab-israeli-conflict-through-numbers/.

army in the history of warfare."[7] Hamas, by contrast, is notorious for building military headquarters under hospitals, for placing its military forces in refugee camps and for using "human shields" comprised of women and children to deter attacks. Hamas's rockets are known to be so inaccurate they cannot be directed against military targets; they can only be used effectively against civilians. In addition, since Hamas's war against Israel was a response to Israel's unilateral withdrawal, it was a criminal aggression responsible for all the subsequent casualties, something the Goldstone Report and the UN Human Rights Council conveniently overlooked.

The Human Rights Council was created in 2006. In its first year, the council listed only one country in the world as violating human rights: Israel. It condemned Israel despite the fact that Israel is the only state in the Middle East that recognizes human rights and protects them. Not one of the world's other 194 countries was even mentioned, including North Korea, Burma, and Iran—the last of which hangs gays from cranes for transgressing the sexual prescriptions of the Koran.[8] The reason for these oversights is no mystery. The UN Human Rights Council has been presided over by representatives of such brutal human rights violators as Libya, China, Saudi Arabia and Cuba, and was such a travesty from its inception that it was boycotted by the United States until Barack Obama decided this year to join its ranks. This decision by the Obama administration, along with its overtures to Syria, Iran, and other noxious regimes, lent a stamp of legitimacy to the hypocrisy of the council and encouraged its malice.

In these sinister developments, which have now stretched over a decade, the world is witnessing a reprise of the 1930s, when the

---

[7]Patrick Goodenough, "Israelis Took Unprecedented Steps to Safeguard Civilians, Says British Officer," *CNS News.com*, October 16, 2009, http://www.cnsnews.com/news/article/israelis-took-unprecedented-steps-safeguard-civilians-says-british-officer.

[8]"Anti-Israel Resolutions at the HRC," *UN Watch*, http://www.unwatch.org/site/c.bdKKISNqEmG/b.3820041/.

Nazis devised a "final solution" to the "Jewish problem" and the civilized world did nothing to halt its implementation. This time, the solution is being proposed in front of the entire international community, which appears unruffled by the prospect. It has turned its collective back on the Jews, and refuses to recognize the gravity of the threat. Moreover, by enforcing the fiction that there is a "peace process" that needs to be brokered between the sides, and ignoring the overt preparation for Israel's destruction by the Palestinian side, the "peacemakers" lend their support to its deadly agenda.

For decades now, Israel has been isolated and alone in the community of nations with one crucial exception. That exception has been the United States, a country on which it has relied for its survival throughout its 60-year history. Every would-be aggressor has understood that the world's most powerful nation was behind Israel and would not let her be destroyed. Every government harboring ill-will toward the Jewish state has had to reckon with the fact that the United States was in Israel's corner. Every vote of condemnation in the United Nations had to confront a veto by the nation that provides its chief financial support.

Until now. In the words of a recent Reuters dispatch, "Under President Barack Obama, the United States no longer provides Israel with automatic support at the United Nations where the Jewish state faces a constant barrage of criticism and condemnation. The subtle but noticeable shift in the U.S. approach to its Middle East ally comes amid what some analysts describe as one of the most serious crises in U.S.-Israel relations in years.[9]

This change first became apparent during an official visit to Jerusalem visit by Vice President Biden earlier this year. On March 9, the vice president arrived for a dinner at the home of the Prime Minister Benjamin Netanyahu nearly two hours late. His tardiness

---

[9]Louis Charbonneau, "UN Rebukes of Israel Permitted in U.S. Policy Shift," *Reuters*, June 8, 2010, http://www.reuters.com/article/2010/06/08/us-israel-usa-un-analysis-idUSTRE6570SP20100608.

was not accidental but a calculated diplomatic slight—specifically, a punishment for Israel's announcement of plans to build 1,600 new homes in a predominantly Jewish section of Jerusalem.[10] The vice president was supposedly embarrassed by the announcement's being made during his visit. In fact the announcement was a routine step, the fourth in a seven-stage bureaucratic approval process for new construction. While its timing might be construed as inopportune, the building of homes in a Jewish neighborhood in Israel's capital city was hardly an issue to create any sort of problem, let alone to cause a rupture between allies. Nonetheless, Israeli officials, conscious of their dependence on their American partners, immediately apologized for any perceived offense.

The Obama administration would have none of it. As severe reproaches of Israel from top U.S. officials followed, the crisis escalated. Secretary of State Hillary Clinton berated Netanyahu, calling Israel's announcement a "deeply negative signal" for U.S.-Israel ties.[11] Senior presidential advisor David Axelrod delivered the same scolding message to an American audience, going on cable news shows to vent the administration's displeasure. Branding Israel's announcement an "affront" and an "insult," Axelrod claimed that Israel had made the "peace process" with the Palestinians much more "difficult."[12]

Unlike Israel's housing announcement, which was made without Netanyahu's knowledge, Washington's response was dictated by President Obama. When the Israeli prime minister arrived in the United States for a meeting with the president that same month, there was no ceremony in the White House Rose Garden and no posing before press cameras—the usual good-will gestures

---

[10]"Biden Came Late to Dinner on Purpose," *Israel National News,* March 11, 2010, http://www.israelnationalnews.com/News/Flash.aspx/182263.

[11]Alastair Macdonald, "Hillary Clinton Berates Netanyahu Over Settlements," *Reuters,* March 16, 2010, http://www.reuters.com/articleidUSN1213959520100312.

[12]"Axelrod: Israel Settlement Approval an 'Affront'; 'Insult'," *ABC News,* March 14, 2010, http://blogs.abcnews.com/politicalpunch/2010/03/axelrod-israel-settlement-approval-an-affront-insult.html.

afforded visiting heads of friendly nations, not to mention long-time allies. The reception was at least as cold in private. When Netanyahu arrived at the White House for what he thought was going to be a dinner with the president, Obama unceremoniously presented him with a list of demands—including an Israeli cessation of all housing construction in East Jerusalem—and curtly abandoned his guest to have dinner with his wife and daughters in the White House residential wing.[13] As Obama left the meeting room, he informed his stunned ally that he would "be around" should the Israeli leader change his mind. As the Israeli press reported afterwards, "There is no humiliation exercise that the Americans did not try on the prime minister and his entourage."[14] *Washington Post* columnist and Middle East expert Jackson Diehl was even more blunt, writing that "Netanyahu is being treated [by Obama] as if he were an unsavory Third World dictator."[15]

Contrary to the administration's insistence that Israel was jeopardizing peace by encroaching on negotiable terrain, the construction site in Jerusalem was anything but disputed territory. Jerusalem is Israel's capital, and the construction site is in Ramat Shlomo, a Jewish neighborhood. Housing construction had been underway in Ramat Shlomo since the early 1990s, and the neighborhood would remain part of Israel in any conceivable peace settlement.[16] Consequently, when Netanyahu had agreed under pressure to a partial ten-month freeze on settlements in the disputed territories, he specifically *excluded* Jerusalem. By its

[13]Adrian Blomfield, "Obama Snubbed Netanyahu for Dinner with Michelle and the Girls, Israelis Claim," *The Telegraph,* March 25, 2010, http://www.telegraph.co.uk/news/worldnews/northamerica/usa/barackobama/7521391/Obama-snubbed-Netanyahu-for-dinner-with-Michelle-and-the-girls-Israelis-claim.html.

[14]Ibid.

[15]Jackson Diehl, "Obama and Netanyahu: Pointless Poison" *The Washington Post,* March 24, 2010, http://voices.washingtonpost.com/postpartisan/2010/03/obama_and_netanyahu_pointless.html.

[16]Abe Selig, "Ramat Shlomo Residents Don't Understand What All the Fuss Is About," *Jerusalem Post,* March 11, 2010, http://www.jpost.com/Israel/Article.aspx?id=170707.

insistence that Israel cease all building in East Jerusalem, it was the Obama administration—not Israel—that was breaking with precedent and opening up the political center of Israel itself to Palestinian claims.

In opposing Israeli construction in a Jewish neighborhood in Jerusalem, the Obama administration embraced a version of Middle Eastern history that directly lent itself to the Arab war against the Jewish state. In the Arab narrative justifying that war, Jerusalem is alleged to occupy a central place in the history of Muslims and Arabs. In the same narrative, Jerusalem is claimed as the capital of a future Palestinian state. But the spiritual centrality of Jerusalem for Muslims is in fact a relatively recent claim and dubious on its face, while the religious claims are by-products of Muslim military conquests.

The Prophet Mohammed never visited Jerusalem, and consequently Jerusalem is never mentioned in the Koran. Today even Islamists regard it as only the third-holiest city in Islam, after Mecca and Medina. It was never the capital of any Arab state. Indeed, for centuries, Jerusalem was a forgotten city to most Arabs, and it was allowed to fall into ruin under Ottoman rule, which lasted until the fall of the Ottomans in the First World War. On a trip to Jerusalem in 1867, Mark Twain had despaired that the city "has lost all its grandeur, and is become a pauper village."[17] Even during Jordan's occupation between 1948 and 1967, Jerusalem was treated like a backwater. Only one Arab leader, Morocco's King Hassan, cared enough to pay a visit to the city that Muslim *jihadis* now suggest is an essential part of their history.[18]

The sudden fracture in the U.S-Israel relationship in March caught the Israeli government off guard. But close observers of the Obama administration would have recognized it as the logical endpoint of a series of markers that had been laid down since

---

[17]Mark Twain, *The Innocents Abroad,* BiblioLife, 2009, p. 393.

[18]Dennis Prager, Joseph Telushkin, *Why the Jews? The Reason for Anti-Semitism,* Simon & Schuster, 1983, p. 168.

Obama's emergence as a leading presidential contender in 2008. With these markers Obama was signaling a major shift in U.S. policy moving toward the Muslim world and America's traditional enemies, and away from allies like Israel. The first sign of this shift was visible during a February 2008 presidential debate when Obama sought to differentiate himself from Hillary Clinton, his then-opponent and future secretary of state, by announcing that unlike her he would be willing to meet with hostile governments "without preconditions." It was a position he justified by asserting that it was critical for the United States to "talk to its enemies." This was a rare example of a campaign promise Obama has kept.[19]

On entering the White House, Obama quickly moved to set a new tone toward the Arab and Muslim world. His very first call to a foreign leader from the Oval Office was to Palestinian president Mahmoud Abbas, and it was not an effort to dissuade Abbas from his support for terrorism or his opposition to the existence of a Jewish state.[20] One of the first interviews Obama gave, in January 2009, was to the Dubai-based television network al-Arabiya. In it, Obama effectively offered an apology to the Arab world for alleged American misdeeds. He assured his interviewer that, with him in charge, Arab states could look to America as a friend. "My job to the Muslim world is to communicate that the Americans are not your enemy," Obama said, adding that the United States "sometimes makes mistakes. We have not been perfect."[21]

It was the first leg of what would become an extensive "apology tour" for America's sins around the world. In April 2009 the

---

[19]Peggy Fikac, "Domestic Issues Dominate Debate in Austin," *Houston Chronicle,* February 22, 2008, http://www.chron.com/disp/story.mpl/front/5561241.html.[20]Robert Farley, "One of Obama's First Calls Was to Palestinian Leader, and Israeli Leader," *Politifact,* May 8, 2009, http://www.politifact.com/truth-o-meter/statements/2009/may/08/chain-email/one-obamas-first-calls-was-palestinian-leader-and-/.

[21]"'Americans Are Not Your Enemy,' Obama Tells Muslims," *CNN,* January 27, 2009, http://www.cnn.com/2009/POLITICS/01/27/obama.arabia/index.html?iref=nextin.

president visited Turkey, a NATO ally, which was rapidly—and alarmingly—becoming an Islamist state. Addressing its parliament, he hailed Turkey as a "true partner" and suggested it was the United States that had been the faithless friend. In a not-so-oblique attack on President Bush, Obama expressed his regret for the "difficulties of these last few years," referring to a strain in relations caused by Turkey's refusal to allow American troops to deploy from Turkish soil during the war in Iraq. Obama lamented that the "trust that binds us has been strained, and I know that strain is shared in many places where the Muslim faith is practiced."

In other words, Turkey's refusal to help America support the Muslim citizens of Iraq and topple a hated tyranny was a response to America's prejudice *against* Muslims.

In his review of past grievances, Obama did not mention the millions of Muslims—including Palestinians in the West Bank and Gaza—who had cheered the 9/11 attacks on U.S. soil by Islamic fanatics. Nor did he complain about the spread of anti-American and anti-Israeli conspiracy theories concerning those attacks in the Muslim world, including Turkey. As recently as 2008, polls found that as many Turks (39 percent) believed the United States or Israel was behind the 9/11 attacks as believed Osama bin Laden and al-Qaeda were the culprits.[22]

Even more worrisome, Obama used the occasion of his Turkish visit to break with the U.S. policy of treating countries that harbor terrorists as hostile nations. President Bush had declared that there would be no room for neutrality in the war against terror—"You are either with us or against us." But Obama now assured his listeners in Turkey, and throughout the Muslim world, that their governments no longer had to choose between America and al-Qaeda. "America's relationship with the Muslim world,"

[22]"Who Was Behind 9/11?," WorldPublicOpinion.org, September 10, 2008, http://www.worldpublicopinion.org/pipa/pdf/sep08/WPO_911_Sep08_quaire.pdf.

Obama said, "cannot and will not be based on opposition to al-Qaeda."[23]

Obama's pandering to Arab and Muslim sensibilities had already been embarrassingly on display a few days earlier, when he took the step, unprecedented for an American president, of making an elaborate bow to Saudi Arabia's King Abdullah, ruler of a nation in which it is illegal to carry a Bible or build a church, or for women to drive automobiles. The incident took place at the G-20 economic summit in London. When critics decried the president's subservient gesture to the Arab despot, the administration was caught by surprise and attempted to deny that it had ever occurred. Inconveniently for White House damage control, a video had captured Obama in full obeisant mode.[24]

The shift in Washington's policy toward the Arab world reached a new level with Obama's speech in Cairo two months later. On the one hand, the president defended the U.S. military campaigns in the Middle East as driven by "necessity", condemned the Holocaust denial and Jew-hatred that are rife in the Arab world, promoted by its governments; and called on Palestinians to abandon violence against Israel. But these statements were accompanied by others that appear particularly troubling in the light of subsequent administration moves. While Obama rightly condemned Holocaust denial, he left the impression that Israel's legitimacy derived solely from the legacy of European anti-Semitism and the Nazis' extermination of six million Jews. This echoed the Arab propaganda claim that Israel is a problem created by Europeans and unfairly imposed on the Arab world. Once again, Obama was bolstering an Arab myth that served to delegitimize the Jewish state.

---

[23]WSJ Staff, "Obama's Remarks to Turkish Parliament," *Wall Street Journal*, April 6, 2009, http://blogs.wsj.com/washwire/2009/04/06/obamas-remarks-to-turkish-parliament/tab/article/.

[24]"Did Barack Obama bow to Saudi King Abdullah?," *Haaretz*, April 9, 2009, http://www.haaretz.com/news/watch-did-barack-obama-bow-to-saudi-king-abdullah-1.273824.

The Holocaust is not merely a European legacy. Arab states such as Iraq and Iran actively sided with Hitler's armies, Arab generals served with Rommel, Hitler's commander in North Africa, while Arab leaders applauded and actively promoted the extermination of the Jews. The founder of the Muslim Brotherhood, Hassan al-Banna, was an admirer of Hitler and had *Mein Kampf* translated into Arabic in the 1930s as a text to guide his followers. The Grand Mufti of Jerusalem and founder of Palestinian nationalism, Haj Amin al-Husseini, was an active and vocal supporter of Hitler's "final solution," and spent the war years in Berlin recruiting Arabs to the Nazi cause. Al-Husseini, a man revered to this day on the West Bank and in Gaza as the George Washington of a Palestinian state, organized anti-Jewish pogroms in the 1920s and 1930s, actively planned to build his own Auschwitz in the Middle East and was thwarted only when Rommel was defeated at El Alamein.

The Arab canard that Israel is Europe's attempt to unload its problem onto the backs of the Arabs ignores—as did Obama—the fact that Jerusalem has been the spiritual capital of the Jewish people for nearly 3,000 years, and that Jews have lived in their historic homeland continuously for all that time. Jerusalem is at the center of the Jewish spiritual tradition, and Jews have been its largest religious community since 1864. Prime Minister Netanyahu was historically accurate when he admonished Obama, saying that "the Jewish people were building Jerusalem 3,000 years ago, and the Jewish people are building Jerusalem today. Jerusalem is not a settlement. It is our capital."

In his Cairo speech, Obama also showed little appreciation for the modern history of Israel. That nation was not built on Arab—let alone "Palestinian"—land. The state of Israel was created out of the ruins of the Turkish empire. In 1922, Great Britain established the state of Jordan out of 80 percent of the Palestine Mandate—a geographical, not an ethnic, designation. The territory in the Mandate had been part of the *Turkish* (not Arab) empire for the previous four hundred years. Then in 1948, a UN "partition plan" provided equal parts of the remaining Turkish land to Arabs and to Jews living on the banks of the Jordan River. In this plan, the Jews were assigned 10 percent of the original Palestine Mandate, while the Arabs received 90 percent. None of this land had belonged to a "Palestinian" nation or a Palestinian entity. In the previous 400 years there had never been a province of the Turkish empire called "Palestine." The entire region out of which Jordan, Iraq, Lebanon, Syria, Israel, Gaza and the West Bank were created was known as "Ottoman Syria."

In what would prove to be a continuing pattern, the Jews accepted the partition's grossly unequal terms—their portion consisted of three unconnected slivers of land, of which 60 percent was arid desert. The Arabs, who had already received 80 percent of the Mandate land, rejected their additional portion, as they would continue to reject any arrangement that would allow for a Jewish state. Immediately, five Arab nations launched a war against the Jews, who repelled the Arab attacks and established a Jewish state.[25] When the fighting ended, the parts of the partition that had been earmarked for the Arabs—namely, the West Bank and Gaza—were annexed by Jordan and Egypt respectively and disappeared from the map.[26] There was no protest from the Arab world at the disappearance of "Palestine" into Jordan and Egypt—no Palestine Liberation Organization, no complaint to the UN. The reason for the silence was that there was no Palestinian identity at the time, no movement for "self-determination," no "Palestinian" people to make a claim. There were Arabs who lived in the region of the Jordan. But they considered themselves inhabitants of Jordan or the Syrian province of the former Ottoman empire. The disappearance of the West Bank and Gaza was an annexation of Arab land by Arab states.

Arab and Western revisionists have turned this history on its head to portray the Jewish war of survival as a racist, imperialist

---

[25]Martin Gilbert, *The Routledge Atlas of the Arab-Israeli Conflict*, Routledge, 2005, pp. 36–37.

[26]Ibid.

plot to expel "Palestinians" from "Palestine." This is an utter distortion of the historical record. The term "Palestine Mandate" is a European reference to a geographical section of the defeated Turkish empire. The claim that there was a Palestinian nation from which ethnic Palestinians were expelled, and which Israel now "occupies" illegally, is a political lie. In 1967, the Arab states attacked Israel again with the express aim of "pushing the Jews into the sea." Again they were defeated. And once again defeat did not prompt the Arab states to make peace or to abandon their efforts to destroy Israel. At an August 1967 summit in Khartoum, Arab leaders declared that they would accept "no peace, no recognition, and no negotiations" with Israel.

This is the permanent Arab war against Israel. It is a war driven by religious and ethnic hate, which is the only durable cause of the conflict in the Middle East.

It is hardly surprising, given this historical reality, that Israel should regard with skepticism the Arab demands that Israel surrender territory it captured in defending itself against Arab aggression. As Prime Minister Netanyahu has said: "What kind of moral position is it to say that the failed aggressor should be given back all the territory from which he launched his attack?" In fact, of no other nation that has been victimized—and victimized repeatedly—by aggressors is such a concession demanded. Yet Israeli concessions—including an agreement not to build houses for its own people in its own capital—are precisely what the Obama administration is demanding as a precondition of peace. It is ostensibly doing so on the dubious assumption that, if only Israel would make further concessions to the Palestinians, peace would be possible. But this assumption flies in the face of 60 years of continuous Arab aggression, including unrelenting terror attacks against Israeli civilians and explicit commitments to wipe out the Jewish state.

The very idea that Israeli settlements—let alone Jewish houses in Jewish neighborhoods—are an obstacle to peace perpetuates the fictitious claims of the Arab cause. There are a million Arabs settled in Israel, and they enjoy more rights as Israeli citizens than do the Arab citizens of any Arab Muslim state. So why are the settlements of a few hundred thousand Jews on the West Bank a problem? The only possible answer is Jew hatred—the desire to make the West Bank *Judenrein,* and ultimately the 60-year Arab campaign to push the Jews into the sea. The Obama administration's pressure on Israel to give up its settlements—or to concede that its capital is disputed terrain—feeds the inherent racism of the Arab cause and undermines Israel's ability to resist the genocidal campaign against it. Such pressure cannot promote peace negotiations when the other party is openly dedicated to Israel's destruction, and has already shown that it will derail even the most generous offers of peace—as when Arafat rejected the Clinton-Barak 2000 plan. Its immediate consequences are to reinforce Palestinian intransigence, escalate Palestinian demands, incite Palestinian violence, and accelerate the drift toward a Middle East war.

Directly following the Obama administration's attacks on Israel's building project in Jerusalem, the Palestinians invoked Israeli intransigence as a pretext for pulling out of the indirect peace talks that had been taking place. Palestinian president Mahmoud Abbas further went on record as refusing to enter into direct talks with Israel unless it instituted an immediate construction freeze in its own capital city. Palestinians had previously participated in talks without that condition, but, as one observer noted, "How could the Palestinian position be softer on Israel than the American position? Of course the Palestinians would have to hold Israel to the newly raised standards of the Obama administration."[27] In this way did the Obama administration further the efforts of the Arabs to dismantle the Jewish state.

Observers of this ominous development warned that, by attacking Israel over settlements, the administration was

---

[27]Richard Baehr, "The Obama Effect in the Muslim World," *The Jewish Policy Center,* Spring 2010, http://www.jewishpolicycenter.org/1628/obama-effect-in-muslim-world.

encouraging a violent buildup that could eventually erupt into a third *intifada.* A Hebrew-speaking Arab protester interviewed on Israeli radio called for armed resistance against Israel's "assault on Jerusalem," declaring that the time had come for a new *intifada.*[28] The call was taken up by Hamas, which declared a "day of rage" to lash out against Israel. Arab rioters protested in the streets, hurled stones at buses, cars and police, and clashed with Israeli security forces. On Israel's Highway 443, connecting Jerusalem with the city of Modi'in, Israeli Arabs firebombed passing motorists, with one attack wounding a father and his nine-month old infant.[29] Arab parliamentarians in the Israeli Knesset, echoing the Obama administration, further fueled the violence. One of them said, "Anyone who builds settlements in Jerusalem is digging a grave for peace."[30]

Even as the new Obama policies were igniting tinderboxes in the Palestinian territories, their most dangerous effects were being felt in Iran. From the beginning of his presidency, Obama had made "reaching out" to the Iranian police state a major part of his approach to the Middle East. In March 2009, Obama addressed a special Persian New Year message to the Iranian people and the leaders of what he called the "Islamic Republic of Iran," itself an ingratiating reference that served to legitimize the totalitarian rule imposed on the country by the 1979 overthrow of the shah. Doubly shameful were Obama's direct appeals to the *mullahs,* whom he urged to move the "Islamic Republic of Iran to take its rightful place in the community of nations."

---

[28]Daniel Gordis, "Will Barack Obama Ignite the Third Intifada?," *danielgordis.org,* March 26, 2010, http://danielgordis.org/2010/03/26/obama-intifada/.

[29]Tzvi Ben Gedalyahu, "Arab Firebomb Wounds Father and Baby Son on Highway 443," *Israel National News,* March 14, 2010, http://www.israelnationalnews.com/News/News.aspx/136490#.VWYN9JvbJJQ.

[30]Liel Kyzer, Fadi Eyadat and Jack Khoury, "IDF Official: Neither Israel nor PA Wants Violence" *Haaretz,* March 16, 2010, http://www.haaretz.com/print-edition/news/idf-official-neither-israel-nor-pa-wants-violence-1.264816.

At the time, Iran's rulers were engaging in surrogate wars against the United States in Iraq and Afghanistan, supplying al-Qaeda and the Taliban with IEDs, which were the principal cause of the American deaths there. The contrast between Obama's appeasement of this enemy and his aggressive displeasure toward a democratic ally could not have been more striking. It sent a dangerous message to the many other dictatorships and hostile forces in the Middle East.

Obama's apologists insist that his message was no different from those that President Bush had previously delivered on the Persian New Year. But an actual reading of Bush's messages reveals the absurdity of the comparison.[31] Unlike Obama, Bush addressed his words directly to the Iranian people, not to the oppressive Iranian regime, which he condemned for pursuing nuclear weapons and depriving its citizens of the right to "live in a free society." The word freedom appeared three times in one of Bush's messages. It did not appear once in Obama's. Confronting Iran's defiance of the world community, its determination to build nuclear weapons and its brutal suppression of its own people, would have interfered with the overtures Obama was making towards a criminal regime.

In May 2009, Obama sent a personal letter to Iran's "supreme leader," the Ayatollah Khamenei, again disregarding his oppressed subjects. The president's letter appealed for better "co-operation in regional and bilateral relations."[32] Khamenei ignored the letter. Then, in mid-June, he mentioned it scornfully in a sermon in which he inveighed against alleged American interference in Iran's rigged elections that month.[33]

---

[31]"Differing U.S. Presidential Statements for Persian New Year," *Washington Post,* March 21, 2009, http://www.washingtonpost.com/wp-dyn/content/article/2009/03/20/AR2009032003512_pf.html.

[32]"Obama Sent Letter to Khamenei Before the Election, Report Says," *The Guardian,* June 24, 2009, http://www.theguardian.com/world/2009/jun/24/khamenei-obama-letter.

[33]Ibid.

Obama's acquiescence in the Iranian regime's brutal suppression of the opposition during its presidential elections demonstrated how far the White House was willing to compromise its values in the interests of an elusive "dialogue" that it had come to value above all else. As pro-democracy protesters, shouting "Death to the dictator!," were being brutally crushed on the streets of Tehran, the Obama administration maintained a deafening silence. There was no official message of solidarity with the demonstrators, no serious admonition to the regime about the right of free assembly, no support for changing a regime that was killing its own citizens while threatening its neighbors. There was no stern warning to an aggressive power that was brazenly defying the international community in racing to acquire nuclear weapons.

After a week of bloodshed and arrests, the closest the administration would come to an official reproach was when Vice President Biden suggested that there was "some real doubt" about Iran's official elections results—in itself a generous understatement.[34] Prior to the election, the victor had run close to his opponent in the polls but, when the ballots were counted, Ahmadinejad won in a landslide, claiming more votes than any politician in Iran's history. However, so that Iran's thugs would not mistake Biden's remark for a policy statement, the vice president made it clear that neither the fraudulent election results nor the continuing repression would sway the Obama administration from its single-minded wooing of the regime. "We are ready to talk," Biden said. Without conditions.[35]

The Iranian mullahs were in no mood to compromise. And why should they be? A year of defiance had cost them nothing, while gaining them precious time to carry out their designs.

[34]http://www.google.com/hostednews/afp/article/ALeqM5j1SSLTI28ydxcunozvJWLBeNmVoA.

[35]http://www.google.com/hostednews/afp/article/ALeqM5j1SSLTI28ydxcunozvJWLBeNmVoA.

Ahmadinejad responded to Biden's wrist-slap by attacking America as a "crippled creature," even while asserting that the U.S. was still an "oppressive system ruling the world." Spurning Washington's outstretched "hand of friendship," the Iranian president baited Obama with an invitation to take part in a debate about "the injustice done by world arrogance to Muslim nations." Speaking at a staged "victory" rally, Ahmadinejad vowed that he would never negotiate with the United States or any foreign power over his country's nuclear ambitions: "That file is shut, forever."[36]

Although it was not clear when Iran would finally be able to produce enough enriched uranium for an operational nuclear weapon, the U.S. military warned in April 2010 that the time frame could be as short as a year. Besides its illicit work on a nuclear weapon, Iran continued to develop a range of missiles that made it a regional and even a global threat. For instance, an unclassified Defense Department report released in April estimated that by 2015 Iran could have a missile capable of striking the United States. With a nuclear arsenal, Iran at last will have a chance to realize its apocalyptic dream of a holy war that will destroy the two countries it calls the source of evil in the world, "the Great Satan and the Little Satan."

Confronted with fresh evidence of Iran's defiance, the Obama administration did not so much stick to its guns as offer to lay them down. In April, Obama announced that the United States was no longer going to develop new nuclear weapons and would not use nuclear weapons to retaliate against countries that attacked the U.S.—even if they had used biological or chemical weapons.[37] The president's policy of unilateral nuclear disarmament did include an exception for rogue states like Iran; but given the administration's track record of backing down in the face of

---

[36]Amir Taheri, "Iran's Clarifying Election," *The Wall Street Journal,* June 15, 2009, http://www.wsj.com/articles/SB124502114089613711.

[37]David E. Sanger and Peter Baker, "Obama Limits When U.S. Would Use Nuclear Arms," *The New York Times,* April 5, 2010, http://www.nytimes.com/2010/04/06/world/06arms.html?_r=0.

Iranian intransigence, it is difficult to imagine that the warning struck fear in the hearts of thc *mullahs.*

With Obama's charm offensive failing, Washington was left without a strategy, a fact Obama's own secretary of defense conceded. In April, the press leaked the contents of a memorandum written by Defense Secretary Robert Gates to the White House four months earlier. According to press reports, the memorandum conceded that the U.S. possessed no effective policy to stop Iran from building a nuclear bomb.

Obama's multiple overtures, his apologies for America's actions in the past and his deference to her enemies in the present have not made the world a safer place. His attempts to make Israel—America's most loyal ally in the Middle East and the region's only democratic state—the culprit in the dramas engulfing the region have encouraged the *jihadi* cause both at home and abroad. It is hardly coincidental, thercforc, that Obama's tcnurc in office has been accompanied by a rash of terrorist assaults. In September 2009, the FBI foiled a plot by three American al-Qaeda recruits to plant homemade bombs on the busiest subway stops in Manhattan during rush hour. According to Attorney General Eric Holder, the attacks would have been the "most serious" since 9/11. In November, army psychiatrist and *jihadi* Major Nidal Malik Hasan went on a shooting rampage at the army base in Ford Hood, Texas, killing 13 people and wounding 32 others. In December, a 23-year *jihadi* from Nigeria was disarmed by passengers as he tried to blow up Northwest flight 253 over Detroit, using explosives he had snuck aboard the plane in his underwear. In May, a Pakistani-born naturalized American citizen, Faisal Shahzad, almost succeeded in turning New York's Times Square into a fiery inferno when he abandoned an SUV rigged to explode there.[38]

[38]"Did Hard Times Create the Times Square Bomber?," *The Telegraph*, May 8, 2010, http://www.telegraph.co.uk/news/worldnews/northamerica/usa/7696765/Did-hard-times-create-the-Times-Square-bomber.html.

In the midst of these attacks by Islamic fanatics, the Obama administration refuses even to recognize the religious nature of the enemy we face. In testimony before Congress, Attorney General Holder repeatedly refused to make a connection between those terrorist acts and any religious belief, although the perpetrators themselves proclaimed their fealty to Islam and the Koran. On a separate occasion, Obama's deputy national security adviser, John Brennan, explained the administration's political correctness: "Nor do we describe our enemy as 'jihadists' or 'Islamists' because *jihad* is a holy struggle, a legitimate tenet of Islam, meaning to purify oneself or one's community, and there is nothing holy or legitimate or Islamic about murdering innocent men, women and children"[39]—even though many Islamic imams are on record as proclaiming that there is.

Obama insists that the U.S. is not at war with Islam. But it is clear that many Muslims, including the leaders of al-Qaeda, Hezbollah, Hamas and Iran, believe that Islam is at war with the United States and Israel. The name of the ruling party in Gaza, with much innocent blood on its hands, is "Hamas," which stands for "Islamic Resistance Movement." While the Obama administration maintains that Israel's enemies are not engaged in a religious war, the Hamas charter declares in the clearest possible terms that it is engaged in a war mandated by the Prophet Mohammed, whose goal is the destruction of Israel and a genocide of its Jews:

The Islamic Resistance Movement aspires to the realization of Allah's promise, no matter how long that should take. The Prophet, Allah bless him and grant him salvation, has said: "The Day of Judgment will not come until Muslims fight the Jews and kill them. When the Jew hides behind the stones and the trees, the

[39]Jillian Bandes, "Brennan: Jihad Is Legitimate Tenet Of Islam," *Townhall.com,* May 28, 2010, http://townhall.com/tipsheet/jillianbandes/2010/05/28/brennan_jihad_is_legitimate_tenet_of_islam.

stones and trees will say, O Muslim, there is a Jew hiding behind me, come and kill him."[40]

And further: "Israel will exist and will continue to exist until Islam will obliterate it, just as it obliterated others before it."[41]

And: "There is no solution for the Palestine question except through *jihad*."[42]

Because of its diminutive size, Israel is a country with little margin for error. Confronted by 300 million hostile Muslim neighbors, its security depends in no small measure on the perception that it has the inalienable support of the world's lone superpower. It is this perception that has been gravely undermined by the Obama administration, with consequences that are already apparent. It is hardly coincidental, for example, that the United Kingdom chose the precise moment of the row over housing in Jerusalem to expel unnamed Israelis from its territory for an alleged connection to the death of a notorious Hamas arms dealer in Dubai. But it is the regional ramifications of this suddenly weakened U.S.-Israel alliance that are truly worrisome.

It is only because Israel has had an American security umbrella that there has been no conventional war against Israel since 1973. If its enemies perceive Israel to have been cast adrift by America, they will be emboldened to try once more the methods that have failed to destroy Israel in the past. Hezbollah is now operating bases and arms depots on Syrian territory, where it is stockpiling long-range Syrian-supplied Scud missiles capable of striking Israeli cities like Jerusalem and Tel Aviv.[43] Egypt has begun staging war games in the Sinai Peninsula using large numbers of infantry and artillery units as well as

---

[40]"Hamas Charter," *MidEastWeb.org,* August 18, 1988, http://www.mideastweb.org/hamas.htm.

[41]Ibid.

[42]Ibid.

[43]Attila Somfalvi, "Netanyahu: Hezbollah operating Scuds from Syria," *ynetnews.com,* May 29, 2010, http://www.ynetnews.com/articles/0,7340,L-3895828,00.html.

warplanes.[44] While Egypt has justified the maneuvers as essential to maintain the readiness of its armed forces, many observers see them as a dress rehearsal for war.

The shift toward Islamic militancy and war preparations on Obama's watch is even more pronounced in Turkey. Turkey was once a staunch NATO ally, and a friend to Israel; but it has been moving for several years in a radical direction under its Islamist prime minister Recep Tayyip Erdogan. Ignoring this development, Obama chose Turkey as the final stop on his first overseas visit as president, and praised it as a "model for the world." Said Obama: "I'm trying to make a statement about the importance of Turkey, not just to the United States but to the world. I think that where there's the most promise of building stronger U.S.-Turkish relations is, in the recognition that Turkey and the United States can build a model partnership in which a predominantly Christian nation, a predominantly Muslim nation—a Western nation and a nation which straddles two continents—that we can create a model international community that is respectful, that is secure, that is prosperous, that there are not tensions—inevitable tensions between cultures—which I think is extraordinarily important."[45]

At the very moment Obama was expressing this vapid hope, his Turkish host was moving his NATO country closer to the *mullahs* of Iran. While Obama was wooing and being rejected by Iran, the *mullahs* were forming an entente with Turkey that would undermine his efforts to keep them from building a nuclear weapon. Just a year after Obama's visit, the Turkish prime minister met with his opposite number in Brazil to conclude a fuel-swapping deal. The deal effectively allowed Iran to continue enriching uranium for a nuclear weapon. With this newly formed

---

[44] "Egyptian Army Conducts Series of War Games on Sinai Peninsula," Haaretz/AP, February 17, 2009, http://www.haaretz.com/news/egyptian-army-conducts-series-of-war-games-on-sinai-peninsula-1.270380.

[45] "Obama Says U.S., Turkey Can Be Model for World," *CNN*, April 6, 2009, http://edition.cnn.com/2009/POLITICS/04/06/obama.turkey/index.html?iref=nextin.

alliance, the *mullahs* would be able to avoid even the ineffective sanctions that the Obama administration had finally come around to considering.[46]

Turkey's embrace of the Middle East's Islamist axis—Syria, Iran, Lebanon, the West Bank and Gaza—occurred simultaneously with an international conference to review the Nuclear Non-Proliferation Treaty. With the United States standing idly by, the conference ignored the chief proliferator, Iran, while singling out Israel as the principal nuclear threat. These ominous developments were the immediate background to the brazen attempt by Hamas and its new patron, Turkey, to break the arms blockade of Gaza, which was a joint effort by Israel and Egypt to prevent weapons from being smuggled into the terrorist state. The six ships that attempted to run the blockade departed from Istanbul and flew under Turkish flags. The flotilla's political camouflage—it described its mission as "humanitarian"—was provided by a Turkish non-governmental organization associated with the United Nations and known by the acronym "IHH." Posing as a humanitarian aid group, the IHH is a well-documented ally of Hamas and al-Qaeda, and was identified in the trial of the "millennium bomber" as playing a key role in the plot to blow up Los Angeles airport. The real mission of the flotilla—to break the weapons blockade—was made transparent when it refused Israel's offer to unload any humanitarian aid it was carrying at the secure port of Ashdod.

On board one of the vessels, the *Mavi Marmara,* were active Turkish terrorists who had been allowed to board without inspection in Istanbul and had vowed on departure to become *jihadi* martyrs.[47] The terrorists armed themselves with steel pipes and

---

[46]"Brazil's Foreign Minister Says Nation Will Oppose, but Respect, Any New Iran Sanctions," *Fox News/AP,* June 1, 2010, http://www.foxnews.com/world/2010/06/01/brazils-foreign-minister-says-nation-oppose-respect-new-iran-sanctions/.

[47]"IDF Names Five Terrorists on Mavi Marmara," *Israel Matzav,* June 7, 2010, http://israelmatzav.blogspot.com/2010/06/idf-names-five-terrorists-on-mavi.html.

knives, and were prepared to attack any Israeli soldiers who boarded the vessel to enforce the blockade. A principal organizer of the operation was the Free Gaza Movement, which had attempted to break the blockade the previous June. Among its leaders were two close friends and political allies of President Obama's: former Weather Underground terrorists William Ayers and Bernardine Dohrn, who paid a visit to the leader of Hamas after the effort failed.[48] Also among its company were major Obama donor and supporter Jodie Evans and British MP George Galloway, Saddam Hussein supporter and founder of the pro-Hamas group *Viva Palestine*—along with many other pro-Hamas activists.[49]

Prior to the incident, the Obama White House had exerted serious pressure on Israel to exercise maximum restraint. Consequently, Israeli authorities did not equip the commandos who boarded the ship with riot gear and tear gas, and their sidearms were holstered.[50] They descended from a helicopter armed with paintball guns, which proved ineffective against the steel bars and knives. They were quickly overwhelmed by what the media would insist on describing as "peace" activists, who stabbed them, beat them with the steel pipes, threw one of them off the deck and stole two firearms which they began shooting until the other soldiers were able to draw their sidearms and fire back. Nine of the belligerents aboard were killed and others wounded; also wounded were six Israeli soldiers, two of whom were in critical condition.[51]

---

[48]"Obama Administration Sabotaging Israel's Defense," *Focus on Jerusalem*, June 6, 2010, http://focusonjerusalem.com/newsroom119 html.

[49]"Iran Offers Escort to Next Gaza Blockade Convoy," *Focus on Jerusalem*, June 6, 2010, http://focusonjerusalem.com/newsroom119.html.

[50]"Israel Says Commandos Carried Paintball Guns" *ABC News*, June 1, 2010, http://www.abc.net.au/news/2010-06-01/israel-says-commandos-carried-paintball-guns/849854.

[51]Yaakov Katz, "Clashes Between Israeli Soldiers and Passengers on Board the Mavi Marmara," *aipnews.com*, June 4, 2010, http://www.aipnews.com/talk/forums/thread-view.asp?tid=14674&posts=2.

An attempt to run a wartime blockade would in other circumstances have resulted in a full armed naval assault. Israel's restraint was rewarded by international media and governments alike describing the confrontation as a brutal attempt to block a humanitarian aid effort. *Jihadis* immediately seized on the event to further their campaign to de-legitimize the Jewish state. This effort was led by Turkey, the very country behind the provocation and thus responsible for the deaths.

Prime Minister Erdogan denounced Israel as guilty of "state terrorism" and called the efforts of the Israelis to defend themselves a "bloody massacre." He then claimed: "The heart of humanity has taken one of the heaviest wounds in history."[42] This was from a man who the previous year had defended Sudanese president Omar al-Bashir when he was indicted by the International Criminal Court for killing half a million Sudanese Christians and non-Arab Muslims.

Erdogan called for a *jihad* against Israel, and threatened that the Turkish navy would escort the next attempt to run the blockade. This threat was seconded by Iran, which vowed to send two "humanitarian aid" ships under escort by the Iranian navy. If carried out, this threat would be, in effect, a declaration of war.[53]

In Hezbollah-controlled Lebanon, a leader of the terrorist organization Fatah, Mounir al-Makdah, said: "The freedom flotilla brings a message of the beginning of the end of Israel." He announced plans for a mass invasion on Israel's northern border, using civilians as human shields. "It could be that they will just break through the border, with their children and their elderly," he explained. "What will Israel be able to do? Even if they kill all

[52]Yitzhak Benhorin, "*The Washington Post:* Investigate Erdogan's Ties with IHH," *ynetnews.com,* June 6, 2010, http://www.ynetnews.com/articles/0,7340,L-3899490,00.html.

[53]Charles Hawley, "Bound for Gaza: German-Jewish Boat to Challenge Israeli Blockade," *Spiegel Online,* June 9, 2010, http://ht.ly/1WdvU.

those who take part in the march, the number of remaining Palestinians will still be more than all the Jews in the world."[54]

Far from voicing alarm at the *jihadi* threats or disapproval of Turkey's aggression, the international community expressed its sympathy for the Islamist runners of the arms blockade. France's president Nicolas Sarkozy deplored Israel's "disproportionate use of force," while Italy's undersecretary of state for foreign affairs, Stefania Craxi, joined the Turks in condemning what she called "the massacre of Gaza." UN secretary general Ban Ki-moon declared himself "shocked" at Israel's actions.[55]

President Obama also failed to condemn Turkey's role in the incident, and insisted instead that Israel allow an international body to investigate its actions. Obama then met with Mahmoud Abbas, to promise $400 million in economic aid to the West Bank and to Gaza—in other words, to shore up the terrorist state and its ruling terrorist party. At the same time, senior officials of the Obama administration began telling foreign governments that the United States would support a UN resolution calling for a commission to investigate Israel's—but not Turkey's or Hamas's—role in the incident.[56]

This paved the way for a reprise of the Goldstone report, which had relied on Hamas sources to condemn Israel's defensive war in Gaza the previous year. It was essentially a demand that Israel's right to self-defense be subject to international approval—some-

---

[54]Hillel Fendel, "Lebanese Threaten Mass March on Israeli Border," *Israel National News,* June 10, 2010, http://www.israelnationalnews.com/News/News.aspx/137992#.VWY1NJvbJJQ.

[55]Daniel Henninger, "Beating Up on Israel," *The Wall Street Journal,* June 3, 2010, http://www.wsj.com/articles/SB10001424052748703561604575282740991794622.

[56]William Kristol, "Obama Administration to Support Anti-Israel Resolution at UN Next Week," *The Weekly Standard,* June 11, 2010, http://www.weeklystandard.com/blogs/sources-obama-administration-support-anti-israel-resolution-un-next-week.

thing no sovereign country could be expected to tolerate.[57] At the same time, the Obama administration was leaning on Israel to end its naval blockade in favor of some "new approach," such as an *international* naval force.[58] This was an even more direct assault on Israel's right to self-defense. Not only did it challenge Israel's fully justified efforts to keep arms and bomb-making materials out of the hands of the Hamas terrorists; it tried to shift responsibility for Israel's security to the same international community that was now savaging the Jewish state for its efforts to stop the flow of arms into the hands of Hamas.

During the year and a half Obama has been in office, he has indeed brought change to America and to the world. He has transformed a nation that had been the world's bulwark of democracy and freedom into an enabler of the very forces that are intent on destroying them. He has helped to isolate America's only ally in the Middle East, its sole democracy and most vulnerable people. And he has brought measurably closer to its nightmare fruition the impending war of annihilation against "crusaders" and Jews that *jihadis* have promised.

---

[57]Anne Bayefsky, "U.S. Interferes With Israel's Gaza Blockade," *Forbes*, June 3, 2010, http://www.forbes.com/2010/06/03/israel-gaza-blockade-obama-opinions-contributors-anne-bayefsky.html.

[58]Isabel Kershner, "Israel Signals New Flexibility on Gaza Shipments," *The New York Times*, June 3, 2010, http://www.nytimes.com/2010/06/04/world/middleeast/04flotilla.html?pagewanted=1&hp.

7

From Shadow Party to Shadow Government

(with John Perazzo)

A watershed moment in George Soros's effort to capture control of the Democratic Party and change the course of American politics came in August 2008 at the party's presidential nominating convention in Denver, Colorado. One of a series of panel discussions staged for the media VIPs and money-men, all of them euphoric at the growing prospect of Barack Obama's victory in the upcoming elections, featured a man named Rob Stein.[1] An aide to Secretary of Commerce Ron Brown during the Clinton administration, Stein was not well known to the public but was locally famous among "progressive" Democrats as a key operative in the network of institutions designed by Soros in an effort to create what Stein himself only half-jokingly referred to as a "vast left-wing conspiracy."

The subject of the panel discussion Stein staged for party movers and shakers in 2008 was "The Colorado Miracle."[2] Everyone in the room knew that the phrase referred to a stunning political development generated virtually overnight by a chain of

---

Originally published on July 8, 2011. Http://www.frontpagemag.com/2011/sara- dogan/freedom-center-re-releases-its-pocket-best- sellers-on-kindle/; The authors wish to thank Adam Schrager and Rob Witwer, authors of *The Blueprint: How the Democrats Won Colorado,* for their insights into *"the Colorado Miracle."*

[1]Rob Stein, http://www.discoverthenetworks.org/individualProfile.asp?indid=2388.

[2]"Excerpt from 'The Blueprint: How the Democrats Won Colorado and Why Republicans Everywhere Should Care'," Fulcrum, 2010, *The Blueprint,* http://blueprintbook.net/?page_id=7.

Soros-funded state organizations. The lineup of state officeholders told the tale. In October 2004, Republicans held both U.S. Senate seats, five of seven congressional seats, the governorship, the secretary of state's office and both houses of the legislature. When the 2008 election was done, the exact opposite would be true, and Colorado would have been changed from a red state to a blue one in one brief election cycle.[3]

Some political commentators would see this transformation as an expression of Western independence and contrarianism or of changing demographics, which had given the state a growing Hispanic population. These and other factors had played a role. But as Stein pointed out in his discussion of the "miracle" just nearing its apotheosis, Colorado had been given a political makeover primarily through a relentless political ground war waged by the Colorado Democracy Alliance, an organization created out of Stein's vision and Soros's money.[4] The Colorado Democracy Alliance had created, in record time, a progressive political infrastructure with one purpose: taking over Colorado politics from the precinct to the statehouse. It had accomplished this by putting together a relentless political blitzkrieg.[5]

Best of all, Stein assured his audience, what had happened in Colorado was an *exportable model* that could be replicated in dozens of other states across the country. The election of Barack Obama might be the immediate goal before them, Stein concluded, but the long-term objective was to take control of the American political system. "The reason we're doing what we're doing..." he said, "and the way we get progressive change is to control government."[6]

---

[3]Ibid.

[4]Democracy Alliance, http://www.discoverthenetworks.org/groupProfile.asp?grpid=7151.

[5]Matthew Vadum, "The Evolving Agenda of George Soros's Democracy Alliance," *Capital Research Center*, September 8, 2008, http://capitalresearch.org/2008/09/the-evolving-agenda-of-george-soross-democracy-alliance/.

[6]Ibid.

Rob Stein was speaking for his patron as well as for himself. Over a twenty-year period, George Soros has been able to exercise unparalleled influence through the network of left-wing political organizations he built—a network so successful that it is a power unto itself and has earned itself a title: the Shadow Party.[7] It is a network that exists in a political penumbra, although it calls for transparency; that works at the edges of the electoral system, although affecting electoral outcomes is its *raison d'être.* Soros's agenda is hidden and his goals are not made public because they are based on a radical vision of social change that most Americans not only reject but fear. But this agenda involving a radical change of American institutions has subverted and taken over the Democratic Party. The Soros agenda, in fact, has become the Obama agenda.

Born in Hungary in 1930 into a deracinated Jewish family, George Soros survived World War II by working as an assistant to an official in the fascist government whose job was to confiscate the property of Jews headed to the gas chambers.[8] After the war, Soros relocated to England, where he attended the London School of Economics and was influenced by one-worldism and the prospect of perfecting humanity through social engineering.[9] But at this point in his life his ideas were subordinate to the desire to make money. After graduating in 1952, Soros joined the London brokerage firm Singer and Friedlander.[10] Four years later, he relocated to New York

---

[7]Shadow Party, http://www.discoverthenetworks.org/viewSubCategory.asp?id=842.

[8]Peter Schweizer, *Do As I Say (Not As I Do): Profiles in Liberal Hypocrisy,* Anchor, 2006, p. 157; Chuck Morse, "George Soros and His Quislings," *World Net Daily,* December 7, 2010, http://www.wnd.com/2010/12/236665/.

[9]"The Official Resource for Information on George Soros," *GeorgeSoros.com,* http://www.georgesoros.com/faqs/entry/georgesoros officialbiography.

[10]David Litterick, "Billionaire Who Broke the Bank of England," *The Telegraph,* September 13, 2002, http://www.telegraph.co.uk/finance/2773265/Billionaire-who-broke-the-Bank-of-England.html.

and eventually found work as a portfolio manager at the firm's investment bank. He brought continental anti-bourgeois and anti-American attitudes with him and later admitted that he only wanted to stay in the U.S. long enough to make his fortune.[11] But business was too good and he became a citizen.

In 1973 Soros set up a private partnership called the Soros Fund, renamed The Quantum Fund in 1979.[12] Its value grew to $381 million by 1980, and more than $1 billion by 1985.[13] As he later said, "Having made it, I could indulge my social concerns."[14] The $3 million he invested in these concerns in 1987 grew to $300 million a year by 1992.[15] During this period, Soros established a series of foundations in Central Asia and Eastern Europe, where projects he had funded hastened the fall of communist regimes and also, as he freely admitted, opened new money-making opportunities for him with the state industries and properties up for grabs.[16] In 1993 Soros established the flagship of his foundation network—the New York City-based Open Society Institute (OSI)—which would support a variety of radical American groups and causes over the next decade, ranging from the legalization of drugs and the promotion of open borders to the creation of a left-wing judiciary—causes that bore his eccentric stamp but also resonated with a growing segment of the Democratic Party.[17]

---

[11]Michael T. Kaufman, *Soros: The Life And Times Of A Messianic Billionaire,* Knopf, 2002, p. 83.

[12]"Soros Fund Management LLC History," (Source: *International Directory of Company Histories,* Vol. 28, St. James Press, 1999), http://www.fundinguniverse.com/company-histories/soros-fund-management-llc-history/.

[13]Peter Schweizer, op. cit., p. 157.

[14]"Rich Man, Wise Man ...," *The Guardian,* March 9, 2002, http://www.theguardian.com/business/2002/mar/10/theobserver.observerbusiness10.

[15]George Soros, *The Bubble of American Supremacy,* Public Affairs, 2003, p. 136.

[16]"Open Society Foundations," http://www.opensocietyfoundations.org/about.

[17]Guide to the George Soros Network, http://www.discoverthenetworks.org/viewSubCategory.asp?id=589.

By the early 1990s, Soros had become close to Bill and Hillary Clinton; "I do now have great access in [the Clinton] administration," he boasted in 1995. "There is no question about this. We actually work together as a team."[18] One point of close collaboration between the Clintons and Soros was health care. Soros had his own reform, promoted by the Open Society Institute, that he saw as compatible with the initiatives which became known as HillaryCare. He called it, with characteristic bluntness, The Project on Death in America.[19] Its rationale was compassionate: to embed hospices and "palliative" care in U.S. health policy. But its basic objective was more pragmatic: rationing care to terminal and seriously ill patients for whom medical attention offered little payoff and who were thus a burden on the system. It was the direct forerunner of the "death panels" of Obamacare that drew fire from the political right in the next decade.

Over a ten-year period, the Open Society Institute would sink $200 million into The Project on Death in America.[20] But Soros was less concerned by the fact that his initiative didn't immediately pay off than he was by the way such socially progressive reforms were defeated in America by unruly free speech. The fate of HillaryCare provided him with an epiphany of how the political system had to be changed if progressive ideas were to triumph.[21]

The Clintons' proposal to nationalize the health care system had been undone in large part by a television ad campaign featuring "Harry and Louise," actors playing a typical American couple voicing their concerns in a series of television spots about the implications of a government takeover of medicine. The campaign

---

[18]Interview with George Soros, The Charlie Rose Show, *PBS*, November 30, 1995, https://www.youtube.com/watch?v=qgSDaTpHkAo.

[19]"Project on Death in America," *Open Society Institute*, January 2001—December 2003, Published 2004, http://www.opensocietyfoundations.org/sites/default/files/a_complete_7.pdf.

[20]Ibid.

[21]David Horowitz and Richard Poe, *The Shadow Party*, op. cit., pp. 131–136.

had cost $14 million, a small sum given what it achieved—undoing the most important initiative of the new administration.[22] The lesson Soros took away from the experience was that he had been putting the cart before the horse. Before pumping money into reforms, he had to clear the field of the unregulated political speech that would always stand in the way of the kinds of progressive (i.e., socialist) solutions to social problems he regarded as critical for the future of America and the world.

There was an answer at hand: campaign finance reform. It had been wafting through American politics with decreasing urgency since Watergate, but was still, many years later, a reform without a constituency. Working with others interested in this issue, Soros would use the institutional network he was beginning to build to create the illusion of a mass movement, so that members of Congress would feel that everywhere they looked—academic institutions, the business community, religious groups—there was a clamor for campaign finance reform.[23]

Over the next few years, Soros would give $12.6 million to the cause of campaign finance reform through the Open Society Institute and push other interested philanthropies, the Pew Charitable Trust chief among them, to accelerate their commitment to this crusade.[24] The juggernaut he had helped form would give large grants to media outlets such as National Public Radio to publicize the cause, and to institutions such as New York University's

---

[22]Natasha Singer, "Harry and Louise Return, with a New Message," *The New York Times,* July 16, 2009, http://www.nytimes.com/2009/07/17/business/media/17adco.html?_r=0.

[23]Richard Poe, "Pewgate: The Battle of the Blogosphere," *RichardPoe.com,* March 25, 2005, http://www.richardpoe.com/2005/ 03/25/pewgate-the-battle-of-the-blogosphere/.

[24]Ryan Sager, "Buying 'Reform': Media Missed Millionaires' Scam," *New York Post,* March 17, 2005, http://archive.frontpagemag.com/readArticle.aspx?ARTID=8649.

Brennan Center to do the legal research, bogus as it later proved to be, that sought to justify the regulation of political speech.[25]

All this paid off in 2002 with the McCain-Feingold Act, which proposed to clean up politics by regulating the kinds and amounts of donations candidates could accept. (Soros had contributed to McCain as well.) The legislation banned "soft" money (unregulated individual contributions) and allowed only limited "hard" money (contributions to political action committees).[26] Soros saw immediately that the main effect of the new law would be twofold: to curb the kind of TV advertising that had killed HillaryCare; and ultimately to limit the influence of the two political parties, which depended on soft money as their basic source of fuel. This would provide the opening for him to step in with his well-funded network and take control of the Democrats' political campaigns.

That goal would be accomplished by funneling money into politics through so-called "527" organizations which would perform the roles—political advertising, get-out-the-vote operations—previously under the control of the Democratic Party, which now lacked the cash to fuel them.[27] (The "527" groups are named for the section of the IRS code allowing them to register with the Federal Election Commission.) The McCain-Feingold law had effectively de-funded both major parties, allowing Soros to step into the breach with a "shadow party" composed of 527 funding entities, radical get-out-the-vote organizations like ACORN, and public-sector unions to pursue Soros's own political agenda.[28]

---

[25]David Tell, "An Appearance of Corruption: The Bogus Research Undergirding Campaign Finance Reform," *The Weekly Standard,* May 26, 2003, Vol. 8, Issue 36, http://www.citizen.org/congress/article_redirect.cfm?ID=9776.

[26]"Campaign Finance Law Quick Reference for Reporters," *Federal Election Commission,* http://www.fec.gov/press/bkgnd/bcra_overview. shtml.

[27]"Section 527" Committees, http://www.discoverthenetworks.org/viewSubCategory.asp?id=813.

[28]Richard Poe, "The Shadow Party: History, Goals, and Activities," *DiscoverTheNetworks,* 2004, http://www.discoverthenetworks.org/Articles/theshadowpartypoe2004.html.

The national reaction to the events of September 11, 2001 convinced Soros that he needed put his plan into effect immediately. He viewed the terrorist attacks as confirmation that what he called "American supremacy" was the number one problem facing the world.[29] Soros detested what he viewed as the arrogance the president displayed when he publicly branded U.S. enemies as "evil"; when the president unapologetically expressed his faith in American exceptionalism; and when he refused to consider the possibility that the terrorists had real grievances and that American imperialism was ultimately responsible for the attacks. Soros maintained that the proper long-term response to 9/11 would be for America to launch a global war on poverty by sending massive amounts of aid to impoverished regions around the world where terrorism flourished. Terrorism, Soros maintained, was the result of a "growing [income] inequality between rich and poor, both within countries and among countries."[30]

Before 9/11 Soros saw his philanthropy as a way of incrementally changing health care, criminal sentencing, drug laws and other social issues he regarded as important. The direction in which he wanted to steer the United States was clear in the radical agendas of the groups that he had been funding for a decade through his Open Society Institute. Those agendas could essentially be distilled down to three overriding themes: the diminution of American power, the subjugation of American sovereignty in favor of one world government, and the implementation of a socialist redistribution of wealth—both within the U.S. and across national borders. But now he decided that the world was immediately endangered by American dominance and that it was essential to change the country fundamentally, overnight as it were rather than over time.

---

[29]George Soros, *The Bubble of American Supremacy: The Costs of Bush's War in Iraq,* Public Affairs, 2003, p. 74; Joy Tiz, "Who's Afraid of the Big Bad Soros," *Canada Free Press,* February 3, 2010, http://canadafreepress.com/index.php/article/19648.

[30]Ibid., p. 94.

Soros believed that the 2004 elections offered the best opportunity to "deflate the bubble of American supremacy."[31] But to accomplish this would require a political apparatus whose like had never been seen in the United States; a network that could not only acquire profound and lasting influence but would do so in such a stealthy manner that Americans would not know what was happening.

There was no official birth announcement when the Shadow Party was launched on July 17, 2003 at El Mirador, George Soros's Southampton, Long Island estate. But it was the most significant development in American politics in decades. At this meeting of political strategists, wealthy donors, left-wing labor leaders and progressive activists, Soros laid out his plan to defeat George Bush in the 2004 presidential election. Present were figures from the Clinton years, such as former Secretary of State Madeline Albright and former White House chief of staff John Podesta; alongside them were "progressive" activists such as Ellen Malcolm, founder and president of EMILY's List, and Carl Pope, executive director of the Sierra Club; along with large donors such as Taco Bell heir Rob McKay, RealNetworks CEO Rob Glaser and Progressive Insurance mogul Peter B. Lewis.[32]

The political operatives Soros had hired to staff the effort believed that Bush could be beaten in 2004 if there were a massive voter turnout of Democrat voters in swing states.[33] Soros pledged the $10 million required to get a new organization started. It was decided to call it America Coming Together. A grass-roots activist group designed to coordinate the Shadow Party's massive get-out-the-vote drive, ACT would raise the money that would allow it to dispatch tens of thousands of volunteers to knock on doors and work phone banks, parlaying the work of left-wing unions,

---

[31]George Soros, "The Bubble of American Supremacy," op. cit., p. 74.

[32]Richard Poe, "Part 1: The Shadow Party," *RichardPoe.com*, October 6, 2005, http://www.richardpoe.com/2005/10/06/part-1-the-shadow-party/.

[33]Ibid.

environmentalists, abortion-rights activists and others into an unprecedented political offensive.

When Soros made his commitment, according to reports that later filtered out of the Southampton meeting, Peter Lewis matched his $10 million, Rob Glaser anteed up $2 million, and Rob McKay put in $1 million.[34] Soon after this summit meeting, Soros also put up $3 million for John Podesta's new think-tank, the Center for American Progress, which would function as the brain trust of the network of institutions that would comprise the Shadow Party.[35] And finally Soros summoned California software developer Wes Boyd for a meeting at his New York office.

In addition to having made a fortune in Silicon Valley, Boyd was also creator of the radical website MoveOn.org, which he had founded during the Clinton impeachment trial to get the nation to "move on" to "more important issues" and since then had made an internet cash cow for left-wing Democrat candidates.[36] Soros offered Boyd a deal. He and Peter Lewis would match up to $5 million for any new money Boyd raised to expand MoveOn's reach for 2004.[37] After all these negotiations were completed, Soros agreed to an interview with *The Washington Post.* "America under Bush is a danger to the world," he declared. "Toppling Bush is the central focus of my life.... And I'm willing to put my money where my mouth is."[38]

While Soros's investment was substantial, it was primarily a catalyst inspiring other left-wing donors to take the new network seriously. As journalist Byron York observed, "After Soros signed

---

[34]Ibid.

[35]Laura Blumenfeld, "Soros's Deep Pockets vs. Bush," *The Washington Post,* November 11, 2003, http://www.axisoflogic.com/artman/publish/Article_3223.shtml; Center For American Progress, http://www.discoverthenetworks.org/groupProfile.asp?grpid=6709.

[36]MoveOn, http://www.discoverthenetworks.org/groupProfile.asp?grpid=6201.

[37]Richard Poe, "Part 1: The Shadow Party," op. cit.

[38]Laura Blumenfeld, "Soros's Deep Pockets vs. Bush," op. cit.

on, contributions started pouring in."[39] America Coming Together and the Media Fund, the organization designed to fight the television "air war" in the coming election, alone took in some $200 million after Soros pledged his $20 million. This type of concentrated money and focused activity was unprecedented in American politics.[40]

By early 2004, scarcely six months after the meeting at the Soros estate, the Shadow Party had taken shape. Its infrastructure was comprised of seven non-profits. In addition to America Coming Together, MoveOn.org, and Podesta's Center for American Progress, the network included America Votes, the Media Fund, Joint Victory Campaign 2004 and the Thunder Road Group. Ostensibly "independent" from each other, these organizations would work synchronously to defeat Bush and implant a progressive agenda in the Democratic Party.

The Shadow Party was the complete package. In the Center for American Progress it had a think tank to explore its important causes, especially what Soros saw as the increasing power of conservatives. The CAP immediately launched Media Matters as an attack site to smear and discredit members of the conservative media, especially those in talk radio and cable news.[41] America Votes, referred to by one of its staffers as a "monster coalition," was designed to coordinate the efforts of all the left-wing groups working at the grassroots to defeat Bush—from ACORN to Planned Parenthood Action Fund, from the Sierra Club to the American Federation of Teachers and the Service Employees International Union. It would manage the "ground war" against Bush, fine-tuning the details down to the precinct level.

The Joint Victory Campaign 2004, formed by onetime Clinton operative Harold Ickes, Jr., was the fundraising entity for the

---

[39]Byron York, *The Vast Left Wing Conspiracy,* Crown Forum, 2005, pp. 86–87.

[40]Ibid.

[41]Media Matter For America, http://www.discoverthenetworks.org/groupProfile.asp?grpid=7150.

Shadow Party.[42] It would ultimately channel more than $53 million into the Shadow Party network, $19.4 million of it to America Coming Together, which focused on high-pressure tactics to register voters and get them to the polls, and another $38.4 million to the Media Fund, also created by Ickes, which would oversee the television attack ads on Bush in the battleground states.[43] Eventually the Media Fund would outspend the Democratic National Committee and shape the political message of the Kerry-Edwards presidential campaign. The Thunder Road Group was the nerve center of the Shadow Party and its unofficial headquarters, coordinating strategy for the Media Fund, America Coming Together, and America Votes through strategic planning, polling, and opposition research.

In addition to its seven core members, the Shadow Party also sheltered in its penumbra at least another 30 well-established left-wing activist groups and labor unions that participated in the America Votes Coalition. Among the better-known of these were ACORN; the AFL-CIO; the American Federation of Teachers; the Association of Trial Lawyers of America; the Defenders of Wildlife Action Fund; EMILY's List; the Human Rights Campaign; the League of Conservation Voters; the NAACP; NARAL Pro-Choice America; the National Education Association; People for the American Way; Planned Parenthood; the Service Employees International Union; and the Sierra Club.[44]

New Mexico's then-governor, Democrat Bill Richardson, observed that these groups were "crucial" to the anti-Bush effort. Because of campaign-finance reform law embodied in McCain-Feingold, Richardson observed, the organizations of the Shadow Party had become "the replacement for the national Democratic

---

[42]Harold Ickes, http://www.discoverthenetworks.org/individualProfile.asp?indid=1624.

[43]David Horowitz and Richard Poe, *The Shadow Party,* op. cit., pp. 199–200.

[44]America Votes, http://www.discoverthenetworks.org/groupProfile.asp?grpid=6527.

Party."[45] And no donor was more heavily invested in these organizations—or in defeating President Bush—than Soros, who contributed $27,080,105 of his personal funds during the 2004 election cycle.[46] Campaign finance reform had led to the biggest infusion of money into politics in American history, and the money was directed by Soros.

In November 2004, the Shadow Party came within a few thousand votes in Ohio of pulling off a victory in the national election. But even in defeat its alteration of the American political landscape was profound. By pushing campaign finance reform, Soros had cut off the Democrats' soft money supply. By forming the Shadow Party, he had provided the Democrats with an alternative source of funding—one which he, and the institutions he had created, controlled. He was in a position to define the agenda of the party, and also to purge it of the small minority of remaining moderates who had survived the McGovern coup of 1972, and to plan for the next election to determine the American future.

As Soros wondered what his next step should be after Bush's reelection, the answer came to him—somewhat unexpectedly—from Democratic political operative Rob Stein, who would play a central role in the "Colorado Miracle," one of the Shadow Party's greatest triumphs and an exhibit piece for its national plan. For the previous two years, Stein had been working in a universe that paralleled the one Soros had created for the 2004 election. Lamenting that he felt as though he was "living in a one-party country" after Republicans had gained eight House seats and two Senate seats in the 2002 midterm elections, Stein had studied the conservative movement to determine why it was winning the political battle.[47]

---

[45]Jeffrey H. Birnbaum, "The New Soft Money," *Fortune,* Vol. 148, Issue 10, November 10, 2003.

[46]Byron York, *The Vast Left Wing Conspiracy,* op. cit., p. 8.

[47]Amanda Carpenter, "New Liberal Alliance Hopes to Replicate Conservatives' Success," *Human Events,* August 26, 2005, http://humanevents.com/2005/08/26/new-liberal-alliance-hopes-to-replicate-conservatives-success/.

After a year of analysis, he concluded that a few influential, wealthy family foundations on the right—notably Scaife, Bradley, Olin, and Coors—had, by creating think tanks such as the Heritage Foundation and American Enterprise Institute and by subsidizing the work of certain intellectuals (such as Charles Murray, whose writings had touched off the movement to end welfare), managed to shape the public debate to a extent that was disproportionate to their relatively modest (and uncoordinated) investment.

Stein put his analysis into a comprehensive PowerPoint presentation titled "The Conservative Message Machine Money Matrix" which mapped out, in painstaking if inflated detail, the conservative movement's networking strategies and funding sources.[48] He showed this presentation—mostly in private meetings—to political leaders, activists, and prospective big-money donors of the left. He hoped to inspire them to join his crusade to build a new organization that would act as a financial clearinghouse dedicated to offsetting the efforts of conservative funders and injecting new life into the progressive movement.

Stein hit pay dirt when he showed made his presentation to Soros early in 2005. After seeing the presentation and talking to Stein, the billionaire staged another summit meeting that April. The venue was in Phoenix, Arizona, but otherwise it resembled the elite get-together a year and a half earlier at Soros's Southampton estate. This time, Soros brought together 70 carefully vetted, likeminded wealthy activists who agreed that conservative politics represented "a fundamental threat to the American way of life" and were ready to do something about it.[49] Thus was born the Democracy Alliance (DA).

---

[48]Ibid.

[49]"Fundraiser McAuliffe Fills His War Chest," *The Washington Times,* March 15, 2009, http://www.washingtontimes.com/news/2009/mar/15/fundraiser-seeks-cash-for-his-own-war-chest/; Matthew Vadum, "Soros Disses Obama At Democracy Alliance Meeting," *Capital Research Center,* November 21, 2010, http://capitalresearch.org/2010/11/soros-disses-obama-at-democracy-alliance-meeting/.

This would be the most exclusive of all the Shadow Party institutions. "Partners" in the Alliance, recruited on an invitation-only basis, would pay an initial $25,000 fee, and $30,000 in yearly dues thereafter. They were also required to donate at least $200,000 annually to groups the Alliance endorsed. Donors were to "pour" these requisite donations into one or more of what Rob Stein referred to as DA's "four buckets": ideas, media, leadership training, and civic engagement. The money was then to be apportioned to approved left-wing groups in each of these categories.[50] Almost pathologically secretive about its membership, the Democracy Alliance is thought to consist of at least 100 donor-partners. The Capital Research Center has managed to compile the names of some of the more significant current and former DA partners, most having ties to Soros that extend beyond their shared membership in the Democracy Alliance.[51] Among them are Peter Lewis, Rob Glaser and Rob McKay, early backers of America Coming Together; Tim Gill, a major funder of gay-rights groups such as the Gay, Lesbian, and Straight Education Network, also supported by Soros; television producer Norman Lear, founder of People for the American Way; and Tides Foundation founder and CEO Drummond Pike.

No grants were pledged at the Democracy Alliance's April 2005 gathering in Phoenix, but at an Atlanta meeting three months later, DA partners pledged $39 million—about a third of which came from George Soros and Peter Lewis.[52] Because the Alliance has largely refrained from providing information about its getting or giving, only a small percentage of its grantees are known to the public. Thus it is impossible to determine precisely how much

[50]Democracy Alliance Membership, http://www.democracyalliance.org/membership%20; Matthew Vadum, op. cit.

[51]Matthew Vadum and James Dellinger, "The Democracy Alliance Does America: The Soros-Founded Plutocrats' Club Forms State Chapters," *Capital Research Center*, December 2008, http://capitalresearch.org/wp-content/uploads/2013/07/FW1208.pdf; Matthew Vadum, op. cit.

[52]Ibid.

money DA has disbursed since its founding. Most estimates, though, place the figure at more than $100 million. Partner Simon Rosenberg, founder of the New Democrat Network, claimed in August 2008 that DA had already "channeled hundreds of millions of dollars into progressive organizations."[53]

The recipients include organizations such as ACORN and Air America, the ill-fated effort to create a left-wing version of talk radio, along with Shadow Party organizations such as Center for American Progress, America Votes, and Media Matters. In the three years following its founding, the Democracy Alliance would establish subchapters in all 50 states. But its most successful effort was in Colorado, where the Colorado Democracy Alliance funded such varied enterprises as liberal think tanks, media "watchdog" groups, ethics groups that bring forth so-called public-interest litigation, voter-mobilization groups, media outlets that attack conservatives, and liberal leadership-training centers. The result was the "Colorado Miracle," which achieved the political equivalent of a sex-change operation in turning a red state blue.

Just two months after the Democratic Party had won control of both houses of Congress in the November 2006 elections, George Soros and then-SEIU president Andrew Stern created Working For Us (WFU), a pro-Democrat PAC. This group does not look favorably upon Democratic centrists. Rather, it aims "to elect lawmakers who support a progressive political agenda"—code for the political left.[54] WFU publishes the names of what it calls the "Top Offenders" among congressional Democrats who fail to support such leftist priorities as "living wage" legislation (a socialist program to raise the minimum wage to potentially unlimited levels), the proliferation of public-sector labor unions, and a single-payer

---

[53]Ibid.; Matthew Vadum and James Dellinger, op. cit.

[54]Working For Us, http://www.discoverthenetworks.org/groupProfile.asp?grpid=7342.

healthcare system which would exert government control over the health of all Americans.

Targeting congressional Democrats whose voting records "are more conservative than their districts," WFU warns that "no bad vote will be overlooked or unpunished."[55] In an effort to promote large-scale income redistribution by means of tax hikes for higher earners, WFU advocates policies that would narrow the economic gulf between the rich and poor. The group's executive director is Steven Rosenthal, a longtime Democratic operative with close ties to the Clinton administration and a co-founder of Soros's America Coming Together. According to Rosenthal, WFU "will encourage Democrats to act like Democrats—and if they don't—they better get out of the way."[56]

What had taken place in Colorado was like a laboratory experiment for the Shadow Party, providing the model for similar coups it plans to stage is other "battleground" states that have experienced similar demographic changes and "cultural revolutions." As early as August 2005, when the Democracy Alliance was just getting off the ground, Soros's Open Society Institute designed a project called the Progressive Legislative Action Network, or PLAN, whose mandate was to furnish state legislatures with prewritten "model" legislation reflecting leftist agendas.[57] A year later, the Democracy Alliance took the next step in the Shadow Party's effort to gain a handhold on the levers of national power by launching a major new initiative called the Secretary of State Project (SoSP), which was set up as an independent "527 committee" devoted to helping Democrats win secretary-of-state elections in

---

[55]Ibid.

[56]Jim Kuhnhenn, "New Coalition Aims to Keep Dems in Check, *Washington Post/AP,* January 23, 2007, http://www.washingtonpost.com/wp-dyn/content/article/2007/01/23/AR2007012300424_pf.html.

[57]Louis Jacobson, "New Organization to Push Liberal Measures In State Legislatures," *Roll Call,* June 23, 2005, http://www.rollcall.com/issues/50_136/-9790-1.html.

crucial "swing" states where the margin of victory in the 2004 presidential election had been 120,000 votes or less.[58]

Why the focus on the Secretary of State, traditionally considered one of the least important jobs in state government? Because whoever fills this position serves as the chief election officer who certifies candidates as well as election results in his or her state.[59]

The holder of this office, then, can potentially play a decisive role in determining the winner of a close election.

The idea for Secretary of State Project had germinated shortly after the 2004 election, when the Shadow Party blamed then-Ohio secretary of state Kenneth Blackwell, a Republican, for John Kerry's defeat. Blackwell had ruled that Ohio, which provided George W. Bush's electoral victory by a relatively slim 118,599-vote margin, would not count provisional ballots—even those submitted by properly registered voters—if they had been submitted at the wrong precinct. Though the U.S. Court of Appeals for the 6th Circuit ultimately upheld Blackwell's decision, the Secretary of State Project's founding members received the ruling with the same bitterness they had felt about the Florida recount which Vice President Al Gore lost to George Bush in the 2000 election, and which was handled by Republican Secretary of State Katherine Harris. Summing up their attitudes, political analyst Matthew Vadum wrote that the Secretary of State Project's leaders and foot soldiers alike "religiously believe that right-leaning secretaries of state helped the GOP steal the presidential elections in Florida in 2000 ... and in Ohio in 2004."[60]

To establish "election protection" against similar outcomes in subsequent political races, the Secretary of State Project targeted

---

[58]Matthew Vadum, "Soros Election Theft Project," *Capital Research Center,* December 4, 2009, http://capitalresearch.org/2009/12/soros-election-theft-project/; Secretary Of State Project, http://www.discoverthenetworks.org/groupProfile.asp?grpid=7487.

[59]"Elections," *Arizona Secretary of State,* http://www.azsos.gov/elections.

[60]Matthew Vadum, "SOS in Minnesota," *American Spectator,* November 7, 2008, http://spectator.org/articles/42654/sos-minnesota.

its funding efforts in 2006 on the secretary-of-state races in seven swing states—Iowa, Minnesota, Nevada, New Mexico, Ohio, Colorado, and Michigan.[61] *USA Today* saw the development, even if it didn't catch sight of the shadowy machinery that had produced it: "The political battle for control of the federal government has opened up a new front: the obscure but vital state offices that determine who votes and how those votes are counted."[62] Because of the relatively mundane nature of most of the Secretary of state's duties, candidates for that office tend to draw fewer (and smaller) donations than do most state-level campaigns. Consequently, even a modest injection of cash from just a handful of dedicated and savvy donors can tip the scales.[63] In 2006, SoSP raised a total of $500,000 for the secretary-of-state candidates whom it supported—a small amount by traditional political fundraising standards, but a weighty amount in comparison to the sums that such candidates had typically garnered in the past. Democrats emerged victorious in five of those seven targeted races—failing only in Michigan and Colorado (where they won two years later as part of the "Miracle.") Politico.com saw the meaning of the Secretary of State Project when it characterized it as "an administrative firewall" designed, "in anticipation of a photo-finish presidential election," to protect Democrats' "electoral interests in ... the most important battleground states."[64]

One beneficiary of the Secretary of State Project funding in 2006 was Democrat Jennifer Brunner of Ohio, who defeated the Shadow Party's bête noire, incumbent Republican Ken Blackwell. Brunner went on to make her influence felt in several ways during the 2008 election cycle. She ruled, for instance, that Ohio

---

[61]Ibid.

[62]Jill Lawrence, "Top Vote Counter Becomes Prize Job—Democrats Focus on Key State Post," *USA Today,* March 24, 2011, http://usatoday30.usatoday.com/printedition/news/20060817/1a_lede17.art.htm.

[63]"SOS in Minnesota," op. cit.

[64]Avi Zenilman, "Secretaries of State Give Dem Firewall," *Politico,* November 2, 2008, http://www.politico.com/news/stories/1008/15105.html.

residents should be permitted, during the designated early-voting period extending from late September to early October, to register *and* vote on the same day.[65] Bruner also sought to effectively invalidate many of the approximately one million absentee-ballot applications that Republican presidential candidate John McCain's campaign had issued. Each of those applications had been printed with a checkbox next to a statement affirming that the voter was a qualified elector. In an effort designed to suppress Republican absentee votes, Brunner maintained that if a registrant failed to check the box—even if he or she signed the form—the application could be rejected. The Ohio Supreme Court subsequently overturned Brunner's directive on grounds that it served "no vital purpose or public interest."[66]

Another key beneficiary of the Secretary of State Project's support in 2006 was Democrat Mark Ritchie, who defeated a two-term incumbent Republican in Minnesota. Ritchie acknowledged his debt to the activists when he said, "I want to thank the Secretary of State Project and its thousands of grass-roots donors for helping to push my campaign over the top."[67] A former community organizer with close ties to ACORN and to the now-defunct radical New Party,[68] Ritchie, like Jennifer Brunner, played a lead role in 2008.

---

[65]"Ohio Battles Over Tuesday's Early Voting," *CBS News/AP,* September 28, 2008, http://www.cbsnews.com/news/ohio-battles-over-tuesdays-early-voting/.

[66]Jim Seigel, "Brunner May Toss Signatures on Payday-lending Ballot Issue—Secretary of State Faces GOP Lawsuit Over Same-day Registration and Voting," *Columbus Dispatch,* September 12, 2008, http://www.dispatch.com/content/stories/local/2008/09/12/payday13.html.

[67]Katherine Kersten, "Could Senate Recount Referee's Résumé Color the Result?," *Star Tribune,* http://www.startribune.com/katherine-kersten-could-senate-recount-referee-s-rsum-color-the-result/34306799/.

[68]"SOS in Minnesota," op. cit.; Trevor Loudon, "Minnesota S.O.S. Helped Found Socialist Party with Ties to President Obama," *New Zeal,* November 12, 2010, http://www.trevorloudon.com/2010/11/mark-ritchie-file-2-minnesota-s-o-s-helped-found-socialist-party-with-ties-to-president-obama/.

When Republican incumbent U.S. Senator Norm Coleman finished 725 votes ahead of Democratic challenger Al Franken, the thin margin of victory triggered an automatic recount. With Ritchie presiding, Coleman's lead gradually dwindled in the ensuing weeks as a result of what journalist Matthew Vadum describes as a long series of "appalling irregularities" that invariably benefited Franken. Among these: during the recount process a number of ballots were suddenly "discovered" in an election judge's car. One Minnesota county similarly "discovered" 100 new votes for Franken and claimed that a clerical error was responsible for the fact that they hadn't been counted before. Another county tallied 177 more votes than it had recorded on Election Day. Yet another county reported 133 fewer votes than its voting machines had originally tabulated.

"Almost every time new ballots materialized, or tallies were updated or corrected, Franken benefitted," writes Vadum.[69] In addition, at least 393 convicted felons voted illegally in two particular Minnesota counties.[70] By the time the recount (and a court challenge by Coleman) had ended in April 2009, Franken held a 312-vote lead and in June was officially declared the victor.[71]

With organizations such as the Democracy Alliance and electoral innovations such as the Secretary of State Project in place, the Shadow Party approached the 2008 presidential election with an integrated organization and singleness of purpose unprecedented in the annals of American politics. It was able to use the Internet to put people in the street; it had think tanks, media organizations, and fundraising arms built to function smoothly in

---

[69]Matthew Vadum, "Fighting Frankenstein," *The American Spectator*, April 14, 2009, http://spectator.org/articles/41783/fighting-frankenstein.

[70]Peter Roff, "Al Franken May Have Won His Senate Seat Through Voter Fraud," *U.S. News*, July 20, 2010, http://www.usnews.com/opinion/blogs/peter-roff/2010/07/20/al-franken-may-have-won-his-senate-seat-through-voter-fraud.

[71]"Fighting Frankenstein," op. cit.; John Fund, "Felons for Franken," *The Wall Street Journal*, July 14, 2010, http://www.wsj.com/articles/SB10001424052748704518904575365063352229680.

the new reality created by campaign finance reform; it had the most sophisticated voter registration—and, for the other side, vote suppression—program yet seen.

It had been widely assumed that Soros would throw the elaborate machinery he had created for seizing power behind the candidacy of Hillary Clinton. After all, the two of them had a relationship going back some 15 years, involving a shared vision about the importance of socializing medicine as a way of expanding government power and regularizing social life. Hillary began the primary season, moreover, as the prohibitive favorite in the fight for the Democrat nomination. But in December 2006 Soros summoned Barack Obama, elected to the U.S. Senate only two years earlier, to a meeting in his New York office. Just a few weeks later—on January 16, 2007 when Obama announced that he would form a presidential exploratory committee—Soros immediately sent the senator a contribution of $2,100, the maximum amount allowable under the new campaign-finance laws he had played so large a role in creating. Later that week, Soros announced that he would support Obama for the Democratic Party's presidential nomination.[72]

Some in the establishment were surprised that he should turn his back on an old friend. But Soros's agenda had always been ideological, not personal. Obama not only shared virtually all of Soros's values, including his antagonism to the Iraq War, but had also risen to prominence in the universe of left-wing networking organizations the Shadow Party had created. Compared to Hillary Clinton, he was a sure thing; a politician who spoke Soros's language and could be counted on to promote the radical causes close to his heart. The Obama campaign was soon staffed, funded and promoted by personnel from the forces Soros had welded into the Shadow Party juggernaut: the left-wing public employees unions, the progressive billionaires, and the ACORN radicals.

---

[72]T. Jefferson, "Soros Exposed: Research on the Progressive Puppet Master," *Glenn Beck*, November 11, 2010, http://www.glennbeck.com/content/articles/article/198/47856/.

Some of the people who sold Obama to America moved in the parochial world of left-wing activism and "community organizing," coming out of organizations such as the Midwest Academy,[73] a major training center for radicals founded by Sixties diehards Heather and Paul Booth,[74] former hardcore members of SDS who had continued the fight above ground when their comrades Billy Ayers and his wife Bernardine Dohrn went underground to launch the Weatherman terror campaign.[75] The Booths chose a more gradual form of revolution whose guidelines were laid down in the radical theories of Saul Alinsky.[76] The Midwest Academy, recipient of a grant from Soros's Open Society Institute, was one of the organizations in which Obama became involved when returning home to Chicago after graduating from Harvard Law.[77]

The future president had also cycled through some of the better-known organizations sheltering under the Shadow Party's political umbrella. The most famous—to become the most notorious in the first year of the Obama presidency—was ACORN,[78] supported for years by Soros's Open Society Institute and other Shadow Party groups.[79] Its agenda, in the words of one critic, was "anti-capitalist

---

[73]Midwest Academy, http://www.discoverthenetworks.org/groupProfile.asp?grpid=6725.

[74]Heather Booth, http://www.discoverthenetworks.org/individualProfile.asp?indid=1641; Paul Booth, http://www.discoverthenetworks.org/individualProfile.asp?indid=2501.

[75]Bill Ayers, http://www.discoverthenetworks.org/individualProfile.asp?indid=2169.

[76]Saul Alinsky, http://www.discoverthenetworks.org/individualProfile.asp?indid=2314.

[77]Midwest Academy, http://www.discoverthenetworks.org/groupProfile.asp?grpid=6725.

[78]Stanley Kurtz, "Inside Obama's Acorn," *National Review,* May 29, 2008, http://www.nationalreview.com/article/224610/inside-obamas-acorn-stanley-kurtz; Stanley Kurtz, "Obama Acorn Cover-up?," *National Review,* October 8, 2008, http://www.nationalreview.com/corner/171642/obama-acorn-cover-stanley-kurtz.

[79]Neil Maghami, "George Soros: The Left's One-Man Message Machine," *Capital Research Center,* November 1, 2006, http://capitalresearch.org/2006/11/george-soros-the-lefts-one-man-message-machine/;

redistributionism" and one of Obama's first jobs had been doing voter registration for the ACORN affiliate, Project Vote.[80]

Then-SEIU President Andrew Stern, the Center for American Progress' John Podesta, and other key figures in the Soros network sat on ACORN's Advisory Council.[81] For his part, Obama, adroitly riding the updrafts of Chicago's left-wing political universe, was the attorney for ACORN's lead election-law cases before joining the Illinois legislature.[82] In 1995, acting as ACORN's attorney, Obama sued to ensure the implementation of an Illinois motor-voter law.[83] When ACORN officially endorsed Obama's presidential candidacy in February 2008, the candidate's campaign gave one of ACORN's front groups $800,000 to fund a voter-registration drive on the senator's behalf.[84] By October, ACORN would be under investigation for voter-registration fraud in 13 states.[85]

In the 2008 campaign, pursuing the Shadow Party's strategy for parlaying the power of institutions within its network, Obama's

---

Matthew Vadum "ACORN: Who Funds the Weather Underground's Little Brother?," *Capital Research Center,* November 2008, http://www.capitalresearch.org/wp-content/uploads/pubs/pdf/v1225222922.pdf.

[80]Editors, "Jive Turkey Rides Again," *National Review Online,* October 10, 2008, http://www.nationalreview.com/article/225951/jive-turkey-rides-again-editors.

[81]Tom Blumer, "ACORN 'Independent Advisory Council' Member Andy Stern Lets Loose on ACORN's Critics; Press Mum," *MRC NewsBusters,* September 21, 2009, http://newsbusters.org/blogs/tom-blumer/2009/09/21/acorn-independent-advisory-council-member-stern-lets-loose-acorns-critic.

[82]Stephanie Strom, "On Obama, Acorn and Voter Registration," *The New York Times,* October 10, 2008, http://www.nytimes.com/2008/10/11/us/politics/11acorn.html?_r=0.

[83]James Simpson, "Barack Obama and the Strategy of Manufactured Crisis," *American Thinker,* September 28, 2008, http://www.americanthinker.com/articles/2008/09/barack_obama_and_the_strategy.html.

[84]Greg Borowski, "ACORN Suspicion Swells as McCain Camp Questions Obama's Ties," *Journal Sentinel,* October 11, 2008, http://www.jsonline.com/news/statepolitics/32432124.html.

[85]Deroy Murdock, "Obama Squirrel Away His Links to ACORN," *National Review,* October 16, 2008, http://www.nationalreview.com/article/226000/obama-squirrels-away-his-links-acorn-deroy-murdock.

presidential campaign furnished Project Vote with a list of donors who had already given the campaign the maximum sum of money permitted by law. In turn, Project Vote representatives contacted those donors and urged them to give contributions to Project Vote, which it could then use to support Obama's candidacy while technically complying with election-law limits on campaign donations.[86] That same year, the Open Society Institute gave Project Vote $400,000.[87] Another boost for Obama came from MoveOn.org. This powerful Soros-affiliated organization dispatched approximately a million volunteers to work on Obama's campaign nationwide—600,000 in battleground states and 400,000 in non-battleground states. In addition, MoveOn registered more than half a million young Obama supporters to vote in the battleground states, while adding a million young people to its membership rolls during the summer of 2008. All told, MoveOn and its members contributed more than $58 million directly to the Obama campaign, while raising and spending at least an additional $30 million in independent election efforts on behalf of other Democrats across the United States.[88]

The Shadow Party succeeded in realizing Soros's dream of putting his man in the White House. With Obama's inauguration, members of the Soros coalition began showing up in high-level jobs in the new administration. One who soon attracted unwanted attention was a self-defined "revolutionary communist" named Van Jones who spent six months as the new president's "green jobs czar" in 2009 before revelations about his background forced him to resign and return to his position as a fellow at Podesta's Center

[86]John Fund, "An Acorn Whistleblower Testifies in Court," *Wall Street Journal,* October 30, 2008, http://www.wsj.com/articles/SB122533169940482893.

[87]Matthew Vadum "ACORN: Who Funds the Weather Underground's Little Brother?," op. cit.

[88]http://techdailydose.nationaljournal.com/2008/11/obama-benefits-from-moveons-88.php.

for American Progress.[89] Before joining Obama, Jones had headed the Ella Baker Center for Human Rights, which had received more than $1 million from the Open Society Institute to pursue its claim that that the American criminal-justice system was racist and therefore to promote "alternatives to incarceration."[90] Over the years, Jones had been a board member of numerous nonprofits funded by the Shadow Party, including the radical environmental group Apollo Alliance, which was launched by the Soros-connected Tides Foundation, as well as Podesta's Center for American Progress.[91] Jones definitely had gotten the Shadow Party message, often urging his fellow leftists by telling them, "I'm willing to forego the cheap satisfaction of the radical pose for the deep satisfaction of radical ends."[92]

A key figure in the Shadow Party entering the Obama White House by the front door was the ubiquitous Andrew Stern, a veteran New Leftist who headed the Service Employees International Union (SEIU), the second-largest labor organization in America. Trained in the tactics of radical activism at the Midwest Academy, Stern had worked with Soros to form America Votes to run the ground war for the Kerry-Edwards ticket. In 2008, Stern's SEIU contributed $60.7 million to help elect Barack Obama to the White House—deploying 100,000 volunteers during the campaign.[93] As of October 30, 2009, scarcely eight months into

---

[89]Van Jones, http://www.discoverthenetworks.org/individualProfile.asp?indid=2406.

[90]"State Realignment Plan Long Overdue but Misses Target," *Ella Baker Center for Human Rights,* September 29, 2011, http://ellabakercenter.org/in-the-news/books-not-bars-justice-system/ella-baker-center-state-realignment-plan-long-overdue-but.

[91]Van Jones, http://www.discoverthenetworks.org/individualProfile.asp?indid=2406.

[92]Glenn Beck, "Van Jones, in His Own Words," *Fox News,* September 1, 2009, http://www.foxnews.com/story/2009/09/01/van-jones-in-his-own-words.html.

[93]Peter Nicholas, "Obama's Curiously Close Labor Friendship," *Los Angeles Times,* June 28, 2009, http://articles.latimes.com/2009/jun/28/nation/na-stern28.

the Obama presidency, the union boss had visited the White House 22 times—more than any other individual.[94]

Almost everywhere one looked in the new administration, members of the Soros inner circle proliferated. Key presidential strategist and advisor David Axelrod, who as much as anyone was responsible for Obama's elections, first to the Senate and then to the Presidency, had received over a quarter of a million dollars for his political consulting firm during the 2004 elections from the Shadow Party's Media Fund.[95] Carol Browner, named by Obama as his "environment czar," was a board member of the Alliance for Climate Protection, the Center for American Progress, and the League of Conservation Voters—all funded by Soros.[96] The SEIU's Anna Burger, vice chair of the Democracy Alliance and "the most powerful women in the labor movement" according to *Fortune* magazine, was appointed to the Obama Economic Recovery Advisory Board.[97] Kevin Jennings, who had established the Boston-area Gay, Lesbian and Straight Education Network (GLSEN) with funding from the Open Society Institute, was named "education czar."[98]

With members of the Shadow Party playing central roles, the Obama White House began to roll out an ideological agenda immediately after the inauguration that involved many of George

---

[94]Jeff Zeleny, "White House Visitor Log Lists Stars and C.E.O.'s," *The New York Times,* October 30, 2009, http://www.nytimes.com/2009/10/31/us/politics/31visitor.html.

[95]Ed Lasky, "The Soros-Axelrod Axis of Astroturf," *American Thinker,* September 27, 2010, http://www.americanthinker.com/blog/2010/09/the_sorosaxelrod_axis_of_astro.html; Ben Smith, "Axelrod and the Outside Groups," *Politico,* September 23, 2010, http://www.politico.com/blogs/bensmith/0910/Axelrod_and_the_outside_groups.html.

[96]Carol Browner, http://www.discoverthenetworks.org/individualProfile.asp?indid=2364.

[97]Anna Burger, *SEIU.org,* http://www.seiu.org/a/ourunion/anna-burger.php; Anna Burger, http://www.discoverthenetworks.org/individualProfile.asp?indid=2445.

[98]Kevin Jennings, *Huffington Post,* http://www.huffingtonpost.com/kevin-jennings; Kevin Jennings, http://www.discoverthenetworks.org/individualProfile.asp?indid=2426.

Soros's signature concerns. Just a few days after Obama was elected, Soros stated: "I think we need a large stimulus package which will provide funds for state and local government to maintain their budgets—because they are not allowed by the constitution to run a deficit. For such a program to be successful, the federal government would need to provide hundreds of billions of dollars. In addition, another infrastructure program is necessary. In total, the cost would be in the 300 to 600 billion-dollar range...." [99] Soon afterwards, as one of the first acts of his presidency, Obama pressured Congress to pass a monumental $787 billion economic-stimulus bill with a text of 1,071 pages which few, if any, legislators had read before voting on. It was based on the radical precept of using social crisis to create radical change, which the Alinskyite groups in Obama's background had made into a theorem and which chief of staff Rahm Emanuel turned into an aphorism: "Never let a good crisis go to waste."[100]

It was first of all a payoff to key Shadow Party elements, in particular public-sector unions, to allow them to remain strong for future elections through the financial crisis. It was also loaded with spending projects Democrats had been unable to fund for years. The stimulus was an opening bid to radically transform American capitalism by channeling populist anger at Wall Street toward support for an expansionist vision of the welfare state based on "social justice"—leftist code for a socialist redistribution of wealth. Obama stressed that it was urgent to pass the stimulus bill at the earliest possible moment, even without full deliberation, so as to forestall any further harm to the U.S. economy. Because of the near-hysterical atmosphere surrounding the flailing economy, it went largely unnoticed that the bill also repealed

---

[99] "SPIEGEL Interview with George Soros," *Spiegel Online International,* November 24, 2008, http://www.spiegel.de/international/business/spiegel-interview-with-george-soros-the-economy-fell-off-the-cliff-a-592268.html.

[100] "Rahm Emanuel: You Never Want a Serious Crisis to Go to Waste," http://www.youtube.com/watch?v=1yeA_kHHLow.

numerous essentials of the 1996 welfare-reform bill which George Soros had so strongly opposed.[101] According to a Heritage Foundation report, 32 percent of the new stimulus bill—or an average of $6,700 in "new means-tested welfare spending" for every poor person in the U.S.—was earmarked for social-welfare programs.[102] Such unprecedented levels of spending did not at all trouble Soros, who justified it with discredited Keynesian doctrine: "At times of recession, running a budget deficit is highly desirable."[103]

Cap-and-trade, Obama's tax-based policy proposal to reduce Americans' consumption of fossil fuels, was a strategy that had been discussed and perfected in the nonprofits associated with the Shadow Party. Under cap-and-trade regulations, companies would be subject to taxes or fees if they exceeded their government-imposed limit for carbon dioxide emissions.[104] Some economists predicted that such legislation, if enacted, would impose colossal costs on businesses—costs that would be passed on to consumers, who in turn would pay anywhere from several hundred to several thousand extra dollars each year in energy costs.[105] But to Soros, the taxpayers' money would be well spent on such a policy. "Dealing with global warming will require a lot of investment," he emphasized, and thus "will be painful" but "at least" it will

---

[101]Faye Fiore, "Gift Aims To Ease Welfare Reform Hit Financier George Soros Donates $50 Million To Help Legal Immigrants," *Los Angeles Times*, October 1, 1996, http://articles.mcall.com/1996-10-01/news/3126013_1_legal-immigrants-welfare-reform-law-rosalind-gold.

[102]Katherine Bradley and Robert Rector, "Welfare Spendathon: House Stimulus Bill Will Cost Taxpayers $787 Billion in New Welfare Spending," *The Heritage Foundation*, February 6, 2009, http://www.heritage.org/research/reports/2009/02/welfare-spendathon-house-stimulus-bill-will-cost-taxpayers-787-billion-in-new-welfare-spending.

[103]"SPIEGEL Interview with George Soros," op. cit.

[104]Cap-And-Trade/Carbon Emissions, http://www.discoverthenetworks.org/viewSubCategory.asp?id=826.

[105]Ben Lieberman, "Beware of Cap and Trade Climate," *The Heritage Foundation*, December 6, 2007, http://www.heritage.org/Research/Reports/2007/12/Beware-of-Cap-and-Trade-Climate-Bills.

enable humankind to "survive and not cook."[106] When asked in 2008 whether he was proposing energy policies that would "create a whole new paradigm for the economic model of the country, of the world," Soros replied, "Yes."[107] During his 2008 presidential campaign, Obama had a comparable moment of candor: "Under my plan of a cap-and-trade system, electricity rates would necessarily skyrocket. Even regardless of what I say about whether coal is good or bad. Because I'm capping greenhouse gases, coal power plants, you know, natural gas, you name it, whatever the plants were, whatever the industry was, they would have to retrofit their operations. That will cost money. They will pass that money on to consumers."[108]

The principal motive underlying the cap-and-trade policies that Obama and Soros support was articulated by Obama's "regulation czar," Cass Sunstein, a leftist law professor and longtime proponent of "distributive justice," whereby America would transfer much of its own wealth to poorer nations as compensation for the alleged harm that U.S. environmental transgressions have allegedly caused in those countries. In language echoing Soros's own pronouncements, Sunstein speculates that "desirable redistribution" can be "accomplished more effectively through climate policy than through direct foreign aid."[109]

Socialized medical care continued to occupy pride of place on the Soros agenda in the years following the defeat of HillaryCare and the inability of his Project on Death to gain traction. Health care was high on the Obama agenda, too, high enough that he focused on it, rather than on the failing economy, in a way that

---

[106]"George Soros—Political/Financial Stances," *KeyWiki*, http://keywiki.org/index.php/George_Soros_-_Political/Financial_Stances.

[107]Ibid.

[108]Mark Tapscott, "Obama: 'Under my Plan … Electricity Rates Would Necessarily Skyrocket'," *Washington Examiner*, November 1, 2008, http://www.washingtonexaminer.com/obama-under-my-plan-…-electricity-rates-would-necessarily-skyrocket/article/136378.

[109]Aaron Klein, "Sunstein: Americans Too Racist for Socialism," *World Net Daily*, October 7, 2009, http://www.wnd.com/2009/10/112243/.

puzzled political observers who failed to appreciate the ideological nature of the new administration. During the political debate over "Obamacare" in 2009 and 2010, one of the most influential pro-reform coalitions backing the president was the Soros-created Health Care for America Now (HCAN), a vast network of organizations supporting a model in which the federal government would be in charge of financing and administering the entire U.S. healthcare system.[110]

HCAN's strategy became the Obama administration's strategy: to try to achieve a "single payer" system by incremental steps that culminated in government control—a full-blown socialist system. The highway to this "solution" would be paved by a "public option"—a government insurance agency to "compete" with existing insurers, so that Americans would be "no longer at the mercy of the private insurance industry."[111] Because such an agency would not need to show a profit in order to remain in business, and because it could tax and regulate its private competitors in whatever fashion it pleased, this "public option" would inevitably force private insurers out of the industry and leave the government as the only alternative. It was a perfect expression of the gradualist strategy of Obama's radical mentor, Saul Alinsky, who counseled a kind of camel's nose-under-the-tent approach—concealing the radical endgame while taking the maximum steps politically feasible at the time. In August 2009, with Obamacare creating widespread grassroots resistance, Soros gave another $5 million to HCAN to promote the administration's campaign and help pass the increasingly unpopular legislation.[112]

---

[110]Health Care For America Now!, http://healthcareforamericanow.org/; Health Care For America Now, http://www.discoverthenetworks.org/groupProfile.asp?grpid=7488.

[111]"About Us," *Health Care For America Now!* http://healthcareforamericanow.org/about-us/.

[112]Ed Morrissey, "Guess Who's Funding ObamaCare Advocates?," *Hot Air,* August 10, 2009, http://hotair.com/archives/2009/08/10/guess-whos-funding-obamacare-advocates/comment-page-1/.

If Obamacare is the one piece of domestic legislation that most bears the stamp of George Soros, the administration's increasing hard line toward Israel is the foreign policy development that most reflects the Soros view of the world beyond Washington. Soros's own ambivalent attitudes about his boyhood, living as a Jew on the edge of the Holocaust, developed into a full-blown hostility to the Jewish state. Just as he perceived American policies to have provoked the anti-American *jihad* and the 9/11 attacks, so he saw Israel as a principal source of anti-Semitism. He has referred to Israel's conflict with the Palestinians as a case of the "victims turning prosecutors."[113] Ignoring the terrorist Hamas's call to kill the Jews and wipe Israel off the face of the earth, Soros has argued that a key to a Mideast peace is "bringing Hamas into the peace process."[114] Soros's views on the Middle East are reflected in a Middle East advocacy group called J Street, which he inspired and funded in 2008.[115] Like other Soros groups, J Street is meant to counter what he regards as a malignant "conservative" organization, in this case the American Israel Public Affairs Committee (AIPAC), roughly 80 percent of whose members are Democrats but not the kind of Democrats that Soros prefers.

J Street has called for "a new direction for American policy in the Middle East" and has cautioned Israel not to be too combative against Hamas, on grounds that the latter "has been the government, law and order, and service provider [in Gaza] since it won the elections in January 2006 and especially since June 2007 when it took complete control."[116] It has also launched over 8,000 unprovoked rocket attacks on Israeli towns and schoolyards in the same period of time.[117] According to J Street, the Mideast conflict

---

113George Soros, "The Bubble of American Supremacy," op. cit., p. 19.

114Soros with Byron Wien and Krisztina Koenen, *Soros on Soros: Staying Ahead of the Curve,* John Wiley and Sons, 1995), p. 241.

115J Street, http://www.discoverthenetworks.org/groupProfile.asp?grpid=7458.

116Ibid.; "Gaza: Ceasefire Now!," *J Street Blog,* December 28, 2008, http://jstreet.org/blog/post/gaza-stop-violence1.

117http://idfspokesperson.com/2009/01/03/rocket-statistics-3-jan-2009/.

is perpetuated chiefly by Israel: "Israel's settlements in the occupied territories have, for over forty years, been an obstacle to peace."[118]

These positions, marking a break with 60 years of American policy towards Israel, are largely indistinguishable from those of the Obama White House. Obama signaled his comfort with J Street's agendas when he sent his then-national security advisor James Jones to deliver the keynote address at the organization's annual conference in October 2009.[119]

Knowing that his comments on Israel made him controversial in the Jewish community, Soros initially tried to conceal his support of J Street from the public for fear that it might alienate other potential backers of the organization. But in September 2010 *The Washington Times* penetrated the veil, revealing that from 2008-2010, Soros and his two children, Jonathan and Andrea, had given a total of $750,000 to J Street and that the organization's advisory council includes a number of individuals with close ties to him.[120] When the streets of Cairo erupted in February 2011 and Obama waffled as Mubarak tried to hold power, Soros quickly moved to give the president a signal to undercut America's unpleasant ally of 40 years and to open the door to the Muslim Brotherhood, a jihadist cult that has spawned 12 terrorist organizations including al-Qaeda and Hamas.[121]

In a *Washington Post* op-ed written during the early stages of the protests, Soros wrote: "President Obama personally and the United States as a country have much to gain by moving out in

---

[118]"Settlements," *J Street,* http://jstreet.org/page/settlements.

[119]P. David Hornick, "Blaming Israel First," *FrontPage Mag,* December 30, 2009, http://www.frontpagemag.com/2009/davidhornik/blaming-israel-first-by-p-david-hornik/.

[120]Eli Lake, "Soros Revealed as Funder of Liberal Jewish-American Lobby," *Washington Times,* September 24, 2010, http://www.washingtontimes.com/news/2010/sep/24/soros-funder-liberal-jewish-american-lobby/; "Advisory Council," *J Street,* http://jstreet.org/supporters/advisory-council.

[121]Muslim Brotherhood, http://www.discoverthenetworks.org/groupProfile.asp?grpid=6386.

front.... Doing so would open the way to peaceful progress in the region. The Muslim Brotherhood's cooperation with Mohamed ElBaradei, the Nobel laureate who is seeking to run for president, is a hopeful sign that it intends to play a constructive role in a democratic political system.... The main stumbling block is Israel.... Fortunately, Obama is not beholden to the religious right, which has carried on a veritable vendetta against him. [And] the American Israel Public Affairs Committee is no longer the sole representative of the Jewish community..."[122]

If George Soros were a lone billionaire, or if the Shadow Party consisted of a few disgruntled billionaires, these facts and achievements would not be so ominous. But the Shadow Party is far more than a reflection of the prejudices of one special interest or one passing generation. It has united the forces of the radical and "liberal" left while expelling moderates from the Democratic Party coalition.

The Shadow Party is the current incarnation of a socialist movement that has been at war with the free-market economy, and the political system based on liberty and individual rights, for more than two hundred years. It is a movement that has learned to conceal its ultimate goal, which is a totalitarian state, in the seductive rhetoric of "progressivism" and "social justice." But its determination to equalize outcomes, its zeal for state power, for government control as the solution to social problems, and its antagonism to America as a defender of freedom are the tell-tale signs of a radical movement whose agenda is to change fundamentally and unalterably the way Americans have lived.

---

[122]George Soros, "Why Obama Has to Get Egypt Right," *GeorgeSoros.com,* February 3, 2011, http://www.georgesoros.com/articles-essays/entry/why_obama_has_to_get_egypt_right.

8

Why I Am Not a Neo-Conservative

When George Bush launched the military campaign to remove Saddam Hussein and enforce Security Council resolution 1441 and sixteen other Security Council resolutions that Saddam had defied, I was for it. I would be for it today. It was a necessary war and a just war. By toppling a monster who had defied international order and who was an obvious threat, Bush did the right thing.

When he named the campaign Operation Iraqi Freedom, I was also an enthusiast. It put the Democratic Party, which soon betrayed the war, and the political left, which instinctively supports America's enemies, on the defensive. When he said he was going to establish democracy in Iraq, I almost believed him. And that seemed to put me in the camp of the neo-conservatives for whom democracy in Iraq was not only a wish but an agenda.

In any case, people labeled me that way, not least because I am a Jew, and "neo-conservative" functions for the ominously expanding anti-Semitic left as a code for self-serving Jews who want to sacrifice American lives for Israel (notwithstanding the fact that the Israelis regarded Iran as the threat rather than Iraq).

Whatever I wrote about the war in support of the democracy agenda, internally I was never a 100 percent believer in the idea

---

Originally published March 23, 2011, http://www.frontpagemag.com/2011/david-horowitz/why-i-am-not-a-neo-conservative/.

that democracy could be so easily implanted in so hostile a soil. I wanted to see Saddam toppled and a non-terrorist-supporting government in his place. I would have settled for that, and for a large U.S. military base as well.

But I allowed myself to get swept up in the Bush-led enthusiasm for a democratic revolution in the Middle East. I remained on board until the Beirut spring began to wither, and I got off when election results in Gaza came in and put a Nazi party into power. That spelled the end of whatever neo-conservative illusions I might have had.

It looks as if we are headed for the same result in Egypt, where the Muslim Brotherhood is poised to win the September elections. The reality is that a totalitarian Islam is the vibrant and increasingly dominant movement in the Arab world. Any elections likely to take place will be on the order of one man, one vote, one time.

Neo-conservatives are now cheering on the Obama administration's reckless intervention in Libya, as though the past ten years have taught them nothing. The nation-building effort in Iraq led to a squandering of American resources and a weakening of American power. Putting a man who is hostile to American power in the White House is not the least aspect of this American decline.

Because of these nation-building delusions, we are still mired in Afghanistan—now the longest war in American history. And we have been plunged into the Middle Eastern maelstrom with no clear agenda or objective.

The Obama Administration, in my view, is the most dangerous administration in American history, and conservatives need to be very clear about the limits and objectives of American power so that they can lead the battle to restore our government to health. To accomplish this, neo-conservatives need to admit they were wrong, and return to the drawing board. They should give up the "neo" and become conservatives again.

9

Occupy Wall Street
(with John Perazzo)

When communism collapsed twenty years ago, its progressive supporters and apologists in the West did not put on sackcloth and ashes and beg forgiveness for the catastrophes they had helped create. Instead, they bided their time and waited until circumstances would conspire to give their socialist fantasies new life. That time has apparently come. All the familiar claims about capitalism and its evil, socialism and its "justice," are being trotted out for a second round. The slogans and demands of this new communism may seem farcical to those who remember the past; but the forces behind it, which include the nation's most powerful unions and some of its biggest philanthropies, make its latest campaign a serious attack on America's foundations.

This basic truth was looming in the background on September 17, 2011, when a group calling itself Occupy Wall Street (OWS) staged a demonstration with 5,000 activists near the hub of New York City's financial district.[1] Their stated purpose was to condemn the "greed" they identified as Wall Street's hallmark, and to express "opposition to the principle that has come to dominate not only our economic lives but our entire lives: profit over and above all else."[2]

Originally published May 1, 2012, http://www.frontpagemag.com/2012/frontpagemag-com/occupy-wall-street-the-communist-movement-reborn/.

[1]Jennie Wood, "Occupy Wall Street," *infoplease,* http://www.infoplease.com/business/occupy-wall-street.html.

[2]Chris, "Why?," *OccupyWallStreet,* September 12, 2011, http://occupywallst.org/article/why/.

This statement encapsulates the credo of the Occupiers' movement. Notable for its ignorance about economics and human nature, it is also informed by the oldest of all socialist myths—that "property is theft." But as history has taught the rest of us, property is in fact the very basis of individual freedom, while socialism is theft.[3]

The claim that corporations elevate "profits over people" is a poisonous myth created by Marx, perpetuated by modern-day radicals like Noam Chomsky and cultural clowns like Michael Moore. In the real world, capitalists must meet people's needs in order to stay in business and make profits. In the real world, corporations make profits only if they lower costs, which actually increases wealth for everyone else (other things being equal). In other words, profits serve people—though you wouldn't learn that in the liberal arts department of any major American university. The Occupy Wall Street movement is simply the old communist shell game: the revived fantasy of a world without money, without classes and without government.

The public debut of the Occupy movement was small by modern protest standards but did not remain so for long. President Obama's sympathizers in the media immediately got behind Occupy Wall Street, seeing it as the rough equivalent of Obama's class-warfare re-election strategy and a potential counterweight to the Tea Party movement. In the first forty days of protests, *The New York Times* and *The Washington Post* together devoted 224 mainly positive articles to the squatters who made up the movement.[4] By early October, news of the "occupations" had gone viral, a lead item on the nightly news spreading to cities nationwide.[5]

---

[3]Reverend Robert A. Sirico, "The Moral Basis for Economic Liberty," *The Heritage Foundation,* July 13, 2010, http://www.heritage.org/research/reports/2010/07/the-moral-basis-for-economic-liberty.

[4]Dan Gainor, "*Post/NYT:* 182,000 Words on Occupy Wall Street and Counting," *MRC NewsBusters,* October 28, 2011, http://newsbusters.org/ blogs/dan-gainor/2011/10/28/postnyt-182000-words-occupy-wall-street-and-counting.

[5]"'Occupy Wall Street' Movement Spreads from New York Across the US," *MercoPress,* October 6, 2011, http://en.mercopress.com/2011/10/06/occupy-wall-street-movement-spreads-from-new-york-across-the-us;

For all the publicity the Occupy movement has gained, its origins and purposes remain obscure, which is exactly what its organizers desire. Officially, OWS claims to have no identifiable leaders, and even makes a fetish of their absence with unison repetitions of every word its "facilitators" utter—a chilling reminder of the monolithic cultures of totalitarian regimes.

OWS portrays itself as a spontaneous eruption of popular anger by grassroots representatives of the "99 percent" who are outraged at the way the "1 percent" have allegedly rigged American society for their own advantage. Spokesmen for the Occupy movement have notably failed to explain how the 1 percent could possibly accomplish this, particularly since powerful representatives of the 1 percent such as George Soros are funding their movement.

Despite the blatant deceptions of the Occupy narrative, media pundits and liberal politicians eagerly repeated it. *New York Times* columnist Thomas Friedman characterized OWS as part of a worldwide pattern of "spontaneous social protests,"[6] while Congresswoman Nancy Pelosi lauded the movement as "young," "spontaneous" and "focused."[7]

Far from being "spontaneous," however, OWS was orchestrated by a long-established network of radical activists. Among them are operatives from ACORN, left-wing philanthropies and socialist unions. OWS is an exercise in serial mendacity—not surprising for a movement that assaults a democracy which created

---

" 'Occupy Wall Street' Now in 25 Cities," *CBS News,* October 10, 2011, http://www.cbsnews.com/news/occupy-wall-street-now-in-25-cities/; Joanna Walters, "Occupy America: Protests against Wall Street and Inequality Hit 70 Cities," *The Guardian,* October 8, 2011, http://www.theguardian.com/world/2011/oct/08/occupy-america-protests-financial-crisis.

[6]Thomas L. Friedman, "Something's Happening Here," *The New York Times,* October 11, 2011, http://www.nytimes.com/2011/10/12/opinion/theres-something-happening-here.html?_r=0.

[7]Wilson, "Nancy Pelosi: Occupy Wall Street Is 'Young', 'Spontaneous', 'Focused'," http://www.glennbeck.com/2011/10/07/nancy-pelosi-occupy-wall-street-is-young-spontaneous-focused/.

readily accessible avenues for redressing grievances, correcting injustices and transferring power.

Off camera, the OWS strategy was explained by one of its organizers, John McGloin: "First you get large numbers of people to join by showing how reasonable you are. Then when the numbers are big enough, they will feel their oats, get impatient, and start demanding more than you could have imagined. (Never underestimate mob mentality.) But if you talk about overthrowing governments, capitalism or wholesale changes, most of the 99 percent will be scared off, and we'll never have the power we need to affect [sic] real change. In order to fight the global corporations I estimate we need a minimum of 15 million Americans on the street. There are not 15 million radical socialist/anarchists in the US. We need people without political agendas, but with anger at corporations."[8]

OWS Founders I: Masters of Deception

The creator of OWS is a 69-year-old Canadian resident named Kalle Lasn, a longtime leftwing filmmaker, radical environmentalist and "student of revolution." Lasn is at war with what he calls "the dog-eat-dog world of capitalism," condemning "consumerism" as "psychologically corrosive" and the American economy as "a destructive system" that has caused "a terrible degradation of our mental environment."[9]

Like all modern radicals, Lasn is above all a nihilist, a destroyer rather than a builder. In 1989, the year the Berlin Wall fell, Lasn

---

[8]Lee Stranahan, "#Occupy Emails Reveal 'Trojan Horse' Strategy to Hide Socialist, Anarchist Goals of #OccupyWallStreet 'Mob','" *Breitbart*, http://www.breitbart.com/big-government/2011/10/20/occupy-emails-reveal-trojan-horse-strategy-to-hide-socialist-anarchist-goals-of-occupy-wallstreet-mob/.

[9]Kalle Lasn, http://www.discoverthenetworks.org/individualProfile.asp?indid=2522; Jules Evans, "Kalle Lasn, Founder of Adbusters, on the Coming Revolution," *Philosophy For Life*, June 16, 2011, http://philosophyforlife.org/kalle-lasn-founder-of-adbusters-on-the-coming-revolution/.

launched a campaign to "wreck" consumerism by creating the Adbusters Media Foundation.[10] This group set out to be a "global network"—now 95,000 strong—of "culture jammers" and "anarchists."[11] Through initiatives such as "Buy Nothing Day," Adbusters encouraged people "stung by consumer culture" to abandon their concerns about money and material possessions. It urged them to sink the economy—in other words, destroy the livelihoods of everyone else.[12]

Adbusters published a *Kick It Over Manifesto,* calling for a "revolution" that will yield "a new economics" not dependent on gross domestic product or any other "fundamentally flawed and incomplete" measure of fiscal health.[13] But of course there is no new economics and nothing to replace the gross domestic product—at least nothing that utopians like Lasn have been able to devise. The *Kick It Over Manifesto* is merely the same siren song to nowhere that radicals have been sounding so disastrously since 1848.

Adbusters is sustained by six-figure grants from the Glaser Progress and Tides Foundations—institutions run by left-wingers willing to fund organizations dedicated to destroying the system that makes their charity possiblc.[14] Tides is heavily bankrolled by George Soros's Open Society Institute.

By his own account, Lasn's inspiration for creating OWS was the so-called "Arab Spring" and its riots, which persuaded him to think that America was likewise "ripe for this type of [mass]

[10]Adbusters Media Foundation, http://www.discoverthenetworks.org/groupProfile.asp?grpid=7695; "Adbusters," *Activist Facts,* https://www.activistfacts.com/organizations/36-adbusters/.

[11]"Adbusters," http://www.adbusters.org/; "Adbusters," *Activist Facts,* op. cit.

[12]"Adbusters—Buy Nothing Day," http://www.adbusters.org/campaigns/bnd; Jules Evans, "Kalle Lasn, Founder of Adbusters, on the Coming Revolution," op. cit.

[13]"Kick It Over Manifesto," *Kick It Over,* http://kickitover.org/kick-it-over/manifesto/.

[14]Between 2001 and 2011, Adbusters received $176,500 and $309,773 from the multimillion-dollar Glaser Progress and Tides Foundations.

rage."[15] Lasn was confident that "despondency" over such concerns as "climate change" and "corruption in Washington" would lead American youth to join a movement for revolutionary change.[16] This was essentially a page taken from Saul Alinsky's *Rules for Radicals,* wherein we read, "Remember: once you organize people around something as commonly agreed upon as pollution, then an organized people is on the move. From there it's a short and natural step to political pollution, to Pentagon pollution."[17] And, according to people like Lasn, to Wall Street pollution.

While the Arab Spring was turning rapidly into a Muslim Brotherhood Winter, Lasn and his Adbusters associates were brainstorming ideas for effecting "regime change" in America.[18] On June 9, 2011, Lasn registered the domain name "OccupyWallStreet.org"[19]—thus giving birth to the movement with which he hoped to "pull the current monster [of capitalism] down."[20]

In July, Lasn and Adbusters posted an "Occupy Wall Street" call to action, aiming to recruit "redeemers, rebels and radicals" to join a mass protest movement "against the greatest corrupter of our democracy: Wall Street, the financial Gomorrah of

---

[15]Kyle Farquharson, "Occupy Everything: The Legacy of the Occupy Wall Street Movement," October 2013, http://blogs.ubc.ca/occupyeverything/files/2013/10/Occupy-Everything-final.doc.

[16]Elizabeth Flock, "Occupy Wall Street: An Interview with Kalle Lasn, the Man Behind it All," *The Washington Post,* October 12, 2011, http://www.washingtonpost.com/blogs/blogpost/post/occupy-wall-street-an-interview-with-kalle-lasn-the-man-behind-it-all/2011/10/12/gIQAC81xfL_blog.html.

[17]Saul Alinsky, *Rules for Radicals: A Pragmatic Primer for Realistic Radicals,* Random House, 1971, p. xxiii; cited in David Horowitz, *Barack Obama's Rules for Revolution: The Alinsky Model,* David Horowitz Freedom Center, 2009, pp. 29–30.

[18]Sam Eifling, "Adbusters' Kalle Lasn Talks About OccupyWallStreet," *The Tyee,* October 7, 2011, http://thetyee.ca/News/2011/10/07/Kalle-Lasn-Occupy-Wall-Street/.

[19]John S. Torell, "Occupy Wall Street—Who Is Behind It" *European-American Evangelistic Crusades,* November 20, 2011, http://www.eaec.org/desk/11-20-2011.htm.

[20]Jules Evans, "Kalle Lasn, Founder of Adbusters, on the Coming Revolution," op. cit.

America."[21] The campaign was to be "a fusion of Tahrir," the square in Cairo where the Egyptian revolt germinated, "with the acampadas of Spain," referring to Spanish protesters who camped out for extended periods in public spaces. Adbusters exhorted its supporters to prepare to "flood into lower Manhattan" on September 17, "set up tents, kitchens, peaceful barricades and occupy Wall Street for a few months," and to do so "with a vengeance."[22]

According to Lasn, "Tahrir succeeded in large part because the people of Egypt made a straightforward ultimatum—that President Hosni Mubarak must go—over and over again until they won." More accurately, Tahrir succeeded because Barack Obama put the weight of the United States behind the effort to push Mubarak out. Adbusters instructed its recruits to "incessantly repeat one simple demand in a plurality of voices."[23] But that demand, explained an Adbusters communiqué, would have to be carefully worded so as to conceal its deeper motives: "Strategically speaking, there is a very real danger that if we naively put our cards on the table and rally around the 'overthrow of capitalism' or some equally outworn utopian slogan, then our Tahrir moment will quickly fizzle into another inconsequential ultra-lefty spectacle soon forgotten."[24]

To guard against this possibility, Lasn knew that his organization would need to articulate "a deceptively simple Trojan Horse demand" that was "specific and doable."[25] Under the slogan "Democracy Not Corporatocracy," Adbusters demanded that Obama "ordain a Presidential Commission tasked with ending the influence money has over our representatives in Washington."[26]

---

[21]"A Shift in Revolutionary Tactics," *Adbusters*, July 13, 2011, https://www.adbusters.org/blogs/adbusters-blog/occupywallstreet.html.
[22]Ibid.
[23]Ibid.
[24]"Can We on the Left Learn Some New Tricks?" *Adbusters*, August 11, 2011, https://www.adbusters.org/blogs/adbusters-blog/occupywall-street-update.html?page=1.
[25]Ibid.
[26]"A Shift in Revolutionary Tactics." op. cit.

The demand went unmet, but the leaders were right in presuming that the president would be an ally. Obama had already injected the class-warfare narrative into the political air as part of his re-election strategy. His speeches were peppered with inflammatory references to the "millionaires and billionaires" and the "corporate jet owners" who allegedly were not paying their "fair share" and were thereby exploiting "working families" and the poor.[27] These were themes that would become central to the message of Occupy Wall Street. From his side, Obama expressed sympathy for the movement, saying that he "understands the frustrations that are being expressed" by the protesters.[28] Speaking in New Hampshire, he told Occupy supporters, "You are the reason I ran for office."[29]

OWS Founders II: Red Wine in New Bottles

The OWS was built on the groundwork that radical leaders had been laying for decades. One of those leaders was Wade Rathke, a Sixties veteran.[30] Rathke had worked with the National Welfare Rights Organization (NWRO), which aimed to "break" the welfare system by recruiting people to overwhelm its rolls and by invading its offices—often violently—to make additional demands that

---

[27]Austin Hill, "The President's Strange Obsession with Millionaires and Billionaires," *Townhall,* September 25, 2011, http://townhall.com/columnists/austinhill/2011/09/25/the_presidents_strange_obsession_with_millionaires_and_billionaires; Lachlan Markay, "Obama Blasts Private Jet Tax Breaks Included in His Own Stimulus," *Daily Signal,* June 29, 2011, http://dailysignal.com/2011/06/29/obama-blasts-private-jet-tax-breaks-created-by-his-own-stimulus/.

[28]Aaron Klein, "Obama: Occupy Wall Street 'Not That Different' From Tea Party Protests," *Klein Online,* November 23, 2011, http://kleinonline.wnd.com/2011/11/23/obama-occupy-wall-street-'not-that-different'-from-tea-party-protests/.

[29]Bernie Becker and Alicia M. Cohn, "Obama Heckled by Protesters at New Hampshire Speech," *The Hill,* November 22, 2011, http://thehill.com/blogs/blog-briefing-room/news/195119-protesters-heckle-obama-at-new-hampshire-speech-on-payroll-tax.

[30]Wade Rathke, http://www.discoverthenetworks.org/individualProfile.asp?indid=1773.

could not be met.[31] In the early 1970s, Rathke founded ACORN, soon to be the largest radical organization in America. ACORN's specialty was voter fraud, conceived as a strategy to break the electoral system. ACORN activists provided a powerful force behind Barack Obama's rise to the Senate in 2004 and his election to the White House in 2008.

OWS was in fact the culmination of the "anti-banking jihad" that Rathke launched in March 2011, calling for "days of rage in ten cities around JP Morgan Chase."[32] Not coincidentally, OWS's inaugural event on September 17 was also widely referred to as a "Day of Rage"[33] and was conducted in conjunction with an affiliated movement known as USDayOfRage. The original "Days of Rage" were a series of riots organized by the terrorist group Weatherman in Chicago in 1969.

Twelve days later, another Sixties radical, Frances Fox Piven,[34] spoke to an OWS rally in New York. It was Piven who had come up with the break-the-system strategy that Rathke's welfare organization adopted. The strategy had actually succeeded, overloading the welfare rolls until it bankrupted the city of New York; Mayor Rudy Giuliani then put an end to the policies that allowed it to happen. Following New York's welfare fiasco, Piven escalated her scheme into a strategy to overload other government agencies

---

[31]National Welfare Rights Organization, http://www.discoverthenetworks.org/groupProfile.asp?grpid=7633.

[32]Aaron Klein, "Revolution Hitting U.S. Streets Tomorrow? Protesters Training to Incite Violence, Resist Arrest, Disrupt Legal System," *Klein Online*, September 15, 2011, http://kleinonline.wnd.com/2011/09/15/revolution-hitting-u-s-streets-tomorrow-protesters-training-to-incite-violence-resist-arrest-disrupt-legal-system/; Matthew Vadum, "Occupy Wall Street Jumps the Shark," *FrontPage Mag*, October 6, 2011, http://www.frontpagemag.com/2011/matthew-vadum/occupy-wall-street-jumps-the-shark/.

[33]Buck Sexton, "The Blaze Reports From Inside the 'Comrade's' Ranks: 'Occupy Wall Street' Day of Rage," *The Blaze*, September 17, 2011, http://www.theblaze.com/stories/2011/09/17/the-blaze-reports-from-inside-the-comrades-ranks-occupy-wall-street-day-of-rage/.

[34]Frances Fox Piven, http://www.discoverthenetworks.org/individualProfile.asp?indid=2505.

with impossible demands, in order to create social chaos and economic collapse.

The Community Reinvestment Act—the cornerstone of the 2008 mortgage crisis—was a triumph of the Piven strategy and of ACORN's political influence in the Democratic Party.[35] But of course radicals like Piven never hold themselves accountable for the damage they cause. At a September 29 OWS rally, Piven instead denounced the "greedy" "thieves" and "cannibals" of the financial industry and claimed that America's budget deficits were so large "because big business and finance has stopped paying taxes."[36] She continued: "Wall Street is the center of the neo-liberal cancer that has spread across the world."[37]

Muscle for OWS was provided by the Service Employees International Union (SEIU) through a board member and longtime left-wing organizer, Stephen Lerner.[38] The SEIU had been a driving force behind the Seattle riots against the World Trade Organization a dozen years before, and had put $60 million into Barack Obama's presidential election campaign.[39] Like the other OWS leaders, Lerner is a dedicated socialist whose declared goal is to "destabilize the folks that are in power and start to rebuild a movement."[40] At a Left Forum held on March 19, 2011, Lerner

[35]"Breaking the System: The Obama Team's Strategy for Changing America," *FrontPage Mag*, October 22, 2010, http://www.frontpagemag.com/2010/frontpagemag-com/breaking-the-system-the-obama-teams-strategy-for-changing-america/.

[36]Robert Stacy McCain, "Organized Ignorance," *American Spectator*, October 31, 2011, http://spectator.org/articles/36657/organized-ignorance; "#OccupyWallStreet—Frances Fox Piven and Russell Simmons Address the General Assembly," http://www.youtube.com/watch?v=VsK2WeO7VbQ&feature=youtu.be.

[37]Ibid.

[38]Stephen Lerner, http://www.discoverthenetworks.org/individualProfile.asp?indid=2525.

[39]Michelle Malkin, "Big Labor's Investment in Obama Pays Off," *Jewish World Review*, May 13, 2009, http://jewishworldreview.com/michelle/malkin051308.php3.

[40]Aaron Klein, "Who's Really Behind Wall Street Protests?," *World Net Daily*, October 2, 2011, http://www.wnd.com/2011/10/351141/.

speculated enthusiastically that if he and his comrades could organize "half a million" homeowners to stage a mass "mortgage strike," refusing to pay their mortgages, they could "put banks at the edge of insolvency again" and "literally cause a new financial crisis."[41] In a similar vein, he urged college graduates to initiate a "debt strike" by refusing to pay their student loans.[42] As with the other OWS radicals, nihilism was the order of the day.

At the Left Forum, Lerner explained: "We are in a transformative stage of what's happening in capitalism ... building something that really has the capacity to disrupt how the system operates." Outlining his strategy to "bring down the stock market" and "interfere" with wealthy people's "ability to be rich," he paraphrased a famous piece of Alinsky advice: "We have to politically isolate them, economically isolate them, and disrupt them." Lerner then disclosed that "a bunch of us around the country" had "decided" that JP Morgan Chase "would be a really good company to hate." As a result, he said, "We are going to roll out over the next couple of months what will hopefully be an exciting campaign about JP Morgan Chase that is really about challenging the power of Wall Street."[43]

Lerner called for "a week" of "civil disobedience" and "direct action" to be carried out "all over the city" of New York in early May. He and his forces would "roll into the JP Morgan shareholder meeting" and then launch "a ten-state mobilization" that would similarly target "bank shareholder meetings around the country." By waging such "brave and heroic battles challenging the power of

---

[41]"Glenn Beck Program," *Beck Cliff Notes*, March 22, 2011, http://beck-cliff-notes.blogspot.com/2011/03/glenn-beck-program-march-22-2011.html.

[42]Henry Blodget, "Caught on Tape: Former SEIU Official Reveals Secret Plan to Destroy JP Morgan, Crash the Stock Market, and Redistribute Wealth In America," *Business Insider*, March 22, 2011, http://www.businessinsider.com/seiu-union-plan-to-destroy-jpmorgan.

[43]Stephen Lerner, http://www.discoverthenetworks.org/individualProfile.asp?indid=2525.

the giant corporations," Lerner said he hoped "to inspire a much bigger movement about redistributing wealth and power."[44]

On September 10—just a week before the first Occupy Wall Street event in Manhattan—Lerner announced that demonstrations would be staged "in Seattle, in L.A., in San Francisco, in Chicago, in New York, in Boston." He emphasized: "We're not going to convince the other side that we're right through intellectual argument. We need to create power, and in a way we need to talk about how we create a crisis for the super rich."[45] On November 17, Lerner's connection to the union movement resulted in the SEIU, the United Federation of Teachers, the Communications Workers of America and other unions endorsing OWS and joining the "March of the 99 Percent."[46]

Another radical who has helped shape OWS is Lisa Fithian, a 50-year-old "community organizer" who specializes in "direct action" tactics and, in the words of one reporter, "operates in the world of anti-globalism anarchists, antiwar protesters, and union activists."[47] Fithian became an activist in the 1980s, when she worked with "Yippie" co-founder Abbie Hoffman at the environmental organization Save the River. She also actively supported the Sandinista communists and protested American aid to the Nicaraguan *contras.* Fithian was the national coordinator of a 1987 demonstration aimed at shutting down CIA headquarters in Langley, Virginia.[48]

---

[44]Ibid.

[45]John Hayward, "Heroes In Need of a Crisis," *Human Events,* September 20, 2011, http://humanevents.com/2011/09/20/heroes-in-need-of-a-crisis/; Trevor Loudon, "Who's Behind Occupy Wall Street?," *New Zeal,* October 25, 2011, http://www.trevorloudon.com/2011/10/who's-behind-occupy-wall-street/.

[46]Raymond Pronk, "Collectivists vs. Individualists: Occupy Wall Street Compared to Tea Party," *Pronk Palisades,* November 17, 2011, https://raymondpronk.wordpress.com/tag/seiu/.

[47]Byron York, "Cindy Sheehan's Radical Strategist," *National Review,* August 29, 2005, http://www.nationalreview.com/article/215275/cindy-sheehans-radical-strategist-byron-york.

[48]Lisa Fithian, http://www.discoverthenetworks.org/individualProfile.asp?indid=2521.

In 1993, Fithian joined the AFL-CIO Organizing Institute. Subsequently, she helped lead direct-action protests against multiple industries (nursing, farming, automobile, hospital, hotel, security, janitorial, laundry, newspaper) in cities across the United States. Many of these protests were marked by lawlessness whose aim was to provoke police into arresting hundreds or even thousands of people.[49]

Fithian, like Stephen Lerner, was a key organizer of the violent "anti-globalization" riots in 1999 that caused the shutdown of the World Trade Organization (WTO) meetings in Seattle.[50] Global capitalism, as Fithian herself has since acknowledged, was the target of the protesters.[51] Afterward, Fithian helped establish the Continental Direct Action Network, a confederation of anarchist groups. In 2003 she organized anti-capitalist protests against a WTO conference in Cancun, Mexico, where the talks similarly collapsed.[52]

Since 2000, Fithian has organized all over the world against such targets as Free Trade Area of the Americas summits, IMF/World Bank meetings, G8 Summits and a World Economic Forum in New York.[53] She currently serves on the national steering committee of United for Peace and Justice,[54] an anti-American organization established by Leslie Cagan, a veteran communist, with the support of the SEIU and other cornerstones of the radical

---

[49]"About Lisa," *Organizing for Power, Organizing for Change,* http://organizingforpower.wordpress.com/movement-history/about-lisa/; Lee Stranahan, "Meet the Anarchist Leaders Behind the 'Leaderless' #Occupy Movement—Part One: Lisa Fithian," *Breitbart,* October 10, 2011, http://biggovernment.com/lstranahan/2011/10/10/meet-the-anarchist-leaders-behind-the-leaderless-occupy-movement-part-one-lisa-fithian/.

[50]"About Lisa," op. cit.

[51]John Sellers, "Battle In Seattle," *Beautiful Trouble,* November 30, 1999, http://beautifultrouble.org/case/battle-in-seattle/.

[52]"About Lisa," op. cit.

[53]Ibid.

[54]Ibid.

left.[55] Fithian has also provided training and support for ACORN, National People's Action and other radical organizations.[56]

Fithian says that she and others in OWS "who are trying to create a new world ... have to dismantle or transform the old order," one dominated by "the corporations [and] the big banks [that] have been destroying this country."[57] In her efforts to "undo all the oppression" whose wellspring is America, she seeks to "create crisis, because crisis is that edge where change is possible."[58] Armed with these goals, Fithian has emerged as the top street-level organizer of the OWS movement and its various urban chapters.[59] In November, Fithian told an interviewer: "There's never been a movement like this," one with such "tremendous potential" to achieve "mass transformation."[60]

Strategy of Deception

Concealing the strategic roles played by these longtime activists and communist nostalgists, Occupy Wall Street officially insists that it is a "leaderless resistance movement" composed of "people of many colors, genders and political persuasions."[61] It claims to be populist rather than radical, a collection of ordinary Americans "fighting back against the oppressive power of major banks and multinational corporations over the democratic process," and

---

[55]Leslie Cagan, http://www.discoverthenetworks.org/individualProfile.asp?indid=629.

[56]"About Lisa," op. cit.

[57]Byron York, "Cindy Sheehan's Radical Strategist," op. cit.; Lee Stranahan, "Meet the Anarchist Leaders Behind the 'Leaderless' #Occupy Movement—Part One: Lisa Fithian," op. cit.

[58]Austin Bunn, "Them Against the World, Part 2," *The New York Times*, November 16, 2003, http://www.nytimes.com/2003/11/16/magazine/them-against-the-world-part-2.html?pagewanted=print&src=pm.

[59]"Lisa Fithian Teaching Radical to Chicago Teachers Union," http://www.youtube.com/watch?v=6BARB-aSqYM.

[60]John Sellers, "Battle In Seattle," op. cit.

[61]"Occupy Movement (Occupy Wall Street)—Chronology of Coverage," *The New York Times*, 2015, http://topics.nytimes.com/top/reference/timestopics/organizations/o/occupy_wall_street/index.html.

against "the role of Wall Street in creating an economic collapse that has caused the greatest recession in generations."[62]

Claiming to be "the 99 percent that will no longer tolerate the greed and corruption of the 1 percent," OWS says that its goal is "creating real change from the bottom up."[63] But the methods it encourages its activists to use in achieving this change—social chaos, lawlessness, violence against citizens and property, and defiance of the representatives of democratic order—belie the benign image. The explosion of anarchy it has fostered is far more corrosive to the democratic process than campaign contributions by Wall Street fat cats—the bulk of which went to Barack Obama in the 2008 election.[64]

While describing itself as a "call for revolution," the original OWS "Call to Action" put the case for its revolution in the most moderate and reasonable terms it could muster: "We want freedom for all, without regards for identity, because we are all people and no other reason should be needed. However, this freedom has largely been taken from the people. . . ."[65]

But just how has freedom been taken from the people? According to the OWS manifesto, through "money" in the hands of the "haves" (as though wealthy people never earned their wealth).[66] It continues: "Money, it has been said, has taken over politics. In truth, we say, money has always been part of the capitalist system.

---

[62]"From Tahrir Square to Times Square: Protests Erupt In Over 1,500 Cities Worldwide," *Occupy Wall Street,* October 16, 2011, http://occupywallst.org/article/tahrir-square-times-square-protests-erupt-over-150/.

[63]"Can Someone Please Explain the Practical Goals of Occupy?," *Occupy Wall Street,* December 29, 2011, http://occupywallst.org/forum/can-someone-please-explain-the-practical-goals-of-/.

[64]Charles Gasparino, *Bought and Paid For: The Unholy Alliance Between Barack Obama and Wall Street,* Sentinel, 2010.

[65]"A Modest Call to Action on This September 17th," *Occupy Wall Street,* September 17, 2011, http://occupywallst.org/article/September_Revolution/.

[66]This is yet another page from the Alinsky manual. Cf. David Horowitz, *Barack Obama's Rules for Revolution: The Alinsky Model,* op. cit., pp. 6, 31, 35.

A system based on the existence of haves and have-nots, where inequality is inherent to the system, will inevitably lead to a situation where the haves find a way to rule, whether by the sword or by the dollar." A better description of capitalism, however, would be a system based on the existence of cans and can-nots, and giving the former freedom to produce without government restraints.

To create "a revolution of the mind as well as of the body politic," the manifesto called for "protests to organize and disrupt the system"; "for workers to not only strike, but seize their workplaces collectively"; and for students and teachers together "to seize the classrooms."[67]

Given such objectives, there was no way that the protesters inspired by OWS would be anything but radicals who had learned nothing from the socialist disasters of recent memory. Nor was there a way for the organizers to control the message and maintain the appearance of a spontaneous and unorganized movement. No sooner had the movement begun than posters and banners bearing anti-capitalist slogans became ubiquitous at the Occupy rallies that spread across the country: "Smash Capitalism," "Capitalism Isn't Working," "Death to Capitalism," "Capitalism = Systematic Exploitation," "F*** Capitalism," "Try Socialism," "Declare War on Banks," "Turn Workers' Anger into Communist Revolution," "This Is the Revolution," "No War but Class War."[68]

The immediate targets of OWS anger were the banks held to be responsible for the financial crisis. The malpractices of Wall Street banks in securitizing bad loans was certainly a prime factor in the economic mess. But the failure of one recently deregulated sector of the economy (deregulated by Democrats and Republicans) was

---

[67]"A Modest Call to Action on This September 17th," op. cit.

[68]"The Occupation of Los Angeles—Part 5," *Ringo's Pictures*, October 13, 2011, http://www.ringospictures.com/index.php?page=20111013; "The Occupation of Los Angeles—Part 3," *Ringo's Pictures*, October 1, 2011, http://www.ringospictures.com/index.php?page=20111002; "The Occupation of Los Angeles—Part 2," *Ringo's Pictures*, October 1, 2011, http://www.ringospictures.com/index.php?page=20111001.

hardly an argument for overthrowing the entire system. Particularly since the anger directed at banks overlooked the pivotal role that ACORN and the left had played in creating the crisis.

The left that organized the OWS protests was the same left that had previously promoted the loosening of banking standards during the Clinton administration, and was the driving force behind the Community Reinvestment Act, which pressured the banks into dropping their credit requirements. This abandonment of banking standards created the bad loans that led to the subprime mortgage crisis, and the banks' securitization of those bad loans, which led to the financial meltdown.[69] All this was a predictable outcome of the "breaking the system" strategy devised by Piven and Rathke and pushed by ACORN and their congressional allies. The goal was to overwhelm the financial system by flooding its books with loans to people who couldn't afford to pay them back. When the banks—out of greed, yes—then securitized the bad loans, the system came crashing down.[70]

The Issue Is Never the Issue

A Sixties activist once said, "The issue is never the issue. The issue is always the revolution."[71] This is the most carefully guarded secret of the left. The plight of the Vietnamese was never the real issue for the Sixties activists who opposed the Vietnam War. When the United States withdrew its forces, the left's concern for the Vietnamese was over as well. When the communist victors they had helped to power began slaughtering the Vietnamese, the left did not organize protests to defend the defenseless. The issue was never the Vietnamese. It was always the

---

[69]Community Reinvestment Act And The Housing Market Crisis Of 2008, http://www.discoverthenetworks.org/viewSubCategory.asp?id=809.

[70]See David Horowitz and Liz Blaine, *Breaking the System: Obama's Strategy for Change*, David Horowitz Freedom Center, 2010.

[71]Cited in Peter Collier and David Horowitz, *Destructive Generation: Second Thoughts About the '60s*, Summit, 1989.

revolution. And the revolution is always about the left's war against America.

The U.S. financial crisis is not the cause of the Occupy Wall Street protests. It is their pretext. The OWS movement is not seeking financial reforms that would address the two principal causes of the collapse: reinstating the Glass-Stegall Act and restricting bank loans to credit-worthy customers. This is not the left's concern. What it wants is revolution, and the revolution it wants is a communist overthrow of the capitalist system.

OWS condemns America as a "ruthless" materialistic society whose chief objective is to "always minimize costs and maximize profits," as though minimizing costs did not spread the wealth to greater and greater numbers of people. OWS condemns capitalism as a system where "lives are commodities to be bought and sold on the open market," which actually describes the slave systems that capitalism replaced. OWS contends that under capitalism "the economic transaction has become the dominant way of relating to the culture and artifacts of human civilization," which is exactly what Marx and other socialists said long ago: that the social nexus had been replaced by a "cash nexus" and communism would fix that.[72]

These residues of communism are the DNA of OWS. In October 2011, the website BigGovernment.com acquired a vast archive of leaked emails containing messages exchanged by the organizers of OWS. The emails revealed the extensive "involvement of socialists, anarchists, and other radicals," as well as "heavy union involvement" in the OWS movement. Further, the emails showed that OWS aims to promote extreme levels of economic and governmental destabilization; to create social unrest throughout the democratic world; and to form alliances with other radical causes, including the Islamic jihadists whose goal is the destruction of Israel and the West. A number of the emails discuss how a "Trojan Horse" strategy—as proposed by Kalle Lasn and John McGloin—

---

[72]Chris, "Why?," op. cit.

could be employed to deceive the public about the Occupy movement's real character and agendas.[73]

The Demonstrations

The organizers of OWS worked hard to portray their movement as being composed of "people who live next door to you" and who have been financially blindsided by the 1 percent who allegedly control America. But *New York* magazine revealed a very different reality in a story published on October 2, 2011. A poll it had conducted with 100 protesters in Manhattan disclosed that half were in their twenties and 35 percent were of the opinion that the U.S. government is "no better than, say, Al Qaeda," while 45 percent said that capitalism "can't be saved" and is "inherently immoral."[74]

In another survey of 200 OWS protesters, 65 percent said the government has a moral responsibility to guarantee all citizens access to affordable health care, a college education and a secure retirement—regardless of the cost; 77 percent supported tax hikes on the wealthiest Americans; 52 percent had participated in earlier political movements; 98 percent endorsed breaking the law to achieve their goals; and 31 percent said they would support violence to promote their agendas. Doug Schoen, the Democratic pollster whose firm conducted the survey, concluded that the OWS activists hold "values that are dangerously out of touch with the broad mass of the American people . . . and are bound by a deep commitment to radical left-wing policies."[75]

---

[73]Thomas Ryan, "The Email Archive of the #OccupyWallStreet Movement: Anarchists, Socialists, Unions, Democrats and Their Plans," *Breitbart*, October 14, 2011, http://www.breitbart.com/big-government/2011/10/14/the-email-archive-of-the-occupywallstreet-movement-anarchists-socialists-unions-democrats-and-their-plans/.

[74]Tracey Samuelson, "Meet the Occupants," *New York Magazine*, October 2, 2011, http://nymag.com/news/intelligencer/topic/occupy-wall-street-2011-10/.

[75]Douglas Schoen, "Polling the Occupy Wall Street Crowd," *Wall Street Journal*, October 18, 2011, http://www.wsj.com/articles/SB10001424052970204479504576637082965745362.

The protesters' first large-scale clash with law enforcement took place on October 1, when a horde of demonstrators shut down traffic on the Brooklyn Bridge for two and a half hours. The action resulted in 700 arrests.[76] Seeking arrest was a calculated OWS tactic. The organizers selected in advance those whom they called their "arrestables:" individuals who projected a desired image of "normalcy."[77] It was all about propaganda, and as real as AstroTurf.

By October 15, likeminded radicals, anarchists and communists were holding rallies in hundreds of cities around the world, a reflection of the fact that this was the reappearance of an international left that was already in place and looking for a pretext to galvanize it. In Rome, tens of thousands of protesters gathered to vent their collective rage violently. As Reuters reported, "Hundreds of hooded, masked demonstrators rampaged in some of the worst violence seen in the Italian capital in years, setting cars ablaze, breaking bank and shop windows and destroying traffic lights and signposts."[78] In Chicago that same day, 175 protesters were arrested, as were another 92 in New York.[79] A featured speaker at an Occupy Los Angeles rally found it an occasion to praise the French Revolution for having "made fundamental transformation," even though "it was bloody." "Ultimately," the speaker told

---

[76]Kevin Sheehan, "Wall St. Protesters Shut Down Brooklyn Bridge," *New York Post,* October 1, 2011, http://nypost.com/2011/10/01/wall-st-protesters-shut-down-brooklyn-bridge/.

[77]Trevor Loudon, "Who's Behind Occupy Wall Street?," op. cit.

[78]Philip Pullella, "Wall Street Protests Go Global; Riots in Rome," *Reuters,* October 15, 2011, http://www.reuters.com/article/2011/10/15/us-protests-idUSTRE79E0FC20111015.

[79]Dawn Rhodes, "175 Chicago Protesters Arrested after Being Told to Leave Grant Park," *Chicago Tribune,* October 16, 2011, http://www.chicagotribune.com/news/local/breaking/chi-occupy-chicago-protesters-relocate-to-grant-park-20111015-story.html#page=1; Cara Buckley and Rachel Donadio, "Buoyed by Wall St. Protests, Rallies Sweep the Globe," *The New York Times,* October 15, 2011, http://www.nytimes.com/2011/10/16/world/occupy-wall-street-protests-worldwide.html?_r=3&hp.

the cheering crowd, "the bourgeoisie won't go without violent means.... Long live revolution! Long live socialism!"[80]

Violence and other forms of criminality soon became commonplace at Occupy Wall Street demonstrations. A cursory Google search brings up news reports of hundreds of separate incidents at OWS sites by late November, including vandalism, extortion, assault, theft, rape, rioting, computer hacking, knife attacks, threatened violence, civil disobedience, the use and trafficking of illegal drugs, public urination and, perhaps most famously, public defecation.[81]

The movement's first homicide was recorded on November 10, when a 25-year-old protester at Occupy Oakland was shot and killed by a man whom other demonstrators described as a "frequent resident" at the camp.[82] This was one of eight deaths that occurred at OWS encampments between late October and early December. The list includes a 35-year-old military veteran who shot himself to death at Occupy Burlington, a man in his 40s who died from a combination of drug abuse and carbon monoxide inside a tent at Occupy Salt Lake City, a man who died of unknown causes inside his tent at Occupy Bloomington, a man in his twenties who was found dead inside a tent at Occupy Oklahoma City, and three others who died from drug and alcohol abuse.[83]

Numerous brutal sexual assaults added to the mayhem. At Occupy Cleveland, a 19-year-old woman was raped while she was

---

[80]Zombie, "Occupy L.A. Speaker: Violence will be Necessary to Achieve Our Goals," *PJ Media,* October 11, 2011, http://pjmedia.com/tatler/2011/10/11/occupy-l-a-speaker-violence-will-be-necessary-to-achieve-our-goals/.

[81]John Nolte, "*Updated* #OccupyWallStreet: The Rap Sheet, So Far," *Breitbart,* October 28, 2011, http://www.breitbart.com/big-journalism/2011/10/28/updated-occupywallstreet-the-rap-sheet-so-far/.

[82]"Southern California—This Just In," *Los Angeles Times,* November 13, 2011, http://latimesblogs.latimes.com/lanow/2011/11/shooting-victim-tied-to-occupy-oakland.html.

[83]"Occupy Movement," *Wikipedia,* Last updated, May 17, 2015, http://en.wikipedia.org/wiki/Occupy_movement (Total deaths = 32; Total injuries = 400+; Total arrests = 7,700+).

inside her tent. At Occupy Baltimore, a woman was raped and robbed by an assailant who subsequently escaped without detection. In New York, an 18-year-old woman was raped by a man who had been working at the protesters' makeshift kitchen at Zuccotti Park, and a female protester was sexually assaulted inside her tent. At Occupy St. Louis, a woman was raped on November 8, and five days later a 23-year-old woman was raped by a 50-year-old man at Occupy Philadelphia. At the Occupy Dallas encampment, a 14-year-old girl was reportedly raped; and in faraway Scotland, a female resident of the Occupy Glasgow camp was sexually assaulted in her tent.[84]

OWS protesters did not confine their criminal activity solely to the Occupy encampment areas; in many cases, they ventured into other neighborhoods to engage in various forms of lawbreaking. In downtown Oakland, California, protesters demonstrated their contempt for corporations by smashing the window of a Men's Wearhouse clothing store.[85] In Fort Collins, Colorado, a 29-year-old protester was arrested for setting fires that destroyed one condominium complex and severely damaged another.[86] In the District of Columbia, occupiers stormed the Washington Convention Center where the conservative political-advocacy group Americans for Prosperity was holding a dinner, and in the process they pushed a 78-year-old woman down a flight of stairs.[87] Also in DC, a 21-year-old OWSer fired a semiautomatic rifle at the White

---

[84]John Nolte, "*Updated* #OccupyWallStreet: The Rap Sheet, So Far," op. cit.

[85]Lonely Conservative, "Despite Support for Occupy Movement, Men's Warehouse Trashed During Oakland Riot," *The Lonely Conservative,* November 3, 2011, http://lonelyconservative.com/2011/11/despite-support-for-occupy-movement-mens-warehouse-trashed-during-oakland-riot/.

[86]"Man Suspected of Setting Fire to Fort Collins Condo Appears In Court," *9News.com,* November 4, 2011, http://archive.9news.com/rss/story.aspx?storyid=227984.

[87]John Hinderaker, "Rampaging Occupiers Attack 78-Year-Old Woman," *PowerLine,* November 5, 2011, http://www.powerlineblog.com/archives/2011/11/rampaging-occupiers-attack-78-year-old-woman.php.

House, striking the presidential residence with at least one bullet.[88]

In Eureka, California, a protester defecated inside a local bank.[89] In New York, demonstrators entered the restroom of a local business, broke the sink, clogged the toilet, and flooded the shop—causing some $3,000 in damages.[90] In Santa Cruz, California, OWSers dumped an estimated 200 pounds of human feces near the county Veterans Memorial Building.[91] In Pennsylvania, a self-identified member of Occupy Philadelphia burglarized a Havertown home.[92]

Some Occupy activists have been investigated for possible ties to terrorist organizations. Chicago OWS leaders Joe Iosbaker and Andy Thayer recently had their homes raided by the FBI on suspicion that they had provided material support to such groups as Hamas and the FARC, a revolutionary Marxist-Leninist organization in Colombia. Notably, Iosbaker in the 1990s was a leader of the New Party, a socialist entity to which then state Senator Barack Obama belonged.[93]

---

[88]"Man Charged with Obama Assassination Attempt," *Freedom Eden*, November 17, 2011, http://freedomeden.blogspot.com/2011/11/oscar-ramiro-ortega-hernandez.html.

[89]Joe Schoffstall, "#Occupy Protest in California: 'Who Pooped on the Bank?!'," *Media Research Center TV*, November 8, 2011, http://www.mrctv.org/videos/occupy-protest-california-who-pooped-bank.

[90]Amber Sutherland, "Occupiers Terrorize Us: Eatery," *New York Post*, November 8, 2011, http://nypost.com/2011/11/08/occupiers-terrorize-us-eatery/.

[91]"Hazmat Crew Called in to Remove 200 lbs of Human Feces Near Occupy Santa Cruz," *Verum Serum*, November 19, 2011, http://www.verumserum.com/?p=33789.

[92]Josh Fernandez, "Police: Havertown Robber Claimed to Be from Occupy Philly," *philly.com*, November 30, 2011, http://articles.philly.com/2011-11-30/news/30459084_1_robber-anonymous-tip-line-havertown.

[93]Jim Hoft, "Occupy Chicago Protest Leaders Are Under Investigation by FBI for Links to Terrorism," *Gateway Pundit*, October 26, 2011, http://www.thegatewaypundit.com/2011/10/occupy-chicago-leaders-are-under-investigation-by-fbi-for-links-to-terrorism/; "Joe Iosbaker," *KeyWiki*, http://keywiki.org/index.php/Joe_Iosbaker; "Andy Thayer," *KeyWiki*, http://keywiki.org/Andy_Thayer.

Violence was integral not only to the protesters' lives but to their intentions as well. A flyer titled "When Should You Shoot a Cop?" was distributed at Occupy Phoenix. In a typically criminal justification for criminal behavior, the flyer asserted that "far more injustice, violence, torture, theft, and outright murder has been committed in the name of 'law enforcement' than has been committed in spite of it." The flyer spells out the course of action this vision of reality demands: "When those violently victimizing the innocent have badges, become a cop-killer.... The next time you hear of a police officer being killed 'in the line of duty,' take a moment to consider the very real possibility that maybe in that case, the 'law enforcer' was the bad guy and the 'cop killer' was the good guy."[94]

In late October, officials in Oakland, California, sought to remove members of OWS from the plaza surrounding City Hall to give municipal workers an opportunity to clean up the mounds of garbage and filth that the protesters had deposited there. When many in the crowd ignored repeated instructions to vacate the premises, police were dispatched to clear out the area.[95] A mob of 400 armed with rocks and bottles tried to reoccupy the site by force, provoking clashes with riot police. Some protesters threw paint at the officers' faces while chanting, "This is why we call you pigs!" Ultimately, 85 provocateurs were arrested, some subdued by clubs and pepper-spray.[96] It was just what the OWS

---

[94]Mike Opelka, "Flyer Found at Occupy Phoenix Ponders: 'When Should You Shoot A Cop?'," *The Blaze,* October 28, 2011, http://www. theblaze.com/stories/2011/10/28/alleged-flyer-at-occupy-phoenix-ponders-when-should-you-shoot-a-cop/; Annette Roberts, "When Should You Shoot a Cop," *clearchannel.com,* October 27, 2011 http://content. clearchannel.com/cc-common/mlib/3359/10/3359_1319803260.pdf.

[95]Jacob Laksin, "Occupy Wall Street Out!," *FrontPage Mag,* October 27, 2011, http://www.frontpagemag.com/2011/jlaksin/occupy-wall-street-out/.

[96]Tiffany Gabbay, "Occupy Oakland Protesters Try to Retake Campsite, Hurl Paint at Police While Chanting 'This Is Why We Call You Pigs'," *The Blaze,* October 25, 2011, http://www.theblaze.com/stories/2011/10/25/occupy-oakland-protesters-try-to-retake-camp-site-hurl-paint-at-police-while-chanting-this-is-why-we-call-you-pigs/.

organizers were hoping for. In Kalle Lasn's words, "police brutality actually helps the movement," by drawing media attention and making the protesters appear to be victims.[97]

Oakland was again the scene of violence on November 2, when hundreds of OWS demonstrators lit a large bonfire with fifteen-foot flames in the middle of a downtown street and successfully shut down operations at one of America's busiest ports. A mob smashed the windows of a Wells Fargo bank, chanting, "Banks got bailed out. We got sold out." The protesters also spray-painted obscenities on an exterior wall and blocked the front door of a nearby Citibank.[98] This incident came just two days after Leo Gerard—international president of United Steelworkers, an advisor to President Obama and a board member of several George Soros–funded political operations–called for even "more militancy."[99] He told an interviewer, "You're damn right Wall Street occupiers speak for us."[100]

Following the Money to Familiar Sources

Two weeks after its launch, OWS retained the Alliance for Global Justice (AGJ) as its fiscal sponsor to manage online donations to

97 Elizabeth Flock, "Occupy Wall Street: An Interview with Kalle Lasn, the Man Behind it All," *Washington Post,* October 12, 2011, http://www.washingtonpost.com/blogs/blogpost/post/occupy-wall-street-an-interview-with-kalle-lasn-the-man-behind-it-all/2011/10/12/gIQAC81xfL_blog.html.

98 Elizabeth Weise, "Oakland Police Clash with Protesters," *USA Today,* November 3, 2011, http://usatoday30.usatoday.com/news/nation/story/2011-11-02/occupy-wall-street-veterans/51046142/1.

99 Aaron Klein, "Obama Advisor Calls for 'More Militancy' In Occupy Protests. Serves on Organizations that Helped Craft President's Healthcare, 'Stimulus' Laws" *Klein Online,* November 4, 2011, http://kleinonline.wnd.com/2011/11/04/obama-advisor-calls-for-more-militancy-in-occupy-protests-serves-on-organizations-that-helped-craft-presidents-healthcare-stimulus-laws/.

100 Jack Coleman, "Union Chief: 'We Need More Militancy ... Blocking Bridges, Occupying Banks'," *Fox News,* November 3, 2011, http://nation.foxnews.com/occupy-wall-street/2011/11/03/union-chief-we-need-more-militancy-blocking-bridges-occupying-banks.

the protesters.[101] AGJ was originally established to support the communist dictatorship in Nicaragua; it continues to underwrite and promote the activities of Marxist movements in Central America. AGJ receives funding from several huge left-wing foundations, including George Soros's Open Society Institute and Tides.[102]

Another key source of financial support for OWS is the online funding site Kickstarter,[103] with additional donations being funneled through WePay.[104] Other monies are contributed by visitors to specific OWS occupation websites. By the beginning of November, OWS had raised $500,000.[105] One of its more famous benefactors was Michael Moore, the filmmaker, who gave $1,000 (of his $50 million net worth) to the cause.[106]

OWS deposits its money in two accounts: one at Amalgamated Bank, which bills itself as "the only 100 percent union-owned bank in the United States," and the other at the People's Federal

---

[101]Alyssa Newcomb, "Human Blunder Loses Occupy Wall Street $144,000," *ABC News*, October 11, 2011, http://abcnews.go.com/blogs/business/2011/10/human-blunder-loses-occupy-wall-street-144000/.

[102]Matthew Vadum, "Occupy Wall Street and Soros' Fingerprints," *FrontPage Mag*, November 4, 2011, http://www.frontpagemag.com/2011/matthew-vadum/occupy-wall-street-and-soros-fingerprints/.

[103]"Occupy Wall Street Media," *KickStarter*, http://www.kickstarter.com/projects/610964639/occupy-wall-street-media.

[104]Neal Ungerleider, "The Stealth Leaders Of Occupy Wall Street," *FastCompany*, http://www.fastcompany.com/1785698/stealth-leaders-occupy-wall-street.

[105]Billy Hallowell, "*AP* Publishes Confusing Article About the Left's Role In Occupy Wall Street," *The Blaze*, November 2, 2011, http://www.theblaze.com/stories/2011/11/02/ap-publishes-confusing-piece-about-the-lefts-role-in-occupy-wall-street/.

[106]Melissa Klein, "Occupy Wall Street Protesters Have Amassed $230,000 and Supplies," *New York Post*, October 16, 2011, http://nypost.com/2011/10/16/occupy-wall-street-protesters-have-amassed-230000-and-supplies/; "How Much Is Michael Moore Worth?," *CelebrityNetWorth*, http://www.celebritynetworth.com/richest-celebrities/directors/michael-moore-net-worth/.

Credit Union.[107] In addition, OWS stores its donated supplies (e.g., blankets, sleeping bags, food, medicine and toiletries) in a cavernous space provided at no cost by the United Federation of Teachers, which has offices in a building near the Zuccotti Park headquarters of OWS's New York regiment.[108] *The Occupied Wall Street Journal,* an OWS publication, is supported by the Independent Media Center,[109] which is funded by the Tides Foundation.[110]

The Socialism of Fools and the OWS Radicals

The German Marxist August Bebel once said that "anti-Semitism is the socialism of fools," but anti-Semitism has recently also become the socialism of the radical left. This left is in full-throated support of the terrorist organizations Hezbollah and Hamas, which have promised "death to Israel" and are partners in the "Boycott, Divest, Sanction" campaign to destroy the Jewish state. The Palestinian Boycott, Divestment and Sanctions National Committee announced at the outset of the protests its "solidarity" with Occupy Wall Street, describing Palestinians as "part of the 99 percent around the world that suffer at the hands of the 1 percent whose greed and ruthless quest for hegemony have led to unspeakable suffering and endless war."[111]

---

[107]Rebecca Rosenberg, "Rain Scatters Occupy Wall Street Protesters," *New York Post,* October 20, 2011, http://nypost.com/2011/10/20/rain-scatters-occupy-wall-street-protesters/; "A Bank for the People Is Born," *Amalgamated Bank,* https://www.amalgamatedbank.com/our-history.

[108]Micah Landau, "UFT Helps Occupy Wall Street," *United Federation of Teachers,* November 10, 2011, http://www.uft.org/news-stories/uft-helps-occupy-wall-street.

[109]Iris Somberg, "$3.6 Million from Soros Backs 'Occupy Wall Street', Media Ignore or Downplay Connection," *MRC NewsBusters,* October 14, 2011, http://newsbusters.org/blogs/iris-somberg/2011/10/14/36-million-soros-aids-groups-support-promote-occupy-wall-street.

[110]Tides Foundation And Tides Center, http://www.discoverthenetworks.org/funderProfile.asp?fndid=5184.

[111]"Occupy Wall Street Not Palestine!," *BDS Movement,* October 14, 2011, http://www.bdsmovement.net/2011/occupy-wall-street-not-palestine-8163#.TtXGeWCoxWN.

OWS anti-Semitism was on display with slogans denouncing "Jewish bankers," "Wall Street Jews," "Jewish billionaires" and "Zionist Jews." Many of its posters featured caricatures of Jewish bankers that bore a striking resemblance to the graphics of Nazi and Arab propaganda campaigns. No OWS leader denounced this Jew-hatred or sought to distance the movement from it.[112] Anti-Semitism has become so much the culture and currency of the left that disagreeing with it would be unthinkable.

One OWS protester, Danny Cline, gained momentary YouTube notoriety when a video was posted showing him abusing an elderly Jew with the taunts: "You're a bum, Jew," "Go back to Israel" and "You got the money ... Jewish man."[113] Another OWS radical stated, "The small ethnic Jewish population in this country, they have a firm grip on America's media [and] finances."[114] In Chicago, Hatem Abudayyeh, executive director of the Arab-American Action Network—an organization founded by the radical PLO propagandist and Obama friend Rashid Khalidi—was a featured OWS speaker. In 2009, the FBI had raided Abudayyeh's home on suspicion of his ties to Hamas. Now he led a cheering crowd in chants of "Free Palestine" and told them, "Israel is beginning to be seen as the criminal pariah state that it is."[115]

At an Occupy L.A. rally, an employee of the Los Angeles Unified School District, Patricia McAllister, told a television reporter,

---

[112]Zombie, "More Anti-Semitism at Occupy Los Angeles," *PJ Media*, October 13, 2011, http://pjmedia.com/tatler/2011/10/13/more-anti-semitism-at-occupy-los-angeles/; "Occupy LA Protester: 'Zionist Jews' Who Run Banks Should Be 'Run Out of This Country'," *Breitbart*, October 15, 2011, http://www.breitbart.com/?s=occupyla-protester-zionist-jews-who-run-banks-should-be-run-out-this-country; "Don Feder & Jeff Katz on Occupy Wall Street Anti-Semitism—October 28, 2011," http://www.youtube.com/watch?v=Ol6voYeh5-k.

[113]"Anti-Semitism at Occupy Wall Street Protest," http://www.youtube.com/watch?v=l3Y9CARUwio.

[114]"Hate at Occupy Wall Street," http://www.youtube.com/watch?v=NIl-RQCPJcew.

[115]Ben Shapiro, "The Anti-Semites of Occupy Wall Street," *FrontPage Mag*, October 26, 2011, http://www.frontpagemag.com/2011/ben-shapiro/the-anti-semites-of-occupy-wall-street/.

"I think that the Zionist Jews who are running these big banks and our Federal Reserve ... need to be run out of this country."[116] McAllister was fired when her school district learned of her comments, but she remained unrepentant: "I think that we should be able to [tell] the truth about what the Jews are doing to this nation, the Zionist Jews, how they control the money system, how they control the markets and everything else.... Jews have been run out of 109 countries throughout history. And we need to run them out of this one." McAllister made these remarks with an Occupy L.A. spokeswoman standing nearby. The spokeswoman refused to condemn McAllister's rhetoric, saying it "doesn't erode our [movement's] credibility, not one bit."[117]

In early November, a contingent of protesters at an Occupy Boston rally marched into the lobby of the building that houses the city's Israeli consulate and held a brief sit-in, chanting, "Hey hey, ho ho! Israeli apartheid's gotta go!" and "Long live the *intifada*!" "Free, free Palestine!" "Viva viva Palestina!" "Not another nickel! Not another dime! No more money for Israel's crimes!" and "Disarm the police, from Israel to Greece!"[118]

The radical anti-Israel group Jewish Voice for Peace distributed flyers at Chicago OWS that said: "Refuse to Pay Taxes. Destroy Israel."[119] Another group, the U.S. Campaign to End the Israeli Occupation, asserted that "the connections between the struggles of Palestinians and the Occupy movement are unmistakable: the

---

[116]Ibid.

[117]Noel Sheppard, "Anti-Semitic Occupy LA Protester Fired by School District, Media Mostly Mum," *MRC NewsBusters*, October 20, 2011, http://newsbusters.org/blogs/noel-sheppard/2011/10/20/anti-semitic-occupy-la-protester-fired-school-district-media-mostly-m.

[118]Ira Stoll, "Occupy Boston Occupies Israeli Consulate," *Future Of Capitali$m*, November 5, 2011, http://www.futureofcapitalism.com/2011/11/occupy-boston-occupies-israeli-consulate#.

[119]Rebel Pundit, "#OccupyChicago Joins 'Destroy Israel' Anti-war, Anti-America 'Peace' March," *Breitbart*, October 14, 2011, http://www.breitbart.com/big-government/2011/10/14/occupychicago-joins-destroy-israel-anti-war—anti-america-peace-march/.

spotlight on privilege and inequality, the mass imprisonment, the police repression, and the people's steadfastness."[120]

The socialism of fools is a credo for those who designed the Occupy Wall Street movement. In 2004, Kalle Lasn authored an *Adbusters* article attacking America's most influential neoconservatives under the title, "Why Won't Anyone Say They Are Jewish?"[121] In a June 2009 article with photo montage, *Adbusters* likened Gaza to the Warsaw ghetto—a Hamas propaganda analogy taken up by the left, aiming to identify Jews with their Nazi murderers.[122]

The OWS leader Lisa Fithian spent several weeks in 2003 working with the International Solidarity Movement, a terrorist support group, in the Palestinian cities of Jenin and Nablus, where she served as a human shield attempting to obstruct Israeli security forces from demolishing the homes and tunnels of Palestinian terrorists.[123] At a protest in Texas on May 31, 2010, Fithian accused Israel of "slaughter[ing] Palestinians every single day in Gaza and the occupied territories," and called for an end to "the U.S. tax dollars that fund that [Israeli] occupation." During the same event, demonstrators chanted, "Long live *intifada!*" and "Palestine will be free, from the river to the sea!"—a Hamas slogan calling for the obliteration of the Jewish state.[124]

The Islamic Republic of Iran, which is the center of international Jew-hatred, has also lined up behind OWS. The country's supreme leader, Ayatollah Ali Khamenei, lauded OWS for having

---

[120]Anna Baltzer, "Tearing Down the Walls from Occupy Oakland to Occupied Palestine," *US Campaign to End the Israeli Occupation,* November 1, 2011, http://www.endtheoccupation.org/article.php?id=3134.

[121]Alana Goodman, "Organizer Behind 'Occupy Wall Street' Has History of Anti-Jewish Writing," *Commentary,* October 13, 2011, https://www.commentarymagazine.com/2011/10/13/occupy-wall-street-kalle-lasn/.

[122]Saeed David Mohammad, "A Ghettoized Gaza Bears Striking Similarities to the Warsaw Ghetto," *AdBusters,* June 9, 2009, https://www.adbusters.org/magazine/83/gaza.html.

[123]"About Lisa," op. cit.

[124]"Lisa Fithian Speaks Out Against Israeli Attacks on Gaza Freedom Flotilla," http://www.youtube.com/watch?v=iWxMbTo8VZg.

"exposed" the "corrupt foundation" of American society, and gleefully predicted that the movement would "grow so that it will bring down the capitalist system and the West."[125] The Iranian armed forces' deputy chief of staff for culture and defense publicity, General Seyed Massoud Jazzayeri, likewise characterized OWS not only as "a revolution and a comprehensive movement against corruption in the U.S.," but as a force that "will no doubt end in the downfall of the Western capitalist system."[126] And a website affiliated with the Iran-created terror group Hezbollah portrayed OWS as a movement that was courageously exposing the "corruption, poverty [and] social inequality in the U.S."[127]

The OWS Network

Given the fact that its objectives so loudly echo those of the international communist left, it is to be expected that Occupy Wall Street would be supported by the Communist Party USA (CPUSA); and, given its anti-Semitism, by the American Nazi Party. Working closely with Occupy Los Angeles are two Southern California communists—veteran party leader Arturo Cambron and his comrade Mario Brito—who declared at the beginning of the protests that OWS was "an international movement" whose goal was "economic justice" and the elimination of the "income inequality the vast majority of Americans" view as "a major problem."[128] In an address to 3,000 attendees at an Occupy Chicago

---

[125]"Khamenei Claims Occupy Wall Street Protests Will Topple US Capitalism," *The Guardian*, October 12, 2011, http://www.theguardian.com/world/2011/oct/12/iran-us-protests-topple-capitalism?newsfeed=true.

[126]"Iran Calls Wall Street Protests 'American Spring'," *USA Today/AP*, October 9, 2011, http://usatoday30.usatoday.com/news/world/story/2011-10-09/iran-wall-street-protest/50713380/1.

[127]"Occupy Wall Street Protesters Plan New Rally," *almoqawama.org*, October 29, 2011, http://almoqawama.org/?a=content.id&id=25867.

[128]Trevor Loudon, "Communists Lead 'Occupy Los Angeles' Movement—Nationwide Takeover Planned," *New Zeal*, October 10, 2011, http://www.trevorloudon.com/2011/10/communists-lead-occupy-los-angeles-movement-nationwide-takeover-planned/.

rally, John Bachtell, a spokesman from the CPUSA's national board, conveyed "greetings and solidarity from the Communist Party" and received a number of loud ovations from the crowd.[129]

Another key OWS ally is the National Lawyers Guild (NLG), from whose ranks came the 200 attorneys who served as volunteer legal observers at OWS events in New York, looking for evidence of overzealous policing.[130] Once the chief legal instrument of the Communist Party USA[131] and a longtime defender of domestic radicals and terrorists, the Lawyers Guild provides representation for the OWS demonstrators who are arrested. The affinity between the two groups is natural, given the NLG mission of promoting "basic change in the structure of our political and [capitalist] economic system"—a system, it claims, where "vast disparities in individual and social wealth" render "neither democracy nor social justice ... possible."[132]

Operatives of the radical organization ACORN (disbanded after a major scandal but still operating under other names) played a major role in organizing the OWS protests nationwide. The Working Families Party (WFP), an ACORN front, helped mobilize the

---

[129]David Martosko, "Red, White and Angry: Communist, Nazi Parties Endorse 'Occupy' Protests," *Daily Caller*, October 17, 2011, http://dailycaller.com/2011/10/17/red-white-and-angry%E2%80%A8-communist-nazi-parties-endorse-occupy-protests/ In addition to official backing from the Communist Party, OWS has been supported by the Revolutionary Communist Party, the Party for Socialism and Liberation, and the Marxist Student Union. OWS has neither declined nor repudiated any of these endorsements.

[130]Claire Zillman, "Meet The Lawyers Keeping an Eye on Occupy Wall Street," *AM Law Daily*, October 18, 2011, http://amlawdaily.typepad.com/amlawdaily/2011/10/meet-occupy-wall-streets-legal-team.html.

[131]National Lawyers Guild, http://www.discoverthenetworks.org/groupProfile.asp?grpid=6162.

[132]"About NLG," *National Lawyers Guild*, http://www.nlg.org/about/; "Our History," *National Lawyers Guild*, http://www.nlg.org/our-history.

demonstrations in New York.[133] WFP organizer Nelini Stamp lauds her organization's effort to bring "revolutionary change" to the "capitalist system" that is "not working for any of us."[134]

Newer offshoots of ACORN such as the New York Communities for Change (NYCC)—led by a longtime ACORN lobbyist Jon Kest—have helped organize OWS demonstrations in lower Manhattan. In Pennsylvania, Action United has participated in the Occupy Pittsburgh rallies. In Florida, Organize Now takes part in Occupy Orlando. The Alliance of Californians for Community Empowerment helps lead the Occupy Los Angeles protests. And New England United for Justice, headed by former ACORN national president Maude Hurd, has participated in the related "Take Back Boston" rallies in Massachusetts.[135]

News reports indicate that New York Communities for Change hired approximately 100 former ACORN-affiliated staffers, paying some of them $100 per day to attend and support OWS demonstrations. Further, NYCC recruited dozens of people from New York homeless shelters and paid them $10 per hour to serve as door-to-door canvassers to collect money for the movement. According to an inside source, top ex-ACORN staffers and current NYCC officials began planning for OWS as early as February 2011: "What people don't understand is that ACORN is

---

[133]Matthew Vadum, "ACORN: Puppet Master of Occupy Wall Street," *FrontPage Mag,* October 11, 2011, http://www.frontpagemag.com/2011/matthew-vadum/acorn-is-behind-occupy-wall-street/.

[134]Trevor Loudon, "Video Exposing How 'Occupy Wall Street' Was Organized from Day One by SEIU/ACORN Front—The Working Family Party, and How They All Tie to the Obama Administration, DNC, Democratic Socialists of America, Tides and George Soros," *New Zeal,* October 7, 2011, http://www.trevorloudon.com/2011/10/video-exposing-how-'occupy-wall-street'-was-organized-from-day-one-by-seiua-corn-front-—the-working-family-party-and-how-they-all-tie-to-the-oba ma-administration-dnc-democr/.

[135]Matthew Vadum, "ACORN: Puppet Master of Occupy Wall Street," op. cit.

behind this—and that this, what's happening now, is all part of the ... plans to go after the banks, Chase in particular."[136]

Another OWS organizer is former ACORN chief executive Bertha Lewis, whose new organization, The Black Institute (TBI), calls its protests "Occupy Black America" and "Occupy The Hood." TBI and several other ACORN reincarnations together organized an event called "New Bottom Line," a financial protest aimed at persuading people to move their money out of major banks.[137] The date set for the withdrawal, November 5, was selected because it is known in the British Commonwealth as "Guy Fawkes Day," named after the man who attempted to blow up Parliament and assassinate King James I in 1605. Fawkes has become an icon of the Occupy demonstrations and the "Anonymous" hacker collective, thus accounting for the large number of stylized Guy Fawkes masks (popularized in the movie *V for Vendetta*) at OWS events.[138]

The October 2011 Movement, based in Washington, D.C., is also an ally of OWS. It calls on the federal government to end all American economic policies "which foster a wealth divide"; to "tax the rich and corporations" at especially high rates so as to diminish the "significant disparities of wealth" that exist between the "extremely wealthy" and "the 99 percent"; to create a single-payer health-care system while expanding social-welfare programs; to devote large sums of money to "creating [public-sector] jobs" while eschewing "spending cuts"; to "end corporate influence over the political process" by banning corporate

---

[136]Jana Winter, "ACORN Playing Behind Scenes Role In 'Occupy' Movement," *Fox News,* October 26, 2011, http://www.foxnews.com/us/2011/10/26/exclusive-acorn-playing-behind-scenes-role-in-occupy-movement/.

[137]Joel B. Pollack, "Email from Lisa Fithian to #OccupyWallStreet Confirms ACORN Role In Occupy's Next Assault on Banks," *Breitbart,* October 26, 2011, http://www.breitbart.com/big-government/2011/10/26/exclusive-email-from-lisa-fithian-to-occupywallstreet-confirms-acorn-role-in-occupys-next-assault-on-banks/.

[138]Ibid.

campaign contributions and establishing a publicly financed campaign system; and to guarantee everyone a "sustainable living wage" and a "publicly-funded" education from preschool through college.[139]

Following the onset of the OWS protests, the left-wing group MoveOn.org announced its plan to launch a protest movement of its own to complement "the amazing work being done by brave Occupy Wall Street protesters," to "end the big banks' excessive influence" and to "Make Wall Street Pay" for its transgressions against "economic justice."[140]

Environmental radicals also joined the OWS movement. Among the most prominent was Bill McKibben, founder of 350.org, who calls the United States the world's chief polluter and derides its "materialism" and "hyperindividualism"—i.e., freedom.[141] In October, as the OWS protests were reaching critical mass, he wrote: "For too long, Wall Street has been occupying the offices of our government, and the cloakrooms of our legislatures.... You could even say Wall Street's been occupying our atmosphere, since any attempt to do anything about climate change always run [sic] afoul of the biggest corporations on the planet. So it's a damned good thing the tables have turned."[142]

The list of prominent leftists supporting OWS is extremely long. Among the more noteworthy are the Marxist cop-killer

---

[139]"Occupy Wall Street," *Popular Resistance*, https://www.popularresistance.org/tag/occupy-wall-street/.

[140]Aaron Klein, "Soros Army Launches Wall Street Assault of Its Own: MoveOn.org Action Campaign Aims to Rebuild U.S. Financial System," *Klein Online*, October 24, 2011, http://kleinonline.wnd.com/2011/10/24/soros-army-launches-wall-street-assault-of-its-own-moveon-org-action-campaign-aims-to-rebuilt-u-s-financial-system-2/.

[141]Bill McKibben, "What a Real, Living, Durable Economy Looks Like," *Powell's*, http://www.powells.com/essays/mckibben.html.

[142]Stephen Lacey, "Climate Activists Stand With Occupy Wall Street Movement," *ThinkProgress*, October 5, 2011, http://thinkprogress.org/romm/2011/10/05/337255/climate-activism-occupy-wall-street-movement/.

Mumia Abu Jamal, who says that OWS's "central focus" is simply "capitalism, greed writ large";[143] the former Obama "green jobs czar" Van Jones, who calls OWS a "beautiful manifestation of moral clarity";[144] and the billionaire financier George Soros, who says he "can understand [the protesters'] sentiment, frankly."[145] Bill Ayers—unrepentant terrorist, Hamas enthusiast and former Obama confidant—described the Occupy movement as a "North American Spring."[146] Ayers lauded the protesters for their "brilliance" and condemned America's "violent culture."[147]

The OWS and the Union Reds

The fact that unions, especially the public employees' unions, have lined up behind Occupy Wall Street reflects the recent subversion of the labor movement by the neo-communists who are behind OWS. During the forty years prior to 1995, the AFL-CIO's two presidents, George Meany (1955–1979) and Lane Kirkland (1979–1995), were known for their centrist liberalism and anti-communism. But when the socialist John Sweeney succeeded Kirkland in 1995, he shifted organized labor's politics dramatically leftward. One of his first orders of business was to repeal an AFL-CIO rule, instituted by

---

[143]"Mumia Abu Jamal on Occupy Wall Street," *Occupy Wall Street*, December 20, 2011, http://occupywallst.org/forum/mumia-abu-jamal-on-occupy-wall-street/; "Mumia Abu-Jamal Speaks on 'Occupy Wall Street'," https://www.youtube.com/watch?v=H-uVrAWS5dk&feature=related: "Mumia Abu Jamal—What Do They Want?," https://www.youtube.com/watch?feature=endscreen&NR=1&v=b7upJglVcNo.

[144]Van Jones, "Defend Occupy Wall Street From Eviction," *The Huffington Post*, October 13, 2011, http://www.huffingtonpost.com/van-jones/occupy-wall-street-eviction_b_1009955.html.

[145]Matthew Vadum "Occupy Wall Street Jumps the Shark," *FrontPage Mag*, October 6, 2011, http://www.frontpagemag.com/2011/matthew-vadum/occupy-wall-street-jumps-the-shark/.

[146]http://www.suntimes.com/news/washington/8211533-452/bill-ayers-rooting-for-the-protesters.html.

[147]Billy Hallowell, "Radical Bill Ayers Speaks to Occupy Chicago Protesters About Revolution & the Tea Party," *The Blaze*, October 26, 2011, http://www.theblaze.com/stories/2011/10/26/radical-bill-ayers-speaks-to-occupy-chicago-protesters-about-revolution-the-tea-party/.

Walter Reuther, that had prohibited communists from becoming leaders of its member unions.[148] A parallel development was the ascendancy of Andrew Stern, a Sixties radical, to the presidency of the Service Employees International Union (SEIU) in 1996.

The leftward shift of the labor movement spurred a dramatic increase in political activism, which was first manifest in the anti-globalization riots that caused the shutdown of the 1999 World Trade Organization (WTO) meetings in Seattle. The AFL-CIO[149] was instrumental in organizing a massive rally.[150] The United Steelworkers union dispatched 1,400 of its members—including top-level officials like Tom Conway, vice president, and Leo Gerard, the international secretary-treasurer at the time—to participate in the disorders whose target was, in effect, international capitalism.[151]

The WTO disturbances foreshadowed some ugly union assaults on the democratic process. In the state of Wisconsin in 2011, Governor Scott Walker, a Republican, sought to address a projected $3.6 billion state budget deficit by loosening the stranglehold of government unions such as the SEIU on the state's politicians and finances.[152] In response to Walker's initiative, tens of thousands of union activists and their supporters invaded the seat of government

---

[148]John Sweeney, http://www.discoverthenetworks.org/individualProfile.asp?indid=2009.

[149]American Federation Of Labor—Congress Of Industrial Organizations, http://www.discoverthenetworks.org/groupProfile.asp?grpid=7507.

[150]Kit Oldham and David Wilma, "After Protestors Fill the Streets and Shut Down the WTO Opening Session, Mayor Paul Schell Declares a State of Emergency and Police Use Tear Gas and Rubber Bullets to Clear Downtown Seattle on November 30, 1999.," *HistoryLink*, October 20, 2009, http://www.historylink.org/index.cfm?DisplayPage=output.cfm&file_id=2142.

[151]Matthew Vadum, "Union Gangsters: Leo Gerard," *FrontPage Mag*, November 11, 2011, http://www.frontpagemag.com/2011/matthew-vadum/union-gangsters-leo-gerard/.

[152]Tina Korbe, "Myths vs. Facts of the Wisconsin Union Protest," *Daily Signal*, February 20, 2011, http://dailysignal.com/2011/02/20/video-myths-vs-facts-of-the-wisconsin-union-protest/; Lachlan Markey, "Liberal Groups Dump More Than $14 Million into Recall Elections," *Daily Signal*, August 8, 2011, http://dailysignal.com/2011/08/08/chart-liberal-groups-dump-more-than-14-million-into-recall-elections/.

in Madison, intent on obstructing the legislation. Screaming mobs of demonstrators stormed the capitol building and physically occupied it, blocking legislators as they entered to cast their votes.[153]

OWS has gained strong support from the SEIU[154] and other government unions such as AFSCME (the Association of Federal, State, County and Municipal Employees)[155] and the United Federation of Teachers. AFL-CIO president Richard Trumka says, "We support the protesters in their determination ... to call for fundamental change."[156]

Support from the Left-wing Media

One reason for the success of the smokescreen that hides the anti-democratic intentions of OWS is the support it can count on from network media and the mainstream press, which has largely portrayed it as a spontaneous uprising independent of any powerful, organized or well-financed influences.

New York Times reporter Natasha Lennard, who according to Politico.com has "played a pivotal role in the media narrative of Occupy Wall Street,"[157] was part of a panel of radicals brought together to discuss the theory, strategy and tactics of the OWS protests.[158] Lisa Simeone, a National Public Radio host, worked as

---

[153]"Crowd Rushing WI Capitol Doors," http://www.youtube.com/watch?v=Df5yT16a_og.

[154]Service Employees International Union, http://www.discoverthenetworks.org/groupProfile.asp?grpid=6535.

[155]American Federation Of State, County, And Municipal Employees, http://www.discoverthenetworks.org/groupProfile.asp?grpid=7515.

[156]Richard Trumka, "Statement by AFL-CIO President Richard Trumka On Occupy Wall Street," *AFL-CIO,* October 5, 2011, http://www.afl-cio.org/Press-Room/Press-Releases/Statement-by-AFL-CIO-President-Richard-Trumka-On-O3.

[157]Keach Hagey, "New Target for 'Occupy Wall Street' Critics: Media," *Politico,* October 25, 2011, http://www.politico.com/news/stories/1011/66764.html.

[158]Lee Stranahan, "*The New York Times* Reporter Natasha Lennard Is #OccupyWallStreet Activist, Supporter," *Breitbart,* October 24, 2011, http://www.breitbart.com/big-journalism/2011/10/24/new-video-reveals-new-york-times-reporter-natasha-lennard-is-occupywallstreet-activist-supporter/.

a spokeswoman for Occupy DC—a chapter of the OWS-affiliated October 2011 Movement—in violation of the network's ethics rules. When questioned by reporters about the matter, Simeone said that because she was a "freelancer" for NPR, she was not obligated to abide by its ethical principles.[159] She added, "Our main focus is that we are against corporatism and militarism.... [W]e are not going to stop acts of civil disobedience... "[160]

In one of many emails contained on a private listserv leaked to BigGovernment.com, MSNBC's Dylan Ratigan advised OWS protesters on how they ought to craft their press statements. "I love what you're doing." he said.[161] In another leaked email, *Rolling Stone's* Matt Taibbi offered a preview of his article "My Advice to the Wall Street Protesters," and expressed his "love" and "support" for OWS, while condemning the "unparalleled thievery and corruption" of Wall Street.[162] The racial arsonist and MSNBC host Al Sharpton made a very public appearance at an OWS rally in Atlanta, where he shouted: "It's time for us to occupy Wall Street, occupy Washington, occupy Alabama."[163]

Barbarism vs. Civilization

As a way of "normalizing" Occupy Wall Street, its supporters have tried to suggest that it is the opposite side of the coin to the Tea

---

[159]Matthew Boyle, "NPR Host Is Occupy DC Spokeswoman," *Daily Caller,* October 19, 2011, http://dailycaller.com/2011/10/19/npr-host-a-spokeswoman-for-occupy-d-c-possible-ethics-violation/.

[160]Wang Fengfeng, "Protestors to 'Occupy' Washington against Corporate Greed," *Xinhua,* October 6, 2011, http://news.xinhuanet.com/english2010/world/2011-10/06/c_131175863.htm; Simeone was later fired by NPR.

[161]Dylan Ratigan, "Dylan Ratigan Goes to Occupy Wall Street in NYC," *Dylan Ratigan,* October 3, 2011, http://www.dylanratigan.com/2011/10/03/dylans-weekend-at-occupywallstreet/.

[162]Matt Taibbi, "My Advice to the Occupy Wall Street Protesters," *Rolling Stone,* October 12, 2011, http://www.rollingstone.com/politics/news/my-advice-to-the-occupy-wall-street-protesters-20111012.

[163]Noel Sheppard, "MSNBC's Sharpton: People Favoring Voter IDs Want to 'Revoke the Voting Rights Act'," *MRC NewsBusters,* October 16, 2011, http://newsbusters.org/blogs/noel-sheppard/2011/10/16/sharpton-people-favoring-voter-ids-want-revoke-voting-rights-act.

Party demonstrations. President Obama has helped to propagate this view, observing that "in some ways" the OWS demonstrations are "not that different from some of the protests that we saw coming from the Tea Party."[164] According to Vice President Joe Biden, OWS and the Tea Party have "a lot in common," in the sense that both "do not think the system is fair."[165] But the Tea Party demonstrations resulted in almost no arrests, in contrast to the 4,800 that took place in the first two months of OWS.[166] The Tea Parties had no rapes, no deaths, no defecations. No $13 million bill for police overtime and cleanup afterward.[167] OWS can be said to be the opposite side of the coin to the Tea Party only in the sense that barbarism is the opposite side of the coin to civilization.

Occupy Wall Street is not a spontaneous uprising of the middle class, as its shadowy leaders have tried to portray it. It is but the latest incarnation of a much older movement —a movement by the far left which tried and failed during the Cold War to create a Soviet America, and which during the sixties tried to bring the "empire" down. It is a destructive movement organized by a new generation of radicals who draw their inspiration from the Marxists and communists who came before them. And, like their predecessors, these radicals have declared war on a system that has produced the freest and most prosperous society the world has ever seen, while promising a utopia that has never existed and never will.

[164]"Obama on Occupy Wall Street, Herman Cain," http://www.youtube.com/watch?v=zC73B8QFaYA.

[165]James Oliphant, "Biden Likens Occupy Wall Street to Tea Party, Blasts BofA," *Los Angeles Times,* October 6, 2011, http://articles.latimes.com/2011/oct/06/news/la-pn-biden-wallstreet-20111006.

[166]"Tea Party Subtopics," *AkDart,* http://akdart.com/obama123.html#WS.

[167]"CCTPP Meeting Minutes, February 14, 2012," *Crystal Coast Tea Party Patriots,* February 14, 2012, http://cctpp.com/?p=2710.

10

How Obama Betrayed America

"If we have to use force, it is because we are America. We are the indispensable nation. We stand tall. We see farther into the future."

—Madeleine Albright, Secretary of State under Bill Clinton

It is a judgment on Barack Obama's timorous, apologetic, irresponsible and ultimately anti-American conduct of foreign affairs that Madeleine Albright's words, spoken little more than 15 years ago, now sound as antique as a pronouncement by Harry Truman at the onset of the Cold War, the great challenge America confronted bravely and without equivocation a generation ago. While Obama has quoted this statement repeatedly to hide his real disdain for his country, he has set in motion policies meant to make America far from indispensable—a diminished nation that "leads from behind," if at all; a nation with a downsized military that is chronically uncertain about its meaning and its mission as it skulks in the wings of the world stage.

Albright's statement was made about Iraq when Democrats were still supporting their country's confrontation with its sadistic dictator Saddam Hussein, and before they defected from the war when its battles were just under way. As a senator, in step with his Democratic colleagues, Obama opposed America's war with Iraq

---

Originally published May 8, 2013, http://www.frontpagemag.com/2013/david-horowitz/how-obama-betrayed-america/; This is also a chapter in Horowitz, *Take No Prisoners: The Battle Plan for Defeating the Left*, Regnery, 2014.

while American troops were still in harm's way, and then opposed the military surge that finally won the victory. As president he presided over the withdrawal of all American forces from Iraq, against the wishes of the Joint Chiefs of Staff who wanted a continuing military presence, paid for with the blood of thousands of American men and women in arms. Obama thus turned that benighted nation over to the malign influences of America's chief enemy in the Middle East, Iran, while betraying every American who gave his or her life for its freedom.

Far from shouldering his responsibility as the commander-in-chief of America's global war on terror and embracing it as this generation's equivalent of the Cold War, Obama showed his distaste for the entire enterprise by dropping the term "War on Terror" and replacing it with an Orwellian phrase—"overseas contingency operations."[1] Minimizing the Islamist threat to the United States is not an oversight of the Obama administration; it is its policy.

It should not have been difficult for Obama to make the nation's defense a priority when he became America's commander-in-chief in January 2009. Eight years earlier, the American homeland had experienced a devastating attack which terrorists have been constantly trying to repeat. Since that dark day, the number of foreign states openly supporting terror has steadily increased, growing even more rapidly during Obama's tenure. Meanwhile the most dangerous Islamist regime—Iran—is being allowed to acquire nuclear weapons, while Washington dithers over pointless negotiations. With secular governments giving way to Islamist regimes in Turkey, Egypt and Iraq, with the Taliban on the rise in Afghanistan and an American withdrawal imminent, the global situation today has eerie parallels to the early Cold War, with implications equally dire. Yet instead of policies that put U.S.

---

[1]Scott Wilson and Al Kamen, "'Global War On Terror' Is Given New Name," *The Washington Post*, March 25, 2009, http://www.washingtonpost.com/wp-dyn/content/article/2009/03/24/AR2009032402818.html.

national security first and are pursued without hesitation or apology, Obama's time in office has been marked by *mea culpas*, retreats, accommodations and even support of Islamist foes—most ominously of the Muslim Brotherhood in Egypt, which with Obama's personal intervention swept aside an American ally and is busily creating a totalitarian state.

In the four years since Obama's first inauguration, almost three times as many Americans have been killed in Afghanistan as in the eight years of the Bush administration. Withdrawal, not victory, has been Obama's goal from the outset, and now is the only outcome possible. During the Obama years, there have been more than 8,000 Islamic terrorist attacks on "infidels" across the globe, a twenty-five percent rise over the years in which the fighting in Iraq was at its height. Yet, in the face of this bloody and intensifying Islamist offensive, Obama has tried to convince the American people that the war against al-Qaeda has been essentially "won"—by him—and that the terrorist threat is subsiding.[2] Denial of the war Islamists have declared on us, and denial of the threat it represents, is the heart of the Obama doctrine that has guided this nation's policies for more than four years.

Obama's desire for rapprochement with Iran's Islamist regime has prompted the administration to drag its feet on the sanctions designed to halt Iran's nuclear program. For the same reason, the president and his administration were silent when hundreds of thousands of Iranians poured into the streets of Teheran to call for an end to the dictatorship and were met by an orgy of violence from the mullahs' thugs. Because of the White House's moral and political timidity, borne out of its denial of the Islamist threat and the guilty conviction that America (presumably an even greater predator) has no right to condemn another nation, this tipping point in Iran tipped the wrong way.

---

[2]"List of Islamic Terror Attacks for the Past 30 Days," *TheReligionof-Piece.com,* http://www.thereligionofpeace.com/index.html#Attacks.

The administration's denial was also egregiously manifest in its response to the massacre of 13 unarmed soldiers at Fort Hood by an Islamic fanatic, Nidal Malik Hasan, who three and a half years later still has not been brought to trial. The Fort Hood terrorist successfully infiltrated the American military and, despite open expressions of hatred against the West, was promoted to U.S. Army major. The Obama administration's Kafkaesque response to an obvious case of Islamist violence against the U.S. was to classify the terrorist attack as an incident of "workplace violence,"[3] and thus to hide the fact that Hasan was a Muslim soldier in a war against the infidels of the West.

This inability to name our enemies was on display again on the eleventh anniversary of 9/11, when jihadists staged demonstrations and launched attacks against the American embassies in Egypt and other Islamic countries. In Libya, al-Qaeda terrorists overran an American consular compound and murdered the American ambassador and three brave warriors. The attack took place in a country that had recently been destabilized by Obama's own intervention to oust its dictator. As senator, Obama had denounced a military intervention in Iraq *on principle,* although unlike his Libyan adventure the Iraq invasion had been authorized by both houses of Congress and a unanimous UN Security Council resolution. As president, he had invoked the principle of non-intervention to justify his passivity in the face of governmental atrocities in Syria and Iran. But in Libya he conducted an unauthorized invasion of a country that posed no threat to the United States and was not, as Syria is, in alliance with the mullahs of Iran and the terrorists of Hezbollah. The chaos that followed Obama's Libyan intervention led directly to the rise of the local al-Qaeda, which planted its flag atop the same American outpost in Benghazi it destroyed, along with our ambassador.

---

[3]"Lawmakers Blast Administration For Calling Fort Hood Massacre 'Workplace Violence'," *Fox News,* December 7, 2011, http://www.foxnews.com/politics/2011/12/06/military-growing-terrorist-target-lawmakers-warn/.

The events in Benghazi were a stark revelation of the consequences of a foreign policy without a moral compass. The battle over the embassy lasted seven hours. Although the president learned about the attack shortly after it began and although the embattled Americans inside the compound begged the White House for help, with U.S. fighter jets in Italy only an hour away, the president, in one of the most shameful acts in the history of that office, denied help by leaving his post, so that only silence answered their desperate calls. The president and his administration then went into cover-up mode—lying to Congress and the American people, pretending for weeks afterwards that the attack was the result of a spontaneous demonstration over an anti-Mohammed internet video, whose director they then threw in jail.

Before his overthrow, dictator Muammar Gaddafi had warned that his demise would unleash the forces of the Islamic jihad not only in his own country but throughout North Africa. This was a prophecy quickly realized. In the aftermath of Obama's intervention, al-Qaeda was able to take control in Mali of an area twice the size of Germany. In Tunisia and Egypt jihadists emerged as the ruling parties, with the acquiescence and even assistance of the Obama administration. In Syria, a savage civil war metastasized unimpeded, killing tens of thousands and eventually pitting a fascist regime allied to Iran against rebel forces largely aligned with al-Qaeda and the Muslim Brotherhood.

As these disasters unfolded, the White House not only failed to oppose the Islamists but armed and enabled them. Obama had previously intervened in Egypt, the largest and most important country in the Middle East, to force the removal of its pro-American leader, Hosni Mubarak. He then promoted the Brotherhood's ascension to power by portraying it as a "moderate" actor in the democratic process. As the Middle East situation deteriorated, the Muslim Brotherhood became the chief beneficiary of America's financial, diplomatic and military support. This same Brotherhood was the driving force behind the Islamist surge, the mentor to Osama bin Laden and the leaders of al-Qaeda, and the creator of

Hamas. Rather than being quarantined, the Brotherhood-dominated government in Cairo now received hundreds of millions of dollars in military aid and F-16 bomber jets from the Obama administration that had facilitated its rise to power.

To allay concerns about the emergence of the Brotherhood, Obama's Secretary of State Hillary Clinton issued the following justification for its acceptance by the White House: "We believe that it is in the interests of the United States to engage with all parties that are peaceful, and committed to non-violence, that intend to compete for the parliament and the presidency."[4] In these words, Clinton was referring to an organization whose spiritual leader, Yusuf al-Qaradawi, had recently called for a second Holocaust of the Jews, and to a party that was calling for the establishment of a Muslim caliphate in Jerusalem and the destruction of the Jewish state.[5] Soon after Clinton's endorsement, the Muslim Brotherhood's presidential candidate, Mohamed Morsi, was elected Egypt's new leader and was referring to Jews as apes and pigs. Secure in the American administration's support, he wasted no time in abolishing the constitution and instituting a dictatorship with no serious protest from the United States. Only months before this destruction of Egypt's civic space by his Islamist party, the new dictator was visited by then Senator John Kerry, shortly to be Hillary Clinton's successor as Secretary of State. Kerry assured the world that the new Muslim Brotherhood regime was "committed to protecting fundamental freedoms."[6]

---

[4]Gadi Adelman, "The Cornerstone of Regional Stability and Peace," *Family Security Matters,* November 27, 2012, http://www.familysecuritymatters.org/publications/detail/the-cornerstone-of-regional-stability-and-peace.

[5]Robert Spencer, "The World's Most Popular Muslim Preacher, Yusuf al-Qaradawi, Asks Allah to Destroy the Jews," *Jihad Watch,* November 18, 2012, http://www.jihadwatch.org/2012/11/the-worlds-most-popular-muslim-preacher-yusuf-al-qaradawi-asks-allah-to-destroy-the-jews.html.

[6]Daniel Greenfield, "John Kerry: Still Wrong After All These Years," *FrontPage Mag,* December 24, 2012, http://www.frontpagemag.com/2012/dgreenfield/john-kerry-still-wrong-after-all-these-years/.

As in Egypt, so in Syria. Both Clinton and Kerry promoted the ruthless dictator Assad as a political reformer and friend of democracy just as he was preparing to launch a war against his own people. Meeting with Assad, Kerry called Syria "an essential player in bringing peace and stability to the region."[7] Shortly thereafter, the dictator began a series of massacres of his own population, which resulted in tens of thousands of fatalities and international calls for a humanitarian intervention—which Obama ignored, just as he had the desperate struggle of the Green Revolution in the streets of Teheran three years earlier. The chaos in Syria has now led to the emergence of al-Qaeda as a leading actor among the rebel forces, under the revealing name "the Islamic State in Iraq and the Levant."[8] The very name indicates the potential scope of the disaster that the Obama administration is presiding over in the Middle East.

Until the "new politics" presidency of Jimmy Carter, the Democratic Party during the Cold War would never have tolerated such abject capitulations to totalitarian forces. And if it had shown such doubts and denial, as the Carter administration did, the Republican Party could have been counted on to defend the morality of American power and carry the fight to the enemy. The Republicans would have done so with the conviction that they were expressing the deepest wishes of the American people who elected them to the presidency all but fourteen of those years since the Second World War. Domestically, the American people preferred Democratic promoters of the welfare state to Republican proponents of fiscal restraint. But the same electorate switched its party vote when it came to protecting the American homeland. While voters made Democrats the majority party in the people's House

---

[7]Daniel Halper, "Kerry a Frequent Visitor with Syrian Dictator Bashar Al-Assad," *Weekly Standard,* December 21, 2012, http://www.weeklystandard.com/blogs/kerry-frequent-visitor-syrian-dictator-bashar-al-assad_690885.html.

[8]"Islamic State of Iraq and the Levant," *Wikipedia,* http://en.wikipedia.org/wiki/Islamic_State_of_Iraq_and_the_Levant.

for 38 of the 42 years of America's Cold War with the Soviet Union, in twenty-eight of those years they elected a Republican to be their commander-in-chief. Moreover, three of the four Democrats who did make it to the White House—Truman, Kennedy and Johnson—were militant anti-Communists and military hawks who held views indistinguishable from Republicans on national security issues.

Given that the most durable lesson of postwar electoral history was that Democrats win national elections on domestic policy and Republicans win when national security issues are at the center of the campaigns, it seems incomprehensible that the Obama administration has been able to degrade American power virtually without Republican opposition. At the Republican Party's 2012 convention in Tampa, its nominee Mitt Romney failed to mention the Islamic jihad and devoted but one sentence to the fact that in order to appease America's enemies Obama had thrown Israel, America's only dependable ally in the region, "under the bus." Romney did not mention Obama's role as enabler of the Muslim Brotherhood or the millions of dollars his administration had given to the Palestinian jihadists on the West Bank and in Gaza, whose official goal was the destruction of Israel and its Jews. He did not mention the calls by Islamist leaders of Egypt and Iran for the destruction of the Jewish state and the completion of the job that Hitler started. Romney addressed exactly two sentences to Obama's appeasement of the Russians, and his abandonment of America's Eastern European allies by reneging on America's commitments to their missile defense. About the Korean peninsula, a flashpoint in national security and a theatre for the current administration's diplomatic dithering, he said nothing.

While Romney failed to confront a vulnerable Obama on national security issues and gave him a pass on his shameful betrayal of his embassy in Benghazi, no other Republican candidate was likely to make the holy war that Islamists are waging against us, and Obama's feckless national security policies, a focal point of their attack. At one time or another, there were a dozen

Republican candidates for the nomination that Romney won and they participated in 19 public debates. There were candidates for social conservatism, candidates for fiscal responsibility and job creation, for libertarian principles and moderate values. But there was not one Republican candidate whose campaign was an aggressive assault on Obama's disastrous national security decisions and how they had imperiled America's interests and its basic safety.

The extent of the Republican retreat on national security was dramatized by an incident that took place a few months before the election, when Representative Michele Bachmann and four other Republican House members sent a letter to the Justice Department's inspector general asking him to look into the possibility of Islamist influence in the Obama administration. The letter expressed concern about State Department policies that "appear to be a result of influence operations conducted by individuals and organizations associated with the Muslim Brotherhood."[9] The letter then listed five specific ways in which Secretary of State Hillary Clinton had actively assisted the Muslim Brotherhood's ascent to power in Egypt, producing a decisive shift in the Middle East towards the jihadist enemies of the United States.

The letter specifically asked for an inquiry into the activities of Huma Abedin, Hillary Clinton's deputy chief of staff and principal adviser on Muslim affairs. It was a reasonable, indeed logical request. Members of Abedin's family—her late father, her mother and her brother—were all identifiable leaders of the Muslim Brotherhood. For twelve years prior to being hired by the State Department, Abedin had worked for an organization founded by a major Brotherhood figure and close associate of Abedin's mother. Abdullah Omar Naseef was wanted by federal authorities in connection with the attack on 9/11 as one of the three principal financiers of

[9]Robert Spencer, "Huma Abedin and the Muslim Brotherhood: Bachmann vs. McCain," *FrontPage Mag*, July 19, 2012, http://www.frontpagemag.com/2012/robert-spencer/huma-abedin-and-the-muslim-brotherhood-bachmann-vs-mccain/.

Osama bin Laden, and a man dedicated to promoting Islamic supremacist doctrines. A second Muslim Brotherhood figure occupying a high place in the Obama administration was Rashad Hussain, deputy associate White House counsel with responsibilities in the areas of national security and Muslim affairs. And there were others.

These Islamists occupied positions of influence in the Obama administration on matters regarding national security and Muslim affairs at a time coinciding with the dramatic rise of the previously outlawed Muslim Brotherhood, which received significant support from the State Department. Yet, when the congressional letter surfaced, Bachmann and her colleagues came under savage attack as McCarthyites and "Islamophobes" whose request for an inquiry was itself un-American. These attacks came not only from *The Washington Post,* leading Democrats, and such well-known apologists for Islamic radicals as Georgetown's John Esposito, but also from Republicans John McCain and John Boehner. Without bothering to address the facts the Bachmann letter presented, McCain said: "When anyone, not least a member of Congress, launches specious and degrading attacks against fellow Americans on the basis of nothing more than fear of who they are and ignorance of what they stand for, it defames the spirit of our nation, and we all grow poorer because of it."[10]

In other words, Bachmann and her colleagues were bigots. Said Boehner, "I don't know Huma, but from everything that I do know of her she has a sterling character. Accusations like this being thrown around are pretty dangerous."[11] In other words, asking rea-

---

[10]Ed O'Keefe, "John McCain Defends Human[sic] Abedin Against Accusations She's Part of Conspiracy," *The Washington Post,* July 18, 2012, http://www.washingtonpost.com/blogs/2chambers/post/john-mccain-defends-huma-abedin-against-accusations-shes-part-of-conspiracy/2012/07/18/gJQAFpxntW_blog.html.

[11]Ed O'Keefe, "John Boehner: Accusations Against Huma Abedin 'Pretty Dangerous'," *The Washington Post,* July 19, 2012, http://www.washingtonpost.com/blogs/2chambers/post/john-boehner-accusations-against-huma-abedin-pretty-dangerous/2012/07/19/gJQAeDT6vW_blog.html.

sonable questions about a Muslim Brotherhood operative at the center of American policy was more dangerous than allowing the connections to the leadership of an organization at war with the United States to remain unexamined.

Why did Republicans exhibit such a lack of conviction on a matter affecting internal and national security issues, traditional pillars of Republican strength? The answer can be found in the way the Republicans allowed themselves over many years to be intimidated, then silenced, while the left established its version of the Iraq War and its lessons. The moment the Republicans lost the national security narrative was in June 2003, just six weeks after the Saddam regime fell. That month, the Democratic Party launched a national television campaign claiming that Bush had lied to lure the American people into a war that was "unnecessary," "immoral" and "illegal." Until that moment, the war in Iraq had been supported by both parties and was regarded by both as a strategic necessity in the larger war on terror. In point of fact, removing Saddam's regime by force had been a specific goal of U.S. policy since October 1998, when Bill Clinton, a Democratic president, signed the Iraqi Liberation Act.

During his reign, Saddam Hussein had launched two aggressive wars, had murdered 300,000 Iraqis, had used chemical weapons on his own citizens and had put in place an active nuclear weapons program thwarted only by his defeat in the first Gulf War. As of 2002, his regime had defied 16 UN Security Council resolutions designed to enforce the Gulf War truce and stop Iraq from pursuing its ambition to possess weapons of mass destruction. In September 2002 the UN Security Council added a new resolution, which gave the regime until December 17, 2002 to comply with its terms or face consequences. When Iraq failed to comply, Bush made the only decision compatible with the preservation of international law and the security of the United States by preparing a pre-emptive invasion to remove the regime and the weapons of mass destruction it was reasonably presumed to possess. The Iraqi dictator was provided the option of leaving the country and averting war. He rejected the offer and the United States-led coalition entered the country on March 19, 2003.[12]

The use of force in Iraq had been authorized by both houses of Congress, including a majority of Democrats in the Senate. It was supported in eloquent speeches by John Kerry, John Edwards, Al Gore and other Democratic leaders. But just three months into the war, they turned against an action they had authorized and began a five-year campaign to delegitimize the conflict, casting America as its villain. It was a fundamental break with the post-World War II bipartisan tradition in foreign policy that had survived even Vietnam. Then, with the support and protection of Democratic legislators, *The New York Times, The Washington Post,* the political left and the national media mounted a relentless five-year propaganda campaign against the war, taking relatively minor incidents like the misbehavior of guards at the Abu Ghraib prison and blowing them up into international scandals damaging their country's prestige and weakening its morale. Every day of the war, *The New York Times* and other left-leaning media provided front-page coverage of America's body counts in Iraq and Afghanistan, and helped to fuel a massive "anti-war" movement which attacked America's fundamental purposes along with its conduct of the war. The goal of these campaigns was to indict America and its leaders as war criminals who posed a threat to the world. *The Times* and *The Post* even leaked classified national security secrets, destroying three major national security programs designed to protect Americans from terrorist attacks.[13]

The principal justification offered by the Democrats for their campaign against the Iraq War was that "Bush lied"[14] in order to

---

[12]This history is recounted in David Horowitz, *Unholy Alliance: Radical Islam and the American Left,* Regnery, 2004.

[13]See David Horowitz & Ben Johnson, *Party of Defeat,* Spence, 2008; Douglas Feith, *War and Decision: Inside the Pentagon at the Dawn of the War on Terrorism,* Harper, 2008.

[14]Mary Mostert, "If Bush Lied about WMD, Kerry and 77% of the Senate Lied Also," *Renew America,* August 16, 2004, http://www.renewamerica.com/columns/mostert/040816; James Kirchick, "The White House Didn't Lie about Iraq," *Los Angeles Times,* June 16, 2008, http://articles.latimes.com/2008/jun/16/opinion/oe-kirchick16.

persuade them to support an invasion that was unnecessary. This claim was the only way Democrats could explain the otherwise inexplicable and unconscionable fact that they turned against a war they had supported. It was only when an antiwar primary candidate, Howard Dean, appeared to be on his way to winning the Democrats' presidential primary that John Kerry and John Edwards—the eventual nominees—reversed themselves on the war. They were followed by the entire party, which suddenly saw a partisan political advantage in attacking Bush over an increasingly difficult situation on the battlefield.

The Democrats' claim that Bush lied was false. Bush could not have lied to John Kerry or the congressional Democrats about WMD's in Iraq because Kerry and other Democrats sat on the Senate and House Intelligence Committees and had access to the same intelligence data that Bush relied on to make his case for the war. When the Democrats authorized and supported the war, they knew everything that Bush knew. The claim that he lied to get their support was itself the biggest lie of the war. Its only purpose was to hide the Democrats' own perfidy in abandoning the nation's mission for partisan gain, and to discredit the president and turn the country against him, at whatever cost, in the hope of winning the 2004 election.

But Republicans didn't lose control of the national security narrative simply because Democrats betrayed a war they had authorized. They had the option of standing fast, as they had done since the attack on Pearl Harbor. Republicans lost control of the narrative because they never held the Democrats accountable for their betrayal. They never suggested that the Democrats' attacks on the war were deceitful and unpatriotic, aiding our enemies and endangering the lives of our troops in the field. The Bush White House failed to defend itself from the attacks, while Republicans as whole failed to expose the Democrats' lie and to describe their reckless accusations as the disloyal propaganda it was. The words "betrayal" and "sabotage"—the appropriate terms for Democrat attacks on the motives of the war—were never employed. Republicans did not accuse Democrats of conducting a campaign to demoralize America's troops in the field, even when Kerry during a presidential debate called it "the wrong war, in the wrong place, at the wrong time."[15] How did that sound to a 19-year-old Marine facing down Islamic terrorists in Fallujah?

The Republicans' failure to defend their president and the troops turned a good war into a bad one. It turned a disloyal opposition into a patriotic cause. It crippled America's ability to protect other people's freedom or even defend its own. If the war against a dictator who had launched two wars, defied 17 UN Security Council resolutions, murdered 300,000 of his own people and schemed to kill a U.S. president was illegitimate and immoral, then American resistance to any outlaw states could be portrayed—and opposed—as reckless and unjustifiable aggressions. In failing to fight the political war over Iraq, Republicans lost their legitimacy as a party that had taken hard, sometimes unpopular steps to protect national security, as they did in the mid-80s when they held the line against Soviet efforts to support Sandinista subversion and a bloody Marxist guerrilla war in El Salvador. Losing—and to some degree failing to fight—the war over the war in Iraq is why Republicans are mute today in matters of foreign policy—why they have not challenged Obama's dangerous course of appeasement and drift, especially in the Middle East.

Although the Joint Chiefs had suggested that a military presence of 20,000 troops in Iraq was necessary to keep it free of Iran's control, the demand for such a presence became problematic when the Republicans allowed the Democrats' narrative of "Bush lied, people died" to prevail. When 2008 presidential candidate John McCain suggested that maintaining troops in a postwar Iraq was a prudent measure, candidate Obama attacked him as a warmonger. "You know," Obama said, "John McCain wants to continue a war

---

[15]Dana Milbank and Spencer S. Hsu, "Cheney: Kerry Victory Is Risky," *The Washington Post,* September 8, 2004, http://www.washingtonpost.com/wp-dyn/articles/A2917-2004Sep7.html.

in Iraq perhaps as long as 100 years."[16] This refrain became a constant theme of the winning Obama campaign—Republicans are warmongers, and dangerous. That is why three years later, when Obama surrendered Iraq to Iran, no Republican dared accuse him of betraying the Americans who gave their lives to make Iraq independent, even though Iraq now fell under the sway of Iran and was providing a land conduit for Iranian weapons headed to Syria.

How far America has fallen—since the time Madeline Albright called us the indispensable nation that stands taller and sees farther—becomes more apparent with each new international crisis. We are not only losing the war with enemies whose stated goal is our destruction. We are led by a political party that constantly finds excuses not to take these enemies seriously, and never needs to account for its disgraceful conduct because its potential opposition is mute. The only way to reverse this trend is to mount a campaign to put Obama's support for the Muslim Brotherhood and appeasement of Iran at the forefront of the political debate; and to educate Americans about the dangers we face. Americans need to become aware of the Islamic supremacist threat, and of the disasters that lie ahead because of Obama's refusal to confront the evil it portends.

[16]Michael Dobbs, "McCain's '100-year War'," *The Washington Post*, April 2, 2008, http://voices.washingtonpost.com/fact-checker/2008/04/mccains_100year_war.html.

11

War and Peace

We are not long emerged from a fifty-year Cold War, which began when the Soviet empire swallowed Eastern Europe and the Baltic states, and ended only when the United States undertook a vast rearmament, and applied enough pressure over enough years to bankrupt the Communist system and force its withdrawal from the occupation. The Russian successor to that empire has just swallowed one of its lost treasures, a sovereign domain in Eastern Europe. The response by our commander-in-chief, Barack Obama, to the rape of Crimea has been to wag his finger and explain to the Russian conqueror that in the 21st century we just don't do things that way: "Russia's leadership is challenging truths that only a few weeks ago seemed self-evident, that in the 21st century the borders of Europe cannot be redrawn with force, that international law matters, that people and nations can make their own decisions about their future."[1]

But words without the force to back them have a tendency to fall on deaf ears. Not surprisingly Obama's pablum made no impression on comrade Putin.

In point of fact, Russia is a second-rate power and strong measures short of war could have dissuaded him from this

---

Originally published March 28, 2014, http://www.frontpagemag.com/2014/david-horowitz/war-peace-in-the-age-of-obama/

[1]"Full Transcript: President Obama Gives Speech Addressing Europe, Russia on March 26," *The Washington Post,* March 26, 2014, http://www.washingtonpost.com/world/transcript-president-obama-gives-speech-addressing-europe-russia-on-march-26/2014/03/26/07ae80ae-b503-11e3-b899-20667de76985_story.html.

transgression. But because Barack Obama is such an embarrassingly weak leader and untrustworthy ally, and has telegraphed so clearly his reluctance to use force, Putin was able to laugh in his face, mass 100,000 troops on the Ukrainian border and prepare to swallow Ukraine itself.

The leader of the free world today is a man who does not believe in the free world or in America's role as its head. In the five years since a Norwegian committee gave him a Nobel Peace Prize for nothing, Obama's posture of weakness and policies of appeasement have made the world a far more dangerous place than it has been since the end of the Cold War, and possibly even at its beginning. From his first day in office Obama has made it clear that he regards America as having wronged its adversaries, while its adversaries have grievances that are justified. It is a view that is conveniently close to Putin's own. As should by now be apparent, America's president is a determined enabler of America's enemies, and equally determined betrayer of her friends. In the five years since he took office he has lost the war in Iraq, abandoning the military presence that thousands of Americans gave their lives to secure, while turning that benighted nation's destiny over to Iran; he has lost the war in Afghanistan by announcing his intention to lose it in advance and by forcing our troops to fight under rules of engagement that tied their hands and got them killed. He has lost Libya by conducting an unauthorized, unilateral and illegal aggression against an American ally, murdering its leader and turning its streets over to mobs of terrorists. In the course of these betrayals, Obama has violated every principle he invoked as a senator to justify his attacks on George Bush's war in Iraq. But then, one needs to remember that Obama is a compulsive and brazen liar on matters foreign as well as domestic.

In the Middle East, Obama has lost Egypt, its largest and most important nation. Until Obama intervened in its internal affairs and overthrew its pro-American president, Egypt had been an American ally for 40 years. In Egypt and throughout the Middle East, Obama and his secretaries Clinton and Kerry have put

American power and influence behind the Muslim Brotherhood—an Islamic terrorist organization with attitudes indistinguishable from the Nazis, except that it claims to take its direction from Allah. The Muslim Brotherhood is the progenitor of al-Qaeda, the creator of Hamas and the source of the global jihad against America and the West. Obama's support for the Brotherhood has not only cost us our Egyptian ally; it has opened the door for Putin's imperial Russia to replace us as the Great Power influence in the region.

On top of these betrayals of America's interests, Obama has systematically appeased our most deadly enemy in the region, the terrorist regime in Iran. In particular, he has conspired to insure that the Iranian mullahs, who have sworn to wipe America and Israel from the face of the earth, are successful in their drive to acquire nuclear weapons. While giving aid and comfort to America's mortal enemies, Obama has turned his back on America's most faithful ally, the only democracy in the Middle East. He has thrown his country's enormous weight behind Islamic radicals whose goal—stated in so many words—is to obliterate the state of Israel and push the Jews who inhabit it into the sea. To finish the job that Hitler started.

For sixty-six years the Arab states and their Palestinian proxies have conducted an unprovoked war of aggression against the Jews. The Palestinian cause is overtly and explicitly genocidal—the destruction of the state of Israel and the cleansing of the entire Arab world of its Yids. The Palestinians have advanced this cause behind the Hitlerian lie that Israel occupies Arab land. Israel was created on land that for four hundred years had belonged to the Turkish Empire, which was not Arab. American Indians have a greater claim to the United States than the Arabs do to the state of Israel.

The Palestinian cause was inspired by the Islamic Nazis of the Muslim Brotherhood. It was created by the war criminal Haj Amin al-Husseini, who served Hitler in Berlin and planned his own Auschwitz for the Jews of the Middle East, thwarted only by

Rommel's defeat at El Alamein. Yet Obama has thrown the full weight of his presidency behind this evil. He has supported the Palestinian demands that Israel retreat to its 1949 borders, which would make their genocidal goal far easier to accomplish. He has demanded that Jews stop building homes for themselves in Jewish Jerusalem, while at the same time he has turned a deaf ear toward the promise of Palestinian leaders that that no Jew will be permitted to live in any territory that Palestinians control. He has acquiesced in Iranian shipments of long-range rockets to the terrorists in Gaza so they can carry out their work of obliterating the Jews. He is a greater enabler of Islamic Nazism than Chamberlain was of Hitler's secular variety.

This is the surreal context of the world we inhabit—where Israel's most important ally is an ally of her enemies; where negotiations designed to facilitate a new Holocaust are called a "peace process;" where an American president provides Iranian Hitlerites with the time and space to acquire nuclear weapons; and where the international dialogue about the Middle East is so constructed by the enemies of the Jews that a rational assessment of the situation has become almost impossible, and a reasonable proposal for improving it difficult to formulate.

12

Obama's Treachery

Barack Obama deliberately set out to lose the war in Iraq, and he did. He defied the advice of his joint chiefs of staff to secure America's formidable military presence and keep 20,000 troops in country, and left Iraq to its own devices and the tender mercies of Teheran. In doing so, he betrayed every American and Iraqi who gave his life to create a free Iraq and keep it out of the clutches of the terrorists. Iraq is now a war zone dominated by the terrorist forces of the Islamic State, whose rise Obama's policies fostered. Both his secretaries of state praised the animal Bashar al-Assad as a "reformer" and a man of "peace," helping him to thwart his domestic opposition. The Islamic State—or ISIS—was born out of the Syrian chaos that ensued.

Far worse was Obama's open support for America's mortal enemy, the Muslim Brotherhood. During the "Arab Spring," Obama put America's weight behind the legitimization of this murderous organization that had been outlawed for 40 years for its assassinations and conspiracies against the Egyptian regime. Secretary of State Clinton gave totally unfounded assurances to the world that the Brotherhood was ready to become part of the democratic process and give up its 90-year holy war against infidels—Jews in particular but also. and explicitly, America. During the Brotherhood's brief tenure as the government in Egypt, Obama gave its genocidal zealots more than a billion dollars in American

---

Originally published August 8, 2014, http://www.nationalreview.com/article/384963/obamas-treachery-and-republican-silence-david-horowitz.

aid and F-16 fighter-bombers that could easily reach Israel's major population centers, which for 60 years the Brotherhood had sworn to destroy.

By his feckless interventions in the Middle East, and his tacit support for the chief organization of Islam's terror war against the West, Obama has set the Middle East on fire. All the violence in the crescent from Gaza to Iraq, including Hamas's genocidal war against Israel, has been encouraged by Obama's support for the Brotherhood and hostility toward the Jewish state. Characteristic of this encouragement was his illegal intervention in Libya, a policy that violated every principle which Obama and the Democrats had invoked to attack President Bush and undermine America's war against the Saddam regime and the terrorists in Iraq. Thanks to Obama, Libya is now in the hands of terrorists and thousands of Libyans are fleeing to Tunisia and Egypt. Thanks to Obama, the Christian communities of Iraq, which date back to the time of Christ, are being decimated and driven into exile.

Because of Obama's aversion to America's role as a keeper of international peace, the tyrant Putin has been able to swallow Crimea and threaten the rest of Ukraine. Since his ascension in 2009, Obama's policies have been responsible for the deaths of tens of thousands of people and will result in the deaths of tens of thousands more. Thanks to his efforts to destroy America's borders, Americans may soon be included in this grim toll. Certainly, Americans are now threatened on their own soil as never before.

Where is the Republican opposition? Why are Republicans still treating Obama as though his were a normal presidency and not a national disgrace? Why are there no indictments of Obama for the carnage he has enabled?

There is one foreign policy area where Republicans have shown some fight: Benghazi. But the fight here has been over an inquiry—important in its own right, but not a political challenge to Obama's efforts to sabotage and degrade the country he is supposed to lead.

We know the basic facts. Obama's team was trying to monitor and recapture the weapons they had helped supply to Islamist militias in Libya. That was Ambassador Stevens's mission. No security was provided because the mission had to be secret and plausibly deniable in the middle of an election in which Obama was running on the cynical lie that the war on terror had been won. ("Al-Qaeda is on the run, and bin Laden is dead."[1]) During the battle waged by American heroes against the terrorists' assault in Benghazi, the president and his secretary of state went AWOL and left these brave Americans to die. Instead of honoring them and hunting down their killers, Obama then took off for a fundraiser in Las Vegas. This was surely the most shameful individual act by a president in history.

Having abandoned these American heroes and their families, Obama and his deputies then lied to the American people about the terrorist attack, blaming it on an anti-Mohammed video, while the president himself used it as an occasion to defend the prophet in a UN address: "The future must not belong to those who slander the prophet of Islam."[2] This series of acts showed Obama's contempt for the American military, contempt for the American people and sympathy for America's enemies, an attitude that he has manifested over and over again.

When will Republicans gather the courage to start speaking truth to power?

---

[1]Ed Henry, "Obama Dropping 'Al Qaeda Is on the Run' from Stump Speech?," *Fox News*, October 17, 2012, http://www.foxnews.com/politics/2012/10/17/obama-dropping-al-qaeda-is-on-run-from-stump-speech/.

[2]"Remarks by the President to the UN General Assembly," *The White House—Office of the Press Secretary*, September 25, 2012, https://www.whitehouse.gov/the-press-office/2012/09/25/remarks-president-un-general-assembly.

13

The Hell That Is the Obama White House

Let me begin by acknowledging that this inspirational title is lifted from a tweet by screen actor James Woods. I will now proceed to explicate it.

Barack Obama is behind every major scandal of his administration, from the betrayal in Benghazi to the use of the IRS as a political weapon against his opponents. How can one know this? Because the culprits haven't been fired. Moreover, if they are serial liars like Susan Rice, they've actually been promoted to posts where their loyalty to the criminal-in-chief can do America and its citizens even more damage. A president faced with a scandal created by underlings behind his back would be naturally furious at their misbehavior, and would want heads to roll. This didn't happen in any of the Obama scandals because their point of origin was the White House itself. Promoting the culprits is a way of keeping them quiet.

To take only one instructive case—what exactly is the IRS scandal about? It is a plan unprecedented in modern American politics to push the political system towards a one-party state by using the government's taxing authority to cripple and destroy the political opposition. The administration's campaign to promote voter fraud by opposing measures to stop it as "racist" is driven by

---

Originally published August 18, 2014, http://www.redstate.com/diary/davidhorowitz/2014/08/18/hell-obama-white-house/.

the same intentions and desire. And why shouldn't Obama want to destroy the two-party system? His presidency is constantly revealing his contempt for the constitutional framework, making law illegally while openly defying an impotent Congress to stop him. Of course every radical hates the Constitution because, as Madison explained in Federalist No. 10, it is designed to thwart "the wicked projects" of redistributing income and destroying free markets.

The same desire to suppress the opposition also drives the war that Obama and the Democrats have waged against America's borders and sovereignty. Their plan is to flood the country with illegals who will be grateful enough for the favor to win them elections and create a permanent majority in their favor. The immediate result of these efforts is that America has no secure southern border, and therefore no border—which has effectively invited criminals and terrorists to come into the country and do its citizens harm.

That brings us to the deepest level of Obama's hell—his anti-American foreign policy. When Obama was re-elected in 2012, the very first thought that came into my head was this: Because of this election, a lot of people are going to be dead. How disastrously right I was. Since their assault on George Bush and their sabotage of the war in Iraq, Obama and the Democrats have created power vacuums in Europe and even more dramatically in the Middle East, where nasty characters have predictably entered to sow ominous seeds for the future.

Take one aspect of this unfolding catastrophe: Obama's lack of response to the slaughter of Christians in Palestine, Egypt and Iraq. Hundreds of thousands of Christians have been slaughtered and driven from their homes in Iraq alone—over half a million by some counts. This is the oldest Christian community in the world, dating back to the time of Christ. Not until a remnant of Yazidi and Christians found themselves trapped on a mountain side, and the world press took note, did Obama make a gesture to help them. Before this, Obama's response to the atrocity was to say and do nothing. Even in his statement announcing a minimal action to save the Yazidi and Christians, the latter were mentioned only once, in passing, while the presidential focus was on the obscure Yazidi.

What this unfeeling response to the slaughter of Christians tells us is that Obama is a pretend Christian, just the way he is a pretend American. What he is, in fact, is a world-class liar. That is because his real agendas are anti-American, anti-Christian, anti-Jewish, and obviously and consistently pro America's third world adversaries to whom he is always apologizing, always appeasing. Obama is forced to lie about his intentions and policies because he couldn't survive politically if he told the truth.

Thus the socialist plot against individual freedom called Obamacare was sold as a charitable attempt to cover the uninsured (which it doesn't), to lower health insurance costs (which it doesn't), and to allow patients to keep their doctors and their plans (which it doesn't). What it actually does is to take away a major element of the freedom that Americans once enjoyed—the freedom to choose how they would care for and protect their lives and not surrender that freedom to government *Diktats*.

This devious, deceitful, power-hungry administration is just as James Woods described it. But it is also a mounting danger for all Americans. Thanks to Obama's global retreat, the terrorists who the president falsely claims are "on the run"[1] are in fact gathering their strength and their weapons of mass destruction until a day comes when they will cross our porous borders and show us what the years of betrayal not only by Obama, but by the whole Democratic Party, have wrought.

---

[1]Fred Lucas, "Obama Has Touted Al Qaeda's Demise 32 Times since Benghazi Attack," *CNS News*, November 1, 2012, http://cnsnews.com/news/article/obama-touts-al-qaeda-s-demise-32-times-benghazi-attack-0.

14

Thank You, ISIS

Beheadings of innocent human beings are unspeakable acts reflecting the savagery of the Islamic "holy war" against the West—against us. Yet despite the intentions of their perpetrators, they have had an unexpected utility. Their gruesome images have entered the living rooms and consciousness of ordinary Americans, and begun to wake them up.

The barbarity of the Islamic movement for world domination has actually been evident for decades: in the suicide bombing of the Marine compound in Lebanon in 1982, in the bombing of the World Trade Center in 1993, in the suicide attacks on Jews—men, women and children—during the second Palestinian *intifada* in 2000, in the 9/11 attacks on the World Trade Center and the Pentagon in 2001, and in the beheadings perpetrated in Iraq by al-Qaeda's Abu al-Zarqawi and the Salafist group known as Ansar al-Islam during the Iraq War. Unfortunately, the response to these barbarities on the part of the Democratic Party and the liberal elites has been to condemn and marginalize anyone who called them barbarous. In their eyes, it is racist to use the word "barbarism" to describe the acts of any Third World people.

To associate Islam with the Islamists is "Islamophobic". President Obama is still comfortably settled in this time warp, denying in so many words that the Islamic State is Islamic. For America's commander-in-chief to make such an obviously moronic statement

---

Originally published October 9, 2014, http://www.nationalreview.com/article/389922/thank-you-isis-david-horowitz.

about his country's enemy in wartime reflects how deeply entrenched is the ideology of protecting Islamists—and jeopardizing the innocent. Even Obama's predecessor, George W. Bush, could not bring himself to describe the West's enemy as Islamic. Fixing on the "war on terror"[1] as a descriptive term was a way of eliding the fact that the savagery was motivated not by nihilism but by faith—Islamic faith. The Obama Democrats have gone even deeper into denial, eliminating "war on terror" from the government vocabulary entirely and replacing it with "overseas contingency operations."

For more than a decade, a handful of conservatives, of whom I was one, tried to sound the alarm about the Islamist threat. For our efforts we were ridiculed, smeared as bigots and marginalized as "Islamophobes." In 2004 I published a book called *Unholy Alliance* about the Islamist movement and the support it was receiving from the American left. For my concern, Harvard professor and Islam expert Noah Feldman dismissed me as a "relic" in *The New York Times Sunday Book Review.* It was the last mention by The *Times* of one of my books.

In 2006 and 2007 I organized nearly 200 "teach-ins" on American campuses, which I called "Islamo-Fascism Awareness" weeks.[2] The idea was to legitimize the hitherto suppressed term "Islamo-fascist" as a description of the enemy confronting us. The demonstrations were attacked by the Muslim Students Association, which is a recruiting organization for the Muslim Brotherhood, and by Students for Justice in Palestine, a front for the terrorist party Hamas. They also inspired the contempt of the liberal left. Joshua Micah Marshall of the Internet site "Talking Points Memo" devoted two YouTube videos to ridiculing me for having the temerity to hold such demonstrations. Campus leftists

---

[1]"Text: President Bush Addresses the Nation," *The Washington Post,* September 20, 2001, http://www.washingtonpost.com/wp-srv/nation/specials/attacked/transcripts/bushaddress_092001.html.

[2]Islamo-Fascism Awareness Week, http://www.discoverthenetworks.org/viewSubCategory.asp?id=750.

attacked the students who organized the speeches and film showings that accompanied them as racists, bigots, and Islamophobes.

As part of these counter-protests, resolutions denouncing critics of Islamic misogyny and terror as "Islamophobes" were unanimously passed by leftist-run student councils at UCLA, UC Santa Barbara, and a dozen other elite schools. Lengthy reports on the menace of Islamophobia targeted me and other speakers at our campus demonstrations. These reports, costing tens of thousands of dollars to produce, were published by FAIR, CAIR, the Southern Poverty Law Center and the Center for American Progress—the brain trust of the Democratic Party.

And then came ISIS. The horrific images of the beheadings, the reports of mass slaughters, and the threats to the American homeland have accomplished what our small contingent of beleaguered conservatives could never have achieved by ourselves. They brought images of these Islamic savages into the living rooms of the American public, and suddenly the acceptable language for describing the enemy began to change. "Savages" and "barbarians" began to roll off the tongues of evening-news anchors and commentators who never would have dreamed of crossing that line before, for fear of offending the politically correct.

Virtually every major Muslim organization in America is an arm of the Muslim Brotherhood, the fountainhead of Islamic terror. Huma Abedin, who was deputy chief of staff to Secretary of State Hillary Clinton (and is still Clinton's confidante and principal aide), comes from a family of Muslim Brotherhood leaders. Yet legislators who have the power to investigate these matters are still intimidated from even raising them.

Language is a weapon in the battle against the threat we face. We cannot fight a war effectively if we cannot name the enemy or describe his methods or examine his influence on our own policy. The Islamic State has created an opportunity for common sense and realism to prevail. The tragedy is that it has taken the slaughter of hundreds of thousands of Muslims and Christians in the Middle East, and the ongoing extermination of the Catholic presence in Iraq, to begin to wake people up. Unfortunately our leaders are still asleep, while our president is manifestly hostile to American purposes and to the military that defends us. Barack Obama identifies more with the Islamic world, which has produced the forces that would destroy us, than he does with the country he is sworn to defend.

15

The Blood on Obama's Hands

When conservatives consider the casualties of Obama's national security policies, their attention is drawn quite naturally to Benghazi. In this shameful episode, the Obama administration sacrificed an ambassador and three American heroes to protect a deceptive presidential campaign message in which Obama claimed that the war against al-Qaeda was over and won.

The facts are these: Ambassador Chris Stevens and three American heroes were sent into an al-Qaeda stomping ground that the British and other diplomatic consulates had already evacuated; they were denied the security they requested; they were then left to die during a seven-hour firefight when their compound was attacked; and finally they were betrayed in death, when Obama and his representatives lied to the world about what had taken place and when he failed to bring their killers to justice as he had mendaciously promised he would.

Benghazi can be seen as the collateral damage caused by presidential lies—and worse, presidential denial— that there is in fact a war that Islamists have declared on America. Instead, Obama insists—in the official language he authorized and still uses —that America's responses to acts of Islamic terror should be described as "overseas contingency operations." If Islamic murders and beheadings take place in the homeland, Obama calls them "workplace violence." Benghazi is also the most shameful presidential abandonment of

---

Originally published October 20, 2014, http://www.redstate.com/diary/DavidHorowitz/2014/10/20/blood-obamas-hands/.

Americans in the field in our history—a disgrace compounded when Obama justified his trade of five Taliban generals for one American deserter by saying Americans don't leave their countrymen on the battlefield, which is precisely what he did in Benghazi. All of which makes right the conservative focus on this terrible event.

But the casualties of Obama's reign in Benghazi are dwarfed by the hundreds of thousands of deaths his policies have caused in Syria and Iraq, and the millions of Iraqis, Syrians and Libyans that those same policies have caused to flee their homes and become homeless in Turkey, Tunisia and other places of refuge. Obama's legacy is defined by his ideological aversion to American power, his rule as the most anti-military president in our history, and his deeds as an "antiwar" activist opposed to the "war on terror" because he believes that America's (and Israel's) policies are the cause of the terrorism and hatred that Islamic fanatics direct against our country.

Because of his ideological opposition to American power, Obama deliberately and openly surrendered America's gains in Iraq, which had been won through the sacrifice of thousands of American lives and tens of thousands of American casualties. By deliberately surrendering America's massive military base in Iraq—a country that borders Syria, Afghanistan and Iran—Obama turned that nation over to the terrorists and to Iran, as his generals and intelligence chief and secretary of defense warned his actions would. Obama disregarded his national security advisers' warnings—as no other American president would have—because he regarded America rather than the terrorists as the threat. In abandoning Iraq and deliberately losing the peace, he betrayed every American and every Iraqi who had paid the ultimate price to keep Iraq out of the hands of the terrorists and the Iranians.

Obama's stubborn refusal to use America's military might—ground forces backed by air power—when Syria's Assad crossed the "red line"[1] Obama had drawn in the sand, created a second

[1]Glenn Kessler, "President Obama and the 'Red Line' on Syria's Chemical Weapons," *Washington Post,* September 6, 2013, http://www.washingtonpost.com/blogs/fact-checker/wp/2013/09/06/president-obama-and-the-red-line-on-syrias-chemical-weapons/.

power vacuum that the terrorists filled, thus leading to the emergence of ISIS. Defenders of Obama will claim that the American public would not have supported a military intervention in Syria even if Obama had ordered one. But why is that? It is because for eleven years, beginning with their assault on "Bush's war"[2] in Iraq, the Democrats have sabotaged the war on terror, claiming that America's use of power for anything but "humanitarian" purposes is illegitimate, dangerous and the root cause of the terrorist threat.

Obama felt justified in conducting an unauthorized, illegal intervention in Libya to overthrow an anti-al Qaeda dictator, saying it was to prevent an invisible threat to civilians there. The result? Al-Qaeda is now a dominant force in Libya, and 1.8 million Libyans—a third of the population—have fled to Tunisia. Another brutal Obama legacy. Yet how firm is Obama's commitment to humanitarian interventions? In Iraq he stood by while more than half a million Christians were either slaughtered or driven into exile by ISIS murderers on their mission to cleanse the earth of infidels.

The Obama presidency has been an unmitigated disaster for Iraqis, Syrians and Libyans. Now that ISIS is in control of territory the size of a state, has access to hundreds of millions of petrol dollars and advanced U.S. ordnance, not to mention chemical weapons that Saddam left behind, it is an impending disaster for Americans at home as well.

---

[2]"Bush's War," *PBS Frontline,* March 24, 2008 http://www.pbs.org/wgbh/pages/frontline/bushswar/. [Funding was provided by the far-left John D. and Catherine T. MacArthur Foundation (http://www.discoverthenetworks.org/funderProfile.asp?fndid=5223) and the far-left Park Foundation (http://www.discoverthenetworks.org/funderProfile.asp?fndid=5391).].

16

How Many Lies?

How many lies have Democrats told to sabotage the war on terror? Start with Obama's claim that the Islamic State of Iraq and Syria (or ISIS) is not Islamic. The so-called war on terror is clearly a self-declared "holy war" that Islamists have declared *on us*. Yet Obama is hostile to this idea and denies that such a war is taking place.

The origin of the Democratic lies that obscure the threat we face can be traced to the Democrats' defection from the war in Iraq, the second front in the so-called "war on terror." "Bush lied, people died" was the disgusting charge with which progressives and Democrats successfully demonized America's commander-in-chief and demoralized the nation as it went to war to take down the terrorist-supporting Saddam regime and defeat Ansar-al-Islam and al-Qaeda in Iraq. The reprehensible claim that Bush lied was concocted by Democrats to justify their defection from a war they had just authorized—betraying their country and the young men and women they had sent into the battlefield.

The Democrats lied in claiming that there were no weapons of mass destruction in Iraq, and that therefore the war was unnecessary and therefore immoral. This was actually two lies in one. In the first place, the decision to go to war wasn't about Saddam's possession of weapons of mass destruction. It was about his determination to build and use weapons of mass destruction and his

---

Originally published November 24, 2014, http://www.frontpagemag.com/2014/david-horowitz/how-many-lies-have-democrats-told-to-sabotage-the-war-on-terror-1/.

violation of 17 Security Council resolutions designed to stop him from doing just that. Saddam violated all 17 of the UN resolutions, beginning with those that constituted the Gulf War Truce and culminating in the ultimatum to disclose and destroy all weapons of mass destruction in his possession. His defiance of that ultimatum is why we went to war with him.

But it was the second lie—that Saddam did not have weapons of mass destruction—which the Democrats used to discredit the president and the war we were fighting. In fact, the Saddam regime did have weapons of mass destruction, including a chemical-weapons storage plant recently discovered by ISIS along with 2500 rockets filled with deadly sarin gas. Here's the report from the *Daily News* of July 9, 2014[1]:

> "A terrorist group bent on turning Iraq into an Islamic state has seized a chemical weapons depot near Baghdad stockpiled with sarin-filled rockets left over from the Saddam Hussein era.... The site, about 35 miles southwest of Baghdad, was once operated by Saddam's army and is believed to contain 2,500 degraded rockets filled with potentially deadly sarin and mustard gas."

Not a single Democrat has apologized for the monstrous defamation campaign they conducted around this lie to cripple their president and their country in a time of war.

The Democrats began their sabotage campaign against the war in Iraq in June 2003, claiming that Bush had lied when he cited a British report that Saddam was seeking fissionable uranium in Niger for his nuclear weapons program. Two official reports, one by the British and the other by the U.S. Senate, confirmed that Bush's statement was correct, but this was long after the Democrats had so demonized America's commander-in-chief that his ability to mobilize American citizens to support the war was

---

[1]Bill Hutchinson, "ISIS Seizes Chemical Weapons Depot Near Baghdad, May Have Access to Deadly Sarin Gas Rockets," *New York Daily News* July 9, 2014, http://www.nydailynews.com/news/world/isis-seizes-chemical-weapons-depot-baghdad-sarin-gas-rockets-article-1.1859934.

severely damaged. No apologies from Democrats or the media, which abetted their lies, in this case either. Here is a recent testimony about the facts of Saddam's quest for fissionable yellowcake uranium:[2]

> "As someone who led the company that transported 550 metric tons of yellowcake uranium—enough to make fourteen Hiroshima-size bombs—from Saddam's nuclear complex in the Iraq War's notorious 'Triangle of Death' for air shipment out of the country, I know Baathist Iraq's WMD potential existed."

Not content with these lies, the left reached into its Marxist pocket for another. The slogan "No Blood for Oil"[3] was a maliciously false claim designed to undermine the moral basis for the war by accusing President Bush of serving the interests of his Texas oil cronies instead of the American people. In the claims of Democrats, corporations in the Republican pocket pushed the country into an imperial war that cost thousands of American and Iraqi lives. But the fact is that despite spending trillions of dollars on a war that cost thousands of American lives, America got no Iraqi oil, which has wound up in the hands of ISIS terrorists and the People's Republic of China. No apologies for this myth either.

Perhaps the most destructive lie that Democrats have used to sabotage the war against the Islamist fanatics is that fighting terrorists creates more of them. Nancy Pelosi actually told 60 Minutes' Steve Croft that if America left Iraq the terrorists would leave, too. The same argument has been used by progressives to oppose a serious military effort to stop ISIS in Syria and Iraq rather than having to fight them here at home. But aggressive pre-emptive war against the terrorists in their homelands rather than ours

---

[2]Carter Andress, "We Drove Saddam's Yellowcake to the Baghdad Airport," *FrontPage Mag,* November 3, 2014, http://www.frontpagemag.com/2014/carter-andress/we-drove-saddams-yellowcake-to-the-baghdad-airport/.

[3]"Opposition to the Iraq War," *Wikipedia,* http://en.wikipedia.org/wiki/Opposition_to_the_Iraq_War.

has the opposite effect, as the victory in Iraq showed before Obama undid it.

The six-year retreat of the Obama administration from the battlefields in Iraq, Syria, Afghanistan, along with its appeasement of the terrorist state of Iran, has created more terrorists than ever. The weakness displayed by what once was the arsenal of democracy, now under the command of an anti-American president, has been a provocation to terrorists. The terror threat that diminished under Bush has grown dramatically under Obama. That is because fighting against terrorists does not produce terrorists. ISIS is able to recruit thousands of new terrorists because Islamist radicals are inspired by what Osama bin Laden called "the strong horse,"[4] by beheadings and the slaughter of Christians without serious reprisal. This is the face of the evil that confronts us; Americans better wake up to that threat before it is too late.

[4]J. T. Hatter, "Obama, The Weak Horse," *American Thinker,* September 14, 2012, http://www.americanthinker.com/articles/2012/09/obama_the_weak_horse.html.

17

Bush Was Right

The Islamic terror attack on the magazine *Charlie Hebdo* was carried out by Muslim criminals who were apparently trained in Yemen. Meanwhile, national security officials are warning of an imminent threat to Europe and the United States from *jihadi* soldiers who are returning from the wars in Syria and Iraq. According to the head of the FBI and other first responders there is no way to stop their re-entry because, after all, they have American passports. Nor is there any way to stop them in Syria and Iraq, since Obama has surrendered both countries to our enemies. The Democratic mayor of New York—ground zero for the Islamic War—has even stopped the surveillance of *jihadi* mosques, the breeding grounds for domestic "lone wolves." And with our southern border shredded by Obama and the Democrats, it's not going to be difficult for foreign *jihadis* to get to their infidel targets. Of course, Obama doesn't like the word "terror" to begin with, let alone "Islamic terror."

Fourteen years after 9/11, it is tragically clear that President Bush was right about the threat we faced, while Democrats have been suicidally wrong. The 9/11 attacks were indeed a salvo in the war Islamists have declared on us; but even now, fourteen years later, Democrats still want to regard such attacks as acts of individual criminality and deal with them through the legal justice system, affording American rights to those who want to destroy

---

Originally published January 9, 2015, http://www.frontpagemag.com/2015/david-horowitz/bush-was-100-right-after-911-1/.

American rights. Why, it might be asked, is the Boston Marathon bomber going to be tried in a criminal court of law, where he will be able to make propaganda for his cause underwritten by his victims? Because Democrats want it that way. It shows we're superior to everybody else.

Nine days after 9/11 President Bush addressed both houses of Congress to outline his response to the terror attacks. This is what he said about states that harbor Islamic terrorists, like Yemen and Syria: "We will pursue nations that provide aid or safe haven to terrorism. Every nation, in every region, now has a decision to make. Either you are with us, or you are with the terrorists. From this day forward, any nation that continues to harbor or support terrorism will be regarded by the United States as a hostile regime."[1]

When the president had completed his remarks, these were precisely the sentences that were singled out for attack by the political left. To progressives, Bush was a tyrant in the making and they took his warning personally: "Either you are with us, or you are with the terrorists." Unfortunately, even though Bush was *not* thinking of them in uttering these words, he might as well have been. When Bush decided to take on the terrorist-supporting, UN-defying regime of Saddam Hussein, Democrats went into full war mode against him, against the "war on terror" and against America's mission to defeat the al-Qaeda armies that had assembled in Iraq. Their sabotage of the war went on for five years, making it impossible for Bush to take on the terror-supporting regimes in Syria, Iran and elsewhere.

The Obama regime is the product of this momentous Democratic defection from America's purposes, from a robust defense of the American homeland, and from a militant response to the war that Islamists have declared on us. Why is there still a free flow of immigration from nations that support or tolerate the Islamist

---

[1] "Text: President Bush Addresses the Nation," op. cit.

armies which are ranged against us? Why isn't our southern border secure? It is because the Obama regime, with support from Democrats in Congress, regards security measures against terror-supporting states to be "Islamophobic," and regards securing our southern border to be xenophobic. Why isn't Obama embracing General el-Sisi and an Egyptian regime that has declared the Islamists to be enemies of the Islamic world? It is because Obama is committed to the Muslim Brotherhood, and against this same Egyptian regime.

Will the massacre in Paris—a repellent assault on free speech in the name of the Prophet Mohammed—wake up the Democrats and the Obama White House, and end their appeasement of Islamic terror? Unfortunately this is unlikely. Their leader is a lifetime, America-despising radical who has shown little appetite for changing course. It remains to be seen whether other Democrats will attribute their recent electoral drubbing to the weak-kneed security policies of the appeaser-in-chief, and find the voice to oppose him. But if they don't, it is a safe bet that this country is in for some bloody consequences.

18

Treasons of the Democrats

The Bolshevik leader Leon Trotsky once described Stalinism as "the perfect theory for gluing up the brain." What he meant to dramatize was the fact that a regime as monstrous as Stalin's, which murdered 40 million people and enslaved many times more, was nonetheless able to persuade progressives and "social justice" advocates all over the world to act as its supporters and defenders.

These enlightened enablers of Stalin's crimes included leading intellectuals of the day, even Nobel Prize winners in the sciences and the arts like Frederic Joliot-Curie and Andre Gide. Brilliant as they were, they were blind to the realities of the Stalinist regime and therefore to the virtues of the societies they lived in.

What glued up their brains was the belief that a brave new world of social justice—a world governed by progressive principles—existed in embryo in Soviet Russia, and had to be defended by any means necessary. As a result of this illusion, they put their talents and prestige at the service of the totalitarian enemies of democracy; acting, in Trotsky's words, as "frontier guards" for the Stalinist empire. They continued their efforts even after the Soviets had conquered Eastern Europe, acquired nuclear weapons and initiated a "cold war" with the West.

This article was published in a somewhat different form by National Review Online; http://www.nationalreview.com/article/429423/left-betrayal-america. See also http://www.frontpagemag.com/fpm/261382/treasons-democrats-david-horowitz.

To the progressives seduced by Stalinism, democratic America represented a greater evil than the barbaric police states of the Soviet bloc. Even half a century later, a progressive culture still refers to the formative phase of the Cold War as years of a "Red Scare"—as though the fifth column of American progressives whose loyalties were to the Soviet enemy, whose members included Soviet spies, were not a matter of serious concern, and as though a nuclear-armed, rapacious Soviet empire did not pose a credible threat.

How were these delusions of otherwise intelligent and well-intentioned people possible? How were otherwise informed individuals able to deny the obvious and support the most brutal and oppressive dictatorship in history? How did they come to view a relatively humane, decent, democratic society like the United States as evil, while regarding the barbarous communist regime as its victim? The answer lies in the identification of Marxism with the promise of social justice and the institution of progressive values, which will take place in a magical socialist future. Defense of the progressive idea trumped recognition of the reactionary fact.

Once the Stalin regime was identified with the imaginary progressive future, everything followed—its status as a persecuted victim, and its adversary's role as a reactionary force standing in the way of the noble aspiration. Every fault of the Stalin regime, every crime it committed—if not denied by progressives—was attributed to the nefarious actions of its enemies, most glaringly the United States. Once a promise of redemption is juxtaposed to an imperfect real-world actor, all of these responses become virtually inevitable. Hence the gluing of the brain.

The Soviet Union is gone, and history has moved on. But the Stalinist dynamic endures as the heritage of a post-Communist left, which remains wedded to fantasies of an impossibly beautiful future that bring it into collision with the flawed American present.

This left is now the dominant force in the Democratic Party. Its extreme disconnect from real-world realities is encapsulated in its support for the transparently racist movement called Black Lives Matter, which attacks law enforcement and defends street predators, excusing their crimes with the alibi that "white supremacists" create the circumstances which make them commit criminal acts. This extremist movement has the "strong support" of the entire spectrum of the "progressive" left—including 46 percent of the Democratic Party, according to a Wall Street Journal/NBC news poll.[1]

Black Lives Matter is a movement built on the fiction that police have declared an open season on innocent blacks. According to progressive fictions, police are the agents of a "white supremacist society"—a claim that alone should make one wary of the sanity of those who advance it. Facts belie the very basis of the claim that there is open hunting season on African Americans. African American males, accounting for 6 percent of the population, are responsible for more than 40 percent of violent crimes. But a Washington Post report on all 980 police shootings of 2015 reveals that only 4 percent of fatal police shootings involved white officers and black victims,[2] while in three-quarters of the incidents cops were either under attack themselves or defending civilians. "In other words," as Michael Walsh observed in the New York Post, they were "doing their jobs."[3]

One such job, done by Officer Darren Wilson in the suburban city of Ferguson, Missouri, became the launching point for the Black Lives Matter movement and its malicious claim that innocent blacks were being wantonly gunned down by racist police. The alleged victim, Michael Brown, had just committed a strong-armed robbery and refused to comply with Wilson's order to surrender. Instead the 300-lb street thug attacked Wilson in his vehicle, tried to wrest his gun from him, and then walked away

---

[1]http://www.wsj.com/articles/most-important-election-2016-feature-deep-and-growing-ideological-divide-1451318440?tesla=y&cb=loggedo.14149387925863266&cb=loggedo.8190284695010632
[2]https://www.washingtonpost.com/graphics/national/police-shootings/
[3]http://nypost.com/2016/01/02/myth-of-the-cop-killing-epidemic/

before turning and charging him. Several warning shots failed to stop Brown, until one killed him.

Ignoring the facts, Black Lives Matter promoted the lie invented by Brown's robbery accomplice—that Brown had his hands up and was attempting to surrender when he was shot. "Hands Up, Don't Shoot" quickly became the anthem of the movement. But this lie was refuted not only by black eyewitnesses testifying before the grand jury, and by forensic evidence, but by a review conducted by the Holder Justice Department, otherwise bent on demonstrating the existence of bigotry in the Ferguson police department.

Meanwhile, Black Lives Matter went about setting fire to Ferguson, causing millions of dollars of damage, because if there was no justice—no hanging of Wilson—there would be no peace, as the now familiar lynch-mob slogan framed it. Black Lives Matter then took its crusade to other cities, most prominently to Baltimore, where a career criminal named Freddie Gray became another cause célèbre.

Gray had suffered fatal injuries inside a police van where only one other captive was present. As Black Lives Matter inspired mobs began to gather in "protest," Baltimore's black Democratic mayor ordered police to stand down, allowing the mobs to destroy millions of dollars of property. The state's black Democratic prosecutor then indicted six officers, three of them African Americans, on various ludicrous charges including first-degree murder, although none except the African American driver had been in the van with Gray.

The immediate result of Black Lives Matter's war on law enforcement was an epidemic of crime, as police officers decided that aggressive law enforcement was dangerous to their careers and lives. Homicides in the St. Louis-Ferguson area and in Baltimore jumped 60 percent, setting records in the annals of criminal mayhem. Virtually all the victims were blacks, revealing the hypocrisy of a movement for which black lives didn't really matter—the attacks on law-enforcement officers, on the "power structure," and on white people were what mattered.

How could any reasonable citizen—let alone one with progressive aspirations—support a roving lynch mob like Black Lives Matter? How could half the Democratic Party support a movement that condemns America as a white supremacist society, disregarding the reality that the president and chief law enforcement officer and thousands of civil servants and elected officials—including the mayors and police chiefs of large urban centers like Memphis, Atlanta and Philadelphia—are black? (In Detroit the new mayor is actually the first white mayor in 40 years, while its police chief is still black.)

You can embrace the absurdity that America is a white supremacist society only if you are afflicted with the illusion that everybody is the same, and that all statistical inequalities affecting African Americans, like high crime rates, are not reflections of culture and character but marks of racist oppression. This particular absurdity—universal as it is among American progressives and the current U.S. Department of Justice—is easily refuted. If statistical disparities proved racism, the National Basketball Association, in which 95 percent of the starting multimillionaires are black, would be an association controlled by black racists, as would the National Football League; while the National Hockey League would be under the thumb of white racists.

Progressives are delusional about black racism and black crime because they are in thrall to the vision of an imaginary progressive future in which social justice will guarantee that every individual outcome is the same. Blindness to the accountability of inner-city populations for their off-the-charts violent crime rates, and their failure to shoulder the responsibilities of parenthood, is as characteristic of the progressive attitude as is its blindness to the betrayal of inner-city communities by Democrats and progressives.

The disgraceful conditions of America's large inner cities are almost entirely the responsibility of these two political actors. Chicago, Detroit, Baltimore, St. Louis and numerous other sites of out-of-control black poverty, failed public school systems and black on black violence are 100-percent controlled by the

Democratic Party and have been for 50 to 100 years. Yet 95 percent of the black vote and 100 percent of the progressive vote continues to go to Democrats who oppress African Americans.

Progressives' sordid history of supporting criminals at home is accompanied by an equally dishonorable record of sympathy for America's enemies abroad. The Iraqi dictator Saddam Hussein was one of the monsters of the 20th century, launching two aggressive wars, dropping poison gas on the Kurds, and murdering 300,000 Iraqi citizens. But more than a million progressives poured into the streets of America to thwart our attempt to depose him. At first, the Democratic leadership supported the Iraq invasion as a just and necessary war. But three months into the war, with American men and women still in harm's way, under pressure from the progressive left they turned against the war they had authorized, and for the next five years conducted a malicious propaganda campaign, worthy of the enemy, to discredit America's intentions and to obstruct its military mission.

Because the Bush administration chose not to defend itself by confronting the treasonous actions of the left—including the exposure and destruction of three national security programs—leftist myths about the Iraq War persist to this day, even in Republican circles. To set the record straight: Bush did not lie to seduce Democrats into supporting the war and could not have done so, since the Democrats had access to the same intelligence he did. The war was not about stockpiles of weapons of mass destruction, as Democrats dishonestly claimed; it was about Saddam's violation of 17 UN Security Council resolutions designed to prevent him from pursuing the WMD weapons programs he had started. The Democrats' betrayal of their country's war effort crippled its progress; and with the election to the presidency of an anti-war leftist in 2008, it led directly to the explosion of terrorism and bloodshed that has since engulfed the Middle East.

Nor was it just the surrender mentality of the Obama administration that fueled these catastrophes. With the full support of the Democratic Party, President Obama embraced the Muslim Brotherhood and America's mortal enemy, Iran, providing its ayatollahs with a path to nuclear weapons and dominance of the region, and causing the Sunni Arab states to prepare for a Middle Eastern civil war.

Just as leftists once acted as propagandists for the Soviet empire, discrediting America's Cold War effort and conducting deceptive campaigns to hide Soviet crimes, so the left today disparages the Islamic threat and opposes security measures necessary to protect the homeland—most alarmingly the sealing of our southern border. Progressives have created seditious "sanctuary cities" which refuse to cooperate with Homeland Security and the immigration laws in more than three hundred outlaw municipalities under Democratic control. Their betrayal has gone unreversed for more than a decade and led to the needless deaths of numerous Americans at the hands of illegal alien criminals, of which there are more than 200,000 inside our jails alone, and obviously many more inside our borders.[4]

Leftists and Democrats have also joined the Islamic propaganda campaign to represent Muslims—whose co-religionists have killed hundreds of thousands of innocents since 9/11 in the name of their religion—as victims of anti-Muslim prejudice, denouncing critics of Islamic terror and proponents of security measures as "Islamophobes" and bigots. In fact, 60 percent of religious hate crimes are directed at Jews, many inspired by the Jew-hatred that forms a core of Islam's religious canon, along with its incitements to war against Christians and other non-Muslim "infidels."

"Imagine where the Jews would be," asks Don Feder, "if a Jewish civil servant and his foreign bride shot up a Christmas party in Southern California. A Jewish psychiatrist murdered 13 and wounded another 30 at Ft. Hood, and two Jewish brothers planted bombs at the finish line of the Boston Marathon." Yet for progressives no heinous act by Islamic terrorists, nor the deafening

---

[4]http://cis.org/ImmigrantCrime

silence by Islamic communities around the atrocities committed in the name of their religion, can prompt them to consider the problematic nature of Islam itself.

Exploiting the myth of anti-Muslim persecution, progressives oppose scrutiny of the Muslim community, including its terror-promoting imams and mosques. They immediately denounce proposals to screen Muslim immigrants as religious bigotry, and thus seal off any rational discussion of the problem. Led by Hillary Clinton and Barack Obama, Democrats have enabled the Islamic assault on free speech, which is a central component of their campaign to create a religious theocracy that circles the globe. Most notoriously the president and his operatives cynically spread the lie that a video about Muhammad was behind the Benghazi terror attack. Speaking like an ayatollah before the UN General Assembly shortly after the attack, Obama declared: "The future must not belong to those who slander the prophet of Islam." What an American president should have said is, "The future must not belong to those who murder in the name of Islam."

By actions such as these, Democrats not only betray the 320 million Americans they are obliged to protect, but encourage the silence of the Muslim community, which has failed to expose the terrorists in its midst, or to condemn the imams and mosques that are preaching hatred of Jews and Christians, while promoting terrorist agendas aimed at Americans.

Our country is at a perilous crossroads, one that is made immeasurably more dangerous by a treacherous national party which blames its own country for the crimes of its enemies; and by a political opposition too feckless and timid to hold its fellow citizens accountable for their treasonous acts.

19

Anti-White Racism: The Hate That Dares Not Speak Its Name

It is a strange election cycle when Republicans go to war with each other with a ferocity rarely manifest when they are confronting Democrats and their progressive agendas. It is especially puzzling because a general consensus has formed on the right that the Democratic Party is moving so far left that its agendas threaten the very foundations of America's social contract. These include a frontal assault on the system of individual rights that the Founders set in place. The left envisions a fundamentally transformed America where individual rights are secondary to the collective rights of races, ethnicities, genders and classes. That is why the particular circumstances of individual acts—such as the ones that led to the death of Michael Brown in Ferguson, for example—don't matter to progressive mobs. It's the races of the actors that do.

This progressive assault is being waged in the name of an "identity politics" that places whites at the bottom of the racial totem pole while holding them responsible for all the sins attributed to Americans but none of their achievements, specifically their success in creating the most tolerant and inclusive society on earth. Identity politics has a long and ugly history under its proper name—fascism—which is another term for the socialism of the

---

Originally published on breitbart.com http://www.breitbart.com/big-journalism/2016/04/26/anti-white-racism-hate-dares-not-speak-name-2/

Volk or nation (as opposed, for example, to the socialism of classes). Today p.c. fascism is an integral feature of the ethos and tactics of the progressive left, which has become the dominant force in the Democratic Party.

Republicans may feel they have the luxury of being nasty towards each other because they fail to grasp that, in the hands of their opponents, politics has become a form of warfare conducted by other means. It is no longer about getting elected and enjoying the perks of office. It is about defaming opponents with the intention of driving them from the public square, so that only the party of "decency" and "compassion" remains standing. Its effect is to traduce the culture of civility that respects dissent, and its logical conclusion is a one-party culture and state.

In this destructive enterprise the left's chief weapon is race, which it uses to attack departures from its orthodoxies as racial bigotry. But even as progressives prosecute this race war, racial bigotry by whites has ceased to be a factor in public life. Progressives deal with this intractable reality by inventing a fictional construct called "institutional racism" to which they attribute all the disparities affecting blacks. "Institutional racism" is a necessary fiction—institutionalized racism has been outlawed for sixty years—because actual racists have become so hard to find.

Even as white racism has become a phenomenon of an insignificant fringe, the left's *accusations* of white racism have escalated to the point of terminal absurdity. Thus Black Lives Matter and other progressive voices describe America as a "white supremacist nation." This accusation is made against a country that outlaws racial discrimination, has twice elected a black president, has recently had a black four-star general head of the Joint Chiefs of Staff, two black secretaries of state, three black national security advisors and two successive black attorneys general, along with thousands of black mayors, city council members, police chiefs and congressmen.

The statement that 2016 America is a "white supremacist" nation is not only the reflection of a deranged hatred for whites. It is an act of hostility towards black America, whose opportunities and rights in this country are greater than in any other under the sun, including every African nation and Caribbean country governed by blacks for hundreds and even thousands of years. The characterization of America as "white supremacist" trivializes the historic sufferings of American blacks, seeks to divorce them from their historic contributions to American culture and society, and depreciates the moral struggles of the civil rights movement that achieved their liberation.

Black Lives Matter—a driving force behind the white supremacist meme—is a roving lynch mob whose premise is the claim that a systematic war is being waged on black people. This claim is deployed to justify riots in the streets, the burning of cities and open incitements to kill police. *(What do we want? Dead cops! When do we want them? Now!)* There is not a shred of evidence to support the claim that there is a hunting season on blacks. Black Lives' blood libel is sustained by portraying black street predators like Michael Brown, Eric Garner and Freddie Gray, who die resisting arrest, as civil rights martyrs.

Here is how Black Lies Matter justifies its rhetorical venom and articulates its political goal: "#BlackLivesMatter is working for a world where Black lives are no longer systematically and intentionally targeted for demise." According to the co-founder of the Black Lives Matter Seattle chapter, Marissa Jenae Johnson, the phrase "All lives matter," which was coined as a response to the original, is a "new racial slur." Her justification: "White Americans have created the conditions that require a phrase like 'Black Likes Matter'.... Do you know how horrific it is to grow up as a child in a world that so hates you? While you're literally being gunned down in the street, while you're being rounded up and mass-incarcerated and forced into prison slavery."

Johnson's racial lies are easily refuted by the facts. White America does not hate black children, and blacks are not being gunned down in the streets by whites or "rounded up" like Jews in Nazi Germany to be forced into "prison slavery." According to a study conducted by *The Washington Post,* last year police officers (who are black and Hispanic and Asian as well as white) killed 662 whites and Hispanics, and 258 blacks. The overwhelming majority of all those police-shooting victims were attacking the officers.

Overall, there were 6,095 black homicide deaths in 2014—the most recent year for which such data are available—compared to only 5,397 homicide deaths for whites and Hispanics who constitute 80 percent of the population. Thus it is true that blacks are being gunned down in numbers far out of proportion to their representation in the population. But the truth Black Lives Matter racists want to obscure is that almost all of those black homicide victims were gunned down by black killers. It is not whites who are gunning down blacks in the streets but other blacks. Moreover, 90 percent of the homicide victims of black killers are black.

In other words, the real oppressors of black communities are the Black Lives Matter movement and its Democratic Party sponsors who are enabling a criminal element in inner city communities to terrorize law-abiding black citizens, while crippling the efforts of law enforcement to protect them.

While blacks are only 13 percent of the population, they commit 38 percent of the violent crimes and over 50 percent of the murders. In Chicago and New York, two of the homicide capitals of America, blacks and Hispanics commit more than 95 percent of the murders. If one removes from the equation the criminal elements of the black and Hispanic populations of this country, America's violent crime rates shrink astronomically until America looks more like European countries whose citizenries have no guns.

Since blacks are 90 percent of the victims of black criminals, it is obvious that crime expert Heather MacDonald is correct when she writes, "The one government agency that is the most dedicated to the proposition that black lives matter is the police."[1] The

[1]Heather MacDonald, "The Myths of Black Lives Matter," http://www.wsj.com/articles/the-myths-of-black-lives-matter-1455235686. The statistics in this section were taken from the same article.

war on police is a war to deprive law-abiding black citizens of their only real protection, since Democratic gun control advocates have already removed from the black and white populations of Chicago, Baltimore and other crime-ridden cities much of their right to bear arms.

According to FBI data, over the past decade 40 percent of cop killers have been black. Officers are killed by blacks at a rate 2.5 times higher than the rate at which blacks are killed by police officers (who are black as well as white). Those blacks killed by police are with few exceptions resisting arrest, do not have their hands up and are not pleading, "Don't shoot."

Yet the sinister propaganda of Black Lives Matter is to suppress and invert these critical facts. That Black Lives Matter is attacking the police who constitute the first line of defense for inner city blacks' reveals the truth about this movement, which is anti-white in its intentions but anti-black in its effects.

In other words, the greatest daily threat to black lives in America is an anti-white racism that has made violent street criminals its civil rights heroes, and multi-racial law enforcement agencies the targets of its hate. It actively suppresses the facts about black and minority criminality by attacking anyone who attempts to raise the issue as racist.

The results of the attacks on police departments were entirely predictable. In the immediate wake of the Ferguson and Baltimore race riots, homicide rates rose 56 percent and 60 percent in those areas and significantly elsewhere as police retreated from the streets while local Democratic officials curtailed anti-crime measures, rewarded the families of career predators like Freddie Gray with six-million-dollar-settlements, and emboldened violent criminals to prey on vulnerable citizens, who are mainly poor and mainly black.

A prime cause of this catastrophic war on police is the vicious propaganda spread by progressive and liberal elites and Democratic Party operatives, beginning with presidential candidates Hillary Clinton and Bernie Sanders. For them, America is still mired in the pre-civil rights era of more than 60 years ago when there was systemic injustice in the criminal justice system, and white attitudes towards blacks were radically different.

How different? In 1960, as commentator Larry Elder has pointed out, 60 percent of Americans said they would never vote for a black president; but in 2008 more than 50 percent of Americans did just that, and did it again in 2012. Moreover, in 1983 a Republican president, Ronald Reagan, made Martin Luther King, Jr.'s birthday the only national holiday honoring an individual American. To do so he eliminated the national holiday specifically honoring George Washington, the father of the country. If that isn't a revolution in attitudes, what is?

Facts, however, don't prevent Black Lives Matters supporters like Ta-Nehisi Coates, America's most pampered racist, from promoting poisonous fictions like this: "And so that beauty that Malcolm pledged us to protect, black beauty, was never celebrated in movies, in television, or in the textbooks I'd seen as a child. Everyone of any import, from Jesus to George Washington, was white."

Coates was born in 1975, and was eight years old when King was honored with the nation's only national holiday honoring an American, and George Washington was sent to the back of the bus. The first motion pictures championing civil rights and equal dignity for blacks—most notably *Home of the Brave*—began appearing in 1949. Sidney Poitier won the Academy Award as best actor for his role in "Lillies of the Field" in 1964. In 1960 Harper Lee's novel about racial justice for blacks won the Pulitzer Prize and went on to sell over 60 million copies. In 1977 television featured "Roots," the epic miniseries about black oppression which was the most widely viewed show of its time. Its episodes were seen by more than 30 million Americans and it won a score of Emmys. As is typical of Black Lives Matter and "social justice" progressives generally, Coates simply lies to sustain his hatred of whites.

Because Coates is the most celebrated of the new racists, he is a perfect emblem of the corruptions of a "liberal" culture, which condemns invisible white racism while defending black criminals who prey on the minority inhabitants of America's inner cities. A principal source of the war on white people generally and law enforcement in particular is our leftwing university and literary culture, which for forty years has taught college students that it is politically correct to hate white people; which fosters a hatred of America so virulent that it has inspired millennials to flock to a lifelong supporter of communist causes like Bernie Sanders; and which has averted its own gaze from this impertinent fact: the largest, most oppressive and most violent inner cities in America are 100-percent controlled by the Democratic Party—the party of slavery and segregation—and have been for fifty to a hundred years. For everything that is wrong in the social environments of America's black poor that policy can affect, Democrats and progressives are responsible.

Ta-Nehisi Coates is a prime product of this cultural sickness. Although he never graduated college, Coates was made a visiting professor at MIT, was offered a column by *The New York Times* (which he turned down) and is currently an editor at one of America's most venerable liberal journals, *The Atlantic.* He is also the recipient of a $625,000 MacArthur "Genius" Award, and this year was given the National Book Award for *Between the World and Me,* accompanied by fawning reviews in *The New York Times* and the rest of the liberal press. The book is written in the form of a letter of advice to his teenage son, to whom he explains that if a black cop kills a black youth (which is what happened to Coates's best friend) that is because the black cop is acting white. In other words, whatever crime is committed by a black person, the white devil made him do it. This is Farrakhanite racism in its purest form.

"White America," explains Coates, "is a syndicate arrayed to protect its exclusive power to dominate and control our bodies." Portraying killings of blacks by police officers as racist business-as-usual, Coates says that "there is nothing uniquely evil" about these officers "endowed with the authority to destroy your body;" they "are merely men enforcing the whims of our country, correctly interpreting its heritage and legacy." America's heritage is killing black people because they are black. America's heritage is slavery—control over black bodies.

Actually—historically speaking—it is black Africa's heritage is to have enslaved black people and delivered control of their bodies to others; America's heritage is to have liberated them.

The historical reality is this: slavery had existed for 3000 years in every country but was never proclaimed immoral until white Christian males in England and America did so towards the end of the 18th century. In 1776 a new nation dedicated itself to the proposition that all men have a God-given right to liberty that no government can take away. Within 90 years of America's declaration, slavery was abolished on this continent at the cost of 350,000 mostly white Union lives, and then—thanks to the English and the Americans—throughout the western hemisphere and large parts of Africa.

This is the truth the left desperately seeks to suppress so it can justify its attacks on a country that has provided not only blacks but all minorities with privileges, rights and opportunities unprecedented in the history of mankind.

Hatred of America and contempt for its guardians among the police and the military is the social gospel of the left. For nearly half a century this hatred has been the unwavering theme of the "progressive" movement in our universities and our streets and in the Democratic Party; its practical agendas are the destruction of the culture of individual liberty and accountability at home, and America's retreat abroad. *This* is what Republicans and all Americans, black and white, should be concerned about and what they should be joining forces to defeat.

Index